ACCOUNTING AND CORPORATE REPORTING - TODAY AND TOMORROW

Edited by **Soner Gokten**

Accounting and Corporate Reporting - Today and Tomorrow
http://dx.doi.org/10.5772/66609
Edited by Soner Gokten

Contributors

Ubaldo Comite, Somnath Debnath, Filiz Angay Kutluk, Helena Isabel B. Saraiva, Maria-Ceu Gaspar Alves, Vítor Gabriel, Seedwell T.M. Sithole, Burak Ozdogan, Mine Aksu, Can Simga Mugan, Ayse Tansel Cetin, Mihriban Coşkun Arslan, Osmar Antonio Bonzanini, Amélia Cristina Ferreira Da Silva, Teresa Gabriela Marques Leite, Pınar Okan Gokten, Beyhan Marsap, Banu Sultanoglu, Yildiz Ozerhan, Ceray Aldemir, Tugba Ucma Uysal, Idil Kaya, Şükran Güngör Tanç, Hakan Vahit Erkutlu, Seyhan Çil Koçyiğit, Figen Öker Türüdüoğlu, Hümeyra Adıgüzel, Tuğçe Uzun Kocamiş, Gülçin Yildirim

Published by InTech
Janeza Trdine 9, 51000 Rijeka, Croatia

Publishing Process Manager Marijana Francetic
Technical Editor SPi Global
Cover InTech Design team

First published September, 2017
Printed in Croatia
Legal deposit, Croatia: National and University Library in Zagreb

Additional hard copies can be obtained from orders@intechopen.com

Accounting and Corporate Reporting - Today and Tomorrow, Edited by Soner Gokten
p. cm.
Print ISBN 978-953-51-3549-4
Online ISBN 978-953-51-3550-0

For EU product safety concerns:
IN TECH d.o.o., Prolaz Marije Krucifikse Kozulić 3, 51000 Rijeka, Croatia,
info@intechopen.com or visit our website at intechopen.com.

Meet the editor

Dr. Gokten is an assistant professor of Accounting and Finance at the Department of Management, Faculty of Economics and Administrative Sciences, Baskent University, Ankara, Turkey. He received his BSBA degree from the Faculty of Economics and Administrative Sciences, Baskent University, Ankara, Turkey, and MBA degree in Finance and PhD degree in Accounting and Finance from the Graduate School of Social Sciences, Gazi University, Ankara, Turkey. He has published several articles, books, book chapters, and conference proceedings. He is serving as a referee to national and international journals, and Dr. Gokten has investment advisory, project finance, and corporate valuation experience in several national and international projects.

Contents

Preface

We have spent a great deal of time on the continued development of accounting and auditing standards, which are used as a primary component of corporate reporting, to reach today's financial reporting framework. However, is it possible to say that, *currently, financial statements provide full and prompt disclosure?* Or *will they still be useful as a primary element with their current structures in corporate reporting?*

Undoubtedly, we are deeply concerned about these issues in recent times.

The traditional perspective, to identify the role of accounting, does not really satisfy the stakeholders of today's business environment. Although, tangible assets (physical capital) are still important for certain industries, value creation dynamics become more dependent on intangible assets, which are derived by the intellectual and human capitals discussed in the endogenous growth theory. In addition, as never before, in order to maintain a livable world, the legitimacy of using natural capital to produce manufactured capital has become one of the main interests of stakeholders. In this sense, stakeholders' increasing demand for information has created a need for contemporary corporate reporting framework, with possible new accounting rules to ensure full disclosure of organization's economic, environmental and social impacts by integrating the financial and nonfinancial information into a single report.

The transformation process of current accounting and corporate reporting principles have different dimensions on accounting rule setting, international standardization, technological issues, behavioral aspects, value relevance, acceptance and adaptation, public sector accounting and accounting profession. Therefore, it is not easy to construct and provide an efficient framework to reach a globally accepted perspective for identifying the new role of accounting: *Saving the planet by creating a globally accepted framework for accounting for sustainability.* Although the recent developments open a new path to change the phase of accounting and corporate reporting as a whole, there is much progress to be made.

This volume contains chapters to discuss the today's and tomorrow's accounting and corporate reporting phenomena in a comprehensive and multidimensional way. Therefore, this book is organized into six sections: 'Achieving Sustainability through Corporate Reporting', 'International Standardization', 'Financial Reporting Quality', 'Accounting Profession and Behavioral Aspects', 'Public Sector Accounting and Reporting', and 'Managerial Accounting'.

I would like to express my sincere gratitude to all of the authors for their high quality contributions. The successful completion of this book has been the result of the cooperation of many people. In the end, I would like to thank the Publishing Process Manager Ms. Marijana Francetic for her support during the publishing process, as well as the Commissioning Editor Ms. Ana Pantar for inviting me to be the editor of this book.

Assistant Professor Soner Gokten
Department of Management
Faculty of Economics and Administrative Sciences
Baskent University
Turkey

Section 1

Achieving Sustainability Through Corporate Reporting

Chapter 1

Paradigm Shift in Corporate Reporting

Pınar Okan Gökten and Beyhan Marşap

Additional information is available at the end of the chapter

http://dx.doi.org/10.5772/intechopen.68832

Abstract

In this paper, we present the evolution of integrated reporting and organizations playing an active role in this process. As a result of the changes, corporate reports including only historical financial information have become insufficient. It has started to be important for the firms to be sensitive towards environment, social capital and governance. For these reasons, authorities started to search for new reporting types. Their aim was to form a report giving detailed (prospective and retrospective) information about the total performance of the firm. Sustainability reports, the starting point of integrated reporting, were established and Global Reporting Initiative (GRI) standards were formed to increase the popularization. Integrated reports aim to supply full disclosure about the firms' strategies, goals and performances. They also respond to the demands and needs of key stakeholders. In order to actualize the financial stability and sustainability, they are necessary. Integrated reports also put related groups into play. So, decision makers become a participant instead of watching the system from outside. In addition, integrated thinking philosophy provides systematic disclosure of value creation, namely how organizations made resource allocations in the past and how they will create value in the future according to their business models.

Keywords: integrated reporting, sustainability reporting, International Integrated Reporting Council, Global Reporting Initiative

1. Introduction

There have been so many changes because of globalisation, developments in technology, rapid population growth, increases in human needs and in the number of environmentally sensitive people. In connection with all these issues, while machine and labour-based production have decreased, information-based production has increased. Also climate changes in negative direction, social responsibility problems and raw material shortages have been observed. As a result of all these changes, traditional financial reports have not kept pace to surroundings.

As traditional financial reports give information about only firms' historical financial positions, they started to be inefficient. In addition to the financial information request, a demand towards non-financial information has also been seen and financial reports giving only financial information have not been preferred any more. Nowadays, in firm evaluation, people do not deal with profit only. They also want to be informed about the environmental sensitivity, future performance, risks and opportunities of the firm. All mentioned changes have led to differentiations in business world.

In order to meet all needs, financial reports started to possess lot of information. This caused confusion and users of financial reports got lost among a lot of information [1]. They could not obtain items that they wanted to learn from reports. This made financial reports useless. Studies had started in order to overcome these problems. Authorities had searched for financial report types having ideal characteristics and meeting needs. Many different types of financial reports have been established by different standard setters in different period of time. As a result, a common view formed a report possessing both financial and nonfinancial information, lacking unnecessary bulk information, being stakeholders' need oriented should be prepared with a standard framework.

A report, considering happiness and welfare of all living things, thinking about future generations and displaying firms' performance related with environmental, social, corporate governance issues, formed and named as sustainability report. But unfortunately, sustainability reports become insufficient in responding the correlation between the firm itself and its business model, strategy and financial situation [2]. In order to overcome this problem, a new reporting type Integrated Reporting (IR) was formed.

As seen in **Figure 1** which is adopted from EY (2014) report [3], the evaluation of corporate reporting has been changed dramatically over the years. In the 1960s, corporate reports referred to financial statements only. Over time, they have become much more contentful. In the early 2000s, sustainability reports have taken place within corporate reports. Nowadays, integrated reports including financial information, governance and remuneration, management

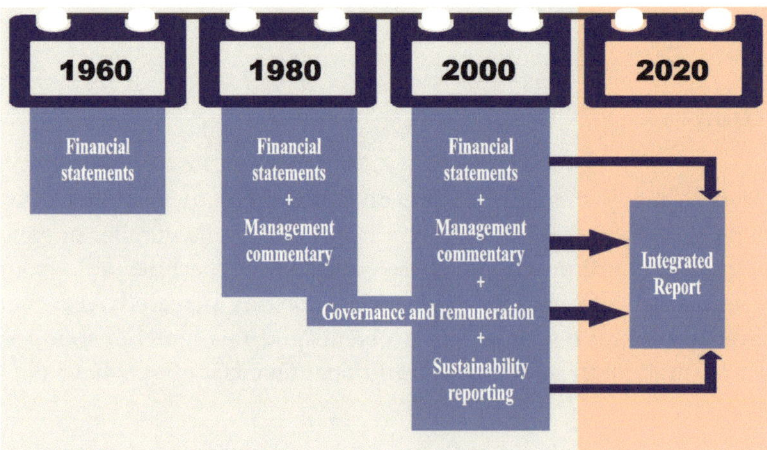

Figure 1. Evaluation of corporate reporting.

commentary and sustainability information become significant in business world. Consequently, it is possible to say that today integrated reports become the pre-eminent form of corporate reports.

In the ongoing sections of this chapter, firstly, sustainability reporting will be subjected as the starting point of IR. Then, the main item IR will be examined in detail with its historical development and its philosophy of integrated thinking.

2. Sustainability reporting

The term of sustainable development was first presented in Brundtland Report of the World Commission on Environment and Development (Brundtland Commission) in 1987. With this term, the importance of guaranteeing the future of new generations was revealed. After that, to be able to respond the changing needs, firms have started to prepare sustainability reports. The important issues about sustainability mentioned in G4 Sustainability Reporting Guidelines are as: "*Sustainability reporting helps organizations to set goals, measure performance, and manage change in order to make their operations more sustainable. A sustainability report conveys disclosures on an organization's impacts—be they positive or negative—on the environment, society and the economy. In doing so, sustainability reporting makes abstract issues tangible and concrete, thereby assisting in understanding and managing the effects of sustainability developments on the organization's activities and strategy*" [4]. Long-term profitability, social justice and environmental protection are the main goals of firms preparing sustainability reports.

With the spread of sustainability, besides financial performance, the importance of social and environmental performances also increased. Therefore, in year 1994, the term "Triple Bottom Line (TBL)" was established by John Elkington regarding to sustainability. TBL consists of three performance dimensions: social, environmental and financial. It has three elements represented as 3Ps. These are:

- People represents the social dimension of TBL
- Planet represents the environmental dimension of TBL
- Profit represents the financial dimension of TBL.

The main goal of TBL is to measure firms' social, environmental and financial performances and to ensure and advance sustainability. The measurement may be actualized by using a shared currency or basing into an index.

The leading organization in the dissemination of sustainability reporting is Global Reporting Initiative (GRI). GRI is an international independent organization that shows the impact of the firms on critical sustainability issues. It has published standards since 2000 in order to form the framework of sustainability reports. The first version of GRI Guidelines named as G1 was published in 2000. In 2002, the second version G2 was published. In 2006, G3 Guidelines was launched. In May 2013, GRI established the fourth generation of Guidelines, G4. Latest revolution of these standards is GRI Sustainability Reporting Standards (or shortly GRI Standards).

GRI Standards are the improved forms of G4 Guidelines. Although there are G4 Guidelines on the basis of GRI Standards, some of the terminologies in G4 have been simplified or changed while passing to GRI Standards. GRI Standards will be mandatory after 1 July 2018. Firms continue to apply G4 Guidelines until that date. Global Sustainability Standards Board (GSSB) is the GRI's independent standard setting body, and it issues GRI Standards. There are three universal standards: GRI 101, GRI 102 and GRI 103. GRI 101 is the starting point and consists of reporting principals.[1] It gives information about how sustainability reports should be prepared according to the standards. GRI 102 mentions the general disclosures related with contextual information. GRI 103 deals with management approach (how you manage).

GRI Standards have also topic specific standards. They have three different main topics as; economic (GRI 200), environmental (GRI 300) and social (GRI 400). They are like bag standards with modular structure and they may be updated, new ones may be added. Firms apply universal standards and in addition to these, they may choose from topic specific standards related with material topics.

In **Figure 2** which is adopted from Chersan study [5], it is possible to see the geographic distribution of reporting according to GRI. While the highest number of reports prepared according to GRI Guidelines is the year 2014 with 3981, the lowest one is the year 1999 with 6.

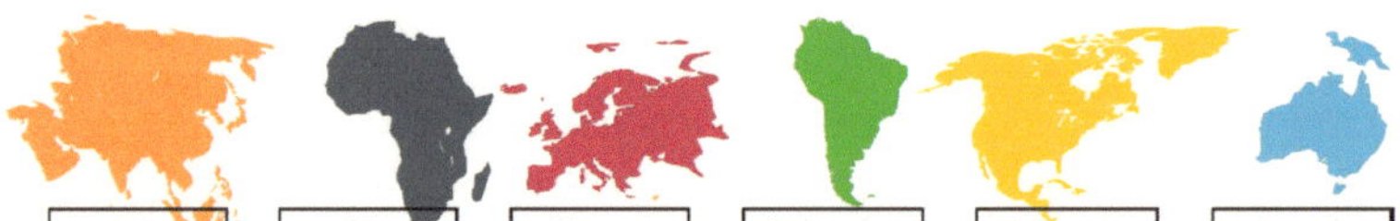

Asia		Africa		Europe		S. America		N. America		Oceania	
1999	1	1999	0	1999	0	1999	0	1999	5	1999	0
2000	7	2000	3	2000	1	2000	1	2000	2	2000	1
2001	1	2001	1	2001	15	2001	2	2001	6	2001	9
2002	3	2002	8	2002	22	2002	9	2002	31	2002	12
2003	3	2003	2	2003	54	2003	5	2003	31	2003	10
2004	8	2004	22	2004	115	2004	9	2004	47	2004	14
2005	29	2005	23	2005	180	2005	17	2005	50	2005	23
2006	39	2006	25	2006	223	2006	51	2006	70	2006	40
2007	85	2007	24	2007	342	2007	80	2007	27	2007	48
2008	185	2008	51	2008	457	2008	141	2008	38	2008	71
2009	304	2009	54	2009	647	2009	189	2009	83	2009	90
2010	367	2010	55	2010	829	2010	258	2010	66	2010	81
2013	1119	2013	167	2013	1344	2013	613	2013	439	2013	122
2014	1183	2014	167	2014	1443	2014	619	2014	453	2014	116
2015	702	2015	47	2015	940	2015	418	2015	274	2015	24

Figure 2. Geographic distribution of reporting according to GRI at world level.

[1]Reporting principals are stakeholder inclusiveness, sustainability context, materiality, completeness, accuracy, balance, clarity, comparability, reliability and timeliness. These have to be taken into account when preparing a sustainability report.

In total, Europe has the highest number of GRI-certified reports. The region with lowest number of reports is Oceania with only 24 firms. On the date of 9 March 2017, according to Sustainability Disclosure Database, totally there are 38,969 reports, 26,004 GRI reports and 10,397 organizations whose reports include sustainability reports [6].

3. Integrated reporting

As a result of increasing needs and changing conditions, both business world and authorities started to be in quest of new reporting types meeting the needs. Especially, stakeholders do not want to examine 150–200 pages reports. This is not useful for them because excessive information obscures critical details. They want to possess clear and concise information at short notice. Integrated reports hold all these features and they can respond to the needs of related groups.

IR contributes to the financial stability and sustainable development by integrating both financial and non-financial information. Actually, IR is more than the combination of financial statements and sustainability reports. It gives a holistic view for the related groups. There may be some problems in adopting IR. As it is research intensive, every business cannot apply it. Also, there is a risk of being so much transparent.

It is possible to examine the components of S&P 500 market value from **Figure 3** which is adopted from Ocean Tomo's 2015 Annual Study [7]. There has been a decrease in firms' tangible assets with the decrease in machine and labour-based production. While in 1975, the intangible asset value of S&P 500 was 17%, it showed a dramatic increase between the years 1975 and 2015 and in 2015, the value of intangible assets became 87%. As a result of this

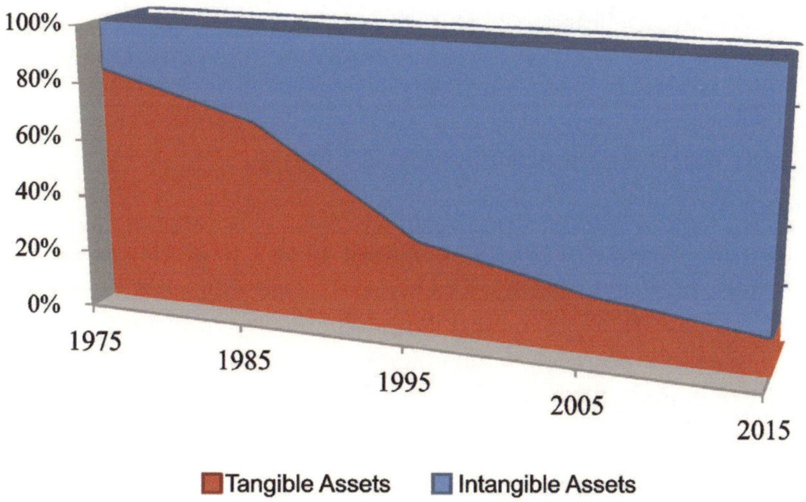

Figure 3. Components of S&P 500 market value.

increase in intangible assets rate, firms understood that they had to give much more information related to intangible assets when compared with past years.

Integrated reporting combines the information referred in traditional financial statements, management commentaries, sustainability reports, governance and remuneration reports and also shows how firms create value in short-medium-long term and the sustaining ability of firms. The term value mentioned here is created for all related groups like stakeholders, investors, government, suppliers, customers, society, creditors etc. The scope of integrated reports differs according to who the value is for. The scope of the report is broader when the value is for society compared with when the value is for investors.

The terms integrated thinking (IT) and IR are interrelated. Integrated thinking is the keystone and philosophy of IR. IT is mainly necessary for an effective IR and it is a kind of broad-minded and prospective thinking. In the study of Churet and Eccles [8], while IR is expressed as the tip and visible part of the iceberg, IT is the below and unseen part. In general, IT understands and interprets how the value creation process will be achieved in short-medium-long term by considering business resources. Long-term thinking, long-term decision making and long-term value creation are actualized by firms started to adopt IT.

Hopwood et al. [9] reveals the benefits of IR as a result of the survey conducted with the pilot enterprises selected in 2010. Eccles and Armbrester [10] and James (2015) [11] are also mentioned that IR avails to firms. On the other hand, Flower [12] and Thomson [13] have negative criticisms related with IR and address the missing aspects of it. Humphrey et al. (2017) [14] builds up a chronological archive data about the development of International Integrated Reporting Council (IIRC) and examines the reasons of high-speed evolution of both IIRC and IR. While Boiral [15] uses the research technique of counter accounting related with sustainability reporting, Rowbottom and Locke (2016) [16] examines the development of IR by using actor network theory. Serafeim [17] mentions that firms producing integrated reports have longer term investors. Chersan [18] examines the firms applying IR standards. He finds that firms implementing IR applications mostly are positioned in South Africa and secondly in European countries. These two regions account for 78% of firms preparing IR in all over the world.

3.1. Historical development process of integrated reporting

In order to understand integrated reporting much better, it is important to examine the historical development process of it as seen in **Figure 4**. In year 1994, King Report on Corporate Governance was established in South Africa in order to encourage firms to report non-financial information. There are also two other King Reports, one of them is King II which was published in 2002 and the other one is King III which was published in 2009. In these reports, the responsibilities of firms clarified as financial, social and environmental issues. Also, issuing annual integrated reports is recommended in King III.

The Prince's Accounting for Sustainability Project was constituted in 2004. Prince of Wales defended that sustainability reports had to be clear, concise and comparable. Prince's idealism was giving the task that saving the planet by the help of accounting [12].

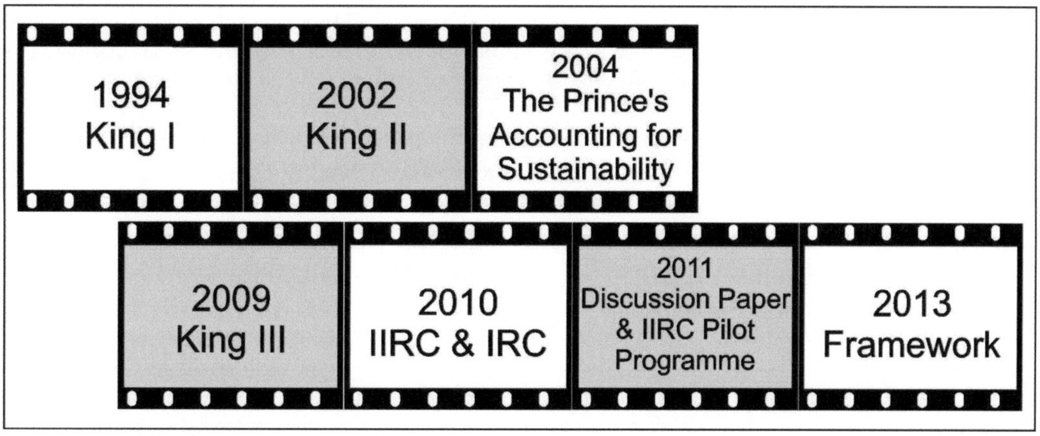

Figure 4. Historical development process of integrated reporting.

International Integrated Reporting Council (IIRC) was formed in August 2010 to actualize sustainability accounting and form a globally accepted framework. IIRC uses social and environmental accounting as a base. There are two leading organizations in the establishment of IIRC: The Prince's Accounting for Sustainability Project and Global Reporting Initiative (GRI). IIRC includes heads of the International Accounting Standards Board (IASB), the Financial Accounting Standards Board (FASB), the International Federation of Accountants (IFAC), the International Organization of Securities Commissions (IOSCO), the CEOs of the 'Big Four' (Deloitte, Ernst & Young, KPMG and PWC), the heads of the major British professional accountancy bodies and the CFOs of major multi-internationals, such as Nestle, Tata and HSBC.

In May 2010, Integrated Reporting Committee (IRC) of South Africa was also formed under the chairmanship of Professor Mervyn King. The main goal of IRC is to provide the best possible practice of integrated reporting in South Africa. The members of the IRC are as follows: Association for Savings and Investment South Africa (ASISA), Banking Association of South Africa (BASA), Batseta (Council of Retirement Funds for South Africa), Business Unity South Africa (BUSA), Chartered Secretaries Southern Africa (CSSA), Financial Services Board (FSB), Institute of Directors in Southern Africa (IoDSA), Institute of Internal Auditors (IIA), Government Employees Pension Fund (GEPF), Johannesburg Stock Exchange (JSE) and South African Institute of Chartered Accountants (SAICA) [19]. IIRC and IRC are leading organizations for the development of IR [20].

South Africa is the first in making the application of IR compulsory (legal obligation) for companies whose shares traded in the stock exchange. In the year 2010, Johannesburg Securities Exchange's (JSE) Listing Requirements were published and companies listed on the JSE either have to issue annual integrated reports (including financial, social and environmental information) or have to explain the reason of not doing so.

In October 2011, IIRC Pilot Programme was announced. This was a 2-year programme and had two parts as Business Network and Investor Network. In Business Network, there were over 100 businesses from 25 countries. They applied IR principles in order to support the development of it. Investor Network, on the hand, had over 35 participants from 12 countries. They were advocators of IR, and they shared their views related with the IR evolution. The IIRC got feedback from this Pilot Programme [21].

In September 2011, Discussion Paper related with integrated reporting was published. After that in 2013, IIRC published the International Integrated Reporting Framework. Framework consists of the guiding principles of integrated reports. These two, especially Framework, shape the integrated reports and are loadstars in the preparation of integrated reports. Shortly, it is possible to mention that King III Report, Discussion Paper and Framework are important references for the ones that will start IR.

In order to increase the importance and application of IR, Memoranda of Understanding (MOU) were signed between IIRC and many other organizations [14]. As mentioned in **Table 1**, it is possible to examine the name of organizations with which MOU was signed and also the signature dates.

3.2. Components of integrated reporting

Integrated reporting has three main components: business model, capitals and value. With all these components, it is possible to imagine IR as a system taking inputs and after operations creating outputs. Business model could be described as: "*Academic research and corporate practice are increasingly addressing the business model as a unit of analysis offering a systemic perspective on how to do business, mainly with the aim of understanding how to improve the ability of companies to create financial value. On the other hand, there is a growing body of literature on business models that provides a range of approaches to characterize their different roles for achieving corporate sustainability*" [22]. Every integrated report has a unique structure. The business model of a firm is extremely important for the integrated report as it shapes integrated report.

The terms referred as inputs and outputs in **Figure 5** [23], are both capitals, second component of IR. When the amount of output capitals is more than the amount of input capitals,

	Name of organization	**Signature date**
Memorandum of Understanding (MOU) signed between IIRC and	International Federation of Accountants (IFAC)	7 September 2012
	International Financial Reporting Standards (IFRS) Foundation	4 February 2013
	International Financial Reporting Standards (IFRS) Foundation	28 November 2014
	Sustainability Accounting Standards Board (SASB)	17 December 2013
	Carbon Disclosure Project (CDP) and Climate Disclosure Standards Board (CDSB)	18 July 2013
	World Intellectual Capital Initiative (WICI)	15 April 2013
	Global Reporting Initiative (GRI)	1 March 2013

Table 1. Memorandum of Understanding (MOU) signed between IIRC and other organizations.

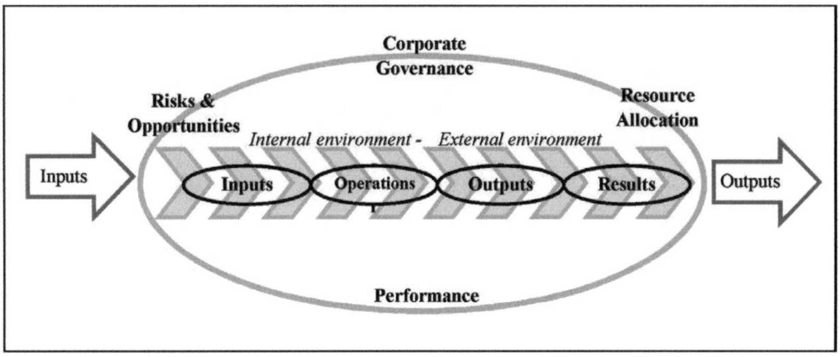

Figure 5. Business model.

we can say that there is a value creation. There are six different categories of capitals. They are financial capital, manufactured capital, human capital, intellectual capital, natural capital and social and relationship capital. Contrary to traditional financial reports, IR does not only take financial capital into consideration, it also deals with other types of capitals. Financial capital can be shortly defined as the pool of funds. Manufactured capital is a kind of human-made capital and machines, buildings, bridges, devices may be good examples of it. Human capital consists of information, skill and ability of employees'. Intellectual capital is a non-physical financial and patent rights, copyrights, licenses, software may be given as examples. Air, water, natural gas, petrol and forests are examples of natural capital. It is necessary to pay attention to the consumption of natural resources especially for future generations. Social and relationship capital is the one constituting well-functioning link, trust and interrelation between individuals and institutions.

Some of the capitals located in integrated report are not owned by the firm. Also, it is possible to make trade-offs between capitals. If the trade-offs affect value creation in a positive manner, then it is rational to do. Let's suppose that there is a decrease in capital X. The firm makes a trade-off from capital X and selects capital Y. As a result of this selection, if an increase in value actualizes, then this means that the firm's decision is right.

Integrated reports have to give information about all capitals affected by the business activities. Briefly, it is possible to specify that firms should report capitals possessed by the firm, influence the firm, controlled by the firm, being both inputs and outputs of the firm.

4. Conclusion

In this chapter, we have tried to show the development process and the paradigm shift in corporate reporting and accounting phenomenon. In today's world, sustainability issues broadly defined in terms of environmental, social and governance gain importance to make effective decisions. Therefore, stakeholders have started to demand summarized corporate reports with comprehensive information that include both financial and non-financial performance. In other words, separate presentation of financial and sustainability information without interconnection has become inadequate in the frame of guidance effectiveness of corporate reporting. In addition, information in order to shape future beliefs has also started to be demanded by stakeholders.

Integrated reporting framework announced in 2013 exhibits the new methodology of corporate reporting to satisfy stakeholders' needs. Its philosophy includes presentation of both financial and non-financial information by providing systematic disclosure of value creation, namely how organizations made resource allocations in the past and how they will create value in the future according to their business models. This new paradigm based on integrated thinking has brought sustainability into the forefront and has redefined the accounting role. Today accounting is no longer simply about producing beneficial financial information. Therefore, accounting as an information system should provide summarized comprehensive information derived by intersection of financial and non-financial performance according to paradigm shift in corporate reporting.

Author details

Pınar Okan Gökten* and Beyhan Marşap

*Address all correspondence to: pinar.okan@gazi.edu.tr

Gazi University, Ankara, Turkey

References

[1] Aras G, Sarıoğlu GU. Kurumsal Raporlamada Yeni Dönem: Entegre Raporlama. 1st ed. Istanbul: TUSIAD; 2015. p. 101

[2] Eccles RG, Serafeim G. Corporate and integrated reporting: A functional perspective. In: Mohrman SA, O'Toole J, Edward EL, editors. Corporate Stewardship: Achieving Sustainable Effectiveness. 1st ed. Sheffield: Greenleaf Publishing; 2015. pp. 156-173

[3] EY (Ernst & Young). Integrated Reporting: Evaluating Value [Internet]. 2014. Available from: http://www.ey.com/Publication/vwLUAssets/EY-Integrated-reporting/$FILE/EY-Integrated-reporting.pdf [Accessed: December 2016]

[4] GRI. G4 Guidelines – Reporting Principles and Standard Disclosures [Internet]. 5 August 2015. Available from: https://www.globalreporting.org/resourcelibrary/G4-Package.zip [Accessed: 17 February, 2017]

[5] Chersan IC. Corporate responsibility reporting according to Global Reporting Initiative: An international comparison. The Audit Financiar Journal. 2016;**14**(136):424-435

[6] GRI. Sustainability Disclosure Database [Internet]. Available from: http://database.globalreporting.org/ [Accessed: 09 March, 2017]

[7] Ocean Tomo. http://www.oceantomo.com/blog/2015/03-05-ocean-tomo-2015-intangible-asset-market-value/ [Internet]. 2015. Available from: http://www.oceantomo.com/blog/2015/03-05-ocean-tomo-2015-intangible-asset-market-value/ [Accessed: 26 November, 2016]

[8] Churet C, Eccles RG. Integrated reporting, quality of management and financial performance. Journal of Applied Corporate Finance. 2014;**26**(1):56-64

[9] Hopwood AG, Unerman J, Fries J. Accounting for sustainability: Practical insights. Earthscan; 2010

[10] Eccles R, Armbrester K. Integrated reporting in the cloud. IESE Insight. 2011;**8**(1):13-20

[11] James ML. The benefits of sustainability and integrated reporting: An investigation of accounting majors' perceptions. Journal of Legal, Ethical and Regulatory Issues. 2015;**18**(1): 1-20

[12] Flower J. The international integrated reporting council: A story of failure. Critical Perspectives on Accounting. 2015;**27**:1-17

[13] Thomson I. But does sustainability need capitalism or an integrated report a commentary on 'The International Integrated Reporting Council: A story of failure' by Flower. Critical Perspectives on Accounting. 2015;**27**:18-22

[14] Humphrey C, O'dwyer B, Unerman J. Re-theorizing the configuration of organizational fields: The IIRC and the pursuit of "enlightened" corporate reporting. Accounting and Business Research. 2017;**47**(1):30-63

[15] Boiral O. Sustainability reports as simulacra? A counter-account of A and A+ GRI reports. Accounting, Auditing & Accountability Journal. 2013;**26**(7):1036-1071

[16] Rowbottom N, Locke J. The emergence of integrated reporting. Accounting and Business Research. 2016;**46**(1):83-115

[17] Serafeim G. Integrated reporting and investor clientele. Journal of Applied Corporate Finance. 2015;**27**(2):34-51

[18] Chersan IC. Study on practices and tendencies in integrated reporting. The Audit Financiar Journal. 2015;**13**(9):108-116

[19] Integrated Reporting Committee (IRC) of South Africa. Reporting on Outcomes: An Information Paper [Internet]. December 2015. Available from: http://www.integratedreportingsa.org/Portals/0/Documents/IRCReportingOutcomesIP.pdf [Accessed: 26 November, 2016]

[20] Abeysekera I. A template for integrated reporting. Emerald Journal of Intellectual Capital. 2013;**14**(2):227-245

[21] IIRC. IIRC Pilot Programme Business Network [Internet]. 2013. Available from: http://integratedreporting.org/wp-content/uploads/2013/11/IIRC-Pilot-Programme-Business-Network-backgrounder-October-2013.pdf [Accessed: 10 February, 2017]

[22] Schaltegger S, Lüdeke-Freund F, Hansen EG. Business models for sustainability a co-evolutionary analysis of sustainable entrepreneurship, innovation, and transformation. Organization & Environment. 2016;**29**(3):264-289

[23] Gökten S. Entegre raporlama yaklaşımı için uygulamaya yönelik sistematik bir öneri. Muhasebe Bilim Dünyası Dergisi. 2016;**18**(4):741-765

Chapter 2

Integrated Reporting: A Template for Energy Companies

Gülçin Yıldırım, Tuğçe Uzun Kocamış and
Figen Öker Türüdüoğlu

Additional information is available at the end of the chapter

http://dx.doi.org/10.5772/intechopen.68921

Abstract

Integrated reporting (IR) is an accelerated corporate reporting approach over the last few years. The idea underlying integrated reporting is to report not only on the company's strategy, management, and financial performance, but also on its social, environmental, and economic impacts. Integrated reporting can also be defined as a holistic report aiming to present annual reports and sustainability reports in a single report, as well as short-, medium-, and long-term goals and strategies of the institution. In the integrated reporting framework prepared by the International Integrated Reporting Council (IIRC), companies aim to make company value measurable and therefore more understandable and comparable by quantifying the environmental and social implications, as well as the financial statements. In this study, firstly the conceptual framework of integrated reporting and the process of extending to integrated reporting, and then the work done in this area in Turkey were given. In the last part of this study, energy companies which are very important in the world trade and which are coming to the agenda due to environmental problems are considered. In this section, integrated reports of seven companies operating in the energy sector and publishing integrated reports are examined. Lastly, it proposes an integrated report template for the Turkish energy sector to contribute to future work.

Keywords: integrated reporting, International Integrated Reporting Council, sustainability reporting, energy companies

1. Introduction

Together with the economies growing in parallel with the globalization trends, it is seen that the financial structures of the enterprises changed and the financial transactions increased in volume and variety. It has become increasingly important that information about business activities is accessible, understandable, reliable, and comparable. The complexity of the business world has led to an increase in requests from companies for information provided in financial performance, management, corporate governance, and sustainability records. Integrated reporting has been developed as a new reporting system in which a firm's strategy, management model, performance, and future expectations can be expressed together in a summarized and understandable way. The purpose of integrated reporting is to ensure that the company's short-, medium-, and long-term future value is expressed by taking into account the company's sustainability results, targets, and expectations, and by linking financial information.

Energy is one of the most important factors in determining the competitiveness of the countries, and the energy sector is an important tool in economic growth. In recent years, energy-environment relation has begun to gain importance in world energy policies. The partnership of these two fields is based on the production of energy for the welfare of the people and the protection of the environment at the same time. In this context, energy companies, in the ever-increasing energy market, are the companies with the highest number of corporations in the world. It is obvious that Turkey cannot stay behind this development.

The interest of the academic and the business world in integrated reporting in Turkey is increasing day by day. Our study summarizes the development process of integrated reporting in the world, including the integrated report proposal for the energy sector where economic and environmental impacts are high.

2. Development of corporate reporting

At the beginning of the 1970s, Adam Smith predicted that the corporate report should act and be responsible for the executive board as a "representative" of a broader set of principles than its shareholders, whose focus is more traditionally the narrower "responsibility" perspective. Therefore, the corporate report suggests greater accountability within the legal rights that lenders, employees, customers, suppliers, the local community, and even the public have for published information [1]. Corporate reporting has undergone significant changes over the last century and is being questioned today whether businesses present their current and future performance correctly [2].

Effective corporate reporting should present a clear strategy and a set of goals for the company based on solid trends and issues, all of the financial risks and opportunities that the company needs to understand and respond to, the sustainability of key stakeholders and relationships that need to be sustained, how the elements of the business model and value chain reflect all, and how they help create environmental and social values [3]. Ideally, reporting should aim to inform the vision and strategy adopted to serve the interests of stakeholders and other factors that may affect future business performance [4].

As seen in **Figure 1**, the corporate reporting process that started with financial reporting has been sustainability reporting in 2000s and eventually integrated reporting. Reporting process is expected to continue with the integrated reporting system.

In summary, when looking at the development of integrated reporting, it is basically possible to mention two cases [6]:

(1) Traditional financial statements and audit reports prepared by the rule-based mandated by different public authorities.

(2) Non-financial reports whose publication is not currently enforced by public authorities and which are focused on environmental and social activities. The main ones of these reports, which have many names and formations in themselves, are social responsibility accounting and sustainability reporting.

At this point, it is worthwhile to focus on sustainability reporting, which is the most important step forward for integrated reporting.

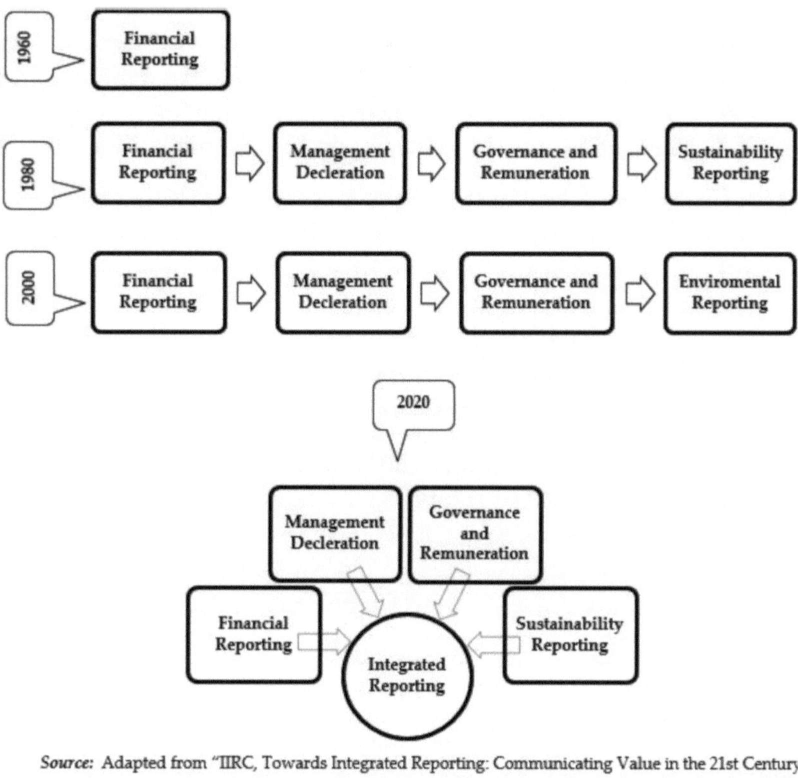

Figure 1. Development of corporate reporting [5]. Source: Adapted from "IIRC, Towards Integrated Reporting: Communicating Value in the 21st Century".

2.1. Sustainability reporting

As a result of the contradiction of "profit" and "social responsibility" in the business world, sustainability concept has gained importance [7]. Sustainability has become one of the foundations of today's business activity. As an integral part of successful financial performance, companies and stakeholders are increasingly interested in sustainable business development. The term "sustainability," together with various meanings and definitions, may be defined as "Sustainability is the impact of the action on the future usability of the future" [8].

It is possible to describe the sustainability report as a report on the economic, environmental, and social impacts of a company or organization's activities.

With sustainability reporting, organizations can measure their economic, environmental, social, and managerial performance and share with information users. In this way, they can set more realistic goals and manage changes more effectively. The sustainability report is the main platform for communicating the positive or negative effects of sustainability performance.

Sustainability reporting is becoming increasingly popular. This can be explained in part by technical developments and the widespread use of the Internet, and as a result, any information about any company can be freely accessed [9]. These developments worry shareholders more about the company's behavior and force businesses to actively participate in the sustainable business development process. The environmental and social accounting disclosures in the report are extremely informative and vital for the companies of certain industries in Europe. Many companies have begun to integrate social and environmental information into their annual reports, or even to publish sustainability or corporate social responsibility reports on their own [8].

The number of companies reporting sustainability performances around the world is increasing [10]. While some companies have included in the activity reports their steps on sustainability, some of them have opened a separate title on their Internet sites to inform their stakeholders and a significant part of them have prepared a separate "sustainability report." In order for companies to be able to open, clear, and transparent sustainability reporting, there are different reporting frameworks accepted around the world. These standards are constantly updated in accordance with stakeholder demands and evolving needs [11].

The need to prepare sustainability reports within a specific standard has emerged at the beginning of the 2000s. Thousands of companies in the world are preparing sustainability reporting, and standards are needed to make a comparative analysis and evaluation in a systematic way. In this regard, companies generally prepare sustainability reports according to the Global Reporting Initiative (GRI) or Global Compact (GC) [12].

World-class reporting frameworks are shown in **Table 1**.

GRI is a world-wide organization with a large number of stakeholders who are not profit-minded. Its mission is to develop globally applicable sustainability reporting rules and to disseminate sustainability reporting by making it routine and comparable as financial reporting. The GRI guide provides a framework for reporting on the environmental, economic, and social activities of companies and the results of these activities [14].

Year	Name of reports	Definitions
1997	Global Reporting Initiative (GRI)	It is the widely accepted initiative about comprehensive reporting in the world. It establishes principles and indicators about economic, environmental and social performance.
1999	AA1000 (AccountAbility 1000)	Account Ability's AA1000 Series of Standards are principles-based Standards and Frameworks used by a broad spectrum of organizations - global businesses, private enterprises, governments and civil societies - to demonstrate leadership and performance in accountability, responsibility and sustainability.
2000	UN Global Compact—UNGC	This contract contains principles for companies to adopt, support and implement a range of core values in the areas of human rights, labor standards, environment and anti-corruption in the area of their impact.
2000	Communication on Progress—COP	Every year, the companies that sign the UN Global Compact must sign "The Communication on Progress" (COP). This declaration is based on the implementation of 10 principles.
2000	The OECD Guidelines for Multinational Enterprises	The OECD Guidelines for Multinational Enterprises are recommendations addressed by governments to multinational enterprises operating in or from adhering countries.
2006	IFC Performance Standards	IFC's Sustainability Framework articulates the Corporation's strategic commitment to sustainable development, and is an integral part of IFC's approach to risk management.
2008	Carbon Disclosure Project—CDP	The CDP works to change the way the business world works in order to mitigate climate change and protect natural resources.
2016	Integrated Reporting—IR	Integrated reporting defines the link between the organization's strategy, management and financial performance and the economic, environmental and social factors in the area in which it operates.
2016	ISO 26000	ISO 26000 aims to contribute to the sustainable development of organizations. The standard encourages legislative harmonization as a requirement of social responsibility, and that the foundation fulfills its legal duties as a basic approach.

Source: [13].

Table 1. Sustainability frameworks.

2.2. Sustainability reporting in Turkey

In 2013, an agreement has been signed between Borsa Istanbul and Ethical Investment Research Services Limited for the calculation of BIST Sustainability Index. Based on the performance of companies in terms of environmental, social, and corporate governance, this index is aimed at increasing the knowledge, understanding, and practices on sustainability issues in Borsa Istanbul companies and also the others throughout Turkey. With the index, companies will be able to meet corporate sustainability performances both in Turkey and globally. The index will allow investors to distinguish and invest in companies that adopt sustainability and corporate social responsibility principles. The BIST Sustainability Index has been calculated and published since November 4, 2014 [15]. **Table 2** shows the companies in the Bist Index.

1	ADEL	ADEL KALEMCİLİK	23	PETKM	PETKİM
2	AKBNK	AKBANK	24	SAHOL	SABANCI HOLDİNG
3	AKSEN	AKSA ENERJİ	25	SISE	SİSE CAM
4	AEFES	ANADOLU EFES	26	HALKB	T. HALK BANKASI
5	ARCLK	ARÇELİK	27	TSKB	T.S.K.B.
6	ASELS	ASELSAN	28	TATGD	TAT GIDA
7	BRISA	BRİSA	29	TAVHL	TAV HAVALİMANLARI
8	CCOLA	COCA COLA İÇECEK	30	TKFEN	TEKFEN HOLDİNG
9	DOHOL	DOĞAN HOLDİNG	31	TOASO	TOFAS OTO. FAB.
10	DOAS	DOĞUS OTOMOTİV	32	TUPRS	TÜPRAS
11	EREGL	EREĞLİ DEMİR CELİK	33	THYAO	TÜRK HAVA YOLLARI
12	FROTO	FORD OTOSAN	34	TTKOM	TÜRK TELEKOM
13	GARAN	GARANTİ BANKASI	35	TTRAK	TÜRK TRAKTÖR
14	GLYHO	GLOBAL YAT. HOLDİNG	36	TCELL	TURKCELL
15	ISCTR	İS BANKASI	37	ULKER	ÜLKER BİSKÜVİ
16	ISGYO	İS GMYO	38	VAKBN	VAKIFLAR BANKASI
17	KCHOL	KOÇ HOLDİNG	39	VESTL	VESTEL
18	KORDS	KORDSA GLOBAL	40	VESBE	VESTEL BEYAZ ESYA
19	MGROS	MİGROS TİCARET	41	YKBNK	YAPI VE KREDİ BANK.
20	NETAS	NETAS TELEKOM.	42	ZOREN	ZORLU ENERJİ
21	OTKAR	OTOKAR			
22	PGSUS	PEGASUS			

Table 2. Companies in the Bist Index in November 2016–October 2017.

There are few studies on sustainability reporting in Turkey. The work done by Topçu and Korkmaz in 2015 is about the phases of integrated reporting in order to achieve the present meaning and try to make some differences with other reports such as corporate governance, environment, and sustainability, especially financial reporting [16].

Aracı and Yuksel reviewed the sustainability reports of 15 organizations who were traded in the BIST Sustainability Index between November 2014 and October 2015, and they found the sustainability report of two organizations prepared in accordance with the GRI reporting principles, eight of these organizations were not prepared in accordance with GRI reporting principles, and four organizations disclose their principles, practices, and activities on sustainability issues to their information users on the Internet site and found that one of the operators included sustainability information in a part of the annual report. They stressed that the use of the GRI G4 reporting principles would be more appropriate for standardization of reporting, transparency, and accountability [17].

Pamukçu and Özdemir examined the sustainability reports of the companies included in Borsa Istanbul Sustainability Index. Among the companies included in the Sustainability Index, they have found that companies have been publishing reports continuously since 2007, and they have come to the conclusion that businesses share their social, environmental, and management performances clearly with their investors as well as financial reporting [18].

Kocamış and Yıldırım examined the corporate portal of sustainability.com which is a communication platform created as a result of the GRI Regional Data Association Agreement. They researched the sustainability applications in Turkey by examining the reports in portal, and they found a total of 136 sustainability reports prepared between 2014 and 2016. One hundred twenty-one of these reports are GRI based [14].

In a study by Gökten on the systematic definition of what the principle view put forward in the framework of integrated reporting implies, a road map has been sought in terms of how the integrated reporting can be done, especially in terms of potential implementers, and it is emphasized that in particular the audit and sustainability reports will be the attachment to the integrated report [19].

3. Integrated reporting

3.1. Definition

With globalization, the results of operations are followed by many groups called financial statement users; investors, customers, suppliers, stakeholders, employees, financial institutions and public authorities. Investment decisions are based on financial decisions. Although financial statements is indispensible, they are not sufficient to meet the needs of the decision makers. They can not reveal the value created by the enterprises in the rapidly changing market conditions [20]. Today, only looking at financial results; it is not possible to attract the attention of potential investors and raise corporate reputation.

In addition to economic effects, business activities have social and environmental impacts. These effects are not sufficiently included in traditional reporting systems. The incomplete aspects of traditional reporting have been tried to be complemented by activity, corporate governance, social responsibility, and sustainability reports that have gained importance in recent years, but reaching and understanding these reports with different dynamics has created problems for decision makers. As a result of these developments, companies have begun to look for ways to express themselves better and the process has brought the business world to a new reporting framework called "Integrated Reporting." Integrated reporting arises from the need to link financial with non-financial information so that financial information users can fully understand the corporate performance of a company and conduct risk analysis of the company. The aim of the integrated report is to ensure that the company's short-, medium-, and long-term future value is expressed by taking into account the company's sustainability results, targets, and expectations and linking them with financial information.

At the end of 2009, the International Integrated Reporting Council (IIRC) was established to serve this purpose. The International Integrated Reporting Council is a worldwide coalition of regulators, companies, investors, non-governmental organizations, and financial experts.

The International Integrated Reporting Council defines integrated reporting as: "Integrated Activity Reporting is the process by which a company's strategy communicates its governance structure, its performance and how its objectives create value in the short, medium and long term."

The integrated report is created by adding additional information about the company's strategy, governance structure, and performance to the existing financial reporting structure. The main objective of integrated reporting is to draw a holistic picture of the company [21].

3.2. Integrated reporting in the world

The integrated reporting concept was introduced in South Africa in 2009 through the corporate governance report King III. The Johannesburg Stock Exchange adopted King III Principles for all companies traded on the stock exchange [22].

In "Accounting for Sustainability-A4S" on December 17, 2009, under the auspices of Prince Charles, the decision to pass integrated reporting and to establish the International Integrated Reporting Council has been taken [23].

The first integrated reports began to be published in 2010, and the first implementation draft of integrated reports was published in 2011 by the IIRC [5]. In this draft, content and principles of integrated reports are included. The IIRC has launched a pilot program in 2012 involving about 100 companies. With this program, until the end of 2013, it was aimed to create the framework of integrated reporting as a new global standard. Eventually, the framework was published in December 2013 [24].

South Africa is the first country to implement integrated reporting. In South Africa, the Integrated Reporting Board has provided the development of integrated reporting with working groups, such as the King's Committee, led by Professor Mervyn King. In South Africa, publicly traded reports are prepared according to the King III guidelines. While not being another country with a mandatory requirement outside South Africa, it is expected that in the future, there will be an increase in the number of voluntary applications and the number of countries that are compulsory.

Parallel to these developments,

- Companies with more than 500 employees in countries subject to the European Union are required to report transparency, sustainability, human rights, corruption, etc. in their annual reports. The transition to integrated reporting, where the topics are located, has begun.

- In the United States, a guide to transparency, sustainability issues related to the integrated reporting was prepared according to the Sustainability Accounting Standards Board (SASB) (Mandatory 10-C form).
- IR studies have started in Brazil, Austria, Japan, and New Zealand [25].

The International Integrated Reporting Council is a global coalition of regulators, investors, companies, standard setters, professional accountancy organizations, and non governmental organisations (NGOs). The IIRC is making efforts to raise awareness about creating value as a next step in the development of corporate reporting. The IIRC defines its mission "The IIRC's mission is to establish integrated reporting and thinking within mainstream business practice as the norm in the public and private sectors" [26]. The IIRC workshops are shared with interested parties at www.integratedreporting.org. On the IIRC portal (http://examples.integratedreporting.org/home), integrated reports are published worldwide. General information on these reports is provided in **Tables 3** and **4**.

Year	2011	2012	2013	2014	2015	2016	Total
Number of reports	46	32	53	86	59	8	284

Table 3. Number of reports published.

Region	Europa	Africa	Asia	South America	Australia	North America	Total
Number of reports	132	81	29	14	14	14	**284**

Table 4. Distribution by region.

3.3. Integrated reporting in Turkey

Turkey is still at an early stage in integrated reporting, just like many other countries. Financial reports in Turkey are presented considering the International Financial Reporting Standards for publicly held companies. Sustainability reporting is carried out within the activity reports or as a separate report. Along with the increasing awareness of sustainability reporting, there is a growing interest in integrated reporting.

The sustainability platform established at the Istanbul Stock Exchange places great emphasis on integrated reporting and conducts awareness raising activities. IIRC's corporate representation in Turkey is conducted by the Corporate Governance Association of Turkey (TKYD) and the Integrated Reporting Working Group formed by the Business World and Sustainable Development Association (SKD Turkey). The working group, which continues its activities to raise awareness in the field of integrated reporting both in the private and public sectors, also carries out activities to improve the framework of reporting [25].

In Turkey, Çimsa Çimento Corporation, and Garanti Bankası Corporation as pilot companies, they carry out integrated reporting studies. The nonprofit Argumental Governance Academy was the first company to publish Turkey's integrated report [27].

3.4. Integrated reporting framework

An integrated reporting framework that integrates financial and non-financial information of organizations with a single report and aims to use common standards is a process that needs to be integrated and that enables the company to periodically report and communicate the value it creates over time.

At the core of the integrated reporting conceptual framework lies the extension of the company's reporting to include all the resources that it uses as input to its business activities. The IIRC defines the term "capital" in six chapters, namely financial, production, intellectual, human, social and relationship, and natural resource to illustrate these sources [28]. In addition, the framework requires the definition of the business model of the company. How the business model and the underlying strategies integrate with these six capital elements must be explained in the report. Another issue that IR differs from traditional financial statements is the need for more forward-looking information, taking into account short-, medium-, and long-term rather than reflecting past transactions and events. In this way, key opportunities and risks are identified and valuable information can be given to stakeholders on the company's future survival capability [29].

The purpose of the framework is to provide guidelines and content items that regulate the total content of an integrated report and to explain the underlying concepts underlying them.

3.4.1. Guiding principles

The following guidelines are used as a basis for preparing an integrated report, which provides information on the content of the report and how it is presented:

- **Strategic focus and future orientation:** An integrated report should provide insight into the strategy of the foundation and its ability to create value in the short, medium and long term, and how it relates to the use and interaction of capital elements.
- **Interlinking information:** An integrated report should provide a holistic picture of the combination of factors that affect the value creation ability of the organization over time, their relationship to each other, and their dependencies.
- **Relations with stakeholders:** An integrated report should provide information on the nature and quality of the relationships established by the stakeholders with the stakeholders and show how the stakeholder understands the legitimate needs and desires of the stakeholders.
- **Materiality:** An integrated report should provide information on issues that significantly affect the ability of the organization to create value in the short, medium, and long term.
- **Be short and simple:** An integrated report should be short and concise.
- **Reliability and completeness:** An integrated report should contain all material aspects, both positive and negative, in a way that is balanced and does not contain any material error.

- **Consistency and comparability:** The information in an integrated report should be presented in a way that (a) is based on a consistent basis over time, and (b) allows the organization to compare with other organizations in terms of their ability to create value over time.

3.4.2. Content items

There are eight content items in an integrated report that are based on each other and do not mutually exclude each other:

- **Corporate overview and external environment:** What is the business that organization is doing and under what conditions does it operate?
- **Corporate governance:** How does the corporate governance structure of the foundation support the ability to create value in the short, medium, and long term?
- **Business model:** What is the establishment business model?
- **Risks and opportunities:** What are the specific risks and opportunities that affect the ability of the establishment to create value in the short, medium, and long term, and how does the organization address them?
- **Strategy and resource transfer:** What is the goal of the establishment and how is it intended to reach it?
- **Performance:** To what extent has the organization achieved its strategic objectives for the period and how have the results influenced the capital items?
- **Overview:** What are the potential difficulties and uncertainties that may arise when implementing the strategy of the establishment and what are the potential impacts of them in terms of their business model and future performance?
- **Based on the presentation:** How does the organization determine the issues to be included in the integrated report and how are these issues being examined or evaluated?

It is possible to say that the integrated reporting principles are consistent with the Fundamental Concepts and Policies of Accounting and are based on the "fair value" approach which is the basis of international financial reporting standards.

4. Examination of integrated reporting application for energy sector

On the basis of ecological economics, nature is not only a passive waste repository and raw material source, but also a manufacturer with its own unique technologies. The ecological economy emphasizes the importance of multidimensional optimization for maximum quality of life in the following dimensions:

- Products and services of nature, environmental conditions
- Social conditions
- Monetized production
- Unmonetized local production (nature or human).

The energy sector that is indispensable in today's world causes many environmental problems in the stages of production, transmission, and consumption. Greenhouse gases and other pollutants are released mostly by energy companies during the energy production, energy consumption, or energy conversion operations. These companies are liable to generate more human-oriented and environmentally sustainable politics while they are maximizing energy supply and consuming energy.

Today, achieving energy which is the basic need is important for economic and social development [30]. The structure of the global energy sector is shaped by environmental factors with the impact of climate change [31]. Energy efficiency policies are one of the areas that need to be addressed sensitively because of the direct relevance of economic growth and social development goals to sustainability, and on the other hand, as a key role in reducing total greenhouse gas emissions.

Fossil fuels (petroleum, natural gas, coal, lignite, asphaltite), hydropower, and nuclear energy, which meet 95% of the world's energy needs, are shown as traditional energy sources of our time. Despite this high utilization rate, because of the limited resources and the negative effects on the environment (fossil fuels, nuclear energy, hydraulics), the use of energy sources that are safer, renewable, and cannot adversely affect the environment and live life became a necessity [32].

Turkey is among the most important energy consumers of the world with its developing economy. In 2014, natural gas Turkey's primary energy demand, which is 123.9 million tons of petroleum equivalent (TPE) (867.3 million barrels), is in the first place with 32.5%, while coal is 29.2%, and petroleum follows them with 28.5% [33].

Within the recent 10-year period, Turkey has emerged as one of the countries with the fastest growing energy demand. After China, Turkey has become the second country with the highest demand to electricity and natural gas. Projections show that Turkey's demand to oil and natural gas will continue to grow in the medium and long term. Due to very limited oil and natural gas reserves, Turkey imported 99% of natural gas mostly from Russia, Iran, and Azerbaijan, and 89 % of oil mostly from Iraq, Iran, and Russia in 2015.

In 2015, Turkey's total energy demand was 264 TWh and met by natural gas 35%, coal 28.5 %, oil 27%, hydro 7%, renewables 2.5% of total demand. According to the official satistics, approximately 25% of total energy demand of Turkey is covered by domestic sources, while 75% is imported from mostly Russia and middle east countries in 2015 [34].

Turkey continues to put intensive efforts on increasing the share of renewable energy sources in the national energy mix and adding nuclear energy to the energy grid, with the aim of reducing energy dependency which is one of the most important issues of many countries.

Issues such as energy saving and efficiency, ensuring energy supply security, reducing risks of external dependence, protecting the environment, and increasing the effectiveness of the challenge against climate change are accepted as the most important components of energy policies [35].

Having important effects on politics and also strategic power, energy industry is in the center of attention throughout the world. With integrated reporting, it is targeted to provide useful information to stakeholders about important issues, including economic, environmental, and social

http://dx.doi.org/10.5772/intechopen.68921

issues that affect the organization's ability to create value. In accordance with the structure of the issuing organization, the reports can be formatted on the basis of guidelines and content items principles. The expectation of information users is essential when preparing the report.

There is no standard format of integrated reporting [36]. It is expected that the integrated report should contain information that is satisfactory to the reader. These information are on

- Organization,
- Governance,
- Opportunities and risks,
- Strategy and resource allocation,
- Business model, and
- Performance.

In this context, the reports of the seven energy companies in Turkey located on the IIRC's online platform are reviewed [37–43]. The integrated report template highlighting the most important issues in this sector is given below (**Tables 5** and **6**).

In this section of study, it is appropriate to refer to the natural capital elements in the IR framework of the energy companies. In the IR framework, natural capital is defined as all renewable and nonrenewable environmental resources and processes that provide goods or services that support the past, current, or future prosperity of an organization. It includes air, water, land, minerals, forests, fossil fuels, agricultural crops and biodiversity, and the others in the coverage of ecosystem.

Sector	Number of report
Basic materials	40
Consumer goods	33
Consumer services	26
Financial services	67
Healthcare	14
Industrials	37
Professional services	11
Public sector	1
Oil and gas	13
Real estate	7
Technology	5
Telecommunication	9
Utilities	21
Total	**284**

Table 5. Sectoral distribution.

Section name	Definition
Organization	- The mission of the company, - Vision, - Ethical values, - Partnership and management structure, - Main activities, - Product services, - Competition structure of the market, - Financial information.
Governance	- Leading staff and management structure of the company, - The expertise and diversity of the managers, - How the institutional culture was created, - Risk management practices.
Opportunities and risks	- Risk factors and uncertainties, - Risk management, - Reduce top risks.
Strategy and resource allocation	- Company strategy, - Company's short, medium and long term strategies, - Resource distribution plans, - Measurement of reaching targets (KPI).
Business model	- Distribution channels, - Innovation policies, - Buildings and other equipment - Human health and safety - Know-how and capabilities - Experience - Relationship with stakeholders (such as organizations, government, society, associations, universities, etc.)
Performance	- Financial sources, - Production source, - Natural capital, - Social and relationship capital, - Intellectual capital, - Human resources

Table 6. Basic presentation topics.

In the integrated reports, natural capital is evaluated as a crucial part of the report which informs the users about what measures are taken to keep the natural resources and which actions are planned to reduce the operations harmful to the environment.

In this study, the reports of seven companies operating in the energy sector [44–50] and publishing integrated reports were examined, and the key performance indicators (KPIs) for the six capital elements under the performance heading were analyzed. KPIs are measurable values that show how effective a company is in achieving its core business objectives. Organizations use KPIs at multiple levels to assess how successful they are in achieving their goals. In this context, IR suggests that quantitative indicators such as KPIs and monetized measures can be extremely useful in explaining how a corporation creates value in an integrated report and how it uses and influences various capital elements. Organizations share the performance of six capital elements by means of their KPIs.

Table 7 shows the key performance indicators (KPI) offered based on energy sector-specific information in the analyzed reports.

Headings	Performance indicators
Financial capital	Sales volume
	Sales revenues
	Operating profit
	Net working capital
	Earnings per share
	Equity profitability
	Earnings increase
	Cash flow from activities
	Investment expenditure
	Cash flow per unit production
	Unit cost per production
	Activity per unit production
	Debt equity ratio
Productive capital	Production volume
	Counterfeit usage rates
	Investment cost
	Change in productive capacity
	Operational efficiency
	Reserves
	Reserve renewal rate
	Unit shipping costs

Headings	Performance indicators
Natural capital	Renewable energy use
	Renewable energy production (mW)
	Renewable energy capacity (mW)
	Energy consumption (mW)
	Operational oil/gas leaks
	Surface water, underground water and network water consumption
	Source based water supply
	Water resources used
	Quantities of drained and recycled water
	Protected areas
	Strategies developed on biodiversity
	Study areas under biodiversity reliance
	Direct and indirect greenhouse gas emissions
	Other ındirect greenhouse gas emissions
	Activities related to greenhouse gas emission reduction
	Ozone drilling emissions ınformation
	Nox, Sox and other air emission types
	Water discharge ınformation
	Total waste volume and disposal methods
	Information on the amount produced or generated water quantities
	Hydrocarbons released to air
	Total waste volume
	Waste drilling studies and ımprovement strategies
	Import, export and transportation wastes
	Settlement areas affected by waste water discharge
Social and relationship capital	Employee satisfaction
	Customer happiness
	Supplier satisfaction
	Unionality rate
	Donations and sponsorships
	Cases and compensation
Intellectual capital	R & D ınvestments
	Patent applications
	Buying patents

Table 7. Performance criteria—basic performance indicators (KPI).

5. Conclusion and recommendations

In the future, integrated reporting is likely to take the place of existing institutional reports. It is important for organizations to decide how to present their financial and non-financial information to the attention of information users. It is appropriate to have different sub-headings for different sectors in integrated reporting because of the fact that there are significant sectoral differences as well as the general framework.

Instead of adding directly the activity report prepared by the companies previously or the sustainability report to integrated report, this report should contain the core information prepared in accordance with the content items.

Businesses that have started to prepare a sustainability report are prepared enterprises for the integrated report preparation. By the integration of financial statements and financial indicators in these reports, integrated reports can be easily prepared.

Integrated reporting for businesses that have not prepared corporate governance and sustainability reporting will require intensive work. Reporting efforts will play a role in motivating self-inquiry, knowledge creation, learning, and various internal control mechanisms for these enterprises and will contribute to the development of enterprises. The companies that do not have experience to prepare the activity reports yet, it would be more appropriate to gradually pass to integrated reporting.

There is not yet an audit framework in Europe and the United States also. Various studies are being carried out in this direction. Firstly, an audit framework should be established by regulatory agencies. The next step should be to identify the auditors to evaluate the non-financial information contained in the integrated reports.

As a result, companies which prepare integrated reports are expected to their corporate image by fulfilling their duty of transparency, accountability, and social responsibility.

Integrated reporting should not be considered as just a report, it is a process that informs all interest groups such as employees, investors, customers, suppliers, trade unions, public institutions, and non-governmental organizations for corporate sustainability and therefore helps to transform and develop society. Businesses should be informed and supported to prepare these reports.

Author details

Gülçin Yıldırım[1], Tuğçe Uzun Kocamış[2] and Figen Öker Türüdüoğlu[1*]

*Address all correspondence to: figenturuduoglu@gmail.com

1 University of Bahçeşehir, İstanbul, Turkey

2 University of Istanbul, İstanbul, Turkey

References

[1] Owen G. Integrated reporting: A review of developments and their implications for the accounting curriculum. Accounting Education: An International Journal. 2013;**22**(4):3 40-356

[2] Massie RK. Accounting and accountability: Integrated reporting and the purpose of the firm. In: Eccles RG, Cheng B, Saltzman D, editors. The Landscape of Integrated Reporting: Reflections and Next Steps. Massachusetts: The President and Fellows of Harvard College; 2010. pp. 2-8

[3] Knight A. Think different. In: Eccles RG, Cheng B, Saltzman D. The Landscape of Integrated Reporting: Reflections and Next steps. Massachusetts: The President and Fellows of Harvard College; 2010. pp. 38-39

[4] Yanık, Serhat ve Türker, İpek. Sürdürülebilirlik ve Sosyal Sorumluluk Raporlamasındaki Gelişmeler (Tümleşik Raporlama). İ.Ü. Siyasal Bilgiler Fakültesi Dergisi. 2012;**47**:291-308

[5] IIRC. Towards integrated reporting: Communicating value in the 21st century. s.l.: IIRC; 2011. Available from: http://integratedreporting.org/wp-content/uploads/2011/09/IR-Discussion-Paper-2011_spreads.pdf

[6] Yaz, DA. Entegre Raporlama (Integrated Reporting). [Online] 13 Ekim 2014. [Quote Date: 20 Kasım 2016.] http://www.finansgundem.com/yazarlar/entegre-rapor lama-integrated-reporting-yazisi/466633

[7] Aydın S. Kurumsal Raporlamanın Evrilme Sürecine İlişkin Bir İrdeleme. Mali Çözüm; 2015. pp. 61-72

[8] Natalja G, Inna S. Survey of sustainability reporting integrated into annual reports of Estonian companies for the years 2007-2010: Based on companies listed on Tallinn Stock Exchange as of October 2011. Procedia Economics and Finance. 2012;**2**:26-34

[9] Akarçay Ç. Sürdürülebilirlik Muhasebesi Standartları Kurulu. Marmara Üniversitesi Öneri Dergisi, Cilt 11. 2014;**42**:1-11

[10] TİSK Proje Ekibi. Herkes İçin Kurumsal Sosyal Sorumluluk Projesi Türkiye Sürdürülebilirlik Raporlaması Ulusal İnceleme Raporu. Ankara: TİSK; 2016

[11] Borsa İstanbul. Şirketler için Sürdürülebilirlik Rehberi. İstanbul: Borsa İstanbul; 2013

[12] IIRC. Towards Integrated Reporting: Communicating Value in the 21st Century. IIRC, 2011. http://integratedreporting.org/wp-content/uploads/2011/09/IR-Discussion-Paper-2011_spreads.pdf.

[13] Önce S, Onay A, Yeşilçelebi G. Corporate sustainability reporting and situation in Turkey. Journal of Economics, Finance and Accounting. 2015;**2**(2):230-252

[14] Kocamış TU, Yıldırım G. Sustainability reporting in Turkey: Analysis of companies in the BIST sustainability index. European Journal of Economics and Business Studies. 2016;**6**(1):41-51

[15] BIST Sustainability Index. İstanbul: Borsa İstanbul. [Online] 20 Aralık 2016. Available from: http://www.borsaistanbul.com/endeksler/bist-pay-endeksleri/surdurulebilirlik-endeksi

[16] Entegre Raporlama: Kavramsal Bir İnceleme. Topçu, Mustafa Kemal ve Korkmaz, Göksel. Dokuz Eylül Üniversitesi İktisadi ve İdari Bilimler Fakültesi Dergisi; 2015. pp. 1-22

[17] Şeffaflık ve Hesap Verilebilirliğin Sağlanmasında Sürdürülerbilirlik Raporları: BİST Sürdürülebilirlik Endeksindeki Şirketlerin Sürdürülebilirlik Raporlarının İncelenmesi. Aracı, Hakan ve Yüksel, Figen. 18 (Özel Sayı-1). Muhasebe Bilim Dünyası Dergisi; 2016. pp. 103-131

[18] Pamukçu F, Özdemir Z. Kurumsal Sürdürülebilir Raporlama Sisteminin Borsa İstanbul Sürdürülebilirlik Endeksi Kapsamındaki İşletmelerde Analizi. Mali Çözüm; 2016. pp. 13-35

[19] Gökten S. Entegre Raporlama Yaklaşımı İçin Uygulamaya Yönelik Sistematik Bir Öneri. Muhasebe Bilim Dünyası Dergisi. 2016; pp. 741-765

[20] Kaya HP. Entegre Raporlama Sisteminin Ortaya Çıkış Sebepleri ve Şirketlere Sağlayacağı Faydalar. 45, Haziran, Muhasebe ve Denetime Bakış Dergisi; 2015. pp. 113-130

[21] Mitchell S. Entegre Raporlamaya Bir Bakış. 19, s.l.: TÜYİD, Hissedar Dergisi, Cilt 1; 2016. pp. 38-39

[22] EY. Integrated Reporting: Elevating Value [Online]. 2014. Available from: http://www.ey.com/Publication/vwLUAssets/EY-Integrated-reporting/$FILE/EY-Integrated-reporting.pdf [Accessed: 5 Kasım 2016]

[23] Pensions Event 2013 [Online]. 2013. Available from: https://www.accountingforsustainability.org/events/resilience-and-the-long-term [Accessed: 5 Kasım 2016]

[24] Sierra-García L, Zorio-Grima A, García-Benau, MA. Stakeholder engagement, corporate social responsibility and integrated reporting: An exploratory study. Corporate Social Responsibility and Environmental Management. 2013;**22**(5):286-304. Available from: http://onlinelibrary.wiley.com/doi/10.1002/csr.1345/abstract.

[25] Ergüden E. Kurumsal Raporlamada Yeni Dönem: Entegre Raporlama. s.l., Ankara: TÜRMOB, 1 Haziran; 2016

[26] [Online]. Available from: http://integratedreporting.org/the-iirc-2/

[27] Argüden Yönetişim Akademisi. Türkiye'nin İlke Entegre Raporu Yayınlandı. İstanbul: s.n., 2016. Available from: https://buvak.org.tr/docs/1477638246_ArgudenAkademi_Entegre_Rapor_Haberi_BUVAKWebsitesi__TR_.pdf

[28] IIRC. Uluslararası IR Çerçevesi [Online]. 2015. Available from: http://integratedreporting.org/wp-content/uploads/2015/03/13-12-08-THE-INTERNATIONAL-IR-FRAMEWORK-Turkish.pdf. http://integratedreporting.org/ [Accessed: 20 Kasım 2016]

[29] Mandy C, et al. The international integrated reporting framework: Key issues and future research opportunities. Journal of International Financial Management & Accounting. 2014;**25**(1):90-119

[30] Ayoola TJ, Olasanmi, OO. Business case for integrated reporting in the Nigerian oil and gas sector. Issues in Social and Environmental Accounting. 2013;30-54

[31] Thermal Power Plants in Turkey. Kıncay, Olcay ve Öztürk, Recep. Energy Sources; 2003. pp. 135-151

[32] Eti Menkul Kıymetler. Enerji Sektörü Raporu. İstanbul: Eti Menkul Kıymetler AŞ; 2008. Available from: http://www.etiyatirim.com/upload/rapor_sektor/SKR_ENERJI_ETIM_060608.pdf

[33] Petrolleri T. Ham Petrol ve Doğalgaz Sektör Raporu. Ankara: Türkiye Petrolleri; 2016

[34] Available from: http://www.mfa.gov.tr/turkeys-energy-strategy.en.mfa

[35] Enerji V. [Online] 2016. Available from: http://www.enerji.gov.tr/tr-TR/Anasayfa [Accessed: 5 Kasım 2016]

[36] KPMG. Integrated Reporting. basım yeri bilinmiyor: KPMG; 2012. Available from: Global/en/IssuesAndInsights/ArticlesPublications/integrated-reporting/Documents/integratedreporting-issue-2.pdf

[37] Ak Enerji. Ak Enerji Sürdürülebilirlik Raporu 2014. İstanbul: Ak Enerji; 2015. Available from: http://www.akenerji.com.tr/Dosya/Dokuman/akenerji_2014_tr_web1.pdf

[38] Aksa Enerji. Aksa Enerji Sürdürülebilirlik Raporu 2015. İstanbul: Finar Kurumsal; 2016. Available from: http://img-aksaenerji.mncdn.com/media/21423/aksa-enerji-2015-yili-surdurulebilirlik-raporu.pdf

[39] Aygaz. Aygaz Sürdülebilirlik Raporu. İstanbul: Aygaz; 2014. Available from: https://www.aygaz.com.tr/Client/Aygaz/AygazSurdurulebilirlikRaporlari/surdurulebilirlik_raporu_2012-2013.pdf

[40] Bursagaz. Bursagaz Sürdülebilirlik Raporu 2011-2013. Bursa: Bursagaz; 2014. Available from: http://www.kurumsalsurdurulebilirlik.com/tr-tr/raporlar/bursagaz-surdurulebilirlik-raporu-2014.aspx

[41] OPET. OPET Sürdülebilirlik Raporu 2012-2013. İstanbul: OPET; 2014. Available from: https://www.opet.com.tr/Files/PDF/SurdurulebilirlikRaporu/2012-2013.pdf

[42] TÜPRAŞ. Kurumsal Sosyal Sorumluluk Raporu 2015. Kocaeli: Tüpraş; 2016. Available from: https://tprstaticfilessa.blob.core.windows.net/assets/uploads/ksra porlari/2015_KSS_TR.pdf

[43] Enerji Z. 2014-2015 Sürdülebilirlik Raporu. İstanbul: Zorlu Enerji; 2016. Available from: http://console22.zorluenerjigrubu.com/Upload/Document/12.7.2016-ZORLUENERJI_2014_2015_Surdurulebilirlik%20Raporu.pdf

[44] BP. Annual Report and Form 20-F 2015. London: Pureprint Group Limited; 2016. Available from: http://www.bp.com/content/dam/bp/pdf/investors/bp-annual-report-and-form-20f-2015.pdf

[45] Cairn Energy. Cairn Energy PLC Annual Report and Accounts 2013. Edinburgh: Emperor; 2014. Available from: http://www.cairnenergy.com/files/reports/annual/ar2013/2013_annual_report.pdf

[46] ENI. Integrated Annual Report. Roma: ENI; 2015. Available from: https://www.eni.com/docs/en_IT/enicom/company/integrated-annual-report-2015.pdf

[47] Rosneft. Annual Report 2013. Moskova: Rosneft; 2014. Available from: http://examples.integratedreporting.org/organisation/109

[48] SASOL. A New Area For SASOL Annual Integrated Report 2014. Johannesburg: SASOL; 2015. Available from: http://www.sasol.com/extras/annual-integrated-report/docs/air/Sasol_AIR_2014_complete.pdf

[49] Tullow Oil PLC. Tullow Oil PLC 2013 Annual Report & Accounts. London: Tullow Oil; 2014

[50] Woodside. Woodside 2011 Annual Report. Perth, WA: Woodside; 2012

Chapter 3

Greening Accounting: An Inevitable Link to Help Firms Connect with Sustainability

Somnath Debnath

Additional information is available at the end of the chapter

http://dx.doi.org/10.5772/67936

Abstract

The last decade has seen developments challenging the abilities of managerial accounting theories in supporting firms with environmental conscious decision-making that are grounded in the expanded accountability of firms toward nature and society. Critical theorists have argued that the shortcomings of the accounting theories to interpret the impacts of business activities on nature have its origin in the missing accounting standards, under-defined contractual boundaries, and the absence of a valid numéraire (monetary equivalency). In this chapter, the author posits that these shortcomings are a legacy of the economic paradigm within which the accounting frameworks operate and would remain so, unless a paradigm change evolves to handle environmental-related considerations on its own, even if it means rewriting rules to generate accounting interpretations of business activities. Instead of offering a methodological solution, this chapter ideates how having "environment" as integral to the accounting paradigm would enable firms in evaluating, accounting, and reporting environmental performance transparently and improve flow of information to help management face sustainability-related challenges better.

Keywords: environmental accounting, ethical rights, externalities, accounting dimensions

1. Introduction

Managerial accounting has evolved over the years as a valuable aid for management to interpret accounting and other organizational inputs and generate information necessary to improve scientific temperament in the decision-making process. However, last two decades have also witnessed developments that challenged its abilities to support sustainability and environment-related issues and help businesses manage societal expectations better. These challenges, in all earnestness, have questioned the efficacy of firms to act as economic agents of society and remain a conduit of continuing progress. The absence of suitable language to comprehensively describe the evolving decision considerations is one end of the problem; inability of current accounting language to satisfy information needs beyond economic viewpoint is proving to be another. Instead of proposing a comprehensive solution to this polyvocal problem, this chapter aims at going beyond the arguments of greening managerial accounting to understand how changes in the core accounting construct might help firms connect better with the sustainability-related issues and shape microlevel application of sustainability to emerge as inherent to the accounting sciences.

2. Sustainability and underlying philosophies: implications for business firms

Sustainability, in simple terms, embodies the eternal principles upholding well-being of mother earth to sustain and improve human and other life forms along with the nonliving world, and enrich natural environment over time. While scientific understanding of energy and matter and how it flows through the diverse activities in nature to support different life forms and abiotic world is inadequate to meaningfully explain its multidimensional nature and long-term ramifications of anthropocentric activities, the ensuing debate within academic disciplines to have largely remained fragmented along the respective epistemological boundaries has been less surprising [1]. Still, some convergence has been witnessed toward acknowledging the need of developing interdisciplinary and transdisciplinary studies to improve understanding of sustainability-related issues (see Abraham [2] in engineering, Bergmann [3] in fine arts, Bosselmann [4] and Mueller [5] in education, Gray [6] in accounting, Stegall [7] in design, Taylor and Theyel [8] in business education, and others). At the same time, critical theorists have argued how increasing materialistic lifestyle and drive to improve economic prosperity of societies have steadily increased the risks of continuing environmental exploits and ecological losses, including loss of biodiversity, global warming, and increasing levels of resource consumption that are seriously threatening intra- and intergenerational equity (supported by the last Millennium Ecosystem Assessment report [9] as well). Jones and Solomon [10] believe that the ecological losses of this era are of the worst type and perhaps can even eclipse previous natural disasters in terms of impact and magnitude, as the twin issues: (a) these being human-induced ones and (b) our inability to understand the impacts in entirety are pushing ecosystem toward a state that is least understood in terms of its life-supporting capabilities. Meanwhile, the inability of global organizations and governments of sovereign countries to push for formal mechanism to uphold accountability of industries toward the impending disaster that can drive significant changes in the behavior of the industries to act responsibly has been equally disturbing. Metcalf and Benn [11] have questioned the "fit for purpose" of corporate firms to continue as the social mechanism of development and changes needed for them to be responsive toward the interconnected, dynamic, economic, environmental, and social systems.

This brings us to the debate if ecological sustenance should be focal to agenda of economic growth and human progress, as ecocentric philosophy proposes, as compared to anthropocentricity that views sustainability as a key to further human existence on this planet. While ecocentric views integrate everything, including our collective knowledge, to improve understanding of our relationship with nature (biotic and abiotic world), anthropocentrism believes the purpose of nature, and its resources are to enrich human life and harness knowledge to serve human needs better [12]. Between these two extremes, the question—how (un)sustainability of human activities is to be viewed against the backdrop of everything else—remains unanswered. In normative terms, sustainability of a region is dependent on pursuing and practicing policies that would sustain ecological balance and natural wealth over time, but to redefine the role of business in effectively participating and supporting the cause, which has hardly been explored, has remained relatively under-defined in ascertaining "what" and "how much" of sustainability should be the responsibility of microlevel entities. This effectively creates a problem for the accounting theories to define "what" needs to be accounted for, even before deciding "how" this could be achieved. To define nature of information needed by firms and its stakeholders to be reflective about the current form of development and how that might be impacting sustainability is also relevant to this discussion. Within the prevailing diversity, how firms and managements could improve their accountabilities toward society and nature would need us to explore advancements in accounting theories and how this could be relevant in helping businesses live up to the challenges of our times (Section 3). This is followed by exploring how accounting sciences would need to rewrite rules to capture environmental impacts of firms and its activities (Section 4), before summarizing how this might change the accounting world for the better (Section 5).

3. Sustainability and critical accounting theories

Firms' need to account for environmental duress due to its economic affairs has been philosophized under the aegis of social and environmental accounting (SEA), where different philosophical approaches have contributed to advance the arguments in favor of improving the nature and state of accounting sciences to support the cause. The context of discussion in this chapter is not to critically examine theoretical approaches that have contributed to advance arguments in favor of environmental accounting but to validate few important ideas that have shaped the need for the accounting theories to play a vital role in supporting sustainability. This includes *ethical approach,* where quasi-public nature of business has been considered as the underlying reason for the firms to partner with the larger issues that the societies are facing today. At the same time, experts have cited *ethical rights theory* to uphold stakeholders' rights to be informed about how firms are handling environmental demands of the society, whereas *instrumentalist approach* of environmental accounting comprises of tools and techniques that can be of significance to translate environment-related risks as a new opportunity for the businesses to pursue and help them generate first mover's opportunity to drive a win-win situation. Here, "environmental accounting" has been referred to reflect the role of accounting and information system to support firms in keeping track of impacts that its activities cause on environment and generate information on the utilization of natural resources like materials, energies, water, and other resources to support information needs of internal and external stakeholders while preserving materiality, traceability, and relevance of such information (improvised from IFAC [13]). Accordingly, more than the empirical aspects of the subject, the following subsections reflect on the systemic ones, including examining how contemporary developments within accounting literature are connected to the issues of environmental sustainability.

3.1. Contemporary developments within the critical accounting theories to support sustainability

We start the discussion with the *ethical approach* that advocates firms to view their obligations toward nature and society as a primary concern and find ways to evolve uncompromising attitude of businesses to uphold this to be a central tenet of existence, simply because "this is the right things to do" (normative view). Even though this view might not always lead to a win-win situation for firms, especially when the outcome(s) of any strategy or opportunity is/are stacked against the economic ones that might have to be sacrificed to pursue environmentally oriented ones, still firms are expected to align their actions and decisions to maximize the overall well-being of everyone concerned [14]. Not only this is impractical from a pragmatic standpoint, such an ideology would have limited impact to bring in a calculative aspect that accounting in general is associated to. The approach closely corresponds to the deep green approach in SEA theories (care for nature in everything we do), which is somewhat contrary to the methods of economic organizations, where economic considerations generally outweigh every other option and even go against the progressive adaptation of environmental sensitivity that the light green approach supports [15]. To exemplify, inadequate methodological support of current knowledge based on evaluating the impacts of doing business and accounting for biodiversity-related losses, permanent loss of natural capital, reduction in inter- and intragenerational equity, and loss of ecological resources, is simply overwhelming. Still, the noticeable part of this approach is to leave the choices and their consequences to the firms, hoping for them to go beyond the disclosures of corporate social responsibility (CSR). Although scholars have supported the use of natural capital theory to understand the built environment and its sustenance in evaluating and accounting for contribution to natural and man-made wealth better [16], the absence of demarcated boundaries of causal relationships and ownership issues introduces the problems in accounting and accountability, where technical complexities to ascertain biodiversity-related losses are still to be resolved [10]. This goes along with the need to also have ecological and/or sustainability accounting standards [17–19].

Subsequent developments within the social and environmental accounting (SEA) theories eased some of the operational limitations of newly introduced approaches by extending its support for voluntary reporting mechanisms that can be used to disseminate information on how firms are/would be contributing to the societal expectations (intent follows action), even when the uncertainty regarding the loci and contents of such broadcasts add to the unresolved questions of traceability and assurance of disseminated information. Further, voluntary reporting remains disconnected from the formal accounting and reporting processes, thereby lending credibility to the widening gap between the accountability of organizations toward environment and the efforts required to promote changes in the overall behavior of firms to incorporate ethical considerations as a part of normal business conduct [20, 21]. Moreover, this has also resulted in institutionalizing multiple reporting platforms like Global Reporting Initiative (GRI), Carbon Disclosure Project (CDP), United Nations Global Compact (UN COMPACT), and Greenhouse Gases (GHG) reporting, not to mention CSR bandwagon, giving way to establish plurality in standards and languages [17, 22, 23] that has overshadowed the need to have fact-based or assured information that Hazelton [24] argues is the information right of citizens, especially where common assets are involved. Without threading out issues like trust and belief that the firms need to address while disseminating information, voluntary reporting could hardly play the role of a catalyst to successfully mediate a meaningful dialogue between the firms and society and to ensue debate regarding firms' contributions to sustainability [15].

The argument here is that in the absence of a systemic integration of environmental *bads* within the voluntary reports, disseminated information rightfully contributes to information asymmetry. To substantiate and highlight the rights of society and stakeholders to be informed about how firms might be operating or contributing to environmental (un)sustainability, which has been a basic premise of the SEA theories, the author invokes the *theory of ethical rights*. As per the ethical rights theory, ethical negatives are not an implied outcome while dealing with the ethical positives, and, instead, it emerges as a response to the corresponding positive right (e.g., right to life can also be viewed as a negative right *not* to be killed) that cannot be considered as belonging to mutually exclusive domains, and instead, develops on the logic to counter each other. Applying this to business would mean for a firm to have a license to operate based on its perceived ability to add value to the society, but it is also to remain open to the scrutiny of society regarding the negative impacts that it might be contributing to, including bearing responsibility of informing stakeholders about the steps being taken to improve the situation. One-sided information, mostly the positive ones that the CSR and voluntary frameworks disseminate, limits the field of view of the users, especially in the absence of corresponding negatives, and contributes to information asymmetry. Unless the claim of positive actions are backed by information on negatives, for example, quantified information on waste, emissions, ethical violations, and the efforts of firms to counter these, and are made available to substantiate the claims, it might appear as a deliberate attempt on the part of the firms to promote certain specific or hidden agenda. SEA theories have remained less overt about the societal rights to be informed about the negative impacts that the businesses are contributing to, in favor of letting it to be an implied one. The contention here is that to be reflective about the *real* worth of a firm, both sets of information (ethical positives as well as negatives) are a necessity, including the feasibility of independently assessing current practices of firms. This will help the stakeholders to remove biasness and evaluate how firms are contributing to the overall well-being of the society and nature.

3.2. Methodological improvements: environmental management accounting (EMA) framework and other techniques

While the ethical approach of SEA theories (from previous subsection) depended on businesses to act in a righteous way so as to improve the overall welfare of the society, it seems wishful and contrary to the real behavior of firms, if learning from the industrial revolution and current state of earth's resources is anything to go by Millennium Ecosystem Assessment [9]. Moreover, in the absence of necessary legal framework to enforce firms to uphold their end of the ethical bargain, firms' motivation to behave ethically and (re)orient its conduct toward superior environmental performance, that the market and society in general would expect and reward, demands a mechanism that can easily be relied on to support internal and external information and decision-making needs of firms [17, 25]. To pursue the argument, this subsection has relied on the instrumental view and explored how the methodological advances from the recent past promoted under the umbrella term of environmental management accounting (EMA) has furthered environmentally conscious methodologies to support decision-making efforts of management, and has improvised the role of accounting in helping firms target costs that are related to generation and prevention of waste. The innovations are not an enactment of the ethical stand but aimed at offering methodological support to businesses in improving environmental risks and achieving win-win outcomes. Developments within EMA did not lead firms to break away from the current goals of business in favor of environmentally superior ones, instead leveraged the innovations to improve outcomes, as instrumentalist approach would expect.

Methodological improvements advanced under the umbrella term of EMA framework [13] have helped firms in dealing with the need of environmentally sensitive information. This included waste accounting and reporting methodology [26] that advocated firms to develop cost drivers to analyze already recorded overheads in the books of accounts and identify environmental-sensitive expenditures that are getting diverted from the value chain [27–29]. A number of case studies experimented with the advancements to support the claim that the firms can improve environmental impacts and bottom line by identifying causal relationship of costs with activities generating waste and effectively control costs as well as waste (lower waste and, hence, improve costs). Another line of development proposed material flow cost accounting (MFCA) and developed waste flows, where valuation of nonproduction outputs (waste) from the production cycles improved visibility around drained resources. Pathbreaking in treating waste equivalent to finished goods, MFCA allocated costs to waste by using the principle of mass balance to generate information on the equivalent economic value being diverted from the organizational value chain [30]. A good number of case studies from around the world experimented with these innovative ideas that culminated in MFCA getting institutionalized as an ISO standard (ISO/DIS 14051) [31].

During the same period, innovative methodologies like environmentally enhanced life cycle costing (E-LCC) and full cost accounting (FCA) breached organizational definition of cost by developing considerations for contingents and intangibles that are less definitive and have traditionally remained outside the formal accounting considerations. Changing paradigm in business environment made these increasingly relevant to managerial decision-making (e.g., new projects, impact of future environmental laws, and others), helping firms to be cognizant of their actions beyond the economic boundary. Subsequent developments within EMA supported environmental costs to include "less tangible costs" that covered out-of-boundary and difficult-to-quantify external costs [13]. While the shifted focus of EMA supported accountability of firms toward externalized liabilities, subsequent studies have not always supported the view [32–34], where experimentation involving out-of-boundary costs in different decision-making situations reported usefulness of expanded views, for example, in evaluating environmental aspects as a physical asset of the firm or to deriving opportunity income by reducing emissions [35, 36]. The new ideas contributed to the growing arsenal of computational and algorithmic solutions that supported legitimacy claims of businesses while remaining disconnected from the epistemological roots of the underlying accounting theories, failing to provide for any foundation to unify environmental accounting as a part of existing management accounting system, as envisioned by Gray and Laughlin [15]. Readers interested in exploring EMA-related developments further can refer to Debnath et al. [37].

3.3. Developments in formal accounting standards to support environmental challenges

With the advent of International Financial Reporting Standards (IFRS) as the global generally accepted accounting principles (GAAP), there have been some advancements in literature in examining how IFRS can help firms handle changing societal expectations better. This subsection is more of a preemptive discussion to emphasize how moving away from country-specific GAAP to IFRS has not diverted the primary focus of financial accounting and reporting from the economic viewpoint that the market system supports. For example, Negash [25] offered a prescriptive treatment how the provisions of IAS 38 (impairments of emission rights), IAS 32 (financial instruments: presentation), and IFRS 7 (financial Instruments: disclosures) can support environmental imperatives that a firm might need to adhere to, where IAS 39 (new IFRS 9) could deal with the presentation, disclosure, recognition, and measurement of financial instruments from the perspectives of carbon trade. Similarly, IFRIC 1 and IFRIC 5 can be used to deal with the financial implications and related liabilities that arise due to decommissioning, rehabilitation, and restoration events of certain industries in certain countries, whereas, IAS 37 can be used to deal with the provisions and contingencies associated with these events. Similar assertions by Firoz and Ansari [38] explained how the aforesaid provisions of IFRS could be used to report material aspects of social and environmental accounting, including accounting and reporting environmental assets (environmental rights and associated values purchased/contracted, actuarial value of insurance or similar risks, and capitalized values in environment-related R&D expenses) and associated liabilities (physical data to quantify aspects toward rehabilitation and restoration of impacted sites and use).

Further reading of these standards reveals the need of a legal framework to reflect: (a) how firms might have chosen to deal with "certain" environmental areas that the law demands (e.g., environmental restoration funds and compliance-related regulations), (b) quantification and possible monetization of impacts resulting from legal compulsions instead of a proactive declaration of externalized liabilities, and (c) how market-based initiatives (e.g., carbon trading and emission rights) would impact accounting, which is also related to disruptions due to initial carbon emission allowance and associated risks of recognizing these as asset in financial accounting [39–41]. Highlighting IFRS' confined boundary to support market mechanism, the author views this to be hardly at an arm's length from the existing financial reporting and of little help to firms and regions where legal support is inadequate, for example, developing and underdeveloped nations.

3.4. What are we missing?

To recapitulate, accounting innovations have supported the legitimacy claims of firms and pursued improvements to achieve lower waste levels and improve bottom lines. At the same time, methodological complexities and under-defined causality made FCA an unviable choice, and only a handful of companies could develop detailed account of extended costs. So, while shift in focus from "accounting" to "accountability" that SEA supported is a good beginning, accounting innovations failed to keep the momentum beyond rhetoric. No surprise, these innovations worked around the existing constraints, instead of challenging the core construct. This abstinence could be due to the perceived equivalence of accounting language with that of the framework itself where *financial accounting* emerges as the only form of accounting, while all other forms are perceived as its feasible extension. This gives rise to the age old dilemma if it is possible to review the theoretical and foundational problems of the accounting sciences by concentrating on specific and narrow area like financial accounting in isolation, without searching for an overall theory that might comprehend all areas of accounting and information system [42]. This chapter searches for a change in the fundamental design in accounting, hoping for improvement in the overall generalization of accounting theory. Next, segment revisits accounting paradigm to explore how environmental concerns can be a part of it.

4. Environment: a missing element of accounting paradigm

To begin with, although we perceive the accounting practices to be restrictive and less caring for environment and sustainability, and we believe that they are not living up to the contemporary challenges, we have to understand that the accounting frameworks are fundamentally designed *not* to be innovative, so as to allow practitioners (accountants) to interpret reality (business events) and offer data and information beyond what is prescribed by the relevant standard(s). Here, the author would like to add that the art and practice of accounting are grounded in its ability to uphold the norms of the framework within which it operates [43]. Accordingly, it is natural for the accountants *not* to interpret business activities to generate information beyond the norms or away from how the accounting frameworks have guided to interpret reality, for example, *not* to highlight if certain activities are or could be potentially discouraging for environment. If the freedom to interpret business events gets disconnected from the guiding principles of accounting, it would result in systematically introducing bias to the entire accounting and reporting process, rendering information artifacts less reliable for decision-making or for any other organizational purposes. In essence, perseverance of an accounting framework in limiting its field of view to highlight accounting interpretations that is narrower than the overall impact of the underlying business event, is not a shortcoming in itself, but inherent to the accounting process that translates business activities into specific accounting information while suppressing noise around it. This brings us to question why the boundaries of the existing frameworks could not be stretched beyond the obvious. The rest of the section follows through on this discussion.

If we consider accounting to be the language to interpret business activities, its enactment is based on the norms and standards that are part of the chosen framework through which the business transactions are analyzed [44], where the theoretical underpinning of the framework provides the generalization of "what account is accounting." In other words, if data and information generated by accounting processes could be considered as symbols, its utility lies in the usefulness that the contents generate within the broader social perspective. As sustainability-related information needs of firms and stakeholders are beyond the economic existence of firms, more so, because it involves environmental and social implications of doing business that brings in concepts like externalities, social costs, and constancy of natural and other types of capitals to the accounting theories, current economic viewpoint would fall short to incorporate these, as the mainstream economics has failed to incorporate externalities and market failure. So, the core viewpoint that an accounting framework supports cannot be reengineered beyond what could be seamlessly integrated within the belief system. Otherwise, the outcomes might result in disruptive changes, severely compromising cost and quality of information.

To substantiate the unidimensionality of accounting framework and its dependency on a core viewpoint that defines its operating boundary, the author would like to cite the origins of cost accounting as a source of valuable insights. Cost accounting evolved as a response to the constraints faced by the decision-makers in extracting information on organizational value creation process from the financial accounting [45]. Management's need of information on the value creation process and actual flow of costs led to the development of cost accounting and its techniques, which grew (mostly) outside the formal structure of financial accounting. By leveraging double-entry principle, cost accounting legitimized materials and resources accounting and satisfied accountability, control, and decision-making needs of management (e.g., financial well-being vs. overhead cost analysis) [46]. Although in due course, the two frameworks merged to form integrated accounting, and represented abstraction of the nominal form of accounting, it is beyond doubt that this commonality is more on account of common measurement scheme (monetary valuation) that they share, as against the purposes they continue to serve. So, it would be unfair to expect the accounting practices to interpret transactions and develop, support, or forecast the (un)sustainability-savvy behavior of firms, especially when this has been neither the intent of the underlying frameworks nor the lingua franca of the mechanism through which the business events are being interpreted. Accordingly, environmental viewpoint would remain a challenge for the existing frameworks to adjust to and natural for them as well to ignore the needs. In order to understand the environmental implications of doing business, accounting theory would have to first conceive environmental viewpoint as a part of its core belief system so as to lay foundations to support corresponding information needs (**Figure 1**).

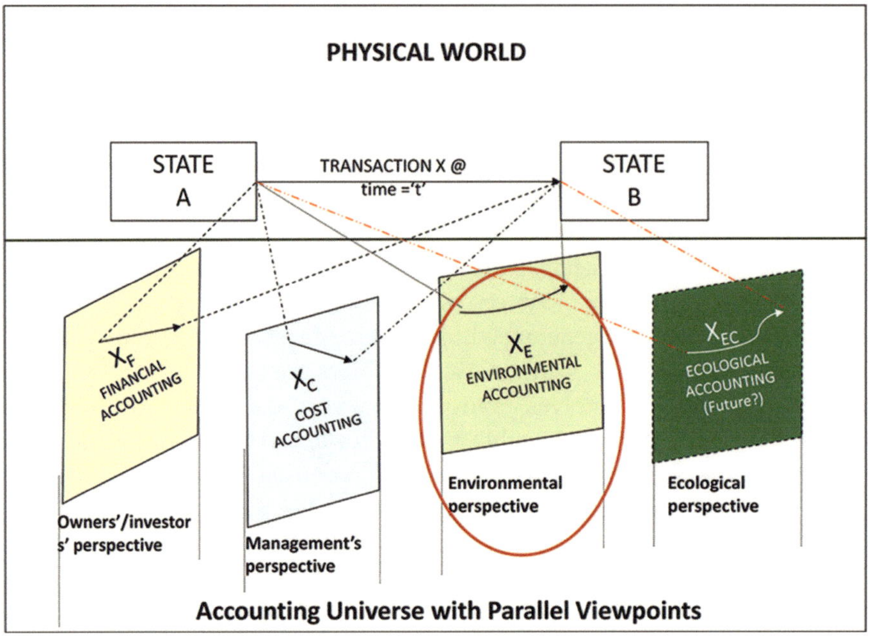

Figure 1. Accounting implications of a transaction within parallel accounting worlds (source: developed by author).

Figure 1 is a schematic representation to reflect that an accounting framework (say X_F) is a mechanism to translate a business transactions (transaction X in time t) in accordance to the norms and principles of the framework (financial accounting in this case) using accounting language that is grounded in the core viewpoint that it supports (owner/shareholder perspective), which would generate information to satisfy the relevant interests of the stakeholders, for example, by evaluating how the entity has been performing within the chosen dimension. We have to understand that the transactional information captured by an accounting system is not the whole truth about it, but a partial view or projection of the transaction on to the respective accounting plane. Accordingly, bookkeeping process would ignore other aspects of the transaction and save for the contextual elements that are relevant in evaluating the implications of the transaction within the chosen framework. Selective acuteness of the accounting paradigm heightens the focus around the intended objective(s), which could be perceived myopic at first, but is a basic necessity for the process to remain aligned to achieve the intended objective. This results in "environment" being a missing element of the prevailing paradigm that needs to be incorporated first (may be within a new framework), where calibrating environment well-being is held central or core to the framework, so as to enable the accounting language and necessary measurement scheme to interpret firm—environment exchange. At this juncture, it would be pertinent to clarify that accounting viewpoint or dimension used interchangeably throughout the chapter reflects isolated boundaries of information needs, conceived to map transactional elements and satisfy information demands, and in no way reflects dimensionality proposed by Ijiri [47].

While the loci to capture environmental impacts of business activities have not been defined for the accounting theories to pursue (Section 2), ethical rights theory can be leveraged (Section 3) by the proposed framework to define how firm-environment exchange might result in ethical negatives that the business activities would generate or subsume, for example, how environmental assets (aspects like waste and emission) impact nature and society (e.g., social and health impacts). Moreover, this can be related to quantify ethical positives to reflect how firms have chosen to deal with them (e.g., improved product design, waste disposal system, and end-of-life product return policy). Using provisional, social, and externalized costs, it is theoretically possible to record externalized liabilities to bring those in within the firm's boundary and integrate within the social contracting process, as theorized [48]. To illustrate, Appendix 1 has tabulated transactions from a case study conducted by the author previously [49] to exemplify how business transactions can be analyzed and evaluated in terms of environmental aspects and impacts and could be used to develop an environmental accounting framework (**Figure 2**). **Figure 2** details a four-step

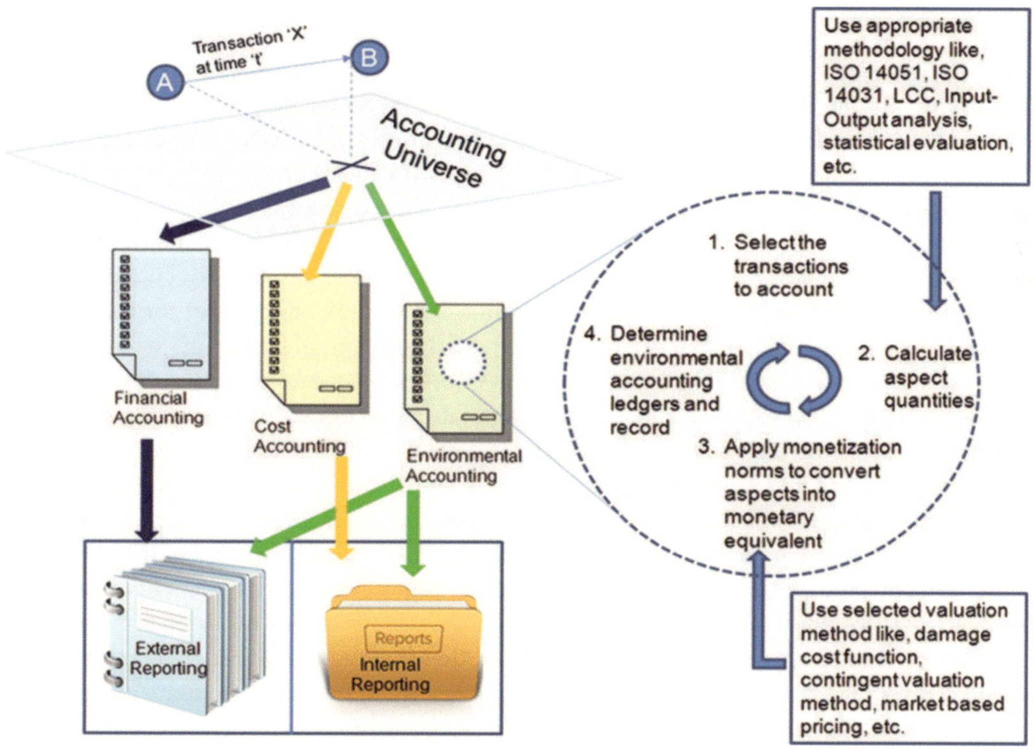

Figure 2. Environmental accounting framework (source: developed by author).

accounting process where suitable environmental technique can be used for quantification of aspects (e.g., ISO 14031, ISO 14051, input-output analysis, life cycle analysis) and suitable monetary conversion (e.g., at cost, at replacement cost, market determined rates, contingent valuation method, cost avoidance method, or any other combinatorial proxy) could be employed to translate these into equivalent externalized costs. The use of multiple methods for quantification and monetization can also be experimented with to improve visibility to the organizational activities.

Although it is natural for us to be critical of the risks associated with the exploratory nature of the framework and under-defined rules, standardization of environmental accounting can be taken up at national or supranational level or could be left for firms to experiment with. This would expand the boundaries of accounting by absolving it from being subservient to the economic interests alone, as also to reduce dependency on monetary unit as the *only* numéraire. Theoretically, this would support in producing ethical-environmental balance sheet in the long run to reflect collective relationship of the company with nature, where instead of measuring profits (economic measure), the question of subsidizing externalities can be raised to define the real profit and sketch future relationships [50, 51].

5. Concluding remarks

For the firms to care for nature and society would require them to manage externalities better (proactive), instead of waiting on the policy enforcements and acting responsibly (reactive). However, proposed methodological improvements from the last decade did not go beyond fulfilling the internal decision-making needs of firms (business as usual) in improving the overall accountability (long-term objectives). In this chapter, the author has argued that the current developments within accounting literature owe its origin to the economic paradigm within which the accounting frameworks operate and serve to satisfy corresponding information needs. Accordingly, pushing the prevailing frameworks to account for the environmental impacts might force the existing frameworks to reengineer beyond what could be seamlessly integrated, resulting in contributing to distorted views and misinformation. To be able to capture the experiences of environmental interactions of firms and support ecological choices of firms, accounting theories would need to evolve *environmental well-being* as one of its core concerns. Considering the limitations of the accounting language to validate transactions using a close-ended approach, this would be fundamental to *account for environment*, where its suitable enactment is expected to institutionalize meanings of the words like "environment" and "externalities" within the accounting process. In an ever complex world, the overall performance of an organization would seldom be judged in the near future by its financial performance alone. Expansion of accounting viewpoints to integrate environment would offer a mechanism to bring calculative aspects of accounting to other dimensions of organizational existence within the equation and support firms to follow sustainability as a natural corollary of accounting.

http://dx.doi.org/10.5772/67936

Appendix 1

Business transaction	Analysis of environmental concerns	Aspects	Impacts
1. Receives 100 MT of raw material say lye against purchase order number PO # 131	Emissions from transportation of the materials	Secondary emissions due to transportation of goods	Eq. environmental load of GHG
2. Dispatch of 1000 MT of banana puree from Mumbai to Rotterdam via ship by Coffee Inc.	Emissions due to the shipment of products	Same as 1	Same as 1
3. Ripening of mangoes in the ripening chamber	Emissions due to the use of electricity purchased from grid	Secondary emission due to shipment of goods	Same as 1
4. Steam used in production generated by briquette boiler	No emission due to the use of biomass fuel	None	None
5. Production of 1000 tons of mango pulp/puree and concentrate	a. Energy consumption	Secondary emissions due to energy consumption	Same as 1
	b. Water	Water drained and not recycled	Social liabilities of not treating wastewater
	c. Solid waste generated	Solid waste transferred to municipality	Social liabilities toward municipal waste management
6. Availing 400 hours of consultancy services toward system development by IT Services Ltd.	a. Energy consumption in software, server, etc.	Same as 5(a)	Same as 5(a)
	b. Traveling of consultants (tCO_2)	Secondary emissions due to traveling	Same as 1
7. Disposal of 100 MT of solid waste through contracted services	Environmental aspect of waste disposal depending on the disposal option	Same as 3(c)	Same as 3(c)
8. Salary and wage disbursement to the employees	Not relevant	No impact	No impact
9. Facility services availed toward cleaning and housekeeping	Environmental aspects of services like water, energy, and emissions are accounted against it	Same as 5(a–c).	Same as 5(a–c)
10. Jobs subcontracted to the service providers	Environmental aspects produced in subcon jobs inventorized	Same as 5(a)	Same as 5(a)
11. Funds invited for investments in new schemes	No impact	None	None

Environmental viewpoint of business transactions from a case study [49].

Author details

Somnath Debnath

Address all correspondence to: sndebnath@yahoo.co.in

Institute of Cost Accountants of India, Kolkata, India

References

[1] Thorén H, Persson J. The philosophy of interdisciplinarity: Sustainability science and problem-feeding. Journal for General Philosophy of Science. 2013;44(2):337-355. DOI:10.1007/s10838-013-9233-5.

[2] Abraham M. Sustainability: Philosophy vs. engineering tools. Environmental Progress. 2006;25(2):87-88. DOI:10.1002/ep.10142.

[3] Bergmann I. What is the role of the arts in the face of this? An exploration in the context of systems thinking and the transition to sustainability. Philosophy Activism Nature. 2007;7:24-32.

[4] Bosselmann K. University and sustainability: Compatible agendas?. Educational Philosophy and Theory. 2001;33(2):167-186. DOI:10.1080/00131850120040546.

[5] Mueller MP. Educational reflections on the "Ecological Crisis": EcoJustice, environmentalism, and sustainability. Science & Education. 2009;18:1031-1056. DOI:10.1007/s11191-008-9179-x.

[6] Gray R. Is accounting for sustainability actually accounting for sustainability...and how would we know? An exploration of narratives of organisations and the planet. Accounting, Organizations and Society. 2010;35:47-62. DOI:10.1016/j.aos.2009.04.006.

[7] Stegall N. Designing for sustainability: A philosophy for ecologically intentional design. Design Issues. 2006;22(2):56-63.

[8] Taylor G, Theyel G. Globalisation, innovation and sustainability: Towards an opportunity-driven design philosophy for graduate business education. Journal of Corporate Citizenship. 2010;39:93-101.

[9] Millennium Ecosystem Assessment. Ecosystems and Human Well Being. Washington: Island Press; 2005.

[10] Jones MJ, Solomon JF. Problematising accounting for biodiversity. Accounting, Auditing & Accountability Journal. 2013;26(5):668-687. DOI:10.1108/AAAJ-03-2013-1255.

[11] Metcalf L, Benn S. The corporation is ailing social technology: Creating a 'fit for purpose' design for sustainability. Journal of Business Ethics. 2012;111(2):195-210. DOI:10.1007/s10551-012-1201-1.

[12] Borland H, Lindgreen A. Sustainability, epistemology, ecocentric business, and marketing strategy: Ideology, reality, and vision. Journal of Business Ethics. 2013;117(1):173-187. DOI:10.1007/s10551-012-1519-8.

[13] IFAC. International Guidance document—Environmental management accounting. New York: International Federation of Accountants; 2005.

[14] Frederiksen CS, Nielsen ME. The Eethical Foundations for CSR. In Corporate Social Responsibility: Challenges, Opportunities and Strategies for 21st Century Leaders. Springer Berlin Heidelberg;2013. pp. 17-33. DOI:10.1007/978-3-642-40975-2_2.

[15] Gray R, Laughlin R. It was 20 years ago today—sgt pepper, accounting, auditing & accountability journal, green accounting and the blue meanies. Accounting, Auditing & Accountability Journal. 2012;25(2):228-255. DOI:10.1108/09513571211198755.

[16] Atkinson G. Sustainability, the capital approach and the built environment. Building Research & Information. 2008;36(3):241-247. DOI:10.1080/09613210801900734.

[17] Akisik O, Gal G. Sustainability in businesses, corporate social responsibility, and accounting standards: An empirical study. International Journal of Accounting & Information Management. 2011;19(3):304-324. DOI:10.1108/18347641111169287.

[18] Aras G, Crowther D. Governance and sustainability: An investigation into the relationship between corporate governance and corporate sustainability. Management Decision. 2008;46(3):433-448. DOI:10.1108/00251740810863870.

[19] Schaltegger S. Information costs, quality of information and stakeholder involvement—the necessity of international standards of ecological accounting. Eco-Management and Auditing. 1997;4:87-97.

[20] Wilburn K, Wilburn R. Using global reporting initiative indicators for CSR programs. Journal of Global responsibility. 2013;4(1):62-75. DOI:10.1108/20412561311324078.

[21] Unerman J, O'Dwyer B. The business case for regulation of corporate social responsibility and accountability. Accounting Forum. 2007;31:332-353. DOI:10.1016/j.accfor.2007.08.002.

[22] Brenna NM, Merkl-Davies DM. Rhetoric and argument in social and environmental reporting: The Dirty Laundry case. Accounting, Auditing & Accountability Journal. 2014;27(4):602-633. DOI:10.1108/AAAJ-04-2013-1333.

[23] Albu N, Albu CN, Dumitru M, Dumitru VF. Plurality or convergence in sustainability reporting. The AMFITEATRU ECONOMIC Journal. 2013;15(Special 7):729-742.

[24] Hazelton J. Accounting as a human right: The case of water information. Accounting, Auditing & Accountability Journal. 2013;26(2):267-311. DOI:10.1108/09513571311303738.

[25] Negash M. IFRS and environmental accounting. Management Research Review. 2012;35(7):577-601. DOI:10.1108/01409171211238811.

[26] UNDSD. Environmental Management Accounting Procedures and Principles. New York: United Nations; 2001.

[27] Hyrslová J, Hájek M. Environmental management accounting in the framework of EMAS II in the Czech Republic. In: Rikhardsson PM, Bennett M, Bouma JJ, Schaltegger S, editors. Implementing Environmental Management Accounting. Dordrecht: Springer; 2005. pp. 279-295.

[28] Jasch C, Danse M. Environmental management accounting pilot projects in Costa Rica. In: Rikhardsson PM, Bennett M, Bouma JJ, Schaltegger S, editors. Implementing Environmental Management Accounting. Dordrecht: Springer; 2005. pp. 343-364.

[29] Staniskis JK, Stasiskiene Z. Environmental management accounting in Lithuania: Exploratory study of current practices, opportunities and strategic intents. Journal of Cleaner Production. 2006;14:1252-1261. DOI:10.1016/j.jclepro.2005.08.009.

[30] Gale R. Environmental management accounting as a reflexive modernization strategy in cleaner production. Journal of Cleaner Production. 2006;14:1228-1236. DOI:10.1016/j.jclepro.2005.08.008.

[31] ISO.org. ISO 14051:2011 Environment Management—Material Flow Cost Accounting—General Framework [Internet]. 2011. Available from http://www.iso.org/iso/catalogue_detail.htm?csnumber=50986 [Accessed:2016-02:01].

[32] Jasch C, Ayres D, Bernaudat L. Environmental management accounting (EMA): Case studies in Honduras—an integrated UNIDO project. Issues in Social and Environmental Accounting. 2010;4(2):89-103.

[33] Laurinkevičiūtė A, Kinderytė L, Stasiškienė Ž. Corporate decision-making in furniture industry: Weight of EMA and a sustainability balanced scorecard. Environmental Research, Engineering and Management. 2008;1(43):69-79.

[34] Lee KH. Carbon accounting for supply chain management in the automobile industry. Journal of Cleaner Production. 2012;36:83-93. DOI:10.1016/j.jclepro.2012.02.023.

[35] Papaspyropoulos KG, Blioumis V, Christodoulou AS, Birtsas PK, Skordas KE. Challenges in implementing environmental management accounting tools: The case of a nonprofit forestry organization. Journal of Cleaner Production. 2012;29-30:132-143. DOI:10.1016/j.jclepro.2012.02.004.

[36] Burritt RL, Herzig C, Tadeo BD. Environmental management accounting for cleaner production: The case of a Philippine rice mill. Journal of Cleaner Production. 2009;17:431-439. DOI:10.1016/j.jclepro.2008.07.005.

[37] Debnath S, Bose SK, Dhalla RS. Environmental management accounting: An overview of its methodological development. International Journal of Business Insight and Transformation. 2011;5(1):44-57.

[38] Firoz M, Ansari AA. Environmental accounting and international financial reporting standards (IFRS). International Journal of Business and Management. 2010;5(10):105-112.

[39] Bebbington J, Larrinaga-González C. Carbon trading: Accounting and reporting issues. European Accounting Review. 2008;17(4):697-717. DOI:10.1080/09638180802489162.

[40] Machado A, Lima FG, Filho AC. Carbon credit storage: A study of how to measure and account posting. Review of Business Research. 2011;11(1):126-133.

[41] Sarkar AN. Emissions trading and carbon credit accounting for sustainable energy development with focus on India. GMJ. 2010;4(1&2):35-62.

[42] Mattessich R. The market value method according to sterling: A review article. Abacus. 1971;7(2):176-193.

[43] Buys P. In Pursuit of a foundational accountancy philosophy. Koers: Bulletin for Christian Scholarship= Koers: Bulletin vir Christelike Wetenskap. 2008;73(3):489-508.

[44] Merino BD. An analysis of the development of accounting knowledge: A pragmatic approach. Accounting, Organizations and Society. 1993;18(2):163-185. DOI:10.1016/0361-3682(93)90032-2.

[45] Edwards JR, Newell E. The development of industrial costs and management accounting before 1850: A survey of evidence. Business History. 1991;33(1):35-57. DOI:10.1080/00076799100000003.

[46] Hoskin KW, Macve RH. Knowing more as knowing less? Alternative histories of cost and management accounting in the U.S. and the U.K. Accounting Historians Journal. 2000;27(1):91-149.

[47] Ijiri Y. Three postulates of momentum accounting. Accounting Horizons. 1987;1:25-34.

[48] Cannon HM, Cannon JN, Köksal AB, Verma S. Accounting for externalities: Harnessing the "Face-In-The-Mirror" phenomenon. Developments in Business Simulation and Experiential Learning. 2013;40:68-73.

[49] Debnath S. Implementing environmental management accounting (EMA): A case study from India. In:Jose PD, editor. Corporations and Sustainability: The South Asian Perspective. London: Greenleaf Publishing; 2016. pp. 28-47.

[50] Hájek M, Pulkrab K, Hyršlová J. Forestry externalities in the environmental management accounting system. Problems of Management in the 21st Century. 2012;5(1):31-45.

[51] Shevchuk V. Assets as accounting, control and analysis objects: Ecology & economic identification and interpretation. Accounting and Finance. 2013(1):66-73.

Chapter 4

Greening Accounting II: Exploring Feasibility of Environmental Accounting Framework

Somnath Debnath

Additional information is available at the end of the chapter

http://dx.doi.org/10.5772/intechopen.68403

Abstract

Exploring the theme of greening accounting in the previous chapter led us to examine the challenges of managerial accounting in supporting firms with the environmentally conscious decision-making and ideate how integrating environmental viewpoint within accounting can be achieved through a new construct that would support firms in integrating 'environmental well-being' as a core concern. In this chapter, the argument is validated by experimenting with a real-life case study and exploring challenges to enact the proposed construct. This not only tests the feasibility of the construct from an accounting perspective, including how information generated through it could be leveraged to meet corresponding information needs of firms without sacrificing transparency and auditability, but also advances the argument of *greening* accounting to redefine how the concerned information needs of firms and stakeholders can be identified and perceived in relation to the micro-level application of sustainability.

Keywords: environmental accounting, double-entry system, externalities, accounting dimensions, case study

1. Introduction

Past decades have witnessed the efforts to integrate 'environmental thinking' within the accounting domain, where contributions from scholars and practitioners theorized how this would enable businesses to significantly reorient their behaviour towards environmental sustainability. In the previous chapter, author highlighted how the efforts in this regard have not moved significantly beyond rhetoric and why *not* having environmental concerns at the core of the prevalent accounting theories is a natural outcome of their existence, as these remain grounded within economic paradigm. This led to conceptualize a new accounting viewpoint as a theoretical solution that would hold environmental care as its core concern, instead of investing resources in retrofitting the existing mechanisms. This chapter validates the argument by experimenting with the proposed construct, so as to test the operational feasibility of environmental accounting (EA) in capturing firm-environment exchange. Leveraging transactions from a real-life case study, the construct could not only build temporal repository of aspects (stock), but also accounted for externalized liabilities of the firm , including how these assets are handled by the firm (flow). This feasibility supports the capability to generate information for firms to improve environmental insight of its processes, products, and decisions while maintaining temporality and auditability. Learning from the study provides inputs on how this could enable accounting to shape the corporate responsiveness of firms towards nature, and redefine the boundaries of accounting theory.

2. Environmental accounting in hospitality business: a case example

To explore the pragmatic elements of EA framework proposed in the previous chapter, this section details how EA can capture firm-environment exchange to integrate externalities by using inputs from a real-life case example (Section 3), before generalizing information produced by such a framework (Section 4) and summarizing learning from the experiment (Section 5).

2.1. The project site

The case study selected to support this experiment was conducted by the author in 2012–13 to study the relevance of environmental management accounting (EMA) in the hospitality sector and to expand the knowledge base with the findings. The study involved understanding the operating environment of two co-located hotels (five-star and three-star) in the western suburbs of Mumbai, India, that are managed by concept hospitality services (CHS facilities, hereafter) (**Figure 1**), and how they managed to reduce the impact on environment. Rationale for using this case study is to generate a view on the working of a firm from an industry where mass-balance is not the primary method to establish input-output link that has not been covered very often in literature. A service organization is expected to improve our understanding of the stock and flow of environmental aspects that differ from the manufacturing organization. Readers interested in the complete case study[1] can refer to Debnath [1]. Due to limited space, only the major features of the case are highlighted here.

2.2. Analysis of key findings

The CHS facilities are Ecotel® certified —certification of environmental and social leadership in hotel/hospitality business [2]—and equipped with the infrastructural and operational arrangements to support environmental conscious operational arrangements. Both the facilities are full-service business hotels and offered boarding/lodging, boutique restaurants, bars,

[1]Out of the three case that the author conducted as a part of his PhD thesis, this one has been selected here to support the argument for *greening* accounting.

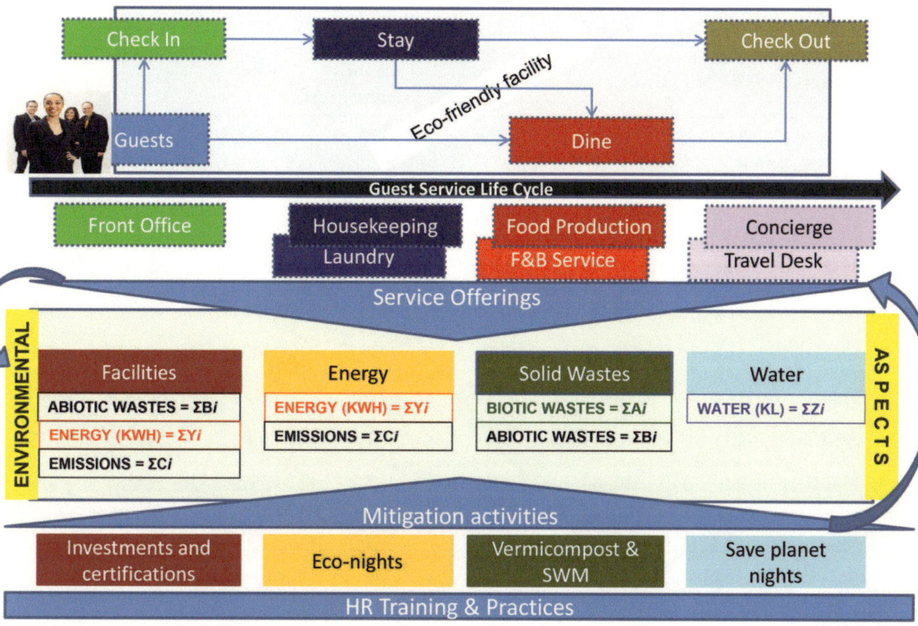

Figure 1. Operational layout of CHS (Sourced from Ref. [1]).

and lounge facilities to the business travellers along with banquet and conference halls for corporate use. Guest service lifecycle covered reservation of rooms and guest check-in, followed by stay, boarding, and checkouts. The amenities and services consumed materials, water, energy and other resources, and produced wastes as outputs. Cumulative waste quantities (solid waste and waste water) reported in **Table 1** were collected from the organizational records, whereas GHG emission due to energy consumptions is as per the norms of GHG accounting [3].

All types of solid waste were segregated at source and collected through a 4-bin system that optimized its reuse/recycling. In regards to disposal of waste, CHS had invested in developing a vermicomposting facility to treat biotic waste that converted waste to compost (bio-fertilizer), which was sold at a nominal rate. Waste categorized and collected as unfit for recycling or reusing (e.g. butter paper, oil cans, etc.) was sent to landfill (a miniscule percentage say, 1–2% by weight). CHS also routed waste water to the community ETP for recycling, from where the treated water (mainly grey water) was received back for further use. CHS had laid pipes to circulate grey water and used it for designated purposes, such as cleaning and gardening. This reduced its operational dependency on fresh water. Complete recycling of organic waste and use of grey water saved CHS from contributing to the environmental impacts that it would have otherwise if waste was disposed using conventional means. However, the tangible savings in social costs cannot be incorporated as a part of EMA construct (**Table 2**). Neither would the liability arising due to waste water generated by laundry services that it outsourced to the external commercial washers. **Table 2** details cost of environmental care for CHS as per EMA norms by keeping it restricted within the organizational boundary.

Month (Units[a])	Food production (Covers)	Garbage (mt)	Linen for wash (Par)	Water consumption (kL)			Energy (kWh)	GHG (tCO2e)
				Supply	Laundry outsourced	Total		
Apr	9069	14.8	43555	4156	7170	11326	347783	341
May	8248	14.1	51949	5140	8507	13647	353394	346
Jun	5283	10.3	35045	5899	5775	11674	332496	326
Jul	5585	10.9	39003	6356	6416	12772	352577	346
Aug	7586	11.1	54359	4906	8916	13822	368708	361
Sep	10111	11.0	45280	5632	7443	13075	357025	350
Oct	8144	11.4	57461	4344	9428	13772	380822	373
Nov	7790	10.7	47311	4041	7761	11802	341721	335
Dec	13434	9.2	52360	8956	8597	17553	347388	340
Total	75250	103.7	426323	49431	70012	119443	3181914	3118

[a]Units: kL—kilo liters; mt—metric tons; kWh—kilo watt-hours; tCO_2e—tons of carbon dioxide equivalent.

Table 1. Monthly consumption of resources.

2.3. EA: accounting for environmental care of CHS

To account for the aspects that CHS business activities generated, monetization norms were needed, so as to journalize these in the EA books. To monetize, valuation methods are used as proxies that would translate the externalized liability corresponding to the aspect. For example, externalized liability due to solid waste disposed through municipal infrastructure

As per EMA	As per the case study	Amount (in INR)
(a) Material waste	Dry and wet garbage—Bottles, packing materials, empty containers, food wastes, and others (100% recycled)—150 mt per annum	0.00
(b) Non-product outputs	Waste water (100% recycled) ~ 45,000 kL per annum	0.00
(c) Waste and pollution prevention costs	Fixed costs per annum of maintaining Ecotel certification Running cost of vermicomposting facility Operating cost of other activities with environmental considerations	250,000 +60,000[a] Unascertainable
(d) R&D expenditure	New initiatives for reducing environmental load	Not available
(e) Less tangible costs	Emission externality of ~ 4.5 $mtCO_2e$ per annum	1,015,000[b]
Total cost		1,325,000

[a]Assumed maintenance cost of vermicomposting facility (1 person @ INR 5000 per month).
[b]Emission costs at INR 225/tCO_2e (USD 4.5 at assumed exchange rate of INR 50/USD) [4].

Table 2. EMA computations for CHS.

is pegged at INR 3500 mt^{-1} as the cost *not* internalized by CHS [5]. Externalized cost included actual cost of disposal incurred by municipalities along with externalities due to GHG generation from organic waste and social costs contributed by the informal sector. Similarly, GHG emission is valued at opportunity cost of market rate at USD 4.5 per tCO_2e (INR 225 at exchange rate of INR 50 per USD) which has been the average rate of carbon for Indian projects in voluntary emission credit market [3]. Waste water has been valued at resource replacement rate of INR 50 kL^{-1}, as followed in other EMA case studies [6]. Accordingly, environmental ledgers are drawn by journalizing entries that followed double-entry system, where respective aspect ledger (of asset nature) is debited to represent the release of specific type of waste to the common pool. These ledgers correspond to the physical nature of the aspects (waste and emissions) and reflect the environmental asset generated by the firm, akin to the finished products. Corresponding credit would go to the respective environmental account (of liability nature) so as to reflect externalized liability. A reversed entry on the other hand would reflect liability that has been annulled due to the changed processes/activities or any other reason. In simple terms, following accounting rules are abstracted from the generalized schematics for EA (as per Appendix 1) and have been used to draw the ledgers (**Tables 3–7**):

(a) Journal entries should be balanced across quantity and value.

(b) One accounting entry would always use same units of measurements.

(c) To account for more than one aspect per business transaction, each aspect would have to have its own journal entry.

(d) In case suitable monetization norm is not available for an aspect, it will remain in physical inventory.

The ledgers are interpreted as under:

(a) Ledger entries are summarized for different periods and represented combined form of t-accounts to record physical and monetary values together. However, firms can maintain separate accounts record aspect inventory and corresponding monetized liability.

Date	Particulars	Qty. (mt)	Debit (INR)	Date	Particulars	Qty. (mt)	Credit (INR)
12/12	To balance c/f	103.7	362,950	04/12	By Env. liability A/c	14.8	51,800
				05/12	By Env. liability A/c	14.1	49,350
				06/12	By Env. liability A/c	10.3	36,050
				07/12	By Env. liability A/c	10.9	38,150
				08/12	By Env. liability A/c	11.1	38,850
				09/12	By Env. liability A/c	11.0	38,500
				10/12	By Env. liability A/c	11.4	39,900
				11/12	By Env. liability A/c	10.7	37,450
				12/12	By Env. liability A/c	9.2	32,200
	Total	103.7	362,950		Total	103.7	362,950

Table 3. Solid waste (externality) T-account.

(b) Credit balance of **Table 3** reflects social externality saved by CHS due to vermicomposting to treat bio-waste, instead of using municipal solid waste disposal system. **Table 4** brings in the supply chain effects into the books of the CHS by performing resource accounting of waste water from outsourced laundry, and accounted it as an environmental liability for CHS. **Table 5** reflects equivalent carbon value of GHG emissions due to energy usage.

(c) Based on the selective performance data, these externalities created environmental obligation of around INR 3.8 million for 26 thousand guest nights (annualized) or INR 147 per guest night (**Table 7**). Accordingly, environmental liability at period-end represents monetized balance (in quantity and monetary terms) to reflect externalities, not annulled.

(d) Management information (**Table 7**) is generated based on data/inputs from the sample ledgers and can be traced back to the individual ledgers, but without positive social externalities due to knowledge sharing by the firms [7] that cannot be quantified due to lack of suitable numeraire.

Date	Particulars	Qty. (kL)	Debit (INR)	Date	Particulars	Qty. (kL)	Credit (INR)
04/12	To Env. liability A/c	7170	358,500	12/12	By balance c/f	70,012	3,506,000
05/12	To Env. liability A/c	8507	425,350				
06/12	To Env. liability A/c	5775	288,750				
07/12	To Env. liability A/c	6416	320,800				
08/12	To Env. liability A/c	8916	445,800				
09/12	To Env. liability A/c	7443	372,150				
10/12	To Env. liability A/c	9428	471,400				
11/12	To Env. liability A/c	7761	388,050				
12/12	To Env. liability A/c	8597	429,500				
	Total	70,012	3,506,000		Total	70,012	3,506,000

Table 4. Waste water (outsourced laundry) T-account.

Date	Particulars	Qty. (tCO_2e)	Debit (INR)	Date	Particulars	Qty. (tCO_2e)	Credit (INR)
04/12	To Env. liability A/c	341	76,725	12/11	By balance c/f	3118	701,550
05/12	To Env. liability A/c	346	77,850				
06/12	To Env. liability A/c	326	73,350				
07/12	To Env. liability A/c	346	77,850				
08/12	To Env. liability A/c	361	81,225				
09/12	To Env. liability A/c	350	78,750				
10/12	To Env. liability A/c	373	83,925				
11/12	To Env. liability A/c	335	75,375				
12/12	To Env. liability A/c	340	76,500				
	Total	3118	701,550		Total	3118	701,550

Table 5. GHG emissions T-account.

Date	Particulars	Qty. (mt)	Debit (INR)	Date	Particulars	Qty. (tCO_2e)	Qty. (kL)	Credit (INR)
12/12	To solid waste A/c	103.7	362,950	12/12	By waste water A/c.	3118	70,012	3,506,000
12/12	To balance c/f		3,844,600	12/12	By emission A/c			701,550
	Total	103.7	4,207,550		Total	3118	70,012	4,207,550

Table 6. Environmental liability control ledger.

Type of activity	Environmental aspects	Savings	Value (in INR)
Vermicomposting	Solid waste	Saved 104 mt reduction in wastes for landfill	+362,950
Composting of floral wastes from festivals	Solid waste	Saved 10 mt (assumed) floral wastes composted	+35,000
Outsourced linen washing	Waste water	Negative cost at replacement rate of water for ~ 70,000 kL per annum	−3,506,000
Use of non-renewable energy sources	Emissions from energy use	Negative costs of ~3.2 $mtCO_2e$	−701,550
Total			−3,809,600

Table 7. Annualized externalized liability of CHS.

3. Systemic integration of externalities within EA framework

This segment explains how EA framework adapts systematic approach of accounting to bookkeep aspects and externalized liability of firm. Although EA is exploratory in here and lacks the breadth and support enjoyed by other established accounting frameworks, which could lead to generate information that has not been studied to remove interpretive bias of decision-makers, especially to reflect how this might help firms to adapt to the changing expectations of the society. Still, it enables firms to compare its environmental performance with the economic ones, and trace its responses through indicators that can be a part of the overall enterprise risk framework.

3.1. Solid waste and its disposal

Waste is an inevitable by-product of any transformation process. Information regarding internal costs incurred in generating and disposing waste could lead to the operational improvements of the firm, as EMA proposed, whereas information on externalized liabilities is expected to improve the firms' response towards permanent cure. Even though having market mechanism to dispose waste, as in developed countries, has resulted in internalization of costs to a certain degree [8], this has also led to institutionalize 'right to waste' that is available for firms at a price, which has not been validated to bring a permanent change in the attitude of firms. Improved information on externalized liabilities through accounting that EA aims for, would push the firms to acknowledge accountability beyond using social infrastructure, where dissemination of *valid* information translates to improved transparency for investors, others stakeholders and society at a large, to appreciate such a behaviour. EA is expected to help firms improve their overall approach towards environmental care by providing a mechanism that can directly reflect its performance in real-time. Conscientious corporate citizens like Interface Global, Patagonia, and 3M (to name a few) have developed sustainable waste reduction techniques by resorting to servicizing, cradle-to-cradle lifecycle, and other initiatives [9]. EA can support firms develop insights about their decisions (e.g. externalized liability for CHS due to landfilled waste that needs a permanent cure) by generating temporal information that remains tied to the source.

3.2. Waste water

Disposal of waste water through local or site-specific effluent treatment plant (ETP) is a common practice for firms, before releasing it to the public drainage system that ultimately releases treated water to the water bodies. However, this has not always been the case, for example, in case of developing and underdeveloped countries, where waste water could be released directly to the water bodies, resulting in severe loss of water resources. At the same time, waste water has not always been reused by developing in-house or community level grey water recycling system, where treated water could be used for reasons other than for drinking or human consumption. Missing legislative support to promote grey water recycling has also hindered the development of necessary infrastructure. With depleting levels of potable water globally and ever rising population, market mechanism to price such a scare resource would hardly do any justice to improve the situation in the long run. Mahadevia and Wolfe [10] have rightly pointed out that the next world war would be fought to control the water resources. The intent of *accounting* for waste water is to help firms understand the stress that they are contributing to within a region, which could lead to business disruptions as well [11]. This could also help firms to participate in improving the disparity within the region so as to be recognized as a valued member of the community that it serves [12].

3.3. Emission and its accounting

Emission of GHGs and non-GHGs has harmful effects on biosphere and contributes to the changing climatic conditions. While GHG accounting is a methodical approach towards inventorizing emissions [3], it remains to be integrated within accounting where loss of temporality might lead to wrong choices, as detailed by the author with reference to a different case study [13], and is universally applicable. In any case, business decisions like moving away from high energy intensive machineries and processes to the lower ones (e.g. installation of bagasse-based boiler instead of using oil-fired boilers or to optimize energy utilization by using technological solutions) depend primarily on the associated economics of it (lowering cost per kg of steam), where environmental outcomes become by-products of the decisions. The argument here is, environmental impact of a business decision can be evaluated better if it could be tied with the performance levels (before and after the effective change), where temporality becomes a natural requirement that EA support. Same is true for carbon trade where accounting of initial emission allowance and other related transactions would need the accountants to separate emissions accounting from corresponding financial impacts, but which cannot be achieved as discussed in previous chapter, unless accounting can guide the practitioners to account for both the areas simultaneously. Author posits that EA supports this delineation and to separately account for temporal generation/savings of emission and the underlying economics, which cannot be dealt in here due to space constraints.

3.4. Approach towards improving environmental care

As compared to EMA, where insights of environmental performance are limited within the organizational boundary of the firms (**Table 2**), EA offers information on the type of aspects and how these are being handled. For example, solid waste account of CHS details saved social cost and is treated as an asset (**Table 3**), whereas waste water account from outsourced laundry (**Table 4**) registered as liability that CHS should be looking into with improved commitment to remain a pro-environmental business that it has declared itself to be. Same is the case of emissions that CHS should be caring for. These insights could not have been possible without letting EA break the boundary of ownership and reflect how firms are contributing to the environmental duress. Although this might not resolve differences that are inherent to the industries in regards to how they operate and/or use resources (e.g. discrete manufacturing vs. hospitality business vs. mining sector), information generated and disseminated by EA could still institutionalize shared vocabulary that is the need of the hour, including devising common terminologies to express how firms might be viewing its performance as compared to others, or in analysing industry specific trends (e.g. environmental care institutionalized by extractive industry as its operating norms). The framework also generalizes the boundary to handle areas that lack computational insights like emission of non-GHG gases (like F-gases) or positive social externalities that CHS generated through the workshops it conducted for other firms to become environmentally friendly, and could be pursued as a part of future research.

4. Externalities, sustainability and accounting generalization

This section assimilates different aspects of the experiment and validates the relevance of information generated by EA in its capacity to support decision-making. While a single case study can never bring the complete set of facts to reflect the uniqueness of different industries, still it offers a good number of points to relate to generalize the capability of EA in generating information of practical relevance to support firms, and can be characterized through the needs of decision-making in managerial accounting.

(a) *Traceability*: EA creates the transactional backbone of environmental aspects to become a part of an information system and offer relevant and verifiable data for environmentally conscious decision-making without losing temporality, transparency and traceability. Traceability links pieces of information to the source event/transaction from a particular time period (e.g. quantity of GHG emission for a quarter) and absolves EMA and corporate management information system from the need of using arbitrary methods to quantify and accumulate information on the environmental aspects and impacts.

(b) *Timeliness*: EA opens the door for the organizations to actively consider externalities as integral to the business activities, and improves transparency in the reporting of ethical negatives, that the previous chapter detailed, as mandatory for voluntary reports to drive ethical positives. Here, an accounting construct can generate information as soon as the underlying activities are recorded and available for its real-time dissemination for decision-making purposes.

(c) *Relevance*: EA allows the existing accounting frameworks to continue in 'as-is' form, which saves time and resources required to modify and institutionalize accounting to care for within a single framework. Relevance of information from managerial decision-making purposes can only be hypothesized here, as its practical utility is yet to be tested, and leaves the door open for future research to address, including how it might support the standards of sustainability and ecological accounting.

(d) *Uniformity*: EA separates the computational complexities of quantification and monetization from the accounting process. Needless to mention, identification of aspects based on the business activities and methods for quantification would need inputs and active cooperation of environmental experts, while accounting of aspects including valuation and ledgerisation can remain within the accounting domain. This not only brings uniformity to the entire process, and seeks active role of environmental management system (EMS) to establish uniformity while interpreting, as well as, disseminating information.

4.1. Valuation of externalities: generalization and cognitive limitations

Valuation of externalities and corresponding limitations to develop it as an acceptable norm in business, has been a lexicon in environmental accounting theories. Methodological improvements in developing verifiable basis of ascertaining cost of waste or in ascertaining corresponding externalities that it contributes to, is expected to support businesses with improved understanding, capturing the impacts in nominal terms and to contribute to the scholarship of ecological modelling [14–16]. However, different class of waste could follow different routes of recycling, reuse, and ultimate disposal (cradle-to-grave), or return to the material cycle (cradle-to-cradle), or anything in between. For example:

Manufacturer →

- (Recyclable waste) Recycler → Reprocessing → Entry to material chain.
- (Hazardous waste) Hazmat handler → Safe disposal.
- (Non-recyclable waste) Municipal disposal → Landfill.
- (End of life) Reclaiming for recycling → Recycler → Disposal.

As evident, each route of disposal would generate separate set of externalities that would be specific to the movement of waste. In other words, even though firms can scan the upstream and downstream supply chains to develop inventory of externalized liabilities, it would remain relative (or incomplete). With loss of causal relationship that waste suffer after entering into the pool of common/public goods, where regional complexities and multiple interaction upon dissemination makes it difficult to trace and capture impacts, quantification and monetization of aspects would results from our contemporary, *not* comprehensive, understanding of the ecological profile of waste. This brings in the cognitive limitations in discovering how waste might interact with different receptors in nature that would always be dynamic, and accordingly, would make it impossible to cover complete set of impacts and costs to be known at any given point of time (**Figure 2**). Other than the layered nature of truth, that would get exposed as collective human knowledge would grow, it would always lead to a certain degree of uncertainty in simultaneous determination of impacts (Δi) within a complex adaptive system, along with the cost (Δc) associated in neutralizing it (analogous to the Heisenberg's uncertainty principle), and is contrary to the deterministic nature of costs and impacts that accounting theories are used to.

Accordingly, we have to acknowledge the boundary of knowledge regarding future impacts of health and ecological effects and related monetary assessment of damage/remediation/restoration to remain outside the collective knowledge base (methodological limitations). Lack of information on exact causal relationship between aspect and impacts that are time-delayed might limit interpretation of damages (cognitive limitations), along with the second and higher order impacts that fail causation (interpretive challenges). This leads to two important conclusions for EA: (a) offering interpretation of business events by accepting probabilistic nature of outcomes as against the deterministic ones, and, (b) to view cost

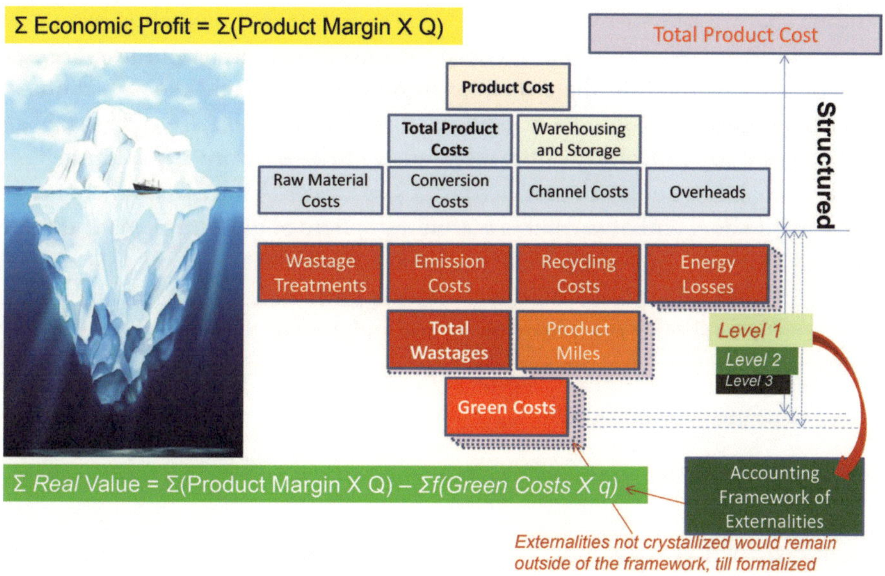

Figure 2. Layered nature of environmental impacts and costs (Sourced by Author).

only as a proxy and not an outcome of elemental interactions. Accordingly, EA would need to support multiple measurements and valuation schemes, holding these as proxies to translate firm-environment exchange.

4.2. Generalized construct of environmental accounting and sustainability

This sub-section explores how EA improves the information base and supports sustainability. Firstly, it is relevant to explain how accounting—a two dimension construct of time and money—has evolved to be the language of business from economic perspectives. EA extends it to the third dimension by bringing in calculative practices of accounting to the domain of firm-environment exchange, aiming to help firms measure its impact on environment and resources. This process also encapsulates stakeholders' demands and organizational interests to help firms identify, understand, and improve environmental performance.

Second, environmental aspects generated by business and its impacts on biosphere are subject to the cognitive limitations of human knowledge, and would remain so, until and unless intricate nature of human activities and corresponding ecological responses across time are well understood. While these cognitive limitations would lead us to explore the complete cycle of natural interaction for the sake of improving scientific accuracy, it also supports layered nature of externalities that limits our 'complete' view. Accordingly, all impacts of an aspect would not be known at all times, and so would our efforts to derive costs to abate or harvest the aspects. Continuing with the argument, externalities generated by waste is not absolute, and instead, would depend on how organizations have chosen to deal with them. So in altruist sense, it is the externalities generated by the chosen path of the waste that should be reflected as the environmental liability of a firm.

With reference to sustainability, this boundary reflects perennial nature of approximate understanding that we humans would have to live with, in regards to how we are engaged with our surroundings. Accordingly, the need for developing an accounting argument that is not dependent on frozen information of constituent elements and their reactions, as traditional accounting practices would have expected, becomes eminent. EA offers an in-principle arrangement to develop repository of the outcomes of firm-environmental interactions while preserving the capabilities of traditional accounting practices. Also, this can help firms review the very first step to deal with it, as that is within the sphere of its control, instead of investing in the efforts to analyse complete cycle, where EA can limit itself to account for the first-order impacts of the interactions. Although, such a view is proximate, it still highlights the important areas where firms should pay attention to, and redefine its accountability towards nature and society.

5. Concluding remarks

An artificial system, like accounting, imitates human requirements to study events for abstracting information so as to generate a map that would help others to navigate and/or interact with the information produced and shared. However, EMA and contemporary sustainability theories are yet to develop a construct to support and measure the *environmental embeddedness* of firms, the *in situ* environmental care with which firms operate, where actions and decisions of a firm are guided by the degree to which firms are upholding their commitments to be environmentally benign as agents of societal progress. While critical theories have advocated to consider the constraints within the accounting capabilities to consider these, albeit theoretically, normative view preferred to look elsewhere, mostly due of the inability of a structure that cannot wrap these challenges within the current form of enactment, pushing the need itself to the fringes of our collective conscience. The two chapters on *greening* accounting aimed at carving a conceptual space for accounting to hold the intent, i.e. having 'environmental well-being' at its core, where accounting language can be leveraged to decipher business transactions in accordance to the needs. While the second part is always easy, it is the first part that is crucial and hopes to pave for enriching accounting, from being a pragmatic solution to uphold accountability that it is ingrained in!

Appendix 1. Schematics for book-keeping environmental aspects generated by business transactions

This section provides scheme to analyse business transactions of a firms from bookkeeping perspective, reflecting how the corresponding business activities might be generating or subsuming environmental assets. While the transaction categories covered here are not exhaustive and can be enhanced subsequently, the accounting schema represents how EA separates environmental dimension of business transactions from the financial/cost accounting-related transactions.

(a) Activities that generate environmental aspects: This category of transactions would result in generation of aspects like emissions, solid waste, waste water, etc. that add to the stock of environmental assets. The corresponding liability would reflect environmental contingency arising due to the addition to common pool, where the accounting treatment would be:

Dr. Environmental asset (aspect type) Aspect Qty X Valuation norm
To Environmental liability (corresponding transaction class)

(b) Sequestration/transfer of environmental aspects: Business activities that would result in sequestering or transferring environmental assets are part of this set. For example, reuse and recycling of food waste using in-house vermicomposting facility or recycling of waste water to improve grey water usage (as CHS did from the case study) to reduce environmental load. Similarly, sale of electricity by utilities would result as transfer-out of GHG load from producer to the consumer(s). Journal entry in this case could be:

In case of sequestration:

Dr. Environmental liability sequestered Aspect Qty saved X Valuation norm

To Environmental Asset (aspect type)

In case of transfer:

Dr. Environmental liability transferred Aspect Qty saved X Valuation norm
To Environmental Asset (aspect type)

(c) Business activities earning environmental credits: Involvement of firms in community activities would result in reducing local waste and save social costs, e.g. reducing community waste by using organizational facilities, thereby helping the business to earn environmental credits. Journal entry in such cases would be to create a credit (or reward):

Dr. Environmental savings generated Aspect Qty X Social costs saved
To Environmental/Social Cost saved

(d) Permit/fees/legal charges/other environmental expenses incurred by business: These transactions are driven by organizational interactions with market and legal system to improve/regulate environmental and social considerations of the firm and would include expenses incurred in purchasing/selling permits and/or licenses, and/or any other expenditure incurred that is/are related to or impacted due to environmental obligations/decisions. These transactions would generally be accounted within the financial books, and can also be EA to accumulate financial impacts supporting environment decisions of firms.

Journal for expenditures:
Dr. Environmental Expenditure (individual head) Amount incurred
To Environmental contingency covered
Journal for income:
Dr. Environmental contingency impacted Amount incurred
To Environmental Income (individual head)

(e) Adjustment transactions in environmental ledgers: These entries would take place within the environmental ledgers to transfer balances, enter corrections, or revalue aspects due to change in quantification and/or valuation norms of the aspects. The journal entry would be:

Dr. Environmental Ledger A Change in value
To Environmental Ledger B

Author details

Somnath Debnath

Address all correspondence to: sndebnath@yahoo.co.in

Institute of Cost Accountants of India, Kolkata, India

References

[1] Debnath S. Integrated waste management framework: a business case. Int. J. of Business Excellence. 2015;8(5):566-83. DOI:10.1504/IJBEX.2015.071278

[2] UNEP Org. Trends in Hotel Certifications and Rating Programs: Guidelines for the Caribbean. [Internet]. 2012. Available from: http://www.cep.unep.org/about-cep/spaw/conservation-and-sustainable-use-of-marine-and-coastal-ecosystems/copy_of_sustainable-tourism [Accessed: 2 February 2016]

[3] WBCSD & WRI. The greenhouse gas Protocol – A corporate accounting and reporting standard. Switzerland: WBCSD & USA: WRI; 2004.

[4] Ecosystem Marketplace & Bloomberg New Energy Finance. Back to the future – State of the voluntary carbon markets 2011[Internet]. 2011. Available from HYPERLINK "http://www.forest-trends.org" www.forest-trends.org [Accessed:2016-02-01]

[5] Debnath S, Bose SK. Exploring full cost accounting approach to evaluate cost of MSW services in India. Resources, Conservation and Recycling. 2014;83:87-95. DOI:10.1016/j.resconrec.2013.12.007

[6] Gale R. Environmental costs at a Canadian paper mill: a case study of Environmental Management Accounting (EMA). Journal of Cleaner Production. 2006;**14**:1237-51. DOI:10.1016/j.jclepro.2005.08.010

[7] Mann SK, Thadani D. ECOTEL version 2.0 - reaching out [Internet]. 2010. Available from http://www.hvs.com/article/4492/ecotelversion20reachingout/ [Accessed:2016-02-01]

[8] Jasch C, Lavicka A. Pilot project on sustainability management accounting with the Styrian automobile cluster. Journal of Cleaner Production. 2006;**14**:1214-1227. DOI: 10.1016/j.jclepro.2005.08.007

[9] Esty DC, Winston AS. Green to Gold: How Smart Companies Use Environmental Strategy to Innovate, Create Value, and Build Competitive Advantage. Hoboken, NJ: John Wiley & Sons, Inc; 2006.

[10] Mahadevia D, Wolfe J. Solid Waste Management in Indian Cities: Status and Emerging Practices. India: Concept Publishing House; 2008.

[11] Hills J, Welford R. Coca-Cola and water in India. Corporate Social Responsibility and Environmental Management. 2005;**12**(3):168-177. DOI: 10.1002/csr.97

[12] Zhang JJ, Joglekar NR, Verma R. Why Multinational Corporations Still Need to Keep It Local: Environment, Operations, and Ownership in the Hospitality Industry. Constructing Green: The Social Structures of Sustainability; 2013.

[13] Debnath S. Expanding environmental management accounting: An experimental construct to integrate material wastes and emission flows. International Journal of Business Information Systems. 2014;**16**(2):119-133. DOI: 10.1504/IJBIS.2014.062834

[14] Atkinson G, Bateman I, Mourato S. Recent advances in the valuation of ecosystem services and biodiversity. Oxford Review of Economic Policy. 2012;**28**(1):22-47. DOI: 10.1093/oxrep/grs007

[15] Laurans Y, Rankovic A, Billé R, Pirard R, Mermet L. Use of ecosystem services economic valuation for decision making, questioning a literature blindspot. Journal of Environmental Management. 2013;**119**:208-219. DOI: 10.1016/j.jenvman.2013.01.008

[16] Ojea E, Martin-Ortega J, Chiabai A. Defining and classifying ecosystem services for economic valuation, the case of forest water services. Environmental Science Policy. 2012;**19-20**:1-15. DOI: 10.1016/j.envsci.2012.02.002

Section 2

International Standardization

Chapter 5

Adaptation of International Accounting Standards: Case of Portugal

Helena Isabel Barroso Saraiva,
Maria-Céu F.G. Alves and Vítor M.S. Gabriel

Additional information is available at the end of the chapter

http://dx.doi.org/10.5772/intechopen.68732

Abstract

This chapter aims to present the results of a broad analysis about the process of accounting standardization in Portugal in order to frame the current situation and the different levels of standardization that characterize it. The methodology followed involves a broad revision of the literature and content analysis on various papers and texts as well on documents directly related with the study topic. It concludes with the identification and characterization of the current levels of accounting standardization and makes reference to the likely scenario of this regulatory framework in the short term. The objective is to understand how the evolution of accounting standards in Portugal has evolved, what the current situation is and its likely evolution in the near future. The chapter is also aimed at contributing to the understanding of the process of adaptation of international accounting standards to the Portuguese reality.

Keywords: accounting standardization, current normative framework, standardization levels, history of standardization, Portugal

1. Introduction

It is generally accepted that the accounting system of a country is determined by its surroundings, whether political, economic, social or legal. Thus, the aim of this chapter is to present a document that can contribute to exposing clearly the actual situation relating to the effort of accounting standardization that has been developed and intensified in recent years and that has led to the consolidation of accounting standards in Portugal.

The evolution of accounting in the current context is characterized by a phenomenon of international harmonization and standardization. In this work, it is understood that standardization *is a process that shows the uniformity of accounting practices while accounting harmonization is a process that addresses more the economic, social and cultural specifics of each country,* given that accounting standardization is a mechanism that contributes to harmonization. It is understood that formal harmonization leads to material harmonization, this being the followed understanding.

The traditional history of accounting is followed, given that research in this area is mainly centred on the origins and evolution of accounting. We have also opted, within this current, to draw upon institutional theory by basing part of the analysis of evolution presented in the role assumed by different landmark institutions at the level of accounting standardization in Portugal. In this sense, taking into account the framework of international organizations that shape the most recent evolution of accounting standardization in Portugal, the perspective is highlighted by North [1], in which the institutions play the rules of the game and the organizations are the operators of change or players.

Thus, the final goal of this chapter is to characterize and analyse the actual scenario at the level of accounting standardization in Portugal. In the present time, when the consolidation of a process of extensive standardization of all sectors of the economy, namely through the expansion of Accounting Financial Report Standards (which is an adaptation from the IFRS), from the private sector of the economy to non-profit sector activities and, in the near future, the approximation of the public sector to the same type of report, seems evident.

This chapter strives to contribute to the understanding of the process of adaptation of the International Accounting Standards (IAS) to the reality in Portugal and the process of adjustment of institutions to international and regional (European) standards, whether at the technical or political level. This situation results in the appearance of different levels of standardization as a consequence of the most recent reform in the realm of accounting harmonization associated with the different levels of depth that the information and financial report assume in entities with different characteristics and with different necessities.

In terms of structure, and after this short introduction, the chapter begins with the presentation of the evolution of the process of standardization in Portugal, through a brief review of the movements that have influenced the area most, from the seventies in the twentieth century to the recent days. Afterwards, a presentation is made on the historical evolution of this process in Portugal from its origins to the present. Then, the current situation in Portugal is presented in more detail, with emphasis on the diverse realities and the framework in terms of accounting standardization. Finally, the main conclusions are stated.

2. Accounting harmonization: Global evolution

There is an evolution based on two different currents of influence, relative to the process of accounting harmonization, normally identified as Anglo Saxon and Continental. This is considered as the means by which a certain country exercises influence on its accounting practices.

Thus, the social and cultural environment implies different frameworks and different accounting practices. The referred differences can be found at various levels:

- at the level of the legal system [2],
- at the level of origin of business financing [3],
- at the level of influence of taxation [4],
- at the level of degree of development of the country [4],
- at the level of cultural factors [5],
- at the level of political influence [6] and
- for other differences [5].

Taking into account this diversity of frameworks and practices in global terms, an immediate consequence is the fact that accounting standardization in different countries and nations does not transmit an image of harmonization.

Thus, because of factors that were previously pointed, initially, there existed a great diversity between practices, which could be standardized at the local level though not harmonized in global terms. This lack of harmony was felt within each one of the major currents (Anglo Saxon and Continental).

However, the need for harmonization was felt and was pressing, essentially, as a result of the globalization of the economy and, by delay of the functioning of financial markets, more concretely, investments in stock exchanges of international values.

In this way, here arose a matter of interest concerning a process that rendered company and organizational financial information intelligible to any stakeholder independent of his location or performance.

Thus, from the moment that this need to develop accounting harmony is identified and assumed as indispensable to the increase in comparability of financial information, the question related to the choice or selection of an organism associated with the emission of accounting norms that can be accepted and generally adopted by all businesses and organizations arises [7–9].

At this point, we need to address questions of legitimacy, representation, independence and performance to which the choice of organism should answer. In this context, the question of institutional theory assumes special importance: this contributes in a significant way to the understanding of accounting standards.

Among the institutions that contributed to the accounting harmonization process, the following can be outlined as relevant in the case under analysis [7–9]:

- **from the perspective of a global context:**
  - the International Accounting Standards Board (IASB), initially influenced by the G4 + 1 group—Group of Accounting Standard Setters, founded in 1994 by

Australia, Canada, the United Kingdom and the United States of America (more specifically the Financial Accounting Standards Board—the FASB) plus New Zealand after a previous phase in which the International Accounting Standards Committee (IASC) had been influenced by the G4; later, in the context of the IASC, the E5 + 2 was created (European Accounting Study Group)—that was founded in 1997 aiming to carry out research and investigation in order to contribute to international harmonization through the IASC within the jurisdiction of the European Union. This last group was composed of five European delegations on the Board of the IASC—France, Germany, Holland, Northern European countries and the United Kingdom—supported by the organisms of national standardization and the European Commission and the FEE—Fédération des Experts-comptables Européens.

- **From the perspective of the regional context:**
    - the European Union (EU)

In a more clear way, we can state that the institutional pressure applied by the EU, in the case of Portugal, was essential in the process of adaptation of norms from the IASB.

3. Accounting standardization in Portugal

Despite the fact that various initiatives had been developed in the nineteenth century with an impact on accounting practices at various levels, the process of accounting standardization in Portugal only began in the twentieth century, complying with the following stages in accordance with the legal instruments used as reference at each stage:

- first stage: approval of the Industrial Contribution Code (ICC) in 1963,
- second stage: approval of the Official Accounting Plan (OAP) in 1977,
- third stage: approval of the second version of the OAP, adjusted in 1989 and
- fourth stage: approval of the System of Accounting Standardization (SAS) in 2009.

The first stage of accounting standardization in Portugal began with the approval of the ICC, which states in Article 22 that 'the rules of accounting' are assumed as the starting point for accounting standardization in the country [10].

Based on this code, accounting began to constitute the basis to find out the real profit of companies, appearing as a reference for the first time for accounting professionals who are designated as 'accounting technicians' in the code. Article 52 of the ICC previews that until attaining legal status in the profession, only those who are considered as accounting technicians are those who formalize their registration in the General Directorate of Contributions and Taxes, following the conditions defined by the Ministry of Finances.

The ICC remained in place until 1988. From 1929, until the date of its creation, the contributions of companies were figured on presumed profit; with the introduction of this code, the taxation was based on the actual profit, a factor that reinforced the relevant role of accounting.

In this phase, and at the same time, the Portuguese Society of Accounting was set up. This society, created in the years of 1945/1946, continued its activity for approximately 40 years, developing activities for the scientific development of accounting and the profession of accountant. This association received special importance due to the fact that it assumed the representation of the country in international organisms, namely in the Union Européenne des Experts Comptables, Économiques et Financiers (UEC), currently known as the FEE.

According to some authors [10], from the mid-fifties of the twentieth century, certain pressures appeared in the direction of establishing standardized practices at the public and private levels with the objective not only of accounting standardization in itself but also in the relationship of this with the fiscal system.

The main characteristics of this first phase are the greater interconnections between accounting, standardization and taxation, proving the fiscal usefulness of accounting. In a corporatist state as Portugal was, at that time, usually accounting is allied with socio-political objectives. In addition, the need to improve public accountability required, by then, more accountants to support the administrative activities of the government. This need seems to have encouraged the development of both accounting education and accounting profession.

The second stage of accounting standardization in Portugal takes place with the publication of the first Accounting Plan in 1977. However, there are some prior moments to the publication of this diploma that must be mentioned to, in our opinion, as being precursors of this; namely, the publication of the General Accounting Plan in 1965 by the National Trade Union of Office Workers of the District of Lisbon; also, the appearance of the General Accounting Plan—in its Preliminary Draft—First Phase, carried out between 1970 and 1973, by the Ministry of Finances and the Tax Collector Institution, with the publication in 1973 of the Preliminary General Accounting Plan by the Centre of Fiscal Studies; finally, the publication of the National Accounting Plan in 1976 by a group of authors who contributed to the Plan.

The importance attributed by the government at the time to the Preliminary Plan presented in 1973, on the initiative of the Ministry of Finances and the Tax Collector Institution, gave rise to a recommendation for its general adoption beginning in 1974. However, this situation ended by not being possible, due to the events related with the 1974 Revolution that occurred in Portugal and to the consequences of the post-revolutionary process.

The first Official Accounting Plan, made official in the Legal Decree 47/77 on February 7, comes from the tradition of continental inspiration on national accounting. This applied to the majority of entities, except credit and insurance institutions. This plan previewed the publication of sectorial plans that, however, were not indeed implemented; it did not preview the consolidation of accounts.

While it was in place, twelve interpretative norms were published. These norms have suffered changes by the following diplomas:

- Legal Decree 74/85, resulting from the introduction of value added tax (VAT),
- Legal Decree 476/85, resulting from the valuation measurements of the final results of the exercises,
- Legal Decree 228/86, resulting from the accounting of currency exchange and
- Legal Decree 27/87, resulting from treasury investments and fixed financial assets.

In this first Accounting Plan, Article 4 refers to the future creation of a regulatory entity: the Commission for Accounting Standardization (CAS), which only some years later formally began to function.

At the time of publication of the first OAP, when the setting up of the CAS was considered, it was assumed by the legal entities that this latter institution should be functioning in the context of the Ministry of Finance as an independent entity in administrative and financial terms. The CAS mission would be '...to secure the functioning and perfecting of the national accounting standardization ...' (Legal Decree number 47/77, Article 4).

Thus, the issue of the implementation of accounting standardization in Portugal has been resolved only in an effective way at the time of publication of a plan by a legal Decree, with the aim of giving legitimacy to the OAP and promoting its use, making it compulsory. This together with the creation of the CAS were determinant questions for the success of the implementation of this formal rule.

In 1986, the year when Portugal joined the EU, the country was obliged to accept European Directives; the CAS had the onus of transposing the Directives that dealt with accounting and adapting those to the internal legal system.

In this way, after an analysis of the previous OAP, the CAS considered that, due to it being outdated, an adjustment to the new reality was valid.

The second stage emerged with the publication of a new Plan, the Legal Decree 401/89, which revoked the previous Legal Decree 47/77 and the remaining complementary legislation. This alteration had as its base the introduction into the national legal framework of changes related to Portugal's adhesion to the EU. The new OAP was enforced to entities covered by the Code for Commercial Companies, excluding banks, insurance companies and financial sector entities. In this new OAP, the role of the CAS is maintained, its mission being that of contributing to the improvement of the quality of financial information.

During the time it was in force, 29 Accounting Directives and five technical interpretations were published by the CAS, right from the beginning of 1991. Successive changes were made to the following diplomas:

- Legal Decree 238/91, relating to the consolidation of accounts,
- Legal Decree 44/99, relating to the system of permanent inventory and demonstration of results by function,
- Legal Decree 79/2003, relating to the system of permanent inventory, the demonstration of cash flow and the demonstration of results by function,

http://dx.doi.org/10.5772/intechopen.68732

- Legal Decree 88/2004—rules of value measurement of some associations and
- Legal Decree 35/2005, relating to the implantation of the European Directive on accounting modernization.

The Accounting Directives were intended to be generally enforced in Portuguese entities and corresponded to the guidelines set out by the EU, being strongly influenced by international accounting standards. However, it was recognized that some Accounting Directives dealt with some issues in a complete way and with others only superficially; in fact, in trying to reduce the content of international standards, the resulting Directives ended up being insufficient and, in some cases, incoherent, apart from out of place.

Despite those negative aspects, it was then settled, precisely through the mechanism of the Accounting Directives, the establishment of a hierarchy of application of the international norms in the Portuguese accounting standard. The supplementary suppression of gaps at the various levels of norms was previewed: material gaps of major importance were not dealt with directly through the Directives. Instead, companies were directed automatically to the IAS in these cases. On the other hand, there was still the problem of many Accounting Directives being, at a certain time, out of date, because apart from having been based on the IAS, these had already been, for the most part, revised, whereas, in turn, the CAS never revised the Accounting Directives.

During this period, more specifically from 1992, legislation appeared for accounting standardization in the public sector of the economy, culminating in the publication of a plan of accounts for the sector, in 1997, through the Legal Decree 232/97. In the following year, the Commission for Accounting Standardization was created for Public Administration, through the Legal Decree 68/98. This Commission functioned in parallel to the CAS for the private sector; it had as its mission to coordinate and accompany the application and perfecting of the Public Administration Plan (PAP) and its sectorial application as well as evaluating the approval, adaptation and alteration of the sectorial plans.

The standardization in the public administration in Portugal is characterized by the creation of sectorial plans, namely for local municipalities, in 1999, for the educational and health sectors, in 2000, and for the system of social security in 2002. Thus, five differentiated plans exist in the public sector that function in a different register from the private one, though the source of inspiration for these public-sector plans had been in fact the OAP.

In addition, in 2002, Legal Regulation 1606/2002 was published by the European Union and in the following year Regulation 1725/2003. Following these, Portugal published the Legal Decree 35/2005. This established that listed national companies used the IAS/IFRS, leaving those not listed to continue to use national standards or the international ones by choice. Apart from this, all companies (listed or not) should continue to elaborate their accounts according to national standards, that is, some companies would have to elaborate two register systems at the same time.

After the publication of Regulation 1606/2002 by the EU, the CAS prepared a document entitled 'Guidelines for a New Model of Accounting Standardization' that was sent for government approval in January 2003 but never reached a final decision. The model understood two levels of accounting standardization: the first, of the European and international nature, was directed at economic entities with greater demands for financial reports in Portugal and the second, of a national nature, was directed at the entities that lacked application of the first level of standardization.

However, in our perspective, in reality, three levels of standardization were envisaged:

- integrating listed companies at the first level, adopting IAS/IFRS,
- the second level would be made up of non-listed companies that would apply the model of Accounting Standardization or alternatively the IAS/IFRS and
- the third level would be made up of companies considered 'small entities (SE)' and would consist of a simplification of the second level for organizations with less necessity in terms of financial reports.

The need for a new System of Accounting Standardization (SAS), is connected with the recognized insufficiency of the OAP for the entities with greater qualitative demand at the financial report level and also the fact that this Plan was lacking technical revision, related to aspects of a conceptual nature. In fact, the standards from IASB and the OAP were not consistent with each other.

In 2009, the **fourth stage** of accounting standardization began in Portugal with the publication of the Legal Decree 158/2009. This approved the SAS and its complementary legislation:

- Ordinance 986/2009 of 7 September with the models of financial demonstrations,
- Ordinance 1011/2009 of 9 September with the new accounts code,
- Notice number 15625/2009, dated 7 September, that presented the conceptual structure,
- Notice number 15653/2009 of 7 September with the two interpretative norms.
- Notice number 15654/2009 of 7 September with the NCRF-PE, wich are the standards applied to small entities.
- Notice number 15655 of 7 September with the group of the 28 NCRF and
- later, Legal Decree number 36-A/2011 of 9 March that defined rules as micro-entities (ME) and Legal Decree number 64/2013 of 13 May that deals with the standardization of the entities in the non-profit sector were emitted.

In 2009, Legal Decree 160/2009 was also emitted in relation to the new CAS and previewed the enforcement mechanism of the accounting norms. According to the CAS, the correct use of the norms and the technical rigorousness, demand in institutional terms, adequate control mechanisms. Enforcement was defined as a system capable of preventing, and later of identifying and correcting, material mistakes or omissions in the application of the standards.

After the introduction of the first OAP, the introduction of the SAS was the most relevant and a significant change in Portuguese accounting standardization that deals with a model based on the IASB but guarantees compatibility with Community Directives in the area of accounting.

According to Ref. [10], this solution, proposed by the CAS, can be considered a 'revolutionary change'. It is in agreement with the definition by North [11]; in that it affects, in legal terms, the alteration of a system based on the continental current in grand part (or in large part) of the entities for a system with an Anglo-Saxon base for all the entities.

As to the presentation of the SAS, four differentiated levels of standardization, in our understanding, were previewed:

- the level of the entities with titles listed, or not, that are applied by obligation or by option to the IAS/IFRS,
- the level of entities that apply by obligation or voluntarily to the Accounting Standards of Financial Report (ASFR)—the Portuguese standards,
- the level of the entities that apply the ASFR-SE: initially presented at the date of emission of the SAS and, later, redefining the concept of the SE, by Law number 20/2010, that widened the concept of the SE and
- the level of the ME embodied in a special regime regulated by Law 35/2010.

Later, the approval of Legal Decree 36-A/2011 consecrated, among others, the measures of approval of the regimes of accounting standardization, for the micro-entities and for the entities of the non-profit sector. The entities covered by the accounting standardization for micro-entities are not bounded by the obligation to present all the financial reports. Thus, the micro-entities are outside the realm of the SNC and correspond, clearly, to the other level of standardization as referred to above.

On the other hand, the regime of accounting standardization is an integral part of the SAS. However, in our understanding, it also corresponds to the other level of standardization as it assumes accounting rules, specifically applied to the entities that proceed as a main activity, non-profit activities and cannot distribute to its members or contributors any economic gain or financial right. A few examples are associations, collective public bodies of an associative type, foundations, clubs, federations and confederations.

Later, through Legal Decree 134/2012, the CAS received the attributes and competences of standardization for the public sector, with the consequent extinction of the Commission of Accounting Standardization of Public Administration; this diploma proceeded to the revision of the structure and composition of the CAS, adapting it to the new competences of standardization for the public sector.

For reasons of systematic clarity and legal security and in order to accommodate the increasing amplitude of structure and tasks, the new legal regime of organization and functioning of the CAS was published, thereby revoking Legal Decree 160/2009, changed by Legal Decree 36-A/2011.

Thus, from this point, it is the responsibility of the CAS to carry out technical work with a view to the approval of a unique System of Public Accounting Standardization (SPAS), adapted to international standards specific to the public sector (IPSAS) and to the national laws in which these matters are regulated.

The legal regime of the organization and functioning of the CAS is now characterized by having as its mission the emission of norms, legal interpretations and recommendations related to the group of entities in the business and in public sector. CAS also aims to establish, in the country, harmonized accounting procedures with the European and international standards of the same nature, contributing to the development of high-quality patterns of information and financial reports of the entities that apply the system of accounting standardization.

As to aspects related to enforcement or regulation and control of the application of accounting norms, the CAS develops the necessary actions so that the accounting norms are effective and adequately applied by the entities subject to them, namely through verification actions on its initiative or through arbitration procedures.

These kinds of procedures also occur in other countries that are making their way into the global harmonization process like, for instance, in Turkey [12].

4. Results: Actual levels of accounting standardization in Portugal

At this point, we will address the actual situation resulting from the activity of all the mentioned institutions: in the present case, the institutions with responsibility at the level of emission and implementation of accounting standards in Portugal. We will give special focus to this kind of institutions.

However, other kinds of institutions also took influence on the process, namely professional associations (i.e. the Chamber of Accounting Technicians) assumed an important role in training and reconverting accounting technicians in the transition to a new and different system [13].

Lehman [14] refers to this as a necessary adaptation of the concept of accounting, which will have to be merged into culture.

We cannot forget that the previous model of accounting current in Portugal was inspired on the continental model, which implied a much closer connection between the organism responsible for the standardization and the political institutions, namely the Ministry of Finances. In this scenario, the sources related with the diverse types of legislation are fundamental elements at the level of accounting standardization, and the institution of reference is, in this case, the government: the only source of standardization is the law.

The legislation as a starting point also happens, in our opinion, with the SAS, which seems to merge with the cultural tradition of the country. However, with the introduction of this new system, the whole framework of accounting has changed:

- the question of emphasis on the historic cost is overcome,
- the principles of prudence and of association to the emphasis on banking interests as the main financier and
- the role previously assumed by the state mainly as a receiver of taxes.

Returning to the initial perspective [1], the organizations also include the role of governments and political entities and their power at the level of global regulatory activity. In the Portuguese case, this assumes special importance because one can interpret how, from the initial proposal of accounting standardization, we evolved to a system that ends up by being, in its nature, quite divergent from that which was initially proposed.

Concluding, it seems clear that at this time, essentially due to the rule of law, ten different levels of accounting standardization are found in Portugal:

- the level of entities with listed titles admitted listed companies,
- that of the entities that apply the range of 28 ASFR,
- that of the entities that apply the ASFR-SE,
- that of the micro-entities,
- that of the non-profit and
- that of the entities in the public sector that, in a general way, can still be doubled into five different levels corresponding to the Public OAP and to sectorial plans.

The current scenario, with the standardization of the public sector still unaltered, presents a fragmented and inconsistent standardization, given that parallel systems based on principles in the private sector and systems based on rules in the public sector coexist.

A change in this situation is previewed for the near future: the convergence of the standards of this sector with the IFRS from IASB, configuring the introduction in the public sector of a system oriented for business accounting with a fundamentally Anglo-American basis.

It is also previewed that, as with private-sector accounting, the sub-system of accounting of management will assume heightened relevance, considering that this branch of accounting is mandatory in the new regulation.

Currently, the existence of a general and a simplified regime is also previewed for the public sector, which seems to indicate that, from the beginning, and if there is no change in this prevision, at a final moment, the levels of standardization will be seven.

Thus, the actual situation, relative to the levels of accounting standardization in Portugal, before the introduction of the SAS and the system that is expected to be implemented in the public sector, is presented according to that shown in **Table 1**.

Analysing **Table 1**, we can conclude that we went from a system with seven differentiated levels of standardization before the introduction of the SAS to a system with ten different levels in reality. In fact, this increase, verified at this point, is obtained through the propagation of levels in the field of the private sector, given that we can verify that in this sector the report needs are of a differentiated nature, depending on the dimension and finality of the entities. In relation to the question of the introduction of standardization in the public sector, predictably, and having no deviation to that which was planned, with the fulfilment of the same, we are faced with a global system made up of seven levels.

Standardization levels	Before the SAS introduction	The SAS	In the near future
Private sector of the economy	Businesses with listed titles	Companies with listed titles—IAS/IFRS	Companies with listed titles—IAS/IFRS
	Private organizations—OAP	Companies in general (not listed)	Companies in general (not listed)
		Small entities	Small entities
		Micro-entities	Micro-entities
	Some of non-profit entities and systems of solidarity and social security	Non-profit entities	Non-profit entities
Public sector of the economy		System of solidarity and social security	SAS—Public administration:
	Central and regional administration	Central and regional administration	**1st Level**
	Local and regional administration	Local and regional administration	and
	Educational system	Educational system	**2nd Level**
	Health system	Health system	

Source: authors.

Table 1. Levels of accounting standardization before the introduction of the SAS currently and in the near future.

For a broader analysis, that encompasses all economic sectors, it would be necessary to refer to other existing levels, which did not experience alterations with the realities analysed in this chapter: those of the banking and financial entities and insurance areas. If we were to take them into consideration, we would have to add two levels in any scenario.

Thus, we can conclude that, up to the present, the process of convergence with the international standards caused in Portugal, among other things, an increase in the levels of existing standardization.

This appears to come up against the fact that the tradition in accounting in Portugal is anchored in the current continental version previously mentioned. This led to, despite having made a choice for a system based on standards, strongly influenced by the Anglo-Saxon framework, in political terms, by implementing a system that, despite being based on these standards, assumes forms of implementation and criteria of functioning more typical of societies based on Roman Law.

The proliferation of diverse levels of standardization in Portugal seems to fit in with the notion of adaptation of harmonization to the specific situation at the local level. The exercise of prerogatives of political power working at this level, in the sense of local/national institutions not losing self-determination in relation to the way in which the entities function and should relate with the Government, conducted to these final solution of several standardization levels.

5. Conclusions

The Portuguese accounting system is traditionally characterized with a system belonging to the continental trend [15], with its strong legislative tradition and by the mighty connection between accounting and fiscal law, patent in the current legislation. Apparently, these characteristics, despite the introduction of a system more influenced by the Anglo-Saxon approach, continue to have a tight preponderance in the Portuguese case. This is not unusual, taking into account that the strategy of the EU is also based on a perspective of accounting harmonization based on legislation and is influenced by political factors.

It is our understanding that this chapter contributes to the understanding of the process of adaptation of international accounting standards to Portuguese reality, having analysed all the factors that shape this evolution; in an institutional perspective, one can verify in practice a multiplication of the levels of accounting standardization—contrary to the expected standardization consequences.

This seems to us as the main contribution of this study for an understanding of the question of adaptations carried out by institutions with power at the national level, adjusting the international and regional standards to the internal reality of a country.

That is, starting from the analysis of the evolution of incremental changes that appeared after the great 'revolution' in the Portuguese accounting system [10], and taking into consideration the activity of the regulatory entities and the role that these entities had after this revolutionary change, an adaptation of this change to the situation and specific characteristics of the country apparently exist, namely through:

- the doubling of the dual system initially previewed for the entities using SAS for a system that distinguishes between small entities and micro-entities—these being outside this dual system;
- the creation of specific rules for the non-profit sector entities, which, although considered as being framed within the context of the SAS, have report systems differentiated from other entities.

Thus, the role of the regulatory entities, at the national level, seems to want to accommodate the question of international harmonization, creating, however, situations of standardization that are more specific and adjusted to the national reality.

Therefore, on one hand, the micro-entities are dealt according to specific norms and are less demanding in terms of reports, perhaps because they are also linked to a form of property that does not require a report that is so transparent as that of other types of entities.

On the other hand, the serious problems the Portuguese economy has been experiencing in the past years have meant that this type of entity has been more protected in terms of public policies—in the sense of expediting the procedures, in such a way as to develop or not penalize the economy any further.

The issue of non-profit entities is also one of the sensitive questions at the national level. In Portugal, a large number of the activities of social nature are developed by private entities. The state or government are large financiers of activities of social nature developed by these entities. In this way, the regulatory institutions understood the existence of special needs at the financial report level.

These two questions seem to us to be related with the pressure brought to bear by the government in the sense of establishing an effort to adapt international standards to the specific characteristics of some entities, so as to achieve greater control either on the evolution of the economic situation or on the functioning of the important role that the non-profit entities develop in social terms.

These pressures could be framed in the theoretical conception of translating ideas and practices that are transformed, interpreted and reformulated during the process of adoption, diffusion or institutionalization.

The Portuguese case seems to indicate that the normative and coercive pressures are more relevant than the pressures of a mimetic character in the development of the legitimation of the changes that occurred in accounting.

This is also one of the conclusions we reach in this study: despite having adopted standards based on the global and the European context, there is an adjustment to the national situation that causes a system that is quite different from the original proposal, based on external influences, introducing, however, in the final solution, specificities related to the functioning of the national economy.

We can still consider that Portugal, in respect to accounting harmonization in both private and public sector entities, has accompanied the route followed by the majority of countries, moving towards international harmonization via legislative initiative and with strong political influence.

Author details

Helena Isabel Barroso Saraiva[1*], Maria-Céu F.G. Alves[2] and Vítor M.S. Gabriel[1]

*Address all correspondence to: helenasaraiva@ipg.pt

1 Polytechnic Institute of Guarda & UDI, Inland Development Center, Guarda, Portugal

2 University of Beira Interior & NECE, Research Unit in Business Sciences, Covilhã, Portugal

References

[1] North DC. Institutions, Institutional Change and Economic Performance. Cambridge: Cambridge University Press; 1990

[2] Nobes C, Mueller G, Gernon H, Meek G. Accounting—An International Perspective. 4th ed. Chicago: Richard D Irwin Inc; 1997

[3] Hill C. Competing in the Global Marketplace. 3rd ed. Boston: Irwin McGraw Hill; 1999

[4] Nobes C, Parker R. Comparative International Accounting. 9th ed. London: Prentice Hall; 2006

[5] Zarzeski M. Spontaneous harmonization effects of culture and market forces on accounting disclosure practices. Accounting Horizons. 1996;**10**(1):18-37

[6] Rodrigues LL, Schmidt P, Santos JL, Fonseca PCD. A research note on accounting in Brazil in the context of political, economic and social transformations, 1860-1964. Accounting History. 2011;**16**(1):111-123

[7] Saraiva HIB, Alves MC, Gabriel VMS. Harmonização contabilística: sua influência na evolução e na atualidade no caso português. In: Proceedings of XVI Encuentro AECA "Recuperación económica: confianza e inversión en Europa"; 25-26 September 2014; Leiria. http://www.aeca1.org/xviencuentroaeca/cd/58e.pdf [Accessed: March 2017]

[8] Saraiva HIB, Alves MC, Gabriel VMS. The roots of the formal process of accounting harmonization, its evolution and its influence in Portugal. De Computis-Revista Española de Historia de la Contabilidad. 2015;**12**(22):172-204

[9] Saraiva HIB, Alves MC, Gabriel VMS. Normalização contabilística em Portugal: a sua evolução e situação atual. In: Proceedings of V Congresso dos TOC; 17-18 September 2015; Lisbon. ISBN: 978-972-9171-86-4. https://www.occ.pt/news/trabalhoscongv/pdf/32.pdf [Accessed: March 2017]

[10] Caria AA, Rodrigues LL. The evolution of financial accounting in Portugal since the 1960s: A new institutional economics perspective. Accounting History. 2014;**19**(1-2):227-254

[11] North DC. Institutional change: A framework of analysis. In: Sjöstrand S, editor. Institutional Change: Theory and Empirical Findings. New York: ME Sharpe Inc.; 1993. pp. 35-42

[12] Gokten S. An audit gap problematic in Turkey: The role of Turkish court of account for semi-public companies. Journal of International Scientific Publications, Economy & Business. 2016;**10**:230-244

[13] Saraiva HIB, Almeida BMV. Normalizacao Contabilistica: o papel das associacoes profissionais em Portugal. In: Proceedings of V Congresso dos TOC; 17—18 September 2015; Lisbon. ISBN: 978-972-9171-86-4. http://bdigital.ipg.pt/dspace/bitstream/10314/2305/1/Ata%20Cientifica_Helena%20Saraiva3.pdf [Accessed: March 2017]

[14] Lehman G. A critical perspective on the harmonisation of accounting in a globalising world. Critical Perspectives on Accounting. 2005;**16**:975-992

[15] Nobes C. An empirical investigation of international accounting principles: A comment. Journal of Accounting Research. 1981;**Spring**:268-280

Chapter 6

M2M-Fair Value Accounting

Yıldız Özerhan and Banu Sultanoğlu

Additional information is available at the end of the chapter

http://dx.doi.org/10.5772/intechopen.68724

Abstract

Since the past 20 years, the value relevance of financial information based on the historical cost method has been widely criticized among the academics and the preparers of financial information. The ongoing debate over the shortcomings of historical cost for ascertaining the worth of assets and liabilities and the rapid spread of fair value measurement for financial reporting has first led to the issuance of Financial Accounting Standard No. 157 *Fair Value Measurements* in September 2006 and then the initialization of fair value measurement project by the International Accounting Standards Board (IASB) and the Financial Accounting Standards Board in 2006 within the convergence project. On May 12, 2011, when the IASB issued IFRS 13 *Fair Value Measurement*, it appears that there has been substantial convergence between IFRS 13 and FASB 157. The purpose of this paper is to comprehensively explain the fair value accounting in accordance with IFRS 13 and describe the types of assets and liabilities that are subject to fair value accounting and their accompanying measurement principles with reference to other IFRSs and the Exposure Draft *Conceptual Framework for Financial Reporting*.

Keywords: fair value measurement, IFRS 13, SFAS 157, M2M accounting, conceptual framework

1. Introduction

Mark-to-market (M2M) or *Fair Value Accounting (FVA)*—the measurement of assets and liabilities at the prevailing price in the market—is considered superior when compared to cost-based accounting for both the initial recognition and the subsequent valuation of economic transactions. In this context, the deficiencies in the value relevance of financial information based on the historical cost method and therefore the urgent need of fair value measurement have been widely discussed by the academics and the preparers of financial information in the past 20 years.

First, Financial Accounting Standards Board (FASB) issued Financial Accounting Standard No. 157: *Fair Value Measurements* in September 2006. Then, especially in the aftermath of the global financial crisis in 2008, the urgent need of common fair value measurement and disclosure requirements in the International Financial Reporting Standards (IFRS) and Generally Accepted Accounting Principles in the United States (US GAAP) has led to a start-up for fair value measurement within the convergence project of International Accounting Standards Board (IASB) and FASB (collectively, the Boards). The goals of the fair value measurement project were [1] to define the fair value more clearly, to set out a single set of measurement requirements and hence reduce complexity and improve consistency, to improve and clarify existing disclosure requirements related to fair value measurements, and to increase the convergence of IFRS and US GAAP. On May 12, 2011, the IASB issued IFRS 13 *Fair Value Measurement* effective for annual periods beginning on or after January 1, 2013 [2]. It appears that there has been substantial convergence between IFRS 13 and FASB 157.

FVA is the practice of accounting that values certain assets and liabilities at their current market value [3]. Especially, for the measurement of financial instruments and the assets and liabilities assumed in a business combination, fair value is accepted to be the most appropriate valuation method. During his speech in the Sixth Symposium on Accounting Research, Paris, France, on December 12, 2016, Hans Hoogervost, the Chairman of IASB, expressed that the cost-based accounting is not a true reflection of long-term equity investments' performance because especially for investors it would be insufficient to reflect the performance of the company and that it would not provide appropriate information to investors' needs. He also stated that the application of fair value accounting would not cause the financial statements to fluctuate, and at the same time, the recognition of gains or losses when the asset is disposed from its cost would have no relation with the prudence principle as those amounts have been accumulated since the previous years.

Also, in the Exposure Draft *Conceptual Framework for Financial Reporting* (ED) ED/2015/3, published on May 28, 2015, the measurement of assets and liabilities was one of the most controversial proposals. After much discussion on this issue, the use of a single measurement basis for valuing assets and liabilities is found to be inadequate in the ED for providing high-quality financial information for the users of the financial statements and the IASB agrees on two measurement bases for assets and liabilities: (1) historical cost and (2) current value (fair value and value in use for assets and fulfillment value for liabilities). It is also emphasized in the ED that the contribution of an asset to the future cash flows of the entity, the way a liability is fulfilled in the future, and the characteristics of assets and liabilities should be taken into consideration for the accurate selection of measurement basis at initial recognition and subsequently [4].

In this study, first, IFRS 13 fair value measurement and then the types of assets and liabilities that are subject to fair value accounting and their accompanying measurement principles with reference to other IFRSs will be explained. Furthermore, the principles that are associated with fair value measurement will also be described in terms of the Exposure Draft *Conceptual Framework for Financial Reporting*.

2. Definition of fair value

Fair value accounting is the measurement of certain assets and liabilities at their current market value through the use of present value of future cash flows associated with an asset or a liability [3]. Fair value is based on the exit price and accordingly defined as *"the price that would be received to sell an asset or paid to transfer a liability in an orderly transaction between market participants at the measurement date"* [IFRS 13:9].

Fair value measurement assumes an orderly transaction between market participants at the measurement date under current market conditions [IFRS 13:15]. An orderly transaction is defined as *"a transaction that assumes exposure to the market for a period before the measurement date to allow for marketing activities that are usual and customary for transactions involving such assets or liabilities; it is not a forced transaction"* [IFRS 13: Appendix A]. The forced transaction referred in this definition could be a forced liquidation or a distressed sale that would not accurately represent the fair value of related asset or liability.

The process of determining the price to be received from the sale of the asset or paid to transfer the liability at the measurement date is a hypothetical forecasting process. It is assumed that the entity will continue its activities in the future in accordance with the concept of "going concern," and based on this assumption, the fair values of assets and liabilities are determined at the measurement date. Hence, an entity's ability to continue as a going concern is essential in fair value measurement.

2.1. Exit price

The hypothetical transaction from the perspective of market participant establishes a basis for estimated price, known as "exit price." An exit price of an asset or a liability is an estimate of the price that would be received to sell an asset or paid to transfer a liability, not the price to buy the asset or to incur the liability (transaction price or entry price) [IFRS 13:2.10]. As market or economic conditions change, those estimates are expected to change and for that reason, until the transaction for the asset or liability is actually realized, the actual price may not be known precisely.

The reason why the exit price is essential for fair value measurement is that it is the best indicator that will represent the anticipation of future cash inflows and outflows associated with the asset and liability from the perspective of market participants at the measurement date [FASB 157:C26]. This means that the management's best estimate of the future economic benefits that are expected from holding an asset is the exit price derived from the market-based data.

The transaction to be fair valued should take place either in the principal market or in the absence of a principal market; the most advantageous market determines the fair value. The *principal market* is the market with the greatest volume and level of activity for the asset or liability from the reporting entity's perspective. *The most advantageous market* is defined as the market that maximizes the amount from the sale of the asset or minimizes the amount to be paid to transfer the liability in the absence of the principal market [IFRS 13: Appendix A].

If a principal market exits for an asset or a liability, the fair value should be based on the price in that market whether determined directly through observation or by a valuation technique. Even if its price is potentially more advantageous in a different market at the measurement date, the fair value should be based on the price in the principle market [IFRS 13:16]. According to this statement, the base for determining the fair value should be the data in the actual market, so with the existence of the principal market, the entity does not have to exhaustively search for all possible markets to discover the most advantageous one. Instead, the reporting entity should use the price in the principal market at the measurement date.

Under IFRS 13, *transaction costs* are not taken into account when determining the exit price since they are not considered attributes of assets or liabilities. These costs are attributable to the disposal of an asset or the transfer of a liability. Therefore, they result directly from that specific transaction and vary depending on the way it happens. Hence, they are more transaction-specific but should be adjusted for in the most advantageous market [IFRS 13:25]. Accordingly, when determining the fair value of an asset, the transaction costs should neither be considered as a deduction from the price available in the principal market nor an addition to the liability amount in the case of a liability transfer. Also, transaction costs do not include transportation costs. However, if the location is a characteristic of the asset or liability being measured (e.g., biological assets), the exit price shall be adjusted for the costs incurred while moving the asset from the current position to that market [IFRS 13:26].

2.2. Market participants

Fair value is a market-based, not an entity-specific measurement, that is, it should be based on the assumptions of market participants for pricing the asset or liability [IFRS 13:22]. Market participants are the buyers and sellers in the principal (or the most advantageous) market for the asset or liability. They are interested in and could benefit from the ownership of a specific asset or liability. Those market participants have the following characteristics (IFRS 13: Appendix A):

- *"buyers and sellers are independent of each other, not related parties, (the term "related parties" is used consistent with its use in IAS 24),"*
- *"they are knowledgeable in the sense that they have reasonable understanding of the asset or liability and the transaction using all available information,"*
- *"they are able to enter into a transaction (must have legal and financial capacity to do so,"*
- *"they are willing to enter into a transaction (not forced to do so)."*

The reporting entity is required to develop a profile of potential market participants instead of identifying specific market participants. The determination of potential market participants is a critical step in the overall determination of fair value. Although it may be easy to determine this profile, in certain other cases, a reporting entity may need to make assumptions about the type of market participant. In the fair value measurement, it is significant to determine the appropriate market and market participants [5].

http://dx.doi.org/10.5772/intechopen.68724

3. Fair value measurement

The objective of fair value measurement is to estimate the price that would be received to sell an asset or paid to transfer a liability in an orderly transaction between market participants at the measurement date [IFRS 13:B2]. The principles to be followed in determining the fair value of assets and liabilities for both initial and subsequent measurement are explained in the next section.

3.1. Measurement

In the measurement of fair value, the entity has to determine all of the following:

(i) The unit of account consistent with a particular asset or liability or a group of assets and liabilities that are being measured.

The determination of how fair value measurement applies depends on the unit of account [IFRS 13:2.4]. The unit of account is the level at which the asset or liability is aggregated or disaggregated in accordance with IFRS applicable for recognition purposes [IFRS 13: Appendix A). Fair value measurement is applied to a particular asset or liability (e.g., an equity investment, a property, plant and equipment (PPE), or an intangible asset). When measuring the fair value of an asset or a liability, the entity should take into account the particular asset or liability's specific characteristics, such as condition, location, and restrictions, if any.

(ii) The appropriate valuation premise to measure for non-financial assets (should be consistent with the "highest and best use").

Fair value is the amount that reflects the perspective of market participants [IFRS 13:29]. From this point of view, the *highest and best use* is the use of market participants to maximize the value of a non-financial asset or a group of assets and liabilities for which the asset is being used. The concept of the highest and best use is not valid for financial assets and liabilities; it is the basis for the fair value measurement of non-financial assets. The use of a non-financial asset at best and at the highest level is provided either by way of use or by exchange. Therefore, the market participant may benefit economically by using it at the highest level or by selling it to another market participant [IFRS 13:27]. The highest and best use takes into consideration the use of asset that is physically possible, legally permissible, and financially feasible.

(iii) The most advantageous market in the absence of the principal market.

If the principal market is available to and accessible by the entity, fair value measurement is conducted by using prices in that market. In the absence of the principal market, the most advantageous market is used for determining the fair value.

(iv) The appropriate valuation technique.

In the measurement of fair value, an appropriate valuation technique should be used that maximizes the use of relevant observable inputs and minimizes the use of unobservable inputs [IFRS 13:61]. The purpose of applying valuation techniques is to estimate the fair value. The three main approaches used as valuation techniques are listed below:

- **Market approach:** uses observable prices and other relevant information derived from market transactions involving identical or similar assets, liabilities or a group of assets and liabilities, such as a business [IFRS 13:B5]. IFRS 13 provides an example of matrix pricing, which is a mathematical method of valuation technique consistent with the market approach [IFRS 13:B5-7].
- **Cost approach:** reflects the current amount that would be needed to replace the service capacity of an asset, that is, the current replacement cost [IFRS 13:B8].
- **Income approach:** uses the valuation techniques to calculate the present value of future amounts based on current market expectations [IFRS 13:B10]. For instance, option-pricing models, residual income valuation method used to measure the fair value of some intangible assets.

(v) Inputs to fair value measurement and the fair value hierarchy.

The fair value standards classify the inputs to fair value measurement in three levels and this classification creates a *"fair value hierarchy."* The hierarchy gives the first priority to the prices of identical assets and liabilities in the active market (e.g., unadjusted quoted prices). The lowest (third) priority is given to unobservable inputs [IFRS 13:72]. The inputs to valuation methods classified below are essential in the measurement of fair value more than the valuation methods:

- **Level 1:** Inputs are *"observable"* because they refer to the quoted prices in the active market of identifiable assets or liabilities that the entity may access at the measurement date. The quoted price in an active market is unadjusted and provides the most reliable evidence of fair value [IFRS 13:77]. If the asset or liability is traded in more than one market, the prices in the principal market are taken into account. In the absence of principal market, the prices in the most advantageous market are used as fair value.
- **Level 2:** Inputs that are observable directly or indirectly with respect to an asset or a liability, other than quoted prices [IFRS 13:81]. These inputs include (a) quoted prices in active market for similar assets or liabilities, (b) quoted prices in markets that are not active for identical or similar assets or liabilities, (c) observable inputs other than quoted prices such as interest rates, and (d) market-corroborated inputs derived principally from or supported by observable market data by correlation or other means.
- **Level 3:** Inputs are *"unobservable"* [IFRS 13:86] so they have the lowest priority. The use of these inputs is allowed where there is no or less market activity for the asset or liability to obtain relevant observable inputs at the measurement date [IFRS 13:87]. The unobservable inputs are generated by the entity itself using the best information available in the circumstances, which might include the entity's own data considering all available information about market participant assumptions. However, in case of other market participants' using different data, the entity's own data should be adjusted [IFRS 13:89]. Long-dated currency swap, a 3-year option on exchange-traded shares, interest rate swap, and cash-generating unit are examples of Level 3 inputs.

To sum up, the entity is required to follow the steps explained above to determine the fair value measurement ("see **Figure 1**").

http://dx.doi.org/10.5772/intechopen.68724

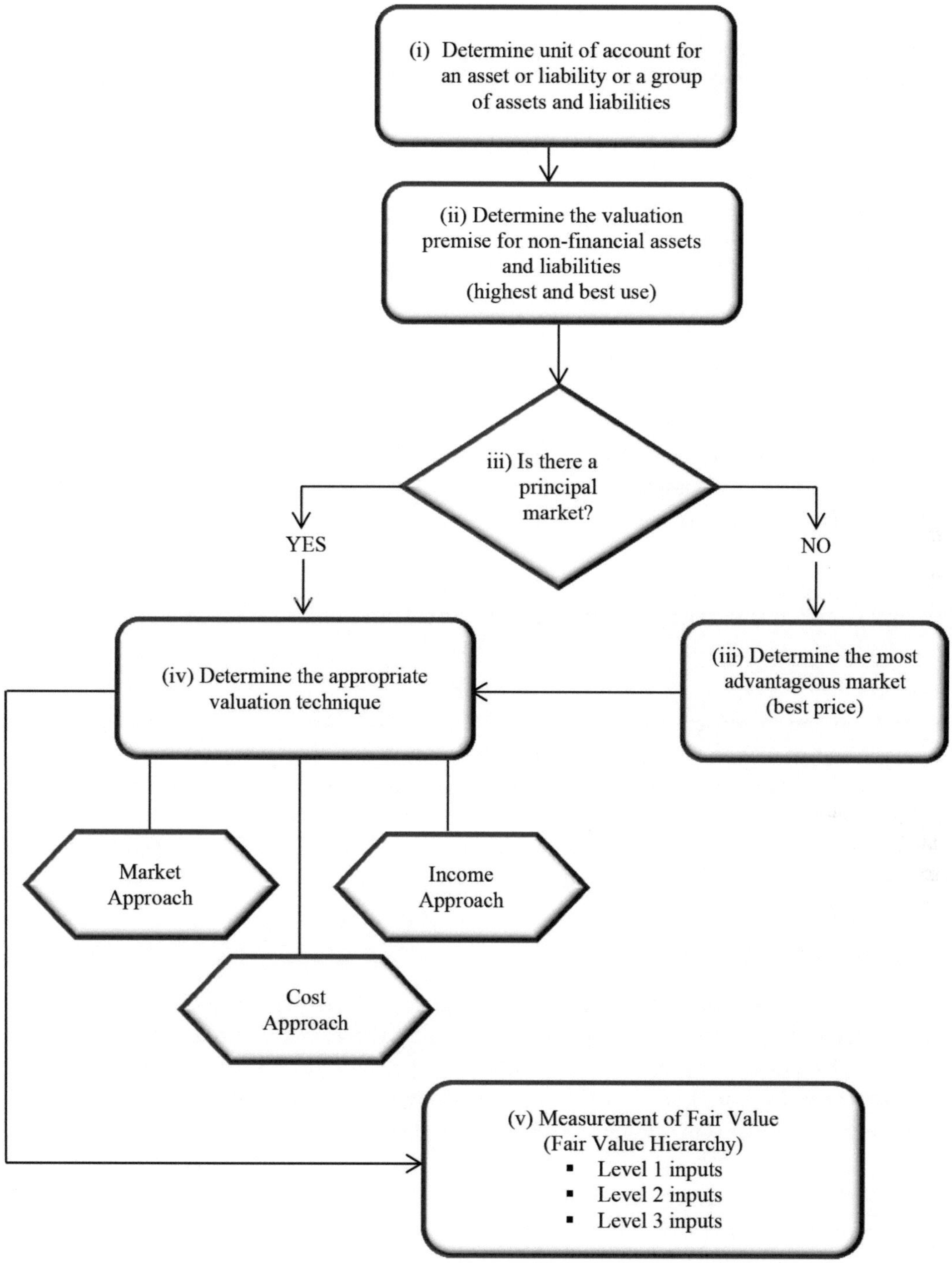

Figure 1. Schematic representation of fair value measurement.

At initial recognition, a general approach is the use of the entry price for the fair value measurement of all assets and liabilities. In many cases, it is assumed that the entry price often reflects the fair value and is thus equal to the exit price at initial recognition. When an asset is acquired or a liability incurred, a change occurs in the transaction involving that asset or liability. The price of such transaction refers to the *entry price* that is paid to acquire the asset or received to assume the liability, whereas the fair value of an asset or a liability is the *exit price* that would be received to sell the asset or paid to transfer the liability. Essentially, the entry price and the exit price are different, in the sense that the prices paid by the buyer and received by the seller are usually not the same because entities do not necessarily sell assets or transfer liabilities at the prices paid to acquire the assets or the prices received to assume the liabilities. There are certain conditions in which the transaction price cannot represent the fair value of an asset or a liability during initial recognition such as [IFRS 13:B4]; a related party transaction, a forced transaction (i.e., seller having financial difficulties), the unit of account for the transaction price does not symbolize the unit of account for the asset or liability being measured or the market in which the transaction is realized and the market in which the reporting entity sells the assets or transfers the liability are different (the principal market or the most advantageous market).

4. Fair value measurements for assets and liabilities (IFRSs)

In accordance with IFRS, certain assets and liabilities are measured at fair value both at initial recognition and in subsequent periods. IFRS 13 addresses *how* to measure the fair value of financial and non-financial assets and liabilities, but it does not prescribe *what* items must be measured at fair value, *when* to measure or *how* to account for subsequent changes in fair value. This section therefore exclusively explains the relevant IFRSs to be considered for each of these requirements. Also, a summary of the measurement of assets and liabilities is given on a tabular form at the end of this section (see **Table 1**).

4.1. Financial assets (IFRS 9)

IFRS 9 divides all financial assets into two groups as soon as the entity becomes a party to the contractual provisions of the instrument—financial assets measured at amortized cost and financial assets measured at fair value where gains and losses are recognized in other comprehensive income (fair value through other comprehensive income, FVTOCI) or recognized in profit or loss (fair value through profit or loss, FVTPL). The entities are required to make this classification for their financial assets at initial recognition by taking into account the entity's *business model* for managing the financial assets and the *contractual cash flow characteristics* of the financial asset. A business model is the way of managing its financial assets by collecting contractual cash flows (hold-to-collect), selling financial assets for trading purpose or collecting contractual cash flows *and* selling financial assets (hold-to-collect and sell) [IFRS 9:4.1.1].

Elements	Measurement	
I. Financial assets (IFRS 9)	**INITIAL**	**SUBSEQUENT**
i. Trade and other receivables	• Transaction price (plus transaction costs) (significant financing component excluded from sales)	• Amortized cost • Impairment provision for credit losses
ii. Debt instruments	• *Fair value* (plus transaction costs)	• **Debt instruments held to collect contractual cash flows** — Amortized cost — Impairment provision for credit losses • **Debt instruments held both to collect contractual cash flows and sell** - *Fair value* (FVTOC)
iii. Equity instruments	• *Fair value* (transaction costs are not included)	• *Fair value* (FVTPL) (FVTOCI is an option for the equity instruments held not for trading purpose)
iv. Derivatives	• *Fair value* (transaction costs are not included)	• *Fair value* (FVTPL)
II. Financial liabilities (IFRS 9)		
i. Financial liabilities measured at amortized cost	• *Fair value* (less transaction costs)	• Amortized cost
ii. Financial liabilities (FVTPL)	• *Fair value*	• *Fair value* (FVTPL)
III. Investments in associates and joint ventures (IAS 28) (IAS 27)	• Acquisition cost (plus transaction costs)	• **Consolidated financial statements** — Equity method • **Separate financial statements** — Measurement at cost — *Fair value measurement* (IFRS 9) — Equity method (IAS 28)
IV. Investments in subsidiaries (IFRS 10) (IAS 27)	• Acquisition cost	• **Consolidated financial statements** - Full consolidation • **Separate financial statements** — Measurement at cost — *Fair value measurement* (IFRS 9) — Equity method (IAS 28)
V. Property, plant, and equipment (IAS 16)	• **Acquisition**—Acquisition cost (financing component excluded unless a qualifying asset) • **Exchange assets**—*Fair value* of the received asset or the asset given up or the carrying amount of the asset given up	• Cost model • Revaluation model (*Fair value*)

Elements	Measurement	
I. Financial assets (IFRS 9)	**INITIAL**	**SUBSEQUENT**
VI. Intangible assets (IAS 38)	• **Acquisition** — Acquisition cost (financing component excluded unless a qualifying asset) • **Business combination** — *Fair value* • **Exchange assets** — *Fair value* of the received asset or the asset given up or the carrying amount of the asset given up • **Government Grant** — *Fair value*	• Cost model • Revaluation model if there is an active market (*Fair value*)
VII. Investment property (IAS 40)	• **Acquisition** — Acquisition cost (financing component excluded unless a qualifying asset)	• Cost model • *Fair value*
VIII. Business combinations (IFRS 3)	• All assets acquired and liabilities assumed in a business combination are measured at acquisition-date fair value • Contingent consideration — *fair value* • Non-controlling interests (NCI) — *Fair value* (full goodwill method) — NCI's proportionate share of net assets of the acquiree	• All acquired assets and liabilities are measured according to the relevant IFRSs.
IX. Agriculture (IAS 41)	Generally measured at *fair value* less costs to sell	

Table 1. Fair value measurements in IFRSs.

If an entity holds a financial asset in order to collect contractual cash flows and the contractual terms of the financial asset give rise to cash flows that are solely payments of principal and interest on the principal amount outstanding on a specified date, then they are called as hold-to-collect business model and measured at amortized cost subsequently [IFRS 9:4.1.2]. *Receivables* and *loans* (*loan receivables with basic features*) are included within the scope of IFRS 15 *Revenue from Contracts* and are measured at transaction price (including transaction costs) at initial recognition, and then classified and accounted for amortized cost in accordance with IFRS 9 subsequently. Conversely, if the objective of an entity is to generate profits by converting the changes in the fair value of the financial assets into cash, the business model of the entity does not hold these assets to collect the contractual cash flows. In other words, if the entity holds financial assets for only trading purposes, that is, to earn profit from the changes in the fair value of financial assets by buying and selling, the financial assets are measured at fair value and valuation differences are recognized in profit or loss (FVTPL).

Debt instruments are carried at fair value plus transaction costs at initial recognition, and then, for subsequent measurement, as stated previously, the entity's *business model* for managing the financial assets and the *contractual cash flow characteristics* of the financial asset must be taken into consideration. Therefore, debt instruments held to collect contractual cash flows are measured at amortized cost, whereas they are measured at fair value with all changes recorded through other comprehensive income in the shareholders' equity (FVTOCI) if they are held within an entity whose objective is achieved by both holding the financial asset in order to collect contractual cash flows and selling the financial asset. All other debt instruments that do not qualify to be measured at amortized cost or FCTOCI must be measured at fair value through profit or loss (FVTPL) [IFRS 9:4.1.4].

Equity instruments are carried at fair value (transaction costs are not included) at initial recognition. The default subsequent measurement for whether quoted or unquoted equities is always the fair value with value changes recognized in profit or loss (FVTPL). IFRS 9 also provides second option, namely "other comprehensive income" option for those equity instruments that are not held for trading and want to present changes in other comprehensive income (FVTOCI). For the unquoted equity instruments, there is no option of measurement with historical cost. *Derivatives* are carried at fair value with value changes recognized in profit or loss (FVTPL).

4.2. Financial liabilities (IFRS 9)

IFRS 9 classifies and divides all financial liabilities into two—financial liabilities measured at amortized cost and financial liabilities measured at fair value where gains and losses are recognized in profit or loss (FVTPL). In accordance with IFRS 9, all financial liabilities are initially measured at fair value. Financial liabilities held for trading are measured through profit or loss and all other financial liabilities are measured at amortized cost unless the fair value option is applied [IFRS 9:4.2.1]. Trade payables, bank borrowings, and loan payables with standard interest rates are examples of financial liabilities that are likely to be classified at amortized cost. FVTPL examples are interest rate swaps and commodity future/option contracts.

4.3. Investments in associates and joint ventures (IAS 28)

According to IAS 28 *Investments in Associates and Joint Ventures*, the investment in an associate or a joint venture is initially recognized at cost (acquisition cost) including transaction costs. On acquisition of the investment in an associate or a joint venture, the goodwill is included in the carrying amount of the investment (implicit goodwill). After acquisition, the implicit goodwill is amortized in the following periods, considering the changes in the relevant accounts. To account for additional depreciation or amortization of the investee's depreciable or amortizable assets, appropriate adjustments to the investor's share of the profits or losses are made based on the excess of their fair values over their carrying amounts at the time the investment was acquired. [IAS 28:23]. For example, for depreciation expense calculated based on the depreciable assets' fair values at the acquisition date or for impairment losses such as for goodwill or property, plant, and equipment, appropriate adjustments should be made to the investor's share of the associate's or joint venture's profit or loss [IAS 28 (2011):32].

In its consolidated financial statements, an investor uses the equity method for investments in associates and joint ventures [IAS 28 (2011):16]. IAS 28 allows the investor to choose an accounting method offered in IAS 27 *Separate Financial Statements* to account for its investments in associates and joint ventures in its separate financial statements. These methods are [IAS 27 (2011):10] as follows:

- measurement at cost or
- fair value measurement in accordance with IFRS 9 or
- using the equity method described in IAS 28.

On the other hand, IAS 28 permits a venture capital organization, mutual fund, unit trust, and similar entities, including investment-linked insurance funds, to measure investments in associates and joint ventures at fair value through profit or loss in accordance with IFRS 9.

4.4. Property, plant, and equipment (IAS 16)

An item of property, plant, and equipment should initially be recorded at cost [IAS 16:15]. PPE is recognized in the statement of financial position through acquisition, in exchange for a non-monetary asset or assets or a combination of monetary and non-monetary assets or self-construction. The cost of PPE acquired in exchange for another asset is measured at the carrying amount of the asset given up unless the fair value of the received asset or the asset given up is reliably measurable [IAS 16:24]. IAS 16 permits two accounting models for subsequent measurement—cost model and revaluation model. In the revaluation model, PPE whose fair value can be reliably measured is carried at a revalued amount, that is, its fair value at the revaluation date of the asset less subsequent depreciation and impairment [IAS 16:31].

4.5. Intangible assets (IAS 38)

The recognition of intangible assets can be done through the following ways:

- **Acquisition:** Intangible assets are initially measured at cost when acquired externally [IAS 38:24].
- **Business combination:** Intangible assets acquired in a business combination are subject to IFRS 3 *Business Combinations* and therefore the cost of that intangible asset is its fair value at the acquisition date. There is a presumption that the fair value (and therefore the cost) of an intangible asset acquired in a business combination can be measured reliably [IAS 38:35].
- **Government grant:** Intangible assets may be acquired free of charge or at a very low price by way of a government grant. In accordance with IAS 20 *Accounting for Government Grants and Disclosure of Government Assistance*, an entity may choose to recognize both the intangible asset and the grant initially at fair value [IAS 38:44].
- **Exchange of assets:** An intangible asset may be recognized in exchange for an asset or a combination of assets. If (a) the exchange transaction is commercial or (b) the fair value of the received asset or the asset given up is reliably measurable, such intangible asset is measured at fair value [IAS 38:45].

- **Internal generation (self-creation):** intangibles internally generated within an entity are classified into (a) research phase and (b) development phase. Expenditures incurred in the research phase are to be recognized as expense and reported in profit or loss, whereas the costs associated with the development phase are capitalized only after technical and commercial feasibility of the asset for sale or use have been established [IAS 38:54 and 38:57]. Therefore, the cost of an intangible asset internally generated is the sum of the expenses capitalized from the development phase [IAS 38:65]. IAS 38 permits two accounting models for subsequent measurement similar to PPE—cost model and revaluation model. In the revaluation model, if the intangible assets have an active market they may be carried at a revalued amount based on fair value less any subsequent amortization and impairment losses [IAS 38:75]. But such active markets are not very common for intangible assets [IAS 38:78]. Examples for such intangibles that may have active markets are production quotas, fishing licences, and taxi licences.

4.6. Investment property (IAS 40)

"Investment property is property (land or a building or part of a building or both) held (by the owner or by the lessee under a finance lease) to earn rentals or for capital appreciation or both" [IAS 40:5]. Investment property is initially measured at cost, including transaction costs [IAS 40:20 and 40:23]. IAS 40 provides two accounting models for subsequent measurement—cost model and fair value model. The best evidence of fair value for an investment property is the current prices in an active market for similar property in the same location and condition and subject to similar lease and other contracts [IAS 40:45]. The entity may consider current prices for properties of a different nature or subject to different conditions, recent prices in less active markets with adjustments to reflect changes in economic conditions, and discounted cash flow projections based on reliable estimates of future cash flows in the absence of such information [IAS 40:46]. Although there are two options for subsequent measurement in IAS 40, the entity shall measure the investment property using the cost model in IAS 16 in case its fair value is not reliably determinable [IAS 40:53].

4.7. Accounting for government grants and disclosure of government assistance (IAS 20)

A government grant may be in the form of a transfer of non-monetary assets, such as land or other resources and it is usual to determine the fair value of the non-monetary asset and to record for both grant and asset at that fair value. In some cases, an alternative method may be used to recognize the asset and the grant at nominal value [IAS 20:23].

4.8. Business combinations (IFRS 3)

IFRS 3 *Business Combinations* define a business combination as a transaction or an event in which an acquirer obtains the control of one or more businesses. Acquisition method is applied to account for business combinations [IFRS 3:4]. In this method, all assets acquired and liabilities assumed in a business combination are measured at acquisition-date fair value [IFRS 3:18]. When measuring all the identifiable assets acquired and the liabilities assumed at fair value in the acquisition method, goodwill or a gain from a bargain purchase may arise. However, there is no explanation for how to determine the fair value of identifiable assets acquired and the liabilities assumed of an entity in IFRS 3. In this respect, the principles under IFRS 13 and relevant IFRSs (standards for assets and liabilities) should be taken into account.[1]

The measurement of an acquirer's pre-combination investment in an acquiree for the case of business combination achieved in stages is done in accordance with other relevant IFRSs (IFRS 9 *Financial Instruments*, IAS 28 *Investments in Associates and Joint Ventures*, and IFRS 11 *Joint Arrangements*). The acquirer re-measures any previously held interest at fair value and takes it into account in the determination of goodwill [IFRS 3:32]. As a result of this re-measurement, the gain or loss is either recognized in profit or loss or other comprehensive income consistent with the previous measurement basis [IFRS 3:42].

In the measurement of non-controlling interests (NCI), IFRS 3 allows an accounting policy choice among the following:

- fair value (sometimes called the full goodwill method), or
- the NCI's proportionate share of net assets of the acquiree.

IFRS 3 allows the acquirer to measure the acquisition-date fair value of a non-controlling interest on the basis of active market prices for the equity shares not held by the acquirer. In the absence of an active market, the acquirer would measure the fair value of the non-controlling interest using other valuation techniques [IFRS 3:B44].

4.9. Agriculture (IAS 41)

Biological assets with the exception of bearer plants, agricultural produce at the point of harvest, and government grants related to these biological assets fall within the scope of IAS 41 *Agriculture*. Under IAS 41, biological assets are generally measured at fair value less costs to sell. However, there are instances when cost can approximate fair value, including when (i) little biological transformation has taken place since the costs were originally incurred or (ii) the impact of biological transformation on price is not expected to be material.

5. Measurement principles in the Exposure Draft *Conceptual Framework for Financial Reporting*

The existing *Conceptual Framework* was initially published by International Accounting Standards Committee in 1989 and describes the basic concepts for the preparation and presentation of financial statements. It is not a standard itself, but has helped the IASB for developing future IFRSs and revising existing ones, as well as a very important reference for the users and preparers.

The *Conceptual Framework* has been widely criticized for its being unclear, for not covering some important concepts and for not being reflective of the IASB's current thinking as

[1]The exceptions would be: contingent liabilities (IAS 37), income taxes (IAS 12), employee benefits (IAS 19), indemnification assets (IFRS 3.27-28), reacquired rights (IFRS 3.29), share-based payment transactions (IFRS 2), and assets held for sale (IFRS 5).

it has been left unchanged and therefore out of date since its inception [6]. Thus, in 2004, the IASB and FASB initiated a joint comprehensive project on the Conceptual Framework (the "Project") with the aim of reviewing and revising the existing one. However, during late 2010, the only one phase of the Project has been finalized and introduced as two chapters (Chapters 1 and 3), namely "The Objective of General Purpose Financial Reporting" and "Qualitative Characteristics of Useful Information" and the Project was abandoned due to the priorities given to other urgent projects. In 2011, the IASB carried out a public consultation and following the feedbacks from many respondents to that consultation, the Project was given the first priority in the IASB's work plan. Consequently, the IASB restarted the Project in 2012 as an IASB-only project. The aim of the Project was to clarify the subjects that are not yet covered, or to explicate the shortcomings in the existing one and focus on the elements of the financial statements, measurement, reporting entity, presentation,and disclosure. In July 2013, a Discussion Paper (DP) *A Review of the Conceptual Framework for Financial Reporting* was issued that set out the IASB's preliminary views on possible amendments to the existing Conceptual Framework [7]. The feedbacks received on this Discussion Paper constitute the infrastructure of the Exposure Draft [8].

Finally, on May 28, 2015, the IASB published the Exposure Draft *Conceptual Framework for Financial Reporting (ED)* ED/2015/3, proposing revisions and amendments for some topical areas in the current one. The purpose of the ED is to fill in the gaps, update the parts that are out of date, and clarify the guidance in some areas. To achieve this, the ED provides key proposals in eight chapters that are mainly on the definitions of an asset and a liability, a guidance on measurement and de-recognition and a framework for presentation and disclosure [9].

Measurement is one of the main proposals discussed initially in the Discussion Paper and then in the ED because the existing Conceptual Framework provides very little guidance on measurement and when particular measurements should be used [DP 6:1]. Measurement is the process of quantifying the amounts of an entity's assets, liabilities, income, and expenses in monetary terms [ED 6:2]. As shown in **Table 1**, there exist various measurement bases for the assets and liabilities in accordance with particular IFRSs. However, many respondents have criticized about the lack of measurement guidelines in the existing Conceptual Framework when difficulties were encountered for the measurement of particular assets or liabilities. Hence, the IASB decided to include this significant issue widely by releasing a "measurement" chapter (Chapter 6) in the ED.

According to Section 6.10 of the DP "*the objective of measurement is to contribute to the faithful representation of relevant information about the resources of the entity, claims against the entity and changes in resources and claims, and about how efficiently and effectively the entity's management and governing board have discharged their responsibilities to use the entity's resources.*" Accordingly, initially Basis for Conclusions Exposure Draft for Financial Reporting and the measurement chapter in the ED focuses on different measurement bases, the information that these measurement bases provide and their advantages and disadvantages [ED 6:4–6:47 and BC 6:15–6:37] [10], and the factors to consider when selecting a measurement basis such as relevance, faithful representation, enhancing qualitative characteristics, and factors specific to initial measurement [ED 6:48–6:73 and BC 6:41–6:68] (see **Figure 2**).

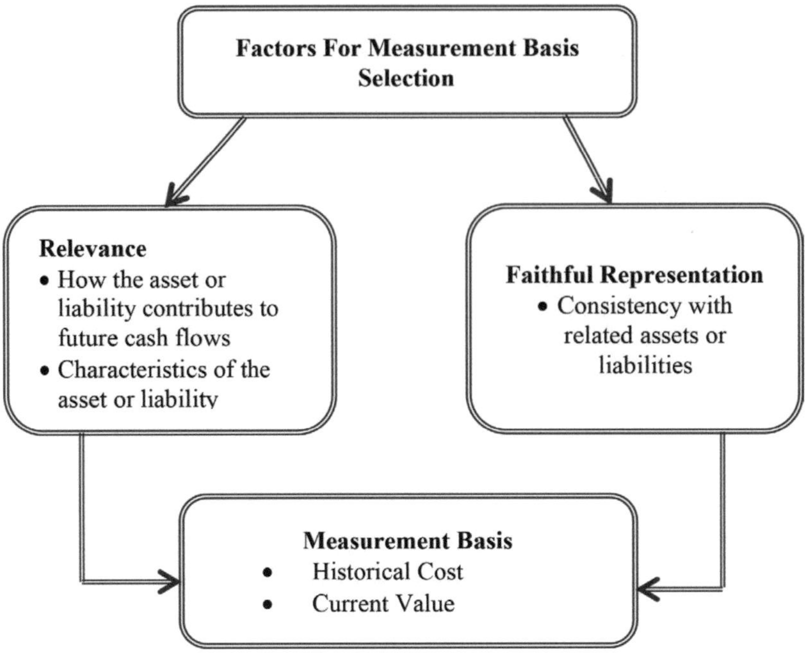

Figure 2. Measurement in Exposure Draft Conceptual Framework.

When developing both the Discussion Paper and the Exposure Draft, the IASB considered whether the *Conceptual Framework* should advocate a single or a default measurement basis but with the consideration of the objective of financial reporting, the qualitative characteristics of useful financial information and the cost constraint, mixed measurement approach is suggested and then proposed in Discussion Paper and Exposure Draft, respectively. It is worth stating the respondents' most common opinions on this issue as [ED 6:74 and 6:75] follows:

a. *"in most cases, the most understandable way to provide the relevant information is to use one measurement in both the statement of financial position and the statement(s) of financial performance, and to use the other measurement basis for disclosure only"*;

b. *"in some cases, more relevant information is provided by using a current value measurement basis in the statement of financial position and a different measurement basis to determine the related income or expenses in the statement of financial performance."*

As a result, selecting measurements by considering either the statement of financial position alone or the statement(s) of profit or loss and other comprehensive income alone does not provide relevant financial information to financial statement users. Instead, it must be taken into consideration that measurement affects both the statement of financial position and the statement(s) of profit or loss and other comprehensive income [ED 6:76].

Paragraphs ED 6:74–6:77 and BC 6:68 discuss situations in which more than one measurement basis is needed to provide relevant information about an asset, liability, income, or expenses.

http://dx.doi.org/10.5772/intechopen.68724

After a long discussion on this issue, the IASB agreed on two categories:

- Historical cost [ED 6:6–6:18 and BC 6:19–BC 6:23] or
- Current value [ED 6:19–6:46 and BC 6:24–BC 6:30]

Cash flow-based measures would then be identified as measurement techniques to estimate the measure of an asset or a liability on a defined measurement basis. Therefore, the ED does not identify those techniques as a separate category of measurement basis, but a tool to estimate either a cost-based measure or a current measure [BC 6:17]. Paragraphs A1–A10 discuss cash flow-based measurement techniques in ED.

5.1. Historical cost

Historical cost measurement provides monetary information about assets, liabilities, income, and expenses based on the information obtained from the transaction or event occurred on that date. It does not reflect changes in prices; instead, it reflects changes such as the consumption (depreciation or amortization) or impairment of assets and the fulfillment of liabilities [ED 6:6].

The ED defines the historical cost of a financial asset (sometimes referred to as amortized cost) and a non-financial asset as the acquisition value plus the transaction costs and the historical cost of a financial liability (again, sometimes referred to as amortized cost) and a non-financial liability as the value of the consideration received to take on the liability less the transaction costs [ED 6:7–6:9]. The subsequent measurement of financial assets and financial liabilities is done at amortized cost that reflects the adjustments for accrual of interest, payments or receipts, and impairment. It is clear that the ED categorizes the amortized cost basis of measurement for financial assets and financial liabilities as a historical cost measurement basis [BC 6:22]. Non-financial asset is adjusted for subsequent depreciation and impairment and non-financial liability is adjusted for accrual of interest, fulfillment of the liability, and onerous liabilities. However, these adjustments for all assets and liabilities do not reflect subsequent changes in prices caused by other factors [ED 6:9].

Historical cost measurement is found to be simpler, easy to understand, and less expensive than using current value measurement bases. On the other hand, historical cost can be difficult to determine when there is no observable transaction price for the asset or liability being measured and subjective to estimate consumption and identify impairment losses or onerous liabilities. Additionally, reporting the similar assets or liabilities that are acquired or incurred at different times in the financial statements at very different amounts can reduce comparability both between reporting entities and within the same reporting entity. For those reasons, the historical cost of an asset or a liability can sometimes be as difficult to apply as a current value [ED 6:15–6:17].

5.2. Current value

Measures based on current value provide monetary information about assets, liabilities, income, and expenses using information that is updated to reflect conditions at the measurement date [ED 6:19]. Current value measurement bases include the following:

- fair value [ED 6:21–6:33] and
- value in use for assets and fulfillment value for liabilities [ED 6:34–6:46].

With respect to *fair value,* it is explained in the ED that the asset or the liability is measured using the same assumptions that market participants would use when pricing each if those market participants act in their economic best interest. In other words, fair value reflects the perspective of market participants [ED 6.22]. Also, transaction costs are not taken into account for fair value measurement of both assets and liabilities. The description of fair value in the ED is consistent with its description in IFRS 13 *Fair Value Measurement* [BC 6.25].

Fair value measurement produces information that has a predictive value, because it reflects market participants' expectations and is priced in a manner that reflects their risk preferences. However, users may not always find information about estimates of changes in expectations of market participants relevant. On the other hand, fair value measurement creates a comparability advantage both between reporting entities and within the same reporting entity as it is determined from market participants' perspective, instead of the perspective of the entity, and is independent of when the asset or the liability was acquired or incurred, identical assets will be measured at the same amount. Furthermore, if there exists an active market for the fair value of an asset or a liability, the fair value measurement is simple, easy to understand, and verifiable. In the absence of a fair value, valuation techniques (sometimes including the use of cash flow-based measurements) may be needed to estimate that fair value but they are not only costly and complex but also subjective and difficult to verify both the inputs and the validity of the process itself. As a consequence, due to the entities' measuring identical assets or liabilities at different amounts, comparability decreases [ED 6:28–6:33].

According to paragraph ED 6:34,*"value in use and fulfilment value are entity-specific values. Value in use is the present value of the cash flows that an entity expects to derive from the continuing use of an asset and from its ultimate disposal. Fulfilment value is the present value of the cash flows that an entity expects to incur as it fulfils a liability."* They reflect the same factors in their measurement as fair value based on factors on entity-specific assumptions rather than assumptions by market participants [ED 6:35]. The descriptions of *value in use and fulfillment value* are derived from the definition of entity-specific current value in IAS 16 *Property, Plant and Equipment.*

In other IFRSs, value in use is used only in determining whether an asset measured at historical cost is impaired, but in the ED it is a separate measurement basis because [BC 6:26]:

- although value in use is used in determining recoverable historical cost, it differs conceptually from historical cost; and
- there may be situations in the future when the IASB decides that an entity should measure an asset using value in use instead of fair value.

Cash flow-based measurement technique is used for both value in use and fulfillment value which may be not only costly and complex but also subjective and difficult to verify both the inputs and the validity of the process itself. As a consequence of this technique, the entities may measure identical assets or liabilities at different amounts which reduces the comparability

[ED 6:43]. Besides, using the perspective of reporting entity may cause differences in the measures of identical assets and liabilities in different entities which again decreases the comparability. By contrast, this problem is not seen in fair value measurement because fair value uses market participant assumptions, in theory, different entities should arrive at identical estimates of fair value for identical items [ED 6:44].

The treatment of transaction costs in the ED is consistent with IFRS 13. The transaction costs incurred in acquiring an asset or taking on a liability are a feature of the original transaction so should be a part of it. Furthermore, if the measure base used is the fair value, fulfillment value, or value in use of an asset or a liability, the measure would not reflect those transaction costs as they do not affect the current value of that asset or liability [BC 6:35].

All things considered, when selecting a measurement basis, whether at initial recognition or subsequently, it is important to consider important factors such as relevance and faithful representation. Additionally, comparability, understandability, and verifiability are enhancing qualitative characteristics for the users of financial statements. To provide relevant information, the following factors should be considered [ED 6:54]:

- Contribution to future cash flows which will depend in part on the nature of the business activities conducted by the entity (e.g., if a property is realized by sale, it will produce cash flows from that sale, but if a property is used in combination with other assets to produce goods and services, it will help produce cash flows from the sale of those goods and services).
- The characteristics of the asset or the liability such as its sensitivity to the changes in the market and effects on the cash flows and other various risk factors that may be attached to the particular asset or liability.

6. Conclusion

Historical cost measurement is exposed to many criticisms that the financial statements prepared on a cost basis do not provide relevant information to the financial statement users due to its lack of fair and true presentation of entities and also causing a gap between the entity's book value and market value. In the past 20 years, there has been an ongoing debate and extensive discussion regarding the value relevance of information when the assets and liabilities are measured at fair value. On the other hand, the most important critique of the fair value is that if there is no active market for assets and liabilities, it may lead to subjective evaluations and cause fluctuations in profit or loss and other comprehensive income.

In other IFRSs where the principles for the measurement and reporting of assets and liabilities are stated, it is also found to be inadequate to use single measurement basis for valuing assets and liabilities and therefore proposes more than one measurement basis (i.e., historical cost, fair value, and net-realizable value). Within this context, IFRS 13 has been issued and in this standard, the fair value is more clearly defined, single set of measurement requirements are established, and hence complexity is reduced and consistency is improved. It also aims to improve and clarify existing disclosure requirements related to fair value measurements and additionally increase the convergence of IFRS and U.S. GAAP.

When assets and liabilities measured at fair value according to relevant IFRSs are analyzed, it is seen that fair value is predominantly used as measurement basis for equity instruments, business combinations, investment properties, and agricultural products. The characteristics of these assets measured at fair value are that significant portion of them have active markets and provide cash flows to the entity through the sale of the asset instead of consumption. Although the revaluation model is proposed for property, plant, and equipment and intangible assets acquired for use in business operations, valuation differences are recognized in other comprehensive income rather than profit or loss. Furthermore, the application of the revaluation model for intangible assets is limited. The absence of an active market for these assets and the difficulties in implementing other valuation techniques make the implementation of revaluation model based on the fair value very limited.

Also, in the Exposure Draft *Conceptual Framework for Financial Reporting*, two measurement bases are agreed on rather than a single one. Selecting the appropriate measurement basis, the contribution of an asset to the future cash flows of the entity, the way a liability is fulfilled in the future and the characteristics of assets and liabilities should be taken into consideration. From that perspective, the measurement of assets acquired for use in business activities rather than sale at historical cost, and that the measurement of assets held for sale at fair value would provide more relevant information to the needs of financial information users. For instance, property, plant, and equipment that is used in operations should be carried at historical cost and will provide more relevant information than its current market price. This application also refers to the notion of prudence principle emphasized in the ED. On the other hand, for all assets the use of a cost-based measurement may not be relevant to the users of financial statements such as derivatives in the group of assets held for sale should be measured at fair value.

To conclude, it is important to recognize that IFRS 13 is the standard that defines fair value and provides a framework for applying fair value measurements when required by IFRS with the intention of increasing consistency, comparability, and hence decreasing complexity. Also, the Exposure Draft *Conceptual Framework for Financial Reporting* finds inadequate to use single measurement basis for providing relevant financial information and therefore proposes two measurement bases: historical cost and current value (i.e., fair value and value in use for assets and fulfillment value for liabilities).

Author details

Yıldız Özerhan[1] and Banu Sultanoğlu[2]*

*Address all correspondence to: sbanu@bilkent.edu.tr

1 Faculty of Economics and Administrative Sciences, Gazi University, Turkey

2 Faculty of Business Administration, Bilkent University, Turkey

References

[1] IFRS 13 Fair Value Measurement. Project Summary and Feedback Statement. May 2011. Available from: http://www.ifrs.org/Current-Projects/IASB-Projects/Fair-Value Measurement/IFRS-13-Fair-ValueMeasurement/Documents/FairValue MeasurementFeedbackstatement_May2011.pdf [Accessed: January 16, 2016]

[2] IFRS 13 Fair Value Measurement. Available from: www.ifrs.org [Accessed: January 16, 2016]

[3] Campbell RL, Owens LA, Robinson DR. Fair Value Accounting from Theory to Practice. 2008. Available from: http://sfmagazine.com/wp-content/uploads/sfarchive/2008/07/Fair-Value-Accountingfrom-Theory-to-Practice.pdf [Accessed: December 16, 2016]

[4] IFRS Exposure Draft for Financial Reporting. May 2015. Available from: www.ifrs.org [Accessed: January 21, 2016]

[5] Fair Value Measurement. 2015 Global Edition-PwC. 2015. Available from: http://www.pwc.com/us/en/cfodirect/assets/pdf/accounting-guides/pwc-fair-value-measurement-2015.pdf [Accessed: January 16, 2016]

[6] EY. IASB Issues the Conceptual Framework Exposure Draft. June 2015. Available from: http://www.ey.com/Publication/vwLUAssets/Applying_IFRS:_IASB_issues_the_Conceptual_Framework_exposure_draft./%24File/Applying-Framework-June2015.pdf [Accessed: January 28, 2016]

[7] IFRS Discussion Paper, July 2013. A Review of the Conceptual Framework for Financial Reporting. 2013. Available from: www.ifrs.org [Accessed: January 21, 2016]

[8] Deloitte. IASB Publishes Exposure Draft of a New Conceptual Framework. May 2015. Available from: https://www.iasplus.com/en/news/2015/05/cf-ed [Accessed: January 21, 2016]

[9] IFRS. Snapshot: Conceptual Framework for Financial Reporting. May 2015. Available from: www.ifrs.org [Accessed: January 28, 2016]

[10] IFRS Basis for Conclusions Exposure Draft for Financial Reporting. May 2015. Available from: www.ifrs.org

Chapter 7

Reporting for Carbon Trading and International Accounting Standards

Figen Öker and Hümeyra Adıgüzel

Additional information is available at the end of the chapter

http://dx.doi.org/10.5772/intechopen.68959

Abstract

During the first commitment period of the Kyoto Protocol, many developed countries were forced to restrict carbon emissions. Flexible mechanisms were initiated to reduce carbon emissions and support clean energy projects. Regulated carbon markets were established to trade carbon premiums produced by these projects by signatory countries, while carbon premiums produced by nonsignatory countries were traded in voluntary markets. Following limited participation in the Kyoto Protocol, by the leadership of European Union, 195 countries presented contributive ideas in Paris Agreement, which is the first-ever universal, legally binding global climate deal. Kyoto Protocol sets commitment targets that have legal force, while the Paris Agreement emphases on consensus building and allows for voluntary and nationally determined targets. Another key difference between Paris Agreement and the Kyoto Protocol is its scope. It does not provide a specific division between developed and developing nations. By means of these changes, trading in voluntary carbon markets is expected to increase due to the higher demand to offset unavoidable carbon emissions. There has been no authoritative guidance published on carbon accounting by the International Accounting Standards Board or the Financial Accounting Standards Board. This study proposes how to measure and report the carbon allowances and carbon credits.

Keywords: carbon credits, emission trading mechanisms, carbon markets, IFRIC-3, International Accounting Standards

1. Introduction

Increased energy demand caused by growth and technological development in the world economy is being met largely from fossil fuel-based sources, which cause increasing emission of greenhouse gases (GHGs) into the atmosphere. Research shows that living conditions will be seriously threatened in the near future if international agreements do not put into force some sanctions to reduce emissions. Thus, the Kyoto Protocol was signed by many developed countries—those most responsible for the currently high GHG levels—in order to restrict future emissions. Flexible mechanisms are developed to enable countries that signed the agreement to fulfill their obligations. These mechanisms are Clean Development Mechanism (CDM), Joint Implementation (JI), and Emissions Trading System (ETS). According to protocol, the carbon credits obtained by organizations in countries which do not have any responsibility to restrict their carbon emissions cannot be a part of flexible mechanisms and can be traded in voluntary markets. Since the Kyoto Protocol went into force, the flexible mechanisms especially the Clean Development Mechanisms have been criticized for failing to produce either meaningful emission reductions or sustainable development benefits in most instances. Following limited participation in the Kyoto Protocol and the lack of agreement in Copenhagen in 2009, at the conference in December 2015, 195 countries adopted the first-ever universal, legally binding global climate deal. Paris Agreement, with its emphasis on consensus building, allows for voluntary and nationally determined targets, and specific climate goals of the agreement are politically encouraged and do not provide a specific division between developed and developing nations. The Paris Agreement is different from previous attempts to reach an international deal on climate, and it requires *all* countries not just the "developed" countries to submit national climate plans.

According to the Paris Agreement, a mechanism is required to contribute to the mitigation of greenhouse gases and support sustainable development. Through this mechanism, which is temporarily called as Sustainable Development Mechanism, parties could collaboratively pursue emission reductions for their Intended Nationally Determined Contributions (INDCs). The Sustainable Development Mechanism will replace the Clean Development Mechanism at the post-Kyoto period (2020). It is much wider in scope because it will be available to all parties as opposed to only Annex-1 parties in Kyoto Protocol.

As a result of emission limitation rates and country quota allocations, countries met new concepts like carbon economy, securitization of carbon, carbon credits, and carbon accounting. Carbon accounting remains an area in which there is no consensus. In 2004, the International Financial Reporting Interpretations Committee (IFRIC) published IFRIC-3 related to the reporting of carbon allowances according to existing International Accounting Standards (IASs), but it caused controversy and was withdrawn 6 months later. After the withdrawal of IFRIC-3, the International Accounting Standards Board (IASB) began a project which is conducted with Financial Accounting Standards Board (FASB), about Emission trading schemes in December 2007. In December 2012, IASB formally reactivated the project as an IASB-only research project and deferred joint work with FASB. In 2015, the project was renamed from "Emission trading schemes" to "Pollutant pricing mechanisms."

This chapter especially focuses on how to report the carbon allowances in accordance with international standards. The remainder of the chapter is organized as follows. Section 2 mentions about Kyoto Protocol and its mechanisms. Section 3 mentions about Paris Agreement and future of the sustainable development. Section 4 briefly mentions about carbon pricing. Section 5 mentions about the reporting of carbon allowances and expenses according to existing IASs and includes two illustrative cases. Finally, Section 6 summarizes the chapter.

2. Kyoto Protocol

The Kyoto Protocol is an attachment of the United Nations Framework Convention on Climate Change (UNFCCC) and was signed by 188 countries. Signatory countries were listed in either Annex-I or Annex-II according to their commitments: Annex-I countries committed themselves to decrease the levels of greenhouse gas emissions by around 5% of 1990 levels over the 2008–2012 period. Annex-II countries, as well as committing to greenhouse gas reduction objectives, were also obliged to give both financial and technological support to developing countries [1]. Fearing a loss of their competitive advantages in international trade, countries such as the United States and China, that are largely responsible for carbon emissions, and newly developing countries such as Turkey, Brazil, and South Korea did not agree to restrict their carbon emissions.

The countries that signed the agreement were required to fulfill their obligations by using a variety of flexible mechanisms such as Clean Development Mechanism (CDM), Joint Implementation (JI), and Emissions Trading System (ETS). Participants are able to obtain carbon credits according to their reduction of carbon emissions and trade them through these mechanisms [2, 3]. While CDM is accessible for the nonAnnex parties of the UNFCCC, JI is applicable for Annex-I parties, which are subject to emission reduction targets as per the obligations of the Protocol for Annex-B parties. **Table 1** shows the parties in the flexible mechanisms.

Flexible mechanisms	Countries		Carbon unit
	Investor	Host country	
Clean Development Mechanism (CDM)	Annex-B parties	NonAnnex parties	Certified emission reduction (CER)
Joint Implementation Mechanism (JI)	Annex-B parties	Annex-B parties	Emission reduction units (ERU)
Emissions Trading System (ETS)	Annex-B parties	Annex-B parties	Assigned amount units (AAU)

Table 1. Kyoto Protocol flexible mechanisms.

Under the Clean Development Mechanism (CDM), industrialized countries, which are party in Annex-B, purchase credits from greenhouse gas emission reduction projects in developing countries (nonAnnex parties) to promote sustainable development in the host country. The procedures are defined under the Kyoto Protocol and are governed by United Nations (UN). Carbon credits under CDM are called as certified emission reduction (CER).

Under Joint Implementation Mechanism (JI), any Annex-I country can invest in an emission reduction project in any other Annex-I country as an alternative to reducing emissions. That mechanism enabled countries to reach their emission reduction targets by using emission reduction units (ERUs) obtained through joint projects in a cheaper way.

The European Union Emissions Trading System (EU ETS), which started operations in 2005, is the first international carbon trading system [4]. Noted that 63% of volume-based carbon transactions were carried out by the EU ETS in 2006 rising to 70% in 2007 [5]. The best-known emission trading mechanisms are "baseline and credit" and "cap and trade," and these operations have been executed by means of regulatory markets.

The carbon credits obtained by organizations in countries which do not have any responsibility to restrict their carbon emissions cannot be a part of flexible mechanisms and can be traded in voluntary markets. According to the agreements, Turkey and some other countries such as the United States and China cannot participate in the regulatory market mechanisms. Organizations in these countries which produce carbon credits trade in voluntary markets.

The voluntary carbon markets emerged to reduce or offset carbon emissions of companies, nonprofit organizations or similar institutions on a voluntary basis. In these markets, operations are carried out on a voluntary basis, regardless of the policies and objectives applied mandatorily under the flexible mechanisms of the Kyoto Protocol. There is no prerequisite for the participation in these markets [6]. Organizations thus develop and implement projects voluntarily to reduce carbon emissions. These emission reductions are certified by competent authorities and exchanged on the over-the-counter (OTC) voluntary carbon markets. Carbon credits in the voluntary market are called as voluntary emission reductions (VERs). Credits from projects in voluntary markets cannot be used by a country which is a party to the Kyoto Protocol to meet emission reduction targets.

Apart from the companies in which the Annex-B countries, which have emission reduction commitments, other companies may want to offset their emissions for several reasons such as to market themselves as "green businesses" to their customers. They reduced their emissions as much as possible and wish to offset their remaining emissions to become carbon neutral by purchasing an equivalent number of carbon credits from voluntary markets. Other important buyers of the carbon credits of voluntary markets are the nongovernmental organizations (NGOs) such as the World Bank to help the global reduction of greenhouse gas emissions and help the sustainable development of the host country. So the most important point for the carbon reduction projects in voluntary markets is that whether project contributes to the sustainable development of the host country.

3. Paris climate conference

Following limited participation in the Kyoto Protocol and the lack of agreement in Copenhagen in 2009, whole world has been searching a common ground of agreement on a global scale to limit global warming. By the leadership of European Union, countries presented much more satisfactory information and contributive ideas in Paris climate conference 2015. Conference was a great success because two big pollutant countries the United States and China contrary to Kyoto agreement acted jointly and showed a constructive attitude.

At the conference in December 2015, 195 countries adopted the first-ever universal, legally binding global climate deal. Before and during the Paris conference, countries submitted comprehensive national climate action plans [7]. The agreement sets out a global action plan to put the world on track to avoid dangerous climate change by limiting global warming to well below 2°C.

The Paris Agreement is an agreement within the United Nations Framework Convention on Climate Change (UNFCCC) dealing with greenhouse gases emissions, mitigation, adaptation, and finance starting in the year 2020. The Paris Agreement basically differs from Kyoto Protocol in two subjects. Unlike the Kyoto Protocol, it does not set some targets forced by legal authorities instead it encourages voluntarily determined targets by the countries [8]. The only requirement under international law is to report and review the targets achieved [9].

Another key difference introduced by Paris Agreement is the scope of the agreement. While the Paris Agreement still emphasizes the principle of "Common but Differentiated Responsibility"—the acknowledgment that different nations has different capacities and duties to climate action—it does not provide a specific division between developed and developing nations. The Paris Agreement is different from previous attempts to reach an international deal on climate change, and it requires *all* countries not just the "developed" countries to submit national climate plans.

Kyoto Protocol differentiated between Annex-1 and nonAnnex-1 countries. In the Paris Agreement, all parties will be required to submit emission reduction plans [10].

The Paris Agreement suggests a market-based mechanism that would allow countries to trade internationally transferred mitigation outcomes. Unlike the Clean Development Mechanism, which is one of the mechanisms of Kyoto Protocol, which was created and used by signatory countries to trade carbon premiums, a market-based mechanism under the Paris Agreement includes all the countries [11].

4. Pricing

Over the last few years, voluntary carbon market participants have reported a maturing market. In this context, while the total transaction volume grew in 2015, buyers paid lower prices across almost all project types. Weighted average prices of carbon premiums dropped dramatically in 2015 compared to 2014 and 2013 [11].

In the light of these pricing dynamics, market participants have recently launched several different initiatives to try to increase prices where they view them as too low. The Fairtrade Climate Standard, the result of a multi-year collaboration between the Gold Standard Foundation and Fairtrade International, launched in December 2015. Just as Fairtrade bananas and cocoa have minimum prices, the standard introduces a price floor for carbon offsets 13 Euros per ton for tree-planting projects, 8.2 Euros per ton for energy efficiency, and 8.1 Euros per ton for clean energy projects. There are some initiaitons to set minimum prices per ton but none have verified yet. Another initiative executed by the World Bank is known as Methane and Climate Change Mitigation-PAF, which aims to organize auctions for buyers to purchase offsets [11].

Although carbon pricing is not in the scope of our study, the price changes in carbon emission markets must be tracked and reflected to the financial reports.

5. Accounting and reporting of carbon trading

After the ratification of the Kyoto Protocol, carbon markets created great excitement and began to be discussed by organizations. However, carbon accounting remains an area in which there is no consensus. There had already been several initiatives in carbon accounting starting from the early 2000s. In 2003, the Emerging Issues Task Force (EITF)[1] brought the topic onto the agenda, but it was removed in a very short time [12]. In 2004, the International Financial Reporting Interpretations Committee (IFRIC) published IFRIC-3 under the heading of regulation and reporting of carbon emissions, but it caused controversy and was withdrawn 6 months later [13]. Due to the lack of mandatory regulations, many companies developed their own accounting policies related to carbon emissions during this period [12].

Carbon allowances and related accounts should be reported in financial statements in accordance with international standards and this duty therefore well within the scope of the accounting standard setters. IFRIC-3 specified accounts and measurements under the "cap and trade" system according to the existing IASs [14]. IFRIC-3 specified that

- emission rights (allowances) are recognized as intangible assets and measured in accordance with IAS 38 *Intangible Assets*,
- if the allowances issued by a government for less than fair value, the difference between the amount paid and fair value of the allowance is accounted as government grant in accordance with IAS 20 *Accounting for Government Grants and Disclosure of Government Assistance*, and
- as a participant produces emissions, a provision for its obligation is recognized to deliver allowances in accordance with IAS 37 *Provisions, Contingent Liabilities and Contingent Assets.*

According to IFRIC-3, the participant recognizes the allowances as an intangible asset at fair value. At the initial recording, because the participant receives this allowance without a payment, it recognizes a grant which is actually deferred revenue in financial statements at the same amount as the allowances. However, after the initial recording, the different measurement bases in the income statement distort the profit or loss. In IFRIC-3, a participant recognizes a provision for its obligation to deliver allowances as emissions are produced and to measure it at the fair value at each reporting date. Nevertheless, this grant is gradually transferred from deferred revenue (liability) to income at its initial value. Another issue is that if the participant prefers to use the fair value model to measure its intangible assets after initial recognition, allowances will change according to the changes in the fair value, while

[1]An organization formed in 1984 by the Financial Accounting Standards Board (FASB) to provide assistance with timely financial reporting. The EITF holds public meetings in order to identify and resolve accounting issues occurring in the financial world.

there will be no change on the liabilities. So the effect of price changes on the asset side of the balance sheet will differ from that on the liability side.

After the withdrawal of IFRIC-3, to guide participants, the IASB began a project about Emission Trading Schemes in December 2007. The project is being conducted with the FASB and aims to develop a comprehensive guidance on accounting for emission trading schemes. The aim of that project is not to result in a new standard, but rather to revise the existing standards (IAS 38, IAS 39, and IAS 20). Up to May 2010, the IASB tentatively decided that an entity should recognize the allowances received free of charge from the government as assets and measure them initially at fair value. Another tentative decision was that the entity recognizes a liability that represents its promise to pay allowances throughout the commitment period irrespective of whether the entity has already emitted.

In December 2012, IASB formally reactivated the project as an IASB-only research project and deferred joint work with FASB. In 2015, the project was renamed from "Emission trading schemes" to "Pollutant pricing mechanisms" to address a variety of schemes that use emissions allowances to manage the emission of pollutants. The board canceled all tentative decisions and makes a fresh start related to the project [15].

5.1. Illustrative example 1

Company A is operating in a developing country and decided to develop a new wind plant project and planned to make an Emission Reduction Purchase Agreement for the emission reductions with Company B which operates in a developed European Union country.

Company B is in the *European Union Emissions Trading Scheme* (EU ETS) and a maximum (cap) amount of greenhouse gases that can be emitted is determined by the authorities. If emission exceeds what is permitted by its allowances, Company B must purchase allowances from others in the *European Union Emissions Trading Scheme* or from a nonAnnex-1 developing country under the Clean Development Mechanism. Conversely, if Company B has performed well at reducing its emissions, it can sell its leftover credits in EU ETS.

By the end of 2014, Company A decided to apply following steps that all carbon finance projects have in the Clean Development Mechanisms (see **Figure 1**).

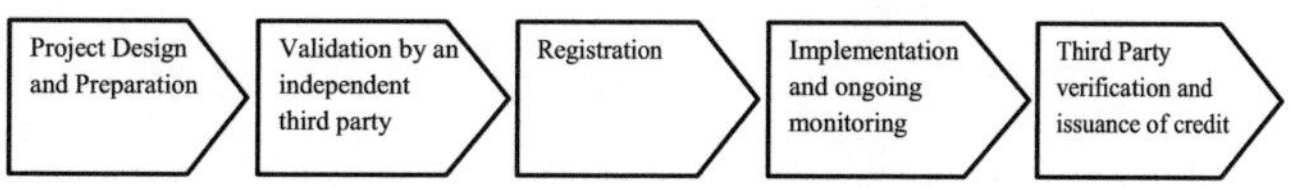

Figure 1. Steps of a carbon finance project under the Clean Development Mechanism.

At the first step, Company A prepared the Project Design Document (PDD) that identifies the details of the project such as the type of the project (energy supply, transport, waste management, etc.), sector background, and expected schedule of the project, financial details, expected environmental benefits, and project-related risks. During the implementation stage of the project, company estimated the greenhouse gas emission reductions (in tons of CO_2) and signed Emission Reduction Purchase Agreement. The difference between the baseline scenario (the amount of emission before the project) and the project scenario computed as the emission reductions achieved through the project. At the end of 2015, the Project Design Document be checked and approved by the independent verifier named Designated Operational Entity (DOE) and by an agency of the government called Designated National Authority (DNA) and Clean Development Mechanism Executive Board. After registration steps, Company A started implementing the project at the beginning of 2016 and signed an Emission Reduction Purchase Agreement with Company B for the emissions traded at $10 per ton of CO_2 for a 7-year period that is renewable twice.

By the end of 2016, the first year of the project's implementation period, actual emission reductions checked by the DOE and Company A received CER (certified emission reduction) for 12,000 tons of CO_2 reduction. Carbon credits were verified by Gold Standard.

Company A incurred following up-front costs during the approval and registration process in 2015:

Project preparation	
• Project assessment cost	$5000
• Document preparation cost	$40,000
• Validation	$30,000
• Legal cost	$3000
Registration fees	2% of the credits

During the project implementation process, Company A also incurred following costs:

Monitoring costs	
• Verification	$5000 per year
• Monitoring	$5000 per year
Issuance fees (deducted by CDM Executive Board)	2% of issued CERs

Company B received a grant of allowances covering 30,000 tons[2] of emissions for 2016 (assigned amount units). But the company has an expectation of 40,000 tons of emissions in a year and signed an Emission Reduction Purchase Agreement for 10,000 tons of CO_2 yearly with Company A for the emission reductions for $10 per ton of CO_2 (certified emission reduction), for a 7-year period that is renewable twice.

The annual cycle for the allocation of allowances and assessment of emissions is a full year of 2016 and company reports semiannually. The fair value of allowances in EU ETS at the reporting dates is given below:

[2]Ton refers to CO2 equivalent ton.

http://dx.doi.org/10.5772/intechopen.68959

Fair value of allowances	
Date	**Price per unit ($ per ton)**
January 1, 2016	12
June 30, 2016	14
December 31, 2016	10

The realized emissions by Company B from January 2016 to June 2016 are 16,000 tons and at June 30 the entity still expects emissions of 40,000 tons until the year end. At the year end, the emissions exceeded the expected amount by 8000 tons. Reporting for Company B under the "cost method" versus "revaluation method" is given in **Tables 2** and **3**.

Date	Accounts	Debit	Credit
January 01, 2016	Emission rights [assigned amount units, (AAU)]	360,000	
	Government grants (deferred revenue)		360,000
	(30,000 tons × $12 = $360,000)		
June 30, 2016	Manufacturing overhead (amortization of emission rights)	192,000*	
	Emission rights (AAU)		192,000
June 30, 2016	Government grants (deferred revenue)	192,000	
	Revenue from government grants		192,000
	(16,000 tons × $12 = $192,000)		
December 31, 2016	Emission rights (certified emission rights (CER))	100,000	
	Cash		100,000
	(10.000 tons × $10 = $100.000)		
December 31, 2016	Loss from impairment of assets	28,000	
	Emission rights (AAU)		28,000
	14,000 tons × ($12–10) = $28,000		
December 31, 2016	Manufacturing overhead (amortization of emission rights)	220,000**	
	Emission rights		220,000
December 12, 2016	Government grants (deferred revenue)	168,000	
	Revenue from government grants		168,000
	(14.000 tons × $12 = $168,000		

Notes: Amortization of the emission rights by using units of production method = (Cost-residual value) × (1/Total tons produced) × Actual tons produced.

*$360,000 × 1/30,000 tons × 16,000 tons = $192,000.

**[$140,000 × 1/14,000 tons × 14,000 tons] + [$100,000 × 1/10,000 tons × 8,000 tons] = $220,000.

Table 2. Reporting for company B under the "cost method".

Date	Accounts	Debit	Credit
January 1, 2016	Emission rights [assigned amount units (AAU)]	360,000	
	Government grants (deferred revenue)		360,000
	(30,000 tons × $12 = $360,000)		
June 30, 2016	Emission rights (AAU)	60,000	
	Intangible assets revaluation fund		60,000
	(30,000 tons × ($14 – $12) = $60,000)		
June 30, 2016	Manufacturing overhead (amortization of emission rights)	224,000*	
	Emission rights (AAU)		224,000
June 30, 2016	Intangible assets revaluation fund	32,000	
	Prior period earnings		32,000
	($60,000 × (16,000 tons/30,000 tons))		
June 30, 2016	Government grants (deferred revenue)	192,000	
	Revenue from $$		192,000
	(16,000 tons × $12 = $192,000)		
December 31, 2016	Emission rights (certified emission rights (CER))	100,000	
	Cash		100,000
	(10,000 tons × $10 = $100,000)		
December 31, 2016	Intangible assets revaluation fund	28,000	
	Loss from impairment of assets	28,000	
	Emission rights (AAU)		56,000
	(14,000 tons × ($14 – $10) = $56.000)		
December 31, 2016	Manufacturing overhead (amortization of emission rights)	220,000**	
	Emission rights		220,000
December 31, 2016	Government grants (deferred revenue)	168,000	
	Revenue from government grants		168,000
	(14,000 tons × $12 = $168,000)		

Notes: Amortization of the emission rights by using units of production method = (Cost-residual value) × (1/Total tons produced) × Actual tons produced.

*$420,000 × (1/30,000 tons) × 16,000 tons = $224,000.

**[$140,000 × (1/14,000 tons) × 14,000 tons] + [$100,000 × 1/10,000 tons × 8,000 tons] = $220,000.

Table 3. Reporting for Company B under the "revaluation method".

According to IAS 20, government grants are recognized in profit or loss systematically in the periods which the entity recognizes expenses for the related costs.

Company B recognizes the allowances as an intangible asset at fair value. Because the company received this allowance as assigned amount units of carbon emissions without a payment, it recognized a grant which is actually deferred revenue in financial statements at the same amount as the allowances. At the reporting date, grant is gradually transferred from deferred revenue (liability) to income at its initial value. According to IAS 38, after initial recognition intangible assets are recorded by using either a cost method or revaluation method. In the cost method, after initial recognition intangible assets should be carried at cost less accumulated amortization and impairment losses. In the example, emission rights are amortized when company emits carbon. At the end of the second period, emission rights are impaired because of the decrease in price to $10 per ton.

According to the Revaluation Model after initial recognition, an intangible asset is carried at a revalued amount. The revalued amount is equal to its fair value at the date of the revaluation unless any subsequent accumulated amortization and any subsequent accumulated impairment losses. The increase in an asset's carrying amount as a result of a revaluation is recognized in other comprehensive income and accumulated in equity. However, the increase need to be recognized in profit or loss in so far as it reverses a revaluation decrease regarding that asset of the same asset previously recognized in profit or loss. If the carrying value of an intangible asset is decreased as a result of a revaluation, the decrease is recognized in profit or loss. However, the decrease is recognized in other comprehensive income in so far as any credit balance in the revaluation fund of that asset.

Transactions related to the carbon project are journalized in **Table 4** in the books of Company A.

Journal entries according to cost method			
Date	**Accounts**	**Debit**	**Credit**
2015	Research & development expenses	78,000	
	Cash		78,000
2015	Research & development expenses	2000	
	Cash		2000
	(Registration fee: (10,000 tons × $10) × 2%)		
2016	Emission rights (CER)	120,000	
	Unearned revenue		120,000
	(12,000 tons × $10)		
2016	Research & development expenses	2400	
	Cash		2400
	(Issuance fee: (12,000 tons × $10) × 2%)		

Journal entries according to cost method			
Date	**Accounts**	**Debit**	**Credit**
2016	Unearned revenue	100,000	
	Revenue from emission reduction projects		100,000
	(10,000 tons × $10)		
2016	Research & development expenses	10,000	
	Cash		10,000
	(Project monitoring costs)		

Table 4. Reporting for company A.

5.2. Illustrative example 2

A Company in Turkey decided to develop an engineering system for low-income families that treats contaminated water. The system reduces the direct release of GHGs into the atmosphere by avoiding the need to burn firewood to boil water. It is estimated that the project will generate more than 20,000 tons of emission reductions per year, the equivalent of taking nearly 350,000 cars off the road for 1 year. Carbon credits obtained through the project cannot be used in a flexible mechanism, so it can be sold in voluntary markets.

In 2016, an Emission Reduction Purchase Agreement (ERPA) was signed with the World Bank for the emission reductions for the purchase of 25,000 tons, $9 per ton of CO_2 during 10 years.

For a voluntary carbon project, the company will apply the same steps as in Clean Development Mechanisms except the approvals by an agency of the government called as Designated National Authority (DNA) and Clean Development Mechanism Executive Board. The company learned that the process of meeting the requirements for a voluntary project is usually easier and shorter than developing a CDM project.

Company prepared the Project Design Document (PDD), which identifies the details of the project, such as the type of the project, sector background, expected schedule of the project, financial details, expected environmental benefits, and project-related risks. Company estimated the greenhouse gas emission reductions in the tons of CO_2 (carbon dioxide) in the baseline scenario (the amount of emission before the project) and the project scenario. The difference between baseline and project scenario will be the emission reductions achieved through the project. At the end of 2015, the Project Design Document then be checked and approved by an independent verifier called as Designated Operational Entity (DOE). After these steps, project is registered and company started implementing it at the beginning of 2016.

In the first year, the amount of emissions reduction achieved through the project is assigned by an independent appraiser as 30,000 tons and carbon credits are verified by Voluntary Gold Standard.

Company incurred following up-front costs during the approval and registration process in 2015:

During project implementation process, Company also incurred following costs:

Reporting under voluntary markets is given in **Table 5**.

Project preparation	
• Project assessment cost	$5000
• Document preparation cost	$35,000
• Validation	$20,000
• Legal cost	$3000
Registration fees	2% of the credits

Monitoring costs	
• Verification	$5000 per year
• Monitoring	$5000 per year
Issuance fees (deducted by voluntary market registries)	30 cents per VER

Date	Accounts	Debit	Credit
2015	Research & development expense	63,000	
	Cash		63,000
	(Project preparation cost)		
2015	Research & development expense	4500	
	Cash		4500
	(Registration fee: (25,000 tons × $9) × 2%)		
2016	Emission rights	270,000	
	Unearned revenue		270,000
	(30,000 tons × $9)		
2016	Research & development expense	9000	
	Cash		9000
	(Issuance fee: 30,000 tons × 30 cents)		
2016	Research & development expense	10,000	
	Cash		10,000
	(monitoring costs)		

Date	Accounts	Debit	Credit
2016	Cash	225,000	
	Emission rights		225,000
	(25,000 tons × $9)		
2016	Unearned revenue	225,000	
	Revenue earned from carbon projects		225,000
	(25,000 tons × $9)		

Table 5. Reporting for carbon credits under voluntary markets.

6. Conclusion

Climate change is one of the biggest challenges of this century. This change affects poor countries more than the developed and rich ones and it is evaluated as human rights intervention. To reduce greenhouse gas emissions, regulatory bodies have been working on this issue and developing some mechanisms. The basic idea of these mechanisms is to create a commercial value referred to as carbon finance by reducing carbon emissions by green projects. These projects can be financed by the companies that emit the higher amount of CO_2 than the proposed amount. In this process, high-carbon-emitting companies help to meet the costs for emission reduction projects. Carbon emission reductions are calculated as the difference between the base case (conventional technology) or "business-as-usual" and the proposed case (clean energy technology) measured in tons of CO_2 per year. This process is regulated through special markets where securitized emission reductions are traded.

Over time, some important steps have been taken in carbon accounting. In 2003, the Emerging Issues Task Force brought the topic onto the agenda, but it was removed in a very short time. In 2004, the International Financial Reporting Interpretations Committee (IFRIC) published IFRIC-3 under the heading of regulation and reporting of carbon emissions. IFRIC-3 specified accounts and measurements under the "cap and trade" system but it caused many controversies and was withdrawn 6 months later. IASB began a project to develop a comprehensive guide for participants about Emission Trading Schemes in December 2007. Up to May 2010, the IASB tentatively decided that an entity should recognize the allowances received free of charge from the government as assets and measure them initially at fair value. Another tentative decision was that the entity recognizes a liability that represents its promise to pay allowances throughout the commitment period irrespective of whether the entity has already emitted.

In December 2012, IASB formally reactivated a project as an IASB-only research project and deferred joint work with FASB. In 2015, the project was renamed from "Emission trading schemes" to "Pollutant pricing mechanisms" to address a variety of schemes that use emissions allowances to manage the emission of pollutants.

In 2015, IASB canceled all tentative decisions and makes a fresh start related to the project. Following this action, staff presents two papers to aid in the further discussion. First, Agenda Paper 6A emphasizes some of the difficulties encountered in earlier approaches. Earlier approaches tried to recognize emission allowances and the related obligations created by the mechanisms in accordance with existing Standards. Second, Agenda Paper 6B provides a simple numerical example of a typical cap-and-trade type of emissions trading scheme to show how different accounting approaches produce different results in the statements. The purpose of the Agenda Paper 6B is to demonstrate the accounting entries and resulting financial statement line items that have developed in the absence of specific guidance in IFRS [16].

This chapter focuses on reporting of carbon emissions. Two examples are designed to show the relevant accounts for regulatory and voluntary markets. In the illustrated examples, emission rights (allowances) are recognized as intangible assets and measured in accordance with IAS 38 Intangible Assets, the difference between the amount paid for the allowance and fair value of the allowance is accounted as government grant in accordance with IAS 20 Accounting for Government Grants and Disclosure of Government Assistance. Emission rights are amortized when company emits carbons and related grant is gradually transferred from deferred revenue to income at its initial value at the end of each reporting date. Due to not having a regulatory guidance yet, this study is expected to contribute to the literature how to measure and report the carbon allowances and carbon credits according to existing International Accounting Standards.

Author details

Figen Öker and Hümeyra Adıgüzel*

*Address all correspondence to: humeyra.adiguzel@eas.bau.edu.tr

Bahçeşehir University, İstanbul, Turkey

References

[1] United Nations Framework Convention on Climate Change UNFCCC. Kyoto Protocol [Internet]. 1997. Available from: http://unfccc.int/essential_background/kyoto_protocol/items/1678.php 5.6.2008

[2] Bailey I. The EU emissions trading scheme. Wiley Interdisciplinary Reviews: Climate Change. 2010;**1**(1):144–153

[3] Mavrakis D, Konidari P. Classification of emissions trading scheme design characteristics. European Environment. 2003;**13**:55. Available from: www.interscience.wiley.com

[4] Tunahan H. Küresel İklim Değişikliğini Azaltmanın Bir Yolu Olarak Karbon Finansmanı. Muhasebe ve Finansman Dergisi. 2010;**46**:47–68

[5] Hamilton K, Sjardin M, Marcello T, Xu G. Forging a Frontier: State of the Voluntary Carbon Markets 2008. New York: Ecosystem Marketplace and New Carbon Finance; 2008

[6] Çevre ve Orman Bakanlığı. Karbon Piyasalarında Ulusal Deneyim ve Geleceğe Bakış [Internet]. 2011. Available from: http://www.undp.org.tr/publicationsDocuments/Karbon_Piyasalarinda_Ulusal_Deneyim_ve_Gelecege_Bakis.pdf

[7] European Commission Web Page- Climate Action- Paris Agreement. Available from: http://ec.europa.eu/clima/policies/international/negotiations/paris_en

[8] Birnie P, Boyle A, Redgwell C. International Law and the Environment. Oxford: OUP; 2009. Chapter 3.

[9] Taraska G. The Paris Climate Agreement. Center for American Progress; 2015

[10] Sinha A. Paris climate talks: Differentiation of developed and developing stays, India happy. 2015

[11] State of the Voluntary Carbon Markets [Internet]. 2016. p.4. Available from: http://www.forest-trends.org/documents/files/doc_5242.pdf

[12] Fornaro JM, Winkelman KA, Glodstein D. Accounting for emissions: Emerging issues and the need for global accounting standards. Journal of Accountancy. July 2009;40–47

[13] Cook A. Emission rights: From costless activity to market operations. Accounting, Organizations and Society. 2009;**34**:456–468

[14] IFRIC-3Emission Rights (2004). International Accounting Standards Board's International Financial Reporting Interpretations Committee. Available from: https://www.iasplus.com/en/standards/ifric/ifric3

[15] IAS Plus [Internet]. 2012. Available from: http://www.IASplus.com/agenda/emission-trading.htm

[16] Pollutant Pricing Mechanisms Project, IFRS Staff Paper, IASB Agenda Reference 6, June 2015. Available from: http://www.ifrs.org/Meetings/MeetingDocs/IASB/2015/June/AP06-Pollutant%20pricing%20mechanisms.pdf

Section 3

Financial Reporting Quality

Chapter 8

Accounting Choices in Corporate Financial Reporting: A Literature Review of Positive Accounting Theory

İdil Kaya

Additional information is available at the end of the chapter

http://dx.doi.org/10.5772/intechopen.68962

Abstract

This chapter aims to put light on the positive accounting theory and related empirical studies and identify its broad contributions to the accounting research. Our objective is to provide a review of positive accounting literature in order to synthesize findings, identify areas of controversy in the literature, and evaluate critiques. Positive research in accounting started coming to prominence around the mid-1960s and had been a vector of paradigm shift within the financial accounting research in the 1970s and 1980s. The positive accounting theory is developed by Watts and Zimmerman and is based on work undertaken in economics and is heavily dependent on the efficient market hypothesis, the capital assets pricing model, and agency theory. The three key hypotheses are bonus plan hypothesis, debt hypothesis, and political cost hypothesis. Nevertheless, PAT has been subjected to severe and numerous criticisms from different perspectives, which are critiques on research methods, its theoretical foundations, its logic on economics' basis, and its reference to philosophy of science. PAT and its hypotheses will continue to be a rich field of empirical research and the basic questions that it raises are still relevant today.

Keywords: positive accounting theory, accounting choice, management compensation hypothesis, debt hypothesis, political cost hypothesis

1. Introduction

Academic studies on the factors that affect a firm's accounting choices triggered a paradigm change in accounting research, altering the nature of literature from prescriptive to predictive. The construct of the new paradigm was first articulated by Ross Watts and Jerold Zimmerman with the publication of their revolutionary articles in *the Accounting Review*—"Towards a Positive Theory of the Determination of Accounting Standards" in 1978 and "The Demand for and Supply of Accounting Theories: The Market for Excuses" in 1979.

The term "Positive Accounting Theory" has come to practise to refer to the accounting theory developed and named by Watts and Zimmerman. The authors seek to appreciate and explain the concept of economic consequences of the interests of managers and financial accounting and reporting. In other words, their major aim is to explain and predict why managers and accountants choose particular accounting methods in preference to others. Furthermore, they assert that firm's attributes, such as leverage and size, are predictive variables of the firm's accounting choice.

In fact, positive research in accounting started coming to prominence around the mid-1960s and had been a vector of paradigm shift within the financial accounting research in the 1970s and 1980s. The term "positive" refers to the theory that attempts to explain and make good predictions of particular phenomena. The positive accounting theory (PAT) relied in great part on work undertaken in economics and was heavily reliant on the efficient market hypothesis, the capital assets pricing model, and agency theory.

PAT has led to a large amount of empirical studies. Positive researchers empirically test their predictions around the bonus plan hypothesis, the debt covenant hypothesis, and the political cost hypothesis. These hypotheses can be used in two distinguished forms of positive accounting theory. The first form is the opportunistic form asserting that managers in electing accounting procedures react to maximize the wealth, and the second form is the efficiency form for good corporate governance.

PAT has been subjected to severe and numerous criticisms from different perspectives, which are critiques on research method, economics base, and reference to philosophy of science. It is said that PAT seeks to predict and explain why managers choose to adopt particular accounting methods in preference to others but says nothing as to which method a firm should use.

We believe that PAT and its hypotheses will continue to be a rich field of empirical research and the basic questions that it raises are still relevant today. This chapter aims to put light on the PAT and related empirical studies and identify its broad contributions to the accounting research. Our objective is to provide a review of extant literature in order to synthesize findings, identify areas of controversy in the literature, and evaluate critiques.

Our literature review is organized around ideas of PAT, its hypotheses, supporters and followers, and finally critiques of this theory. The remaining part of this chapter proceeds as follows: We first examine the forces that give rise to this theory. We then investigate its foundations using the works of Watts and Zimmerman. We describe how empirical studies added unique insights into its development. Some criticisms are evaluated. Finally, we outline and discuss the significant contribution of PAT to our understanding of corporate reporting practices. We conclude that this theory has generated several useful insights on managers' reporting decisions.

2. The paradigm change in accounting research: the origins of positive accounting theory

In this section, we examine the forces and the publications that had a major impact on the emergence of PAT. This theory is based on work undertaken in economics and is heavily dependent on the efficient market hypothesis, the capital assets pricing model, and agency theory.

Positive research began in early 1960s and opened a new era in accounting literature, using economic models and statistical processing in empirical studies. The first serious discussions and analyses of positive research on accounting emerged in late 1960s with the pioneering studies of Ball and Brown [1] and Beaver [2]. These two seminal publications provide significant evidence of the information content in accounting earnings announcements, i.e., the earnings reflect some of the information in security prices. They gave rise to a huge literature of capital markets research [3].

A significant number of academic publications investigated the determinants of the shift in paradigm from narrative to positive research. Major findings offered by these studies are as follows.

- Research methodologies have been developed based on the "hypothesis formulating and testing" [4, 5].
- With the emergence of computers, large new databases of financial information would be readily accessible for researchers [4, 6].
- The concept of "economic consequences" has been investigated. This concept is defined by Zeff as "the impact of accounting reports on the decision-making behaviour of business, governments, and creditors" [7, 8].
- New academic journals have been established and they adopt the selection policy of empirical researches [9].
- The development of behavioural science enabled to analyse managers' accounting choices [6, 9].
- Generous research grants have been provided to new generation of accounting researchers that applied empirical research methods [9].

It is said that two reports on US business education were the impetus for those changes [4, 5]. In 1959, R.A. Gordon and James E. Howell published "Higher education for business" and Franck C. Pierson published "The education of American Business men". The former report was commissioned by Ford Foundation and the latter by Carnegie Foundation. Besides their recommendations on teaching methods, these authors stressed the need to develop research based on the formulation and testing of the hypotheses. They also describe the resources necessary to advance the level of business studies.

Another significant explanation of the PAT's development is the strong influence of several academic works on positive economic theory, efficient markets hypothesis, CAPM, agency theory, and capital markets researches (**Table 1**). Watts and Zimmerman aimed to develop an economic-based accounting theory and they advance an empirical methodology that focus on economics-based explanations and predictions of accounting practice. Boland and Gordon assert that this economic-based accounting theory is a combination of Milton Friedman's instrumentalism and Paul Samuelson's positivism [15]. They also add that Watts and Zimmerman practise the methodology as that of the Chicago School economists [6, 15].

In 1976, the publication of Jensen and Merckling's article on agency theory had a major impact on PAT [14]. In agency theory, the firm is analysed as "a nexus of contracts" and this concept is accepted by positive accounting research. The contracts are produced with the aim of guarantee that all parties, acting in their own self-interest, are at the same time motivated towards maximizing the firm's value. PAT accentuates the function of accounting in reducing agency costs and its essential role in an efficient corporate governance structure [4].

Authors	Contribution
Friedman [10]	Friedman (1953) described positive science in economics.
Fama [11]	He introduced and subsequently made major contribution to the efficient markets hypothesis.
Sharpe [12] and Lintner [13]	They developed the capital asset pricing model (CAPM).
Ball and Brown [1]	They found significantly positive correlation between the sign of the abnormal stock return and the sign of the earnings change over the firm's previous year's earnings.
Beaver [2]	The author examined the variability of stock returns and trading volume around earnings announcements. He found that the flow of info increase in the earnings announcement periods.
Jensen and Merckling [14]	The authors investigated managerial behaviour, agency costs, and ownership structure in the context of the firm.

Table 1. Academic literatures that were the impetus for PAT.

3. The development of positive accounting theory

In this section, we examine the development of the PAT, the contribution of major works of Watts and Zimmerman, and the hypotheses of this theory.

The construct of PAT was first articulated by Watts and Zimmerman and popularized in their book: positive accounting theory [6, 16]. **Table 2** shows major works of Watts and Zimmerman in this issue. They adopted the label "positive" from the economics to distinguish accounting research aimed at understanding accounting from research directed at generating prescriptions. They investigated the role of accounting theory in determining accounting practice and build a theory intending to be a positive theory (Watts & Zimmerman, p. 274) [5], i.e.,

> *"a theory capable of explaining the factors determining the extant accounting literature, predicting how research will change as the underlying factors change, and explaining the role of theories in the determination of accounting standards. It is not normative or prescriptive".*

http://dx.doi.org/10.5772/intechopen.68962

Authors	Contribution
Watts and Zimmerman [16]	This pioneering article outlined many of the problems posed by regulatory capture. The authors announce that ultimately, they seek to develop a positive theory of the determination of accounting standards. They believe that management plays a central role in the determination of standards. They examine factors affecting management wealth which are taxes, political costs, regulation, information production and management compensation plans. They find that the political cost factor is important in affecting management's attitude.
Watts and Zimmerman [17]	This paper analyses; • The demands for accounting theories in an unregulated economy than in a regulated economy, i.e., the additional demands generated by government intervention; and • The supply of accounting theory.
Watts and Zimmerman [6]	This book is written and used for second year M.B.A and Ph.D. audience. Authors review the theory and methodology of the economic-based literature in accounting. EMH and CAPM are explained. The important role of EMH in accounting research is emphasized. CAPM is used as the valuation method. The methodologies of the empirical studies in the development of the literature are explained. Analyses end syntheses are provided on the different issues. These are forecasting earnings, contracting process, compensation plans, debt contracts, political process, empirical tests of accounting choice, stock price tests of the theory, and the theory's application to auditing.
Watts and Zimmerman [5]	This paper examines and evaluated the evolution and state of PAT and criticisms of positive accounting research. The authors responded to most of the published critiques on issues relating to research method and philosophy of science. Opportunistic and efficiency perspectives of PAT are distinguished.

Table 2. Major works of Watts and Zimmerman.

Watts and Zimmerman reviewed the theory and methodology of the economic-based literature in accounting in their prominent book dated 1986 [6]. In this book written and used for second year M.B.A and Ph.D. audience, the authors point the important role of efficient market hypothesis in accounting research; they use CAPM as the valuation method. They explain the methodology of the empirical studies in the development of the literature. They also provide analyses end syntheses on forecasting earnings, contracting process, compensation plans, debt contracts, political process, empirical tests of accounting choice, stock price tests of the theory, and the theory's application to auditing [6].

According to Watts and Zimmerman, the "property rights" theory adopted by positive accounting researchers assumes that the firm is a nexus of contracts between self-interested individuals. PAT highlighted the importance of contracting costs, including information, agency, bankruptcy, and lobbying costs [5, 6].

In 1990, after more than a decade since the publication of 1978 and 1979 articles, the authors examined and evaluated the evolution and state of PAT and criticisms of positive accounting research in their article "Positive Accounting Theory: A Ten Year Perspective", in the accounting review. They emphasized that their two pioneering papers contributed to a literature that has uncovered empirical regularities in accounting practice and they responded to most of the published critiques [5]. In evaluating the contribution of this article to the literature, Watts and Zimmerman asset that:

> *"The literature explains why accounting is used and provides a framework for predicting accounting choices. Choices are not made in terms of "better measurement" of some accounting construct, such as earnings. Choices are made in terms of individual objectives and the effects of accounting methods on the achievement of those objectives".*

Watts and Zimmerman identified three essential hypotheses. These are bonus plan hypothesis (or management compensation hypothesis), the debt/equity hypothesis (or debt hypothesis), and political cost hypothesis [5]. According to management compensation hypothesis, managers with bonus plans anchored to earnings are more likely to adopt accounting methods that increase current period's reported income. The debt hypothesis predicts that the higher the firm's debt/equity ratio, the more likely managers use accounting methods that increase earnings. As far as political costs hypothesis is concerned, it is assumed that if managers are under political scrutiny, they are likely to adopt accounting methods that reduce reported income [4].

4. Literature relating to the PAT

In this section, we examine the PAT literature. A considerable amount of literature has been published on PAT. Numerous empirical studies tested its hypotheses, provided important evidence, and contributed to the theory.

PAT literature focuses on management's motives for financial reporting choices, using economic models and statistical processing, when there are agency costs and information asymmetry. It attempts to explain and predict firm accounting choices as a part of the firm's overall need to minimize its cost of capital and other contracting costs, applying methods and techniques from economics. Opportunistic attitudes and behaviours of managers and their impacts on accounting policy choices have been investigated widely in positive research and this led to a rich body of empirical studies on earnings management. A wide range of the literature incorporates both ex ante contracting efficiency incentives with ex post redistributive effects. The methodology of this literature is the methodology of economics, finance, and science generally [5]. **Table 3** provides an overview of these empirical researches and their research area.

http://dx.doi.org/10.5772/intechopen.68962

Beattie et al. state that this literature implicitly assumes that the market is inefficient and relies on bottom line accounting numbers and does not show interest in methods used to produce them [18]. According to Healy and Palepu (p. 419) [19],

> *"Empirical studies of positive accounting studies test whether managers make accounting method changes or accrual estimates to reduce the costs of violating bond covenants written in terms of accounting numbers, to increase the value of earnings-based bonuses under compensation contracts, or to reduce the likelihood of implicit or explicit taxes".*

On the other hand, Healy and Palepu assert that PAT studies generated several interesting empirical regularities regarding management accounting choice but there is ambiguity on the interpretation of this evidence [19].

Authors	Research area
Ball, Kothari and Watts [20]	Determinants of the relationship between earnings changes and stock return.
Beattie [18]	Relationship between extraordinary items and income smoothing.
Christie [21]	Cross-sectional analysis.
Christie [22]	Evidence on contracting and size hypotheses.
De Angelo [23]	Study of the accounting numbers as market value substitutes in managerial buyouts of public stockholders.
Dechow [24]	The role of accounting accruals in earnings and cash flows.
Dechow and Sloan [25]	Executive incentives and the horizon problem.
Dechow, Sloan and Sweeney [26]	Detection of earnings management.
Dechow, Kothari and Watts [27]	The relation between earnings and cash flows.
Dechow, Ge and Schrand [28]	Proxies in earnings quality.
Healy [29]	The effect of bonus schemes on accounting decisions. Description of "taking a bath" or Big Bath concept.
Healy and Palepu [19]	Information asymmetry, corporate disclosure, and the capital markets.
Kothari [3]	Review of capital markets research in accounting.
Lys and Sohn [30]	The association between revisions of financial analysts' earnings forecasts and security price changes.
Nagar, Nanda and Wysocki [31]	Discretionary disclosure and stock-based incentives.
Sweeney [32]	Debt-covenant violations and managers.
Verrecchia [33]	Discretionary disclosure.
Zang [34]	The contracting benefits of accounting conservatism to lenders and borrowers.

Table 3. Literature constructed on the PAT.

5. Criticisms from different perspectives

In this section, we summarize and analyse the literature having critical comments on PAT. The literature developed since the first publication of Watts and Zimmerman articles in 1978.

PAT has been subject to a continuous and endless stream of criticisms since it first emerged in late 1970s. The critiques are from different perspectives. These are critiques related to its theoretical foundations, its logic on economics' basis, its research methods, and critiques on its reference to philosophy of science [15, 35]. It has been defended that this theory is scientifically wrong and its predictions do not always hold. Christenson (p. 18) asserts that [36]:

> *"By arguing that their theories admit exceptions, Watts and Zimmerman condemn them as insignificant and useless".*

In an examination of PAT methodology with a critical look, Christenson argues that he prefers to use the name "the Rochester School" referring to authors' affiliation instead of PAT [36]. Furthermore, he asserts that this discipline should be denominated "sociology of accounting" since it is about describing, predicting, and explaining the behaviours of managers and accountants. **Table 4** presents an overview of some criticisms.

R. J. Chambers, preeminent normative theorist, criticises the PAT in an aggressive manner, begins his article with the so-called positive accounting theory and continue with the label "PA cult" referring to positive accounting theorists [37]. Chambers [37]asserts that:

> *"The verbal adornments of the cult — 'positive', 'empirical', 'scientific', 'economics based' and so on — its rituals, its congregations, its sanctions and its cohesion, drew a galaxy of followers into orbit about the Chicago-Rochester axis".*

The other major criticisms are as follows:

- The theory does not provide prescription to improve accounting practice [4, 40].
- Its fundamental assumption that all action is driven by self-interest is flawy.
- It focuses only in a single motive. Complex nature of shareholders and managers behaviour is not regarded in the analysis [4, 38].
- Measurements and proxies being used in its empirical researches have a simplistic nature [38].
- The banking and global financial crisis in 2008 raised doubts on the efficient market hypothesis [4].

Authors	Critiques
Boland and Gordon [15]	The authors examined economics-based critiques and those based on philosophy of science. They conclude that critiques on philosophy of science may not be very effective but the critiques on the limitations of equilibrium-based economic analysis are valid.
Chambers [37]	The author criticise PAT in a harsh style. He argues that PAT does not embrace the substance of accounting; and the PA literature deals with only firms having publicly traded security, i.e., a very small part of the accounting theory and practices. He criticises the theorists to spawn new journals to publish PAT literature.
Christenson [36]	The author provides a critical evaluation on the label and the methodology of the theory.
Fields, Lys and Vincent [38]	They criticise that PAT focuses only in a single motive. They argue that complex nature of shareholders and managers behaviour is not regarded in the analysis and the proxies used in empirical studies are simplistic.
Milne [35]	The author criticises the theory in the context of political costs and social disclosure analyses.
Mouck [39]	A critical examination of Watts and Zimmerman's works and their use of the rhetoric of science is provided.
Sterling [40]	The author argues that PAT is subjected to scrutiny; its pillars (value-free study and accounting practices) are found to be insubstantial.

Table 4. Some criticisms of the PAT.

6. Conclusion

Positive research began in early 1960s and triggered a paradigm shift in accounting literature, using economic models and statistical processing in empirical studies. The PAT is developed by Watts and Zimmerman and is based on work undertaken in economics and is heavily dependent on the efficient market hypothesis, the capital assets pricing model and agency theory. Watts and Zimmerman founded *Journal of Accounting and Economics* in 1978. The three key hypotheses are bonus plan hypothesis, debt hypothesis, and political cost hypothesis.

Management compensation contracts, capital structure of the firm and its exposure to political scrutiny have been the main areas of researches that are concerned with explaining and predicting accounting practice. These three aspects of the theory-oriented main stream researches in accounting allowed accounting researchers to expand the boundaries of their studies to align with theories in the field of economics and management. Positive researchers introduced new rational from the economics literature to analyse the implications of the efficient market hypothesis for disclosure regulation, to investigate the stock price effects of changes in accounting procedures, and to study the variables that are related to contract political costs.

PAT has been also subjected to severe and numerous criticisms on its research methods, its theoretical foundations, its logic on economics' basis, and its reference to philosophy of science.

Acknowledgements

The author is grateful for the support provided by Galatasaray University Research Fund. [Grant number 16.102.002].

Author details

İdil Kaya

Address all correspondence to: ikaya@gsu.edu.tr

Galatasaray University, Istanbul, Turkey

References

[1] Ball R, Brown P. An empirical evaluation of accounting income numbers. Journal of Accounting Research. 1968;**6**:159-177

[2] Beaver WH. The information content of annual earnings announcements. Journal of Accounting Research. 1968;**6**(3):67-92

[3] Kothari SP. Capital markets research in accounting. Journal of Accounting and Economics. 2001 Sept;**31**(1-3):105-231

[4] Deegan, C, Unerman, J. Financial Accounting Theory, 2nd European ed. Glasgow: McGraw-Hill; 2011

[5] Watts R, Zimmerman J. Positive accounting theory: A ten year perspective. Accounting Review. 1990 Jan;**65**(1):131-156

[6] Watts R, Zimmerman J. Positive Accounting Theory. New Jersey: Prentice-Hall; 1986

[7] Zeff SA. The rise of economic consequences. The Journal of Accountancy. 1978 Dec; **146**(6):56-63

[8] Scott WR. Financial Accounting Theory. 6th ed. Toronto: Pearson; 2012

[9] Jeanjean T, Ramirez C. Back to the origins of positive theories: A contribution to an analysis of paradigm changes in accounting research. Accounting In Europe. 2009 June; **6**(1):107-126

[10] Friedman M, The Methodology of Positive Economics, Essays in Positive Economics. Chicago: University of Chicago Press, reprinted by Phoenix Books, Chicago; 1953;1966

[11] Fama E, The behavior of stock market prices. Journal of Business. 1965;**38**:34-105

[12] Sharpe WF. Capital assets prices: A theory of market equilibrium under conditions of risk. The Journal of Finance. 1964;**19**:425-442

[13] Lintner J. The valuation of risky assets and the selection of risky investments in stock portfolios and capital budgets. Review of Economics and Statistics. 1965 Feb;**47**(1):13-37

[14] Jensen M, Meckling W. Theory of the firm: Managerial behavior, agency costs and ownership structure. Journal of Financial Economics. 1976;**3**:305-360

[15] Boland L, Gordon I. Criticizing positive accounting theory. Contemporary Accounting Research. 1992 Fall;**9**(1):142-170

[16] Watts R, Zimmerman J. Towards a positive theory of the determination of accounting standards. Accounting Review. 1978 Jan;**53**(1):112

[17] Watts R, Zimmerman J. The demand for and supply of accounting theories: The market for excuses. Accounting Review. 1979 Apr;**54**(2):273

[18] Beattie V, Brown S, Ewers D, John B, Manson S, Turner M, et al. Extraordinary items and income smooting: A positive accounting approach. Journal of Business Finance & Accounting. 1994 Sep;**21**(6):791-811

[19] Healy P, Palepu K. Information asymmetry, corporate disclosure, and the capital markets: A review of the empirical disclosure literature. The Journal of Accounting and Economics. 2001 Sept;**31**(1-3):405-440

[20] Ball R, Kothari S, Watts R, Economic determinants of the relation between earnings changes and stock returns. The Accounting Review. 1993;**68**:622-638

[21] Christie AA. On cross-sectional analysis in accounting research. Journal of Accounting & Economics. 1987;**9**(3):231-258

[22] Christie AA, Aggregation of test statistics: An evaluation of the evidence on contracting and size hypotheses. Journal of Accounting & Economics. 1990;**12**:15-36

[23] De Angelo L, Accounting numbers as market value substitutes: A study of managerial buyouts of public stockholders. The Accounting Review. 1986;**61**:400-420

[24] Dechow P. Accounting earnings and cash flows as measures of firm performance: The role of accounting accruals. Journal of Accounting and Economics. 1994;**18**:3-42

[25] Dechow P, Sloan R. Executive incentives and the horizon problem: An empirical investigation. Journal of Accounting and Economics. 1991;**14**:51-89

[26] Dechow P, Sloan R, Sweeney A. Detecting earnings management. The Accounting Review. 1995;**70**:3-42

[27] Dechow P, Kothari S, Watts R. The relation between earnings and cash flows. Journal of Accounting and Economics. 1998;**25**:133-168

[28] Dechow P, Ge W, Schrand C. Understanding earnings quality: A review of the proxies, their determinants and their consequences. Journal of Accounting and Economics. 2010 Jan;**50**(2-3):344-401

[29] Healy P. The effect of bonus schemes on accounting decisions. Journal of Accounting and Economics. 1985;**7**:85-107

[30] Lys T, Sohn S. The association between revisions of financial analysts' earnings forecasts and security price changes. Journal of Accounting and Economics. 1990;**13**:341-363.

[31] Nagar V, Nanda D, Wysocki P. Discretionary disclosure and stock-based incentives. Journal of Accounting and Economics. 2003 Jan;**34**(1-3):283-309

[32] Sweeney A P. Debt-covenant violations and managers accounting responses. Journal of Accounting and Economics. 1994;**17**:281-308

[33] Verrecchia R E. Discretionary disclosure. Journal of Accounting and Economics. 1983;**5**:179-194

[34] Zhang J. The contracting benefits of accounting conservatism to lenders and borrowers. The Journal of Accounting and Economics. 2008;**45**(1):27-54

[35] Milne M. Positive accounting theory, political costs and social disclosure analyses: A critical look. Critical Perspectives on Accounting. 2002 June;**13**(3):369

[36] Christenson C. The methodology of positive accounting. Accounting Review. 1983 Jan;**58**(1):1

[37] Chambers R. Positive accounting theory and the PA cult. Abacus. 1993 Mar; **29**(1):1-26

[38] Fields TD, Lys TZ, Vincent L. Empirical research on accounting choice. Journal of Accounting and Economics. 2001; **31**(1-3):255-307

[39] Mouck T. The rhetoric of science and the rhetoric of revolt in the "Story" of positive accounting theory. Accounting, Auditing & Accountability Journal. 1992 Sep;**5**(4):35

[40] Sterling R. Positive accounting: An assessment. Abacus. 1990 Sep;**26**(2):97-135

Chapter 9

Value Relevance of Accounting Data in an Emerging Market: Did Accounting Reforms Make a Difference?

Mine Aksu, Ayse Tansel Cetin and
Can Simga Mugan

Additional information is available at the end of the chapter

http://dx.doi.org/10.5772/intechopen.69103

Abstract

This study investigates the association of accounting earnings (NI) and book value of equity (BV) with stock prices in Istanbul Stock Exchange (ISE), currently Borsa Istanbul (BIST), during the 1992–2006 period. We also explore the effect of accounting reforms on value relevance that is measured as the strength of the association between a firm's NI and BV and its market value. We specifically investigate the impact of the Turkish Uniform Chart of Accounts (1994), mandatory inflation accounting, consolidations and voluntary (2003–2004), and the mandatory (2005) adoption of International Financial Reporting Standards (IFRS). We hypothesize that these reforms have reduced information asymmetry and thus are expected to enhance the value relevance of accounting information. We find strong evidence that the Ohlson model is a valid model, and BV is more value relevant than NI in BIST. We also find that inflation accounting and consolidations have enhanced the value relevance of BV, while IFRS has increased the value relevance of NI, but reduced that of BV. We contribute to the debate by exploiting the unique sequence of reforms, to come up with comparative value relevance testing designs and interesting results for all major reforms, which we believe will be instructive for researchers and for all emerging and developed economies undergoing similar reforms and best practices.

Keywords: value relevance, net income, book value of equity, IFRS, inflation accounting, financial statements

1. Introduction

This study examines the cross-sectional and intertemporal association between accounting numbers and firm value and explores the impact of accounting reforms on this relationship by using an unbalanced panel data set of 116 firms traded in the then Istanbul Stock Exchange (ISE), now Borsa Istanbul (BIST), over the period 1992–2006. We base our study on prior research on the value relevance of accounting numbers and the consequences of accounting reforms and the worldwide efforts to converge accounting standards. More informative accounting standards and measurement bases, and improvements in disclosure reduce the information asymmetry among stakeholders of the firm. The idea that these improvements would lead to reported accounting numbers that better reflect the firm's fundamentals and, thus, strengthen the association between security prices and accounting numbers, form the basis of our argument.

Our first objective is to investigate the informativeness of financial statement bottom lines of net income (NI) and book value of equity (BV), the most important summary measures in financial statements (F/S) over a lengthy sample period of 15 years. Second, we compare value relevance in the pre-reform and reform periods to observe the overall impact of accounting reforms on value relevance. We specifically explore the value relevance of accounting numbers generated by the Uniform Chart of Accounts promulgated in 1994, the mandatory adoption of general price level accounting and consolidations in group firms in 2003–2004, the voluntary adoption of International Financial Reporting Standards (IFRS) by a subsample of firms during 2003–2004, and the mandatory adoption of IFRS by all public firms traded in the stock exchange in 2005.

Throughout the study, our main hypothesis is that firms that adopt higher quality accounting standards and more informative reporting and disclosure practices will have higher quality accounting numbers in the sense that their net incomes and equity book values will be more closely associated with stock prices. This, in turn, is expected to give rise to more efficient markets and better informed minority shareholders, which is expected to mitigate the expropriation of minority shareholders by concentrated family ownership, which leads to an important agency problem in Turkish firms and other emerging markets (EM).

We use an empirical specification of Ohlson's seminal theoretical accounting valuation model in [1] to estimate the association between firm value and the accounting bottom lines of NI and BV. We carry out subperiod and subsample tests and compare their R^2s to measure differences in value relevance. We also estimate pooled regressions with multiplicative interaction terms that measure the incremental effect of the periods or reforms in question on the coefficients of NI and BV. Our results indicate that the model in [1] is a valid model, and BV is generally more value relevant than NI in the BIST during the sample period. Furthermore, there is some evidence that inflation accounting (IFRS) has enhanced the value relevance of BV (NI). Consolidations, on the other hand, do not seem to have any incremental explanatory power in explaining the changes in stock prices.

Although this relationship has been tested on Turkish data (for example, see [2–4]), this chapter uses a much longer sample period, which allows us to evaluate the impact of a series of accounting reforms on the strength of the association. Moreover, this is the first study to exploit the interesting sequence of accounting and financial disclosure reforms that follow one another during the 2003–2006 period, to come up with comparative value relevance testing designs and results for all major voluntary and mandatory reforms, which we believe will be instructive for all emerging markets and developed economies also undergoing similar reforms and best practices.

2. Motivation: Turkish financial reporting setting

Turkish accounting reforms and data provide a unique setting to study the impact of accounting reforms cross-sectionally and longitudinally over our sample period. First, limiting the study to a single country and to a series of consecutive reforms that followed one another within a short time period allows one to control for country-specific institutional-, cultural-, and market-based differences and mitigates model validity problems due to possible structural changes in model variables over time. Second, Turkey is one of the few countries in the world where only partial inflation accounting alongside historical cost has been used in spite of the high inflation rates experienced in especially the earlier part of our sample period (1992–2002).[1] Starting in 1986, plant asset costs reported in the balance sheets have been annually adjusted using a single index established by the Ministry of Finance. This practice may have mitigating effects on the value relevance of inflation accounting applied in 2003 and 2004. Third, a mandatory Uniform Chart of Accounts adopted by the Ministry of Finance in 1994 has fully harmonized the different account titles, numbers, and formats used in F/S to enhance comparability between the F/S prepared by the Turkish firms. This has certainly made the financial statements more consistent and comparable, but impacted only their form, rather than the substance. Hence, it will be interesting to see if this reform will enhance value relevance as strongly as the later reforms that have changed the accounting numbers themselves. Fourth, in response to globalization and accession to the European Union (EU), the regulatory body of traded companies, the Capital Markets Board (CMB), allowed the companies to apply IFRS as published by the International Accounting Standards Board (IASB) or to use the IFRS-based standards published by the CMB in 2003 (promulgated by Regulation Series XI, No. 25).[2] Companies voluntarily adopted these standards in 2003 and 2004; and then in 2005, CMB required all publicly traded companies to adopt IFRS as accepted by the EU. Hence, this setting will allow us to test if the IFRS numbers have any incremental explanatory power over inflation adjusted numbers, reported by different firms, during the same 2-year period. Finally, the voluntary adoption of IFRS in 2003–2004, immediately followed by its mandatory adoption in 2005, allows comparison of the value relevance of voluntary versus mandatory IFRS. Researchers can easily access the historical cost financial statements with plant asset revaluations, inflation-adjusted financial statements, and IFRS-converged (voluntary and mandatory) financial statements for most publicly traded firms on the BIST website. These reforms are depicted on a time line in **Figure 1**.

---

[1] Turkey has been grappling with very high levels of inflation since three decades. In our sample period, inflation rate has ranged from a high of 126% in 1999 to the lowest level of 9.5% in 2005. It has significantly decreased to single digits or low teens, as a result of economic reforms of the previous and current government, during our reform period of 2003–2006.

[2] In essence, the standards published by CMB are the same as IFRS as they are direct translations, except a few instances related to tax-based rules. Until the translations are completed, firms used the original IFRSs. For more detail on the exact accounting differences between the two, see [52].

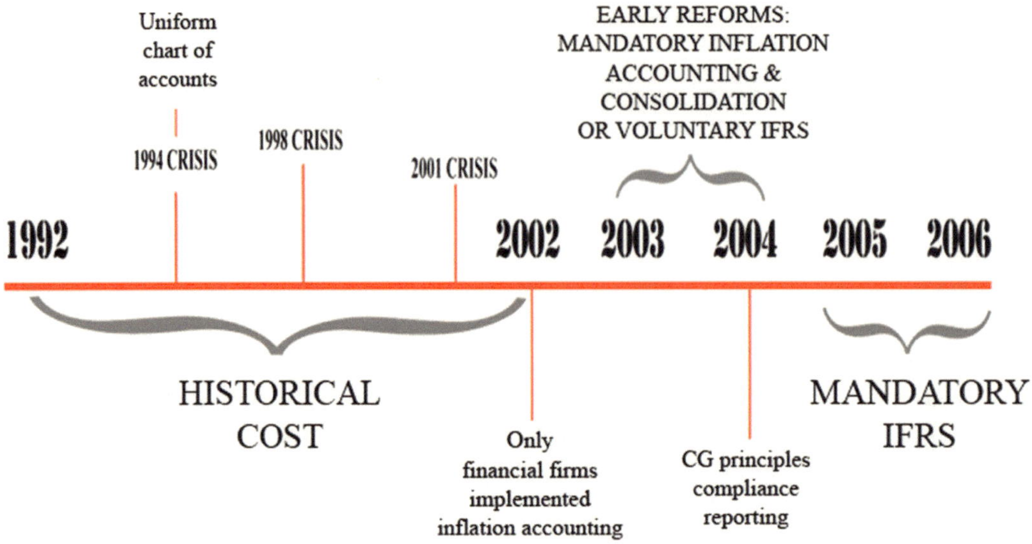

Figure 1. Timeline of accounting reforms in the BIST.

3. Prior research

Among the vast amount of prior literature on accounting valuation models, quality of accounting numbers, and disclosure practices, we will mostly review the work that has used [1] the seminal Ohlson model in estimating the impact of accounting reforms on the relation between accounting numbers and firm value.

3.1. Value relevance of accounting numbers

Researchers have been trying to link accounting numbers to firm value since the two seminal studies [5, 6] that found a significant price and volume reaction to earnings announcements in the USA. The value relevance of the bottom lines of financial statements, net income and owners' equity, was later formalized and modeled in these three seminal studies: [1, 7, 8]. We use both net income and owner's equity in our empirical implementation of the Ohlson's model since their theoretical model and its empirical applications suggest that both of these reported numbers are priced as shown in [1, 9–11].

Since these pioneering studies, there has been a proliferation of empirical work on value relevance. Some studies have found that the value relevance of financial reports is sensitive to country-specific factors as in [12] and firm-specific factors as in [13]. Furthermore, in [14, 15], it has been observed that the value relevance of F/S is weaker and BV is more value relevant than NI in Code Law countries. Since Turkey is a Code Law country in the French tradition, it will be interesting to see if these observations hold in Turkey.

Researchers have also measured value relevance over time and observed that the informativeness of accounting numbers, especially that of earnings, has declined [11, 16, 17]. With the expectation that value relevance will decline under crisis, several studies investigate value relevance under adverse economic conditions as in [18], in loss years and as financial health decreases [19–21], and as earnings/book value ratio changes [22]. Most results point out that there has been a decline in the value relevance of earnings, compensated by an increase in that of book value, especially under such adverse conditions.

In addition to the research in more efficient developed markets, recent research on value relevance has tapped the unique regulatory, financial, and accounting environments of emerging markets (EM) to gain insight into some unanswered questions. To name a few, [23] examines value relevance of accounting numbers in Middle East and North Africa (MENA) countries [24], in the Korean chaebols [25], in Tunisia [18], during the Mexican financial crises [26], in the Czech Republic, and [27] in different segments of the Chinese market, with no conclusive results.

3.2. Value relevance of accounting reforms

Prior research on value relevance of inflation-adjusted accounting data has been inconclusive. Most of this research has been conducted in the USA around the time of the promulgation of SFAS 33, which required large companies to disclose supplementary information on the impact of changing prices on the firm. For example, while [28, 29] found that inflation-adjusted NI is not more value relevant than historical cost NI, [30] concludes that inflation adjustment has incremental explanatory power and [31] found that their predictive power is higher. In [32], the authors use an earnings and book value model and report that inflation-adjusted numbers prepared in accordance with Mexican accounting rules and US Generally Accepted Accounting Principles (GAAP) are both value relevant. The only study based on Turkish firms is [2], where the authors find that inflation-adjusted accounting numbers of 2003, required to be reported in 2004, alongside 2004 inflation-adjusted numbers for comparative purposes, and their 2003 historical cost counterparts are both value relevant.

Similarly, most of the research on the value relevance of IFRS-based accounting numbers has been carried out in developed markets. [33] shows that disclosure quality has increased significantly under both mandatory and voluntary adoption of IFRS. [34] found that the application of International Accounting Standards (IAS) leads to higher accounting quality. In [35–37], the authors found that the book value becomes more relevant than earnings when voluntary IAS adaptors are investigated in Germany, Greece, and some other European countries in separate studies. In [38, 39], incremental value relevance of book value increases during the voluntary adoption of IFRS in European countries.

Some studies such as [40] find that accounting reforms improve the value relevance of earnings and other accounting measures, whereas others fail to find any significant increase in value relevance of NI and BV as a result of accounting reforms [41, 42]. In [43], the authors investigate the effects of voluntary and mandatory IFRS adoption in 16 European countries and find that during the mandatory transition period, the largest improvement takes place in the information environment of firms that have already voluntarily adopted IFRS.

One of the major accounting changes in Turkey is the consolidation requirement that started in 2003. Previous research on the effect of consolidation on the value relevance of accounting numbers is scant. In [44], the authors find that consolidated accounting numbers in Spain are more value relevant than the parent company disclosure alone where book value has higher value relevance than earnings. Similarly, using Finnish accounting data for domestic and foreign investors, [45] found that consolidated data provide more useful information to both types of investors.

3.3. Value relevance studies using Turkish data

Investigating the contemporaneous relationship between net income and stock returns, [46, 47] found that both levels and changes in earnings explain the changes in stock returns. [23] is noteworthy as it examines the association between value relevance and country and firm-specific characteristics of seven countries in the Middle East, including 90 Turkish firms. They find that disclosure quality enhances this relationship in both financial and non-financial firms. In [3, 4], the authors find that NI/share and BV/share are both significant and explain 57.5% of the variation in stock prices, but there is a steep decline in the value relevance of both variables during the 2000–2001 financial crisis that has increased the incidence of losses. In summary, only [2–4] have used both book values and earnings in their tests of value relevance in the BIST. However, none of these papers investigate the specific impact of any of the accounting and financial reporting reforms we examine in this study.

4. The hypotheses

Our primary expectation is that the higher the quality of accounting information in reflecting the true economic fundamentals of the firm, across countries and across firms, the more informative NI and BVE would be of security prices. The following are the specific hypotheses to be tested, all presented in the alternative form:

H_1: Net income (NI) and book value of equity (BV) are expected to be positively associated with firm value over the sample period of 1992–2006.

H_2: The relationship is expected to get stronger after the start of the accounting reforms in 2003.

H_3: The value relevance of NI and BVE is expected to have improved as a result of the Uniform Accounting System promulgated by the Ministry of Finance in 1994, unless it is perceived as just a change in form, not substance.

H_4: Firms that have voluntarily used inflation accounting (general price-level accounting) in 2003 and 2004 have more informative NI and BV, unless the inflation rate is perceived to be immaterial by market participants in those years.

H_5: The firms that voluntarily adopted IFRS in 2003 and 2004 have more informative NI and BV.

H_6: The value relevance of NI and BV has improved after IFRS became mandatory starting fiscal year 2005.

H_7: Consolidating the accounts of the subsidiaries with that of the parent firm increases the value relevance of parents' accounting numbers.

H_8: We expect value relevance to be lower in crisis periods and in loss firms.

5. Sample, data, and methods of analysis

In this study, we use a panel data set of stock prices and financial statement data for BIST-100 firms traded in Borsa Istanbul over the years 1992–2006. Without considering the missing data leading to missing observations, our sample of BIST firms consists of 116 firms (mainly BIST-100 index firms) leading to a sample size of 1386 firm years, one of the largest data sets used in tests on BIST firms. The financial statement variables are manually collected from the BIST website, whereas the stock prices are obtained from a financial research and investment firm: http://www.analiz.com.

Our basic methodology in measuring the quality of accounting numbers (i.e., their value relevance) is borrowed from the theoretical accounting valuation model derived in the seminal works in [1, 7, 8]. They posit that the accounting bottom line numbers of earnings and book value of equity inform us about firm value because they both help in forecasting future expected earnings. Accordingly, [1] models firm value as a function of current book value, PV, of expected excess earnings and other orthogonal value relevant non-accounting information.

In our empirical application, we use both NI and BVE because both the theoretical model and its extant empirical applications suggest that both bottom line accounting numbers are priced [1, 9–11]. Prior research found higher value relevance for BV in Code Law countries and in risky economic environments and also provided evidence that the role of NI has diminished while BVE became a more important determinant of equity value over time in [11, 48], in financially distressed firms with losses, and when earnings/book value is low in [10, 19, 21, 22]. Following [49, 50], we take the natural log of both the dependent and the independent variables which took care of the nonlinearity and extreme skewness in the relationships and led to residuals that satisfy the assumptions of linear regression analysis.[3] The general log-log model specifications estimated for the sample period are as follows:

$$MVE_{it} = \beta_{0t} + \beta_{1t} BVE_{it} + \beta_{2t} Ni_{it} + \varepsilon_{it} \tag{1}$$

where i and t denote firms and years; MVE = close price on March 31_{t+1} * # of shares; BVE = book value of equity, December 31_t; NI = Net income, December 31_t; and Ln transformation is used for all the model variables.

---

[3] First, we tried taking logs of one variable at a time, but the econometric problems were not solved until we tried the log-log model. In the sensitivity analysis section, we also present some of the results under the usual specification $P_{it} = \beta_{0t} + \beta_{1t} BVE_{it} + \beta_{2t} NI_{it} + \beta_{4t} NIdummy_{it}$ * NI+ ε_{it}, where price is regressed against BV and NI. In this specification, the variables are deflated by number of shares, to control for size differences between firms, and we use a net loss dummy to examine the incremental informativeness of losses.

In all specifications and the tables presented below, reporting the results of value-relevance regressions, we assume a random walk process for residual income and hence use current year income as a proxy for the PV of future residual incomes, as assumed in many empirical adaptations of the model. To control for year-specific effects that might confound the results, we use year dummies in regressions pooled across time. Only (+) NI observations are included when natural log transformation is undertaken for nonlinearities and skewness in the data and correction for size differences. We also drop the influential extreme observations based on the Cook's D procedure to ameliorate their effect on the regression line. Furthermore, White's correction is used to obtain standard errors and P values corrected for heteroscedasticity.

In terms of design, we first compare value relevance of accounting numbers in the relevant subsamples we want to compare (e.g., in firms that have and that have not adopted IFRS) where we measure statistical significance of the differences with adjusted R^2 comparisons using Cramer's procedure in [51]. We also estimate pooled regressions with multiplicative interaction terms to capture the significance of the incremental effects of reforms on the coefficients of BV and NI. That is, we let NI and BVE interact with a "year" or "type of reform" dummy to capture the incremental effect of reform years or a specific reform on the slopes of NI and BVE:

$$MVE_{it} = \beta_0 + \beta_{1t}BVE_{it} + \beta_{2t}NI_{it} + \beta_{3t}Dummy_tBVE_{it} + \beta_{4t}Dummy_tNI_{it} + \varepsilon_{it} \quad (2)$$

where $Dummy_t$ = 1, if the firm reports in a particular year or if the firm adopts a particular reform, used to capture the incremental effect of the year or accounting reform on the slopes of NI and BE, and 0, otherwise.

6. Results

6.1. Sample and descriptive statistics

Our sample is composed of both financial and non-financial BIST-100 index firms for which we have stock price and financial statement data over the period 1992–2006. In total, we have 239 firm-year observations for financial firms and 1147 for non-financial firms over the sample period. In our sample for 1992–2003 period, there are 135 financial firms and 765 non-financial firms that have used the historical cost for measurement basis. During the reform years 2003–2006, the number of firms using different accounting standards or measurement basis are as follows: In 2003 and 2004, there are 25 financial and 31 non-financial firms that have used inflation adjustment only; the number of firms that have used inflation adjustment and consolidation at the same period amounts to 25 and 84, respectively; and during the same year, the number of firms which voluntarily applied IFRS are 3 for financial and 79 for non-financial firms. For the 2005–2006 period, the number of sample firms that have applied IFRS mandatorily amounts to 51 and 188 for financial and non-financial firms, respectively.

Table 1 reports the means, medians, standard deviations of the dependent variable price/share and the independent variables NI, BVE, and the number of loss firms in each sample year. We

Year	Price			BV/sh			NI/sh			Number of loss firms
	Mean	Median	Std. Dev.	Mean	Median	Std. Dev.	Mean	Median	Std. Dev.	
1992[1]	6,79	2,71	*10,15*	2,84	2,49	*1,38*	0,69	0,51	*0,74*	3
1993[1]	17,25	8,10	*31,21*	3,87	3,04	*2,62*	1,40	1,00	*1,71*	4
1994[1]	24,11	12,00	*47,74*	4,87	2,99	*8,01*	2,13	0,83	*7,11*	**6**
1995[1]	19,85	13,50	*22,92*	4,62	3,46	*3,84*	1,45	1,13	*3,20*	2
1996[1]	30,41	17,12	*46,56*	5,94	3,51	*7,89*	2,44	0,96	*6,30*	2
1997[1]	44,05	13,00	*95,86*	8,26	3,97	*15,45*	3,83	1,27	*12,09*	2
1998[1]	36,70	8,00	*111,02*	10,37	3,93	*23,98*	3,88	0,96	*15,50*	8
1999[1]	65,72	15,87	*225,84*	10,08	2,77	*37,97*	3,72	0,60	*19,21*	15
2000[1]	31,34	5,85	*144,93*	10,72	2,96	*45,99*	3,10	0,49	*18,53*	11
2001[1]	51,75	5,40	*304,93*	15,47	2,35	*80,93*	6,28	0,08	***50,80***	**44**
2002[1]	20,79	3,67	*138,62*	10,58	2,65	*56,86*	0,55	0,36	*2,83*	**20**
2003[1]	70,30	4,58	*405,70*	23,23	2,83	*110,70*	1,38	0,65	*3,29*	5
2003[2]	104,17	4,73	*516,65*	42,57	4,09	*185,17*	0,95	0,16	*4,48*	8
2003[3]	10,30	4,73	*18,70*	9,93	4,63	*15,97*	1,03	0,56	*1,62*	15
2003[4]	15,84	9,25	*21,42*	10,70	4,37	*15,63*	1,85	1,09	*2,80*	1
2003[5]	6,99	4,29	*7,27*	5,77	3,40	*6,92*	0,94	0,54	*1,59*	3
2004[2]	13,07	4,72	*32,29*	6,79	2,68	*9,17*	0,23	0,25	*1,20*	8
2004[3]	10,20	3,77	*24,14*	8,73	3,16	*15,74*	0,93	0,47	*1,41*	**16**
2004[4]	15,01	7,07	*22,47*	10,71	5,17	*17,91*	1,36	0,75	*2,25*	**1**
2004[5]	5,76	3,75	*6,95*	4,35	3,17	*5,55*	0,54	0,30	*1,14*	**5**
2005[6]	20,40	7,22	*36,73*	7,75	3,21	*11,88*	0,71	0,37	*1,76*	**10**
2005[7]	11,51	5,75	*20,15*	6,10	3,25	*11,03*	0,73	0,36	*1,32*	**19**
2006[6]	17,29	6,25	*30,41*	7,12	3,21	*10,66*	0,98	0,55	*1,19*	3
2006[7]	8,73	5,15	*13,42*	5,70	3,33	*11,24*	0,71	0,34	*1,33*	13

Mean, median, and standard deviations for the dependent variable, price, and independent variables BV/sh (book value of owner's equity per share) and NI/sh (net income/share) for each year in the sample period 1992–2006.
[1] Historical cost.
[2] Mandatory inf., adjustment.
[3]Mandatory inf. adjustment and consolidation.
[4]Voluntary IFRS (unconsolidated).
[5] Voluntary IFRS (consolidated).
[6] Mandatory IFRS (unconsolidated).
[7] Mandatory IFRS (consolidated).

Table 1. Descriptive statistics.

observe that NI/share seems to be lower in the financial crisis years of 1994 and 1998, the number of loss firms are the highest in the financial crisis year of 2001, and the standard deviations are high in general and even higher during the 1997–2003 period.

6.2. Yearly cross-sectional regression results: 1992–2006

As explained in Section 5, in all the tables reported henceforth, the regression coefficients of NI and BV and White's robust *p* values (***$p < 0.01$, **$p < 0.05$, and *$p < 0.1$) are based on an empirical specification of the seminal accounting valuation model of Ohlson. Natural log transformation is undertaken for nonlinearities and skewness in the data and correction for size. Hence, only (+) NI observations are included. Cook's D is used to trim the outlier influential observations.

Table 2 depicts the yearly average value relevance of accounting bottom lines for each year during the 1992–2002 pre-reform and the 2003–2006 reform periods, respectively. The pre-reform period constitutes the years in which a rules-based, mainly tax based, historical cost basis of accounting was used. The average value relevance results in pooled regressions across all years indicate strong informativeness for both NI and BV ($R^2 = 0.89$). Hence, we can state that our accounting valuation model is valid for BIST firms during our sample period. In the years 2003 and 2004, firms were required to use inflation accounting and consolidations (if they are parent firms) unless the firm has voluntarily adopted IFRS. Both prior to and during reform years, the explanatory power of our valuation model is high with R^2s ranging from 60 to 91.6%, highest in the years 2003–2006.

A crude comparison of R^2s in the pre- and post-reform period shows that while explanatory power remains constant at around 80% in the pre-reform historical cost period until 2003 (when it decreases to 60%), it increases to around 89% each year after 2003. Just based on this comparison, we can infer that the reforms have slightly improved value relevance as measured by R^2s of the yearly regressions. We also observe that BVE consistently has the expected positive, significant (*P* value = 0.00) coefficient during both pre-and post-reform periods. NI also has the expected positive and significant coefficient in the pre-reform and post-reform periods. However, it is not significant in 2001 and 2002, indicating a drop in value relevance of NI during the financial crisis of 2001 and NI resuming its significance in 2003.[4]

In **Table 3**, Panel A, we pool the relevant years and compare the significance of the coefficients of the accounting variables and the overall R^2 validity of our model in the pre- versus post-reform periods and during voluntary IFRS (2003–2004) versus mandatory IFRS (2005–2006) reform periods by using subgroup analysis. The regressions using all the 10-year cross-sectional and time series pre-reform data from 1992 to 2002 and the more recent pre-reform period 1999–2002, which is of equal length to the reform period, yield positive and highly significant coefficients for both BVE and NI, and the adjusted R^2 of the two regressions are 87% and 65%, respectively. In the reform period and its two stages (early voluntary reforms of 2003 and 2004 and the mandatory IFRS period of 2005 and 2006), we have a valid model and highly significant (+) coefficients for BVE and NI, both significant at $\alpha = 0.00$, consistent with the results of our yearly analysis. However, the coefficient for NI (BV) increases (decreases) in the

[4] Prior to ln transformation of the variables, we added a negative NI dummy for loss firms to the model with NI/share and BV/share. The coefficients of net loss dummy were either insignificant or barely significant or had a (−) sign in some years both prior to and during the reforms.

Variable	Year					
	1992HC	1993HC	1994HC	1995HC	1996HC	1997HC
Ln NI	0.631***	0.618***	0.254***	0.433***	0.462***	0.442***
Ln BV	0.278**	0.424***	0.637***	0.343***	0.457***	0.564***
Constant	2.520***	1.031	3.273***	5.165***	3.207***	1.681
No. of observations (n)	43	51	51	60	63	71
Adj. R^2	0.799	0.735	0.780	0.740	0.796	0.775
	1998HC	1999HC	2000HC	2001HC	2002 HC	2003 HC
Ln NI	0.476***	0.109*	0.314***	0.063	0.077	0.278***
Ln BV	0.693***	0.945***	0.664***	1.142***	1.023***	0.495***
Constant	−1.418	0.868	1.554	−2.953*	−1.526	5.065***
No. of observations (n)	68	67	84	50	68	39
Adj. R^2	0.808	0.787	0.719	0.772	0.783	0.603
		2003 EarlyREF	2004 EarlyREF	2005IFRS	2006IFRS	1992–2006
Ln NI		0.238***	0.184***	0.467***	0.317***	0.351***
Ln BV		0.763***	0.840***	0.477***	0.648***	0.574***
Constant		0.618	0.064	2.769***	1.815**	2.660***
#of obs. (n)		72	74	83	92	1057
Adj. R^2		0.883	0.902	0.916	0.865	0.893

Model: $Ln(MV_t) = \beta_{0t} + \beta_{1t}\, Ln(NI_t) + \beta_{2t}\, Ln\ (BV_t)$; White's robust p values.
*** $p < 0.01$; ** $p < 0.05$; and * $p < 0.1$.
HC: Historical cost based on local standards; EarlyREF: NI and BV based on mandatory inflation adjustment and consolidation or voluntary IFRS; and IFRS: Mandatory IFRS adoption.

Table 2. The time series of value relevance of accounting numbers in the ISE (1992–2006).

mandatory IFRS period. In this panel, we also use the Cramer's procedure in [51] to test the significance of the difference in the pre- and post-reform R^2 s. The Z-value test statistic comparing the R^2 for the pre-reform period 1992–2002 (1999–2002) versus 2003–2006 reform period is significant at $\alpha = 0.10$ ($\alpha = 0.01$), respectively.

In this panel, we also use an interactive dummy =1 if the firm reporting in these years is a financial firm to see if the value relevance results over the HC and reform periods are different for financial firms. Indeed, we find that financial firms have a significantly lower coefficient for NI under the HC period while a significantly higher one under the reform period of 2003–2006. Thus, we accept H2 and conclude that the reforms have significantly improved value relevance as measured by the significant increase in R^2 in the reform period.

In Panel B, we statistically test the incremental effect of all the reforms undertaken during 2003–2006 on the coefficients for positive NI firms. This time, we pool the data for the

Panel A. Subperiod tests: pre-reform and reform periods and the incremental effect of financial firms. *Model:* $Ln(MV_t) = \beta_{0t} + \beta_{1t}\, Ln(NI_t) + \beta_{2t}\, Ln\,(BV_t) + \beta_{3t}\, FINdummy{*}Ln\,(NI) + \beta_{4t} FINdummy{*}Ln\,(BV)$

Variable	Period				
	1992–2002 HC	**1999–2002 HC**	**2003–2006 REF**	**2003–2004 EarlyREF**	**2005–2006 IFRS**
Ln NI	0.445***	0.174***	0.231***	0.175***	0.297***
Ln BV	0.556***	0.799***	0.745***	0.855***	0.627***
FINdummy*Ln NI	−0.156*	0.075	0.196**	0.159	0.242***
FINdummy*Ln BV	0.097	−0.110	−0.169**	−0.143	−0.210**
Constant	1.746***	1.687**	1.328***	−0.123	2.677***
No. of observations	681	269	324	151	176
Adjusted R^2	0.872	0.654	0.867	0.866	0.873
Bootstrapping Std. Err.	0.011	.0339	0.014		
Z^*	1.57[1]	6.82[2]			

White's robust *p values* (*** $p < 0.01$; ** $p < 0.05$; and * $p < 0.1$).
HC: Historical cost based on local standards; EarlyREF: NI and BV based on mandatory inflation adjustment and consolidation or voluntary IFRS; and IFRS: Mandatory IFRS adoption.
[1]Z^* value for the significance of the difference between R^2 of HC (1992–2002) versus R^2 of REF (2002–2006) is calculated using Cramer's [51] procedure and is significant at $\alpha = 0.10$.
[2]Z^* value for the significance of the difference between R^2 of HC (1999–2002) versus R^2 of REF (2002–2006) is calculated using Cramer's [51] procedure and is significant at $\alpha = 0.01$.

Panel B. Pooled regressions: the interaction effect of reform period 2003–2006 on coefficients of NI and BV. *Model:* $Ln(MV) = \beta_0 + \beta_1{*}Ln(NI) + \beta_2{*}All\ Reforms{*}Ln(NI) + \beta_3{*}\ Ln(BV) + \beta_4{*}\ All\ Reforms{*}Ln(BV) + \beta_i{*}Year\ Dummy_i$

Dependent variable: Ln(MV)	**Positive NI**	
Variables	Coefficient	*P* value
Ln(NI)	0.317***	(0.000)
All Reforms*Ln(NI)	−0.084	(0.108)
Ln(BV)	0.677***	(0.000)
All Reforms*Ln(BV)	0.060	(0.210)
Constant	0.928***	(0.000)
No. of observations	1010	
Adjusted R^2	0.933	

*** $p < 0.01$; ** $p < 0.05$; and * $p < 0.1$.
Base category for "all reforms " interaction variables: historical c.
Year fixed effects are included in the regressions as dummy variables.

Table 3. The effect of the reform periods versus historical cost on value relevance.

subgroups which we ran separately in Panel A, and add a multiplicative reform period interaction term for NI and BV to capture the incremental effect of the 2003–2006, all reforms period, on the coefficients of NI and BV. In the regressions pooled across 1992–2006, we find that the coefficient of BV is not significantly changed during the reforms period 2003–2006 since the coefficient of the BV interaction term is not significant. Although R^2 has significantly increased in all reforms period, the coefficients of BV and NI have not changed significantly.

6.3. The impact of specific accounting reforms

We next investigate the impact of separate voluntary and mandatory accounting reforms during the sample period. Our yearly regressions in **Table 4** indicate that the overall explanatory power of the model does not seem to increase after 1994, the year firms start using the Uniform Accounting System promulgated by the Ministry of Finance (R^2 increases from around 0.74 to 0.78) in 1994. Our findings do not support H3, and we conclude that the consistency in the format and account titles of financial reports has not increased value relevance of NI or BV. Form does not seem to be as important as the substance in financial statements.

Table 4 depicts the results for each separate reform that took place one after the other starting 2003. We use subgroup analyses and pooled regressions with interaction terms for specific reforms and reform periods. Panel A includes subgroup comparisons of regression results on companies using the different accounting methods. Compared to a large 11-year sample of 900 firm-year observations under HC, value relevance (R^2) significantly drops for firms using inflation accounting in 2003–2004 from 87 to 83%, but then significantly increases under voluntary IFRS. The increase in R^2 is significant compared to both HC and inflation accounting. However, no significant difference in value relevance is observed between voluntary versus mandatory IFRS periods and accordingly, we reject H6.

Next, we pool all the firms using HC, inflation accounting, and IFRS across our sample period and estimate a regression model with different interaction dummies for firms using inflation accounting and both mandatory and voluntary IFRS to see the incremental impact of these two reforms on the coefficients of NI and BV. In Panel B, we again observe that inflation accounting significantly decreases the value relevance of NI, while it significantly increases that of BV. In contrast, IFRS does not significantly impact the already significant coefficients of BV or NI. To compare the incremental change in value relevance under IFRS compared to inflation accounting, we next pool the firms using these methods between 2002 and 2006 and use interaction dummies with BV and NI, which acquire a value of 1 if the firm has used IFRS during this time period. The results in Panel C strongly indicate that IFRS significantly increases ($\alpha = 0.00$) the insignificant coefficient of NI under inflation accounting and hence makes it significant and significantly reduces (again at $\alpha = 0.00$) the highly significant value relevance of BV under inflation accounting.

In Panel D, we use subsample tests to evaluate the difference in value relevance under historical cost versus inflation accounting versus voluntary IFRS, all measured during the early reform years of 2003 and 2004. These two years are the only ones some firms reported under both historical cost and inflation accounting while some other firms voluntarily reported under IFRS. Since the years are held constant, we expect stronger results in Panel D. Compared to local historical cost standards, inflation-adjusted NI and BV are significantly more value relevant as the adjusted R^2 of 89% is significantly higher at $\alpha = 0.05$ compared to 62% for firms using HC. Similarly, overall value relevance, measured by the significance of the difference in adjusted R^2, is significantly higher at $\alpha = 0.05$ under voluntary IFRS than under HC. To summarize **Table 4**, historical cost NI and BV have been value relevant across our sample period. Inflation accounting required and experimented with for only 2 years has significantly increased (decreased) the value relevance of BV (NI), whereas IFRS regulation leads to increase in value relevance for NI and not for BV.

Panel A. Subgroup analysis of different accounting reforms. The incremental value relevance of financial firms. *Model:* $Ln(MV_t) = \beta_{0t} + \beta_{1t} Ln(NI_t) + \beta_{2t} Ln(BV_t) + \beta_{3t} FINdummy*Ln(NI) + \beta_{4t} FINdummy*Ln(BV)$

Variable	**Standard**				
	Historical cost (1992–2003)	**Inflation accounting (2003–2004)**	**Voluntary IFRS (2003–2004)**	**Mandatory IFRS (2005–2006)**	**IFRS (2003–2006)**
Ln NI	0.440***	0.020	0.338***	0.297***	0.298***
Ln BV	0.550***	0.964***	0.617***	0.627***	0.642***
FIN*Ln NI	−0.150*	0.029	0.256	0.242***	0.260***
FIN*Ln BV	0.095	−0.032	−0.213	−0.210**	−0.220***
Constant	1.892***	0.272	1.882**	2.677***	2.275***
No. of observations	720	97	72	176	243
Adjusted R^2	0.876	0.830	0.878	0.873	0.879
Bootstrapping Std. Err.	0.010	0.039	0.016	0.017	0.012
Z^*			2.24–2.60	1.19	1.80

White's robust *p values* (*** $p < 0.01$; ** $p < 0.05$; and * $p < 0.1$).
All Z^* values are calculated using Cramer's [51] procedure.
The Z^* values of 2.24 (1.8) for the significance of the difference between R^2 of inflation accounting in 2003 and 2004 versus R^2 of voluntary IFRS in 2003 and 2004 (IFRS in 2003–2006) are significant at α= 0.05 (at α = 0.10).
Z^* value for the significance of the difference between R^2 of historical cost (1992–2003) versus R^2 of voluntary IFRS (2003–2006) is 2.60 and it is significant at α= 0.05.
Z^* value for the significance of the difference between R^2 of voluntary IFRS (2003 and 2004) versus R^2 of mandatory IFRS (2005 and 2006) is 1.19 and it is not significant.

In 2003 and 2004, parent firms were for the first time required to report consolidated financial reports regardless of the accounting standards they use. In 2005 and 2006, again group firms had to consolidate the accounts since they were required to use IFRS. Furthermore, during 2002–2006, the Banking Regulation and Supervision Agency (BDDK) required all banks to report both consolidated and solo financial statements while using either inflation accounting or IFRS in 2003 and 2004. We again run subgroup and pooled regressions to try to disentangle the value relevance impact of consolidations. The results are reported in **Table 5**.

Panel B. Pooled regressions with interaction dummies for accounting reforms (inflation accounting and all IFRS versus HC). *Model:* $Ln(MV)= \beta_0 + \beta_1*Ln(NI) + \beta_2*InfAdj.*Ln(NI) + \beta_3*IFRS(All)*Ln(NI) + \beta_4*Ln(BV) + \beta_5*InfAdj.*Ln(BV) + \beta_6*IFRS(All)*Ln(BV) + \beta_i*Year\ Dummies_i$

Dependent variable: Ln(MV)	Positive NI	
Variables	**Coefficient**	***P* value**
Ln(NI)	0.309***	(0.000)
InfAdj.*Ln(NI)	−0.256***	(0.001)
IFRS(All)*Ln(NI)	0.021	(0.674)
Ln(BV)	0.687***	(0.000)
InfAdj.*Ln(BV)	0.198***	(0.004)
IFRS(All)*Ln(BV)	−0.033	(0.478)
Constant	0.861***	(0.001)
Observations	1016	
Adjusted R^2	0.932	

*** $p < 0.01$; ** $p < 0.05$; and * $p < 0.1$.
Base category for "Accounting Standard " interaction variables: Historical cost.
Year fixed effects are included in the regressions as dummy variables.

Panel C. Pooled regressions with interaction dummies for all IFRS versus inflation accounting. *Model:* $Ln(MV)= \beta_0 + \beta_1*Ln(NI) + \beta_2* IFRS(All)*Ln(NI) + \beta_3*Ln(BV) + \beta_4* IFRS(All)*Ln(BV)$

Dependent Variable: Ln(MV)		
Variables	**Coefficient**	***P* value**
Ln(NI)	−0.015	(0.817)
IFRS(All)*Ln(NI)	0.321***	(0.000)
Ln(BV)	0.928***	(0.000)
IFRS(All)*Ln(BV)	−0.257***	(0.000)
Constant	1.569***	(0.000)
Observations	337	
Adjusted R^2	0.866	

***$p < 0.01$; **$p < 0.05$; and *$p < 0.1$.
Base category for "Accounting Standard " interaction variables: Inflation adjustment.
The influential observations are dropped based on the Cook's statistics.
Due to the heteroscedasticity problem, White correction method is implemented in order to obtain corrected p values.

In Panel A, we compare the solo and consolidated accounting numbers of only banks during the 2002–2006 period, holding the firms and years constant. To our surprise, we observe that consolidated parent NI is not significant, while their consolidated BV is highly significant,

Panel D. Subsample comparisons of historical cost versus inflation accounting versus voluntary IFRS for 2003–2004 period[1] *Model:* $Ln(MV_t) = \beta_{0t} + \beta_{1t} Ln(NI_t) + \beta_{2t} Ln(BV_t)$

Variable	Accounting standard and year		
	Historical cost (2003–2004)	**Inflation accounting (2003–2004)**	**Voluntary IFRS (2003–2004)**
Ln NI	0.297***	0.137**	0.163**
Ln BV	0.489***	0.834***	0.800***
Constant	4.892***	0.878	1.358**
No. of observations (n)	42	71	68
Adj. R^2	0.617	0.889	0.909
Bootstrapping Std. Err.	0.106	0.027	0.015
Z*		2.486[2]	2.727[3]

[1]2003 and 2004 are the only years in which some firms reported under both historical cost and inflation accounting, and some other firms reported under voluntary IFRS. Since the year is kept constant, we get stronger results in Panel D. Comparisons for only year 2003 provide similar significant differences.
[2]Z* value for the significance of the difference between R^2 under historical cost (2003–2004) versus R^2 under inflation accounting (2003–2004) is calculated using Cramer's [51] procedure and it is significant at $\alpha = 0.05$.
[3]Z* value for the significance of the difference between R^2 under historical cost (2003–2004) versus R^2 under voluntary IFRS (2003–2004) is calculated using Cramer's [51] procedure and it is significant at $\alpha = 0.01$.

Table 4. Value relevance of different accounting reforms.

indicating that reporting ownership of net assets of subsidiaries and recording of goodwill are informative, while the group net income is somehow garbled and useless. In Panel B, we pool the solo and consolidated accounting numbers of all banks across the same time period and use a consolidation dummy equal to 1 if the bank reports consolidated results. The results show no incremental value relevance for either BV or NI. Considering the results may be different for financial firms as evidenced in **Tables 3** and **4**, Panel A, we next compare all parent firms that had reported solo financial statements in 2001 and 2002, with their consolidated reports in 2003 and 2004 when they were required to report consolidated financial statements for the first time. The results in Panel C show that historical cost solo NI of these parent firms was not value relevant in 2001 and 2002, while their BV was significantly value relevant. In the next two columns, we compare the consolidated accounting numbers of parents who consolidate while using inflation accounting and those who consolidate within IFRS. Both groups report significantly higher R^2s of 85% compared to the solo HC accounting bottom lines (73%) and have significant positive coefficients for both NI and BV. To control for the possible value relevance impact of using either inflation adjustment or IFRS in these reform years for these consolidated parents, we pool all consolidated parents and run two pooled regressions, one with an inflation dummy and the other with an IFRS dummy to control for their effects on value relevance. Untabulated results show that they neither have any value relevance. We conclude that non-financial parent firms have more value relevant bottom lines when they reflect the results of consolidations compared to their solo bottom lines.

Panel A. Subgroup comparison of consolidated versus solo NI and BV (financial firms). *Model:* $Ln(MV_t) = \beta_{0t} + \beta_{1t}\, Ln(NI_t) + \beta_{2t}\, Ln\, (BV_t)$

Variables	Solo (2002–2006)	Consolidated (2002–2006)
Ln NI	0.401**	0.169
Ln BV	0.707***	0.954***
Constant	−0.955	−1.811
No. of observations (n)	43	43
Adj. R^2	0.902	0.881
Bootstrapping Std. Err.	*0.019*	*0.030*
Z*	−0.586	

First financial firms are used to test the effect of consolidation as Banking Regulation and Supervision Agency (BDDK) required banks to report both consolidated and solo financial statements during 2002–2006
White's robust p values (*** $p < 0.01$; ** $p < 0.05$; and * $p < 0.1$).

Panel B. Pooled regressions with interaction dummies for consolidated versus solo NI and BV Base category for reform dummy interaction variables: unconsolidated NI and BV (financial firms). *Model:* $Ln(MV) = \beta_0 + \beta_1{}^*Ln(NI) + \beta_2{}^*\, Cons{}^*Ln\, (NI) + \beta_3{}^*Ln(BV) + \beta_4{}^*\, Cons\, {}^*Ln(BV)$

Variables	Coefficient	P value
Ln(NI)	0.287	(0.155)
Consolidated*Ln(NI)	−0.233	(0.332)
Ln(BV)	0.822***	(0.000)
Consolidated *Ln(BV)	0.214	(0.325)
Constant	−1.322	(0.340)
Observations	88	
Adjusted R^2	0.822	

*** $p < 0.01$, ** $p < 0.05$, * $p < 0.1$.
Z* value for the significance of the difference between R^2 of consolidated financial statements versus R^2 of solo financial statements is calculated using Cramer's [51] procedure and is not significant.

Panel C. Comparison of HC solo NI and BV of parent firms in 2001 and 2002 with consolidated NI and BV of same firms in 2003 and 2004 (only non-financial firms). *Model:* $Ln(MV) = \beta_0 + \beta_1{}^*Ln(NI) + \beta_2{}^*Ln(BV) + \beta_3{}^*\, Inf.Cons{}^*Ln(NI) + \beta_4{}^*\, Inf.\, Cons{}^*Ln(BV) + B_5{}^*IFRSCON{}^*Ln(NI) + B_6{}^*IFRSCON{}^*Ln(BV)$

Variable	Solo HC 2001–2002	Cons with INF Dummy	Cons with IFRS Dummy
Ln NI	0.126	0.276**	0.304***
Ln BV	1.133***	0.779***	0.740***
Inf.Cons*Ln NI		0.027	
Inf.Cons*Ln BV		−0.038	

Panel C. Comparison of HC solo NI and BV of parent firms in 2001 and 2002 with consolidated NI and BV of same firms in 2003 and 2004 (only non-financial firms). *Model:* $Ln(MV)= \beta_0 + \beta_1{*}Ln(NI) + \beta_2{*}Ln(BV) + \beta_3{*}\ Inf.Cons{*}Ln(NI) + \beta_4{*}\ Inf.Cons{*}Ln(BV) + B_5{*}IFRSCON{*}Ln(NI) + B_6{*}IFRSCON{*}Ln(BV)$

Variable	Solo HC 2001–2002	Cons with INF Dummy	Cons with IFRS Dummy
IFRSCONS*Ln NI			−0.027
IFRSCONS*Ln BV			0.038
Constant	−4.200***	−0.303	−0.303
Observations	66	75	75
Adjusted R^2	0.728	0.856	0.854

Table 5. The effect of consolidated versus solo accounting numbers.

7. Sensitivity tests

Here, we also present some of the results for the regressions we estimated under the following usual specification:

$$P_{it} = \beta_{0t} + \beta_{1t}BVE_{it} + \beta_{2t}NI_{it} + \beta_{4t}NIdummy_{it} \times NI + \varepsilon_i. \quad (3)$$

In this specification, we do not use the log-log specification, which we used in previous analysis. Instead, the variables are deflated by the number of shares to control for size differences between firms, and we use a net loss dummy to examine the incremental informativeness of losses. Our main untabulated results, highlighting only the differences from the current results under ln transformation, are the following: (a) The Uniform Accounting System of 1994 increases the value relevance of accounting numbers (R^2 increases from around 0.40 to 0.80 in the year 1994 and remains around there in future years); (b) we find no overall discernable effect for the voluntary adoption of inflation accounting and IFRS during 2003 and 2004; (c) there is stronger indication in these tests that there is some learning going on as the 2005 and 2006 results under mandatory IFRS, after some firms have experienced with voluntary IFRS, are significant for both NI and BV. The results are the strongest in 2006 as the firms have had the time to apply IFRS and the market participants learned how to interpret the numbers under the new standards and the valuation implications of more informative and transparent disclosure practices; (d) Since we are able to include loss firms in these regressions, we have interesting results for loss firms. First value relevance is much lower in loss firms, and the coefficient of NI is either not significant or has an (−) sign in all years, whereas BV is highly significant for loss firms. These results strongly support prior research on loss firms. What is more interesting is that we observe a strong (+) coefficient on the NI dummy large enough to change the (−) sign of the NI coefficient to (+).

8. Conclusion and discussion

The study contributes to the extant literature on the value relevance of accounting numbers and the research on the consequences of disclosure intensity and financial reporting reforms by

http://dx.doi.org/10.5772/intechopen.69103

studying the Turkish market which has several unique characteristics that make the study particularly interesting. To our knowledge, this is the first study to explore the relationship between equity values and NI and BV over such a lengthy period of time and also provide time series evidence of the effects of a series of regulatory interventions. We investigate the following reforms: i) The use of the Uniform Chart of Accounts in 1994; ii) the mandatory use of general price level accounting, which better reflects the current purchasing power of the currency in periods of high inflation in 2003 and 2004; iii) the concurrent requirement for consolidation of parent firms' accounts with those of its subsidiaries; iv) first voluntary (2003-2004), and then mandatory (2005 and 2006) adoption of IFRS in more than 100 countries in the world, and finally, v) the CG Principles compliance reporting, promulgated on a comply or explain basis, in 2004.[5]

In summary, we find that NI and BE are highly value relevant over the sample years in the BIST, with BV leading the way during the full period. While the Uniform Accounting System of 1994 has not increased the value relevance of accounting numbers, we find that both bottom lines have had very significant coefficients over the historical cost period that extended until 2003 (with the exception of NI losing its value relevance around the crisis year of 2001). We find that in general, the value relevance of accounting numbers has increased slightly during the reform period. Experimenting with mandatory inflation accounting has reduced the value relevance of NI while increasing it for BV, while tests on consolidation accounting indicate the informativeness of the elimination of intercompany transactions and combination of net assets. Adoption of IFRS has an opposite effect, increasing the value relevance of NI, but reducing that of BV. This is good because it may signal Turkey's coming of age as a more developed country in which NI is generally more value relevant prior studies. Consolidation of group accounts, on the other hand, has increased value relevance of accounts of all parent firms, with the exception of banks. We conjecture that the slow impact on value relevance of IFRS may be due to the fact that either the preparers have not yet mastered preparing the financial statements in line with IFRS in the early reform years investigated or the market participants are yet unable to assess the revaluation implications of IFRS.

The results should be of interest to preparers of financial statements, international, and local policy makers including accounting standard setters, and investors at a time when debate on the usefulness of convergence to IFRS and other corporate governance and disclosure reforms has been continuing. As future research, we intend to examine the effect of other CG attributes (family versus non-family ownership, cross-equity ownership, float rate, foreign or institutional shareholdings) on the value relevance of accounting numbers. These independent variables are also expected to mitigate the agency problem related to the expropriation of minority

[5] We also investigated the effect of Corporate Governance Principles compliance reporting, promulgated on a comply or explain basis in 2004, leading to significant progress in the transparency and disclosure (TD) scores of BIST firms measured using S&P methodology over the 2003–2006 period, particularly with regard to financial information and ownership structure disclosures in the annual reports of listed companies [53]. Using the BIST firms in our sample with TD scores, we created two subsamples of high and low TD score firms and compared value relevance of NI and BE in these two subsamples. We find that the value relevance of NI is higher in both 2004 and 2006, and value relevance of BV is significant only in high TD firms in 2005 and 2006, indicating that complying with the corporate governance principles have increased the value relevance of the financial statements of these firms.

shareholders by concentrated family owners the BIST, and thus are expected to enhance the value relevance of accounting information.

Acknowledgements

This study was carried out as part of a TUBITAK (Scientific and Technological Research Council of Turkey) project, grant number 108K364. We are indebted to TUBITAK for their financial support. We also like to thank Tuncer Vatansever of *Analiz.com.tr* for the market-based data they made available and our project assistants Pinar Cingoz and Erdal Aydin, for their thorough and invaluable support in data collection and statistical analysis. This chapter was presented at the American Accounting Association (AAA), Ohio Regional Meeting in March 2009, the Annual Asian Academic Accounting Association Conference held in Istanbul in November 2009, and the AAA Annual Meeting and Conference on Teaching and Learning in Accounting held in New York in August 2009, and we are thankful to the session participants in these conferences for their comments and suggestions.

Author details

Mine Aksu[1]*, Ayse Tansel Cetin[2] and Can Simga Mugan[3]

*Address all correspondence to: maksu@sabanciuniv.edu

1 School of Management, Sabanci University, Orhanli/Tuzla, Istanbul, Turkey

2 Department of Business Administration, Faculty of Economics and Administrative Sciences, Yalova University, Yalova, Turkey

3 Department of Business Administration, Faculty of Business, Izmir University of Economics, Izmir, Turkey

References

[1] Ohlson J. Earnings, book values and dividends in security valuation. Contemporary Accounting Research. 1995;**11**(2):661–688

[2] Kirkulak B, Balsari C K. Value relevance of inflation-adjusted equity and income. The International Journal of Accounting. 2009; 44: 363–377

[3] Senel K, Nural I, Pamukçu B. Is capital structure a significant determinant for value relevance from İstanbul Stock Exchange. Working paper [Internet]. 2004. Available from: http://www.u-cergy.fr/AFFI_2004/IMG/pdf/NURAL.pdf [Accessed: March 11, 2009]

[4] Anandarajan A, Hasan I, Isık I, McCarthy C. The role of earnings and book values in pricing stocks: Evidence from Turkey. Advances in International Accounting. 2006;**19**:59–89

[5] Beaver WH. The information content of annual earnings announcements. Journal of Accounting Research. 1968;**6**:67–92

[6] Ball R, Brown P. An empirical evaluation of accounting income numbers. Journal of Accounting Research. 1968;Autumn:159–178

[7] Ohlson J. The theory of value and earnings, and an introduction to the Ball-Brown analysis. Contemporary Accounting Research. 1991;**8**(1):1–19

[8] Feltham G, Ohlson J. Valuation and clean surplus accounting for operating and financial activities. Contemporary Accounting Research. 1995;**11**(Spring):689–731

[9] Ohlson J, Penman S. Disaggregated accounting data as explanatory variables for returns. Journal of Accounting, Auditing & Finance. 1992;**7**(4):553–573

[10] Penman SH. A synthesis of equity valuation techniques and the terminal value calculation for the dividend discount model. Review of Accounting Studies. 1997;**2**:303–323

[11] Collins DW, Maydew EL, Weiss IS. Changes in the value-relevance of earnings and book values over the past forty years. Journal of Accounting & Economics. 1997;**24**:39–67

[12] Ali A, Hwang L. Country-specific factors related to financial reporting and the value relevance of accounting data. Journal of Accounting Research. 2000;**38**(1):1–21

[13] Warfield TD, Wild KL. Managerial ownership, accounting choices, and informativeness of earnings. Journal of Accounting and Economics. 1995;**20**(1):61–91

[14] Hung M. Accounting standards and value relevance of financial statements: An international analysis. Journal of Accounting & Economics. 2001;**30**:401–420

[15] Arce M, Mora A. Empirical evidence of the effect of European accounting differences on the stock market valuation of earnings and book value. European Accounting Review. 2002;**11**(3):573–599

[16] Lev B, Zarowin P. The boundaries of financial reporting and how to extend them. Journal of Accounting Research. 1999;**37**(2):353–385

[17] Francis J, Schipper K. Have financial statements lost their relevance?. Journal of Accounting Research. 1999;**37**(2):319–352

[18] Davis Friday PY, Gordon EA. The Effect of Macroeconomic Changes on the Value Relevance of Accounting Information: The Case of Mexico and the 1995 Financial Crisis. [Internet]. 2002. Available from: http://papers.ssrn.com/sol3/papers.cfm?abstract_id=322762 [Accessed: June 2, 2015]

[19] Barth ME, Beaver WH, Landsman W. Relative valuation roles of equity book value and net income as function of financial health. Journal of Accounting and Economics. 1998;**25**:1–34

[20] Collins DW, Pincus M, Xie H. Equity valuation and negative earnings: The role of book value of equity. The Accounting Review. 1999;**74**(January):29–61

[21] Franzen L. The nature of losses and the value relevance of earnings. Working Paper. Texas: University of Texas at Dallas; 2002

[22] Burgstahler D, Dichev I. Earnings, adaptation, and equity value. Accounting Review. 1997;**72**(2):187–215

[23] Hasan I, Anandarahan A. Transparency and Value Relevance: The Experience of Some Mena Countries [Internet]. 2003. Available from: http://www.erf.org.eg/CMS/getFile.php?id=635 [Accessed: March 21, 2010]

[24] Bae KH, Jeong SW. The value relevance of earnings and book-value, ownership structure and business group affiliation: Evidence from Korean business groups. Journal of Business, Accounting and Finance. 2007;**34**(5–6):740–766

[25] Naceur SB, Goaied M. The value relevance of accounting and financial information: panel data evidence. Applied Financial Economics. 2004;**14**:1219–1224

[26] Hellstrom K. The value relevance of financial accounting information in a transition economy: The case of the Czech Republic. European Accounting Review. 2006;**15**(3):325–349

[27] Sami H, Zhou H. A comparison of value relevance of accounting information in different segments of the Chinese Stock Market. The International Journal of Accounting. 2004;**39**: 403–427

[28] Beaver WH, Griffin PA, Landsman WR. The incremental information content of replacement cost earnings. Journal of Accounting and Economics. 1982;**4**:15–39

[29] Ketz JE. The effect of general price-level adjustments on the predictive ability of financial ratios. Journal of Accounting Research. 1978;**16**:273–284

[30] Bublitz B, Frecka TJ, McKeown JC. Market association test and FASB Statement no.33 disclosures: A reexamination. Journal of Accounting Research. 1985;**23**:(Suppl):1/23

[31] Sami H, Curatola AP, Trapnell JE. Evidence on the predictive ability of inflation-adjusted earnings measures. Contemporary Accounting Research. 1989;**5**:556–574

[32] Davis-Friday PY, Rivera JM. Inflation accounting and 20-F disclosures: Evidence from Mexico. Accounting Horizons. 2000;**14**(2):113–135

[33] Daske H, Gebhardt G. International financial reporting standards and experts' perceptions of disclosure quality. Abacus. 2006;**42**(3–4):461–498

[34] Barth M, Landsman W, Lang MH. International accounting standards and accounting quality. Journal of Accounting Research. 2008;**46**(3):467–498

[35] Hung M, Subramanyam K. Financial statement effects of adopting international accounting standards: The case of Germany. Review of Accounting Studies. 2007;**12**:623–657

[36] Stergios A, Athanasios V, Nikolaos D. Financial statement effects of adopting International Accounting Standards: The case of Greece. Working Paper. Greece: University of Macedonia; 2007

[37] Capkun V, Cazavan-Jeny A, Jeanjean T, Weiss LA. Transition to IFRS: Value Relevance and Earnings Management [Internet]. 2007. Available from: http://www.econ.kuleuven.ac.be/eng/tew/academic/afi/events/arnn/PDFPatrickB/jeanjean.pdf [Accessed: May 8, 2010]

[38] Paananen M, Lin H. The Development of Value Relevance of IAS and IFRS Over Time: The Case of Germany. Working Paper [Internet]. 2007. University of Hertfordshire. Available from: http://papers.ssrn.com/sol3/papers.cfm?abstract_id=1066604 [Accessed: January 20, 2015]

[39] Daske H, Hail L, Leuz C, Verdi R. Mandatory IFRS reporting around the world: Early evidence on the economic consequences. Journal of Accounting Research. 2008;**46** (5):1085–1142

[40] Naceur SB, Nachi V. Does the Tunisian Accounting Reform Improve The Value Relevance of Financial Information? [Internet]. 2006. Available from: http://papers.ssrn.com/sol3/papers.cfm?abstract_id=888922 [Accessed: October 4, 2015]

[41] Habib A, Weil S. The impact of regulatory reform on the value-relevance of accounting information: Evidence from the 1993 regulatory reforms in New Zealand. Advances in Accounting, Incorporating Advances in International Accounting. 2008;**24**:227–236

[42] Tsalavoutas I, André P, Evans, L. Transition to IFRS and Value Relevance in a Small But Developed Market: A Look at Greek Evidence [Internet]. 2008. Available from: http://ssrn.com/abstract=1286474 [Accessed: October 4, 2015]

[43] Horton J, Serafeim G, Serafeim I. Does Mandatory IFRS Adoption Improve the Information Environment? [Internet]. 2008. Available from: http://ssrn.com/abstract=1264101 [Accessed: August 2, 2011]

[44] Abad C, Laffarga J, Garcia-Borbolla A, Larrdn M, Pinero M, Garrod N. An evaluation of the value relevance of consolidated versus unconsolidated accounting information: evidence from quoted Spanish firms. Journal of International Financial Management and Accounting. 2000;**11**(3):156–177

[45] Niskanen J, Kinnunenb J, Kasanenb E. The value relevance of IAS reconciliation components: Empirical evidence from Finland. Journal of Accounting and Public Policy. 2000;**19** (2):119–137

[46] Ozer G. Firma değerlenmesinde muhasebe kârlarının rolü: İMKB'de deneysel bir araştırma. İktisat, İşletme ve Finans. 2002;**17**(201):112–122

[47] Ozer G, Yucel R. Bir yıldan uzun ölçüm dönemlerinin düzey ve değişim modelleri açısından muhasebe karları ile hisse senedi fiyatları arasındaki ilişki üzerine etkisi. Muhasebe ve Denetime Bakış. 2005;**14**:1–22

[48] Ramesh K, Thiagarajan R. Inter-temporal decline in earnings response coefficients. Working Paper. Evanston, IL: Northwestern University; 1995

[49] Hand J. The Value Relevance of Financial Statements Within and Across Private and Public Equity Markets [Internet]. 2003. Available from: http://papers.ssrn.com/sol3/papers.cfm?abstract_id=484382 [Accessed: October 4, 2015]

[50] Hand J. The value relevance of financial statements in the venture capital market. The Accounting Review. 2005;**80**(2):613–648

[51] Cramer J. Mean and variance of R^2 in small and moderate samples. Journal of Econometrics. 1987;**35**:253–266.

[52] Simga-Mugan C, Hosal-Akman N. Convergence to international financial reporting standards: The case of Turkey. International Journal of Accounting, Auditing and Performance Evaluation. 2005;**2**(1–2):127–139

[53] Aksu M, Espahbodi H. The impact of IFRS adoption and corporate governance principles on transparency and disclosure: The case of Istanbul stock exchange. Emerging Markets Finance and Trade (SSCI). 2016;**52**(4):1030–1028. Published on line Sept. 18, 2015, in print April 2016. DOI: 10.1080/1540496X.2014.998570

Section 4

Accounting Profession and Behavioral Aspects

Chapter 10

Associativism of Accounting Professionals

Osmar Antonio Bonzanini,
Amélia Cristina Ferreira da Silva and
Teresa Gabriela Marques Leite

Additional information is available at the end of the chapter

http://dx.doi.org/10.5772/intechopen.68711

Abstract

This chapter aims to discuss the role of professional accounting associations and orders in relation to the current context of accounting training. It is intended, with this, to broaden the discussion about the performance of these professional entities, since they are placed as of public interest. Its work with the universities, aiming to interfere in the training process of future professionals, whether by the application of evidence of access to the profession or by direct and indirect influence in the construction of the curricular contents intended to form the accountants, must be thought openly and free of ideological load. Thus, it is considered important to analyze the aspects of the relationship between universities and such class entities, in order to know if there is a disinterested relationship or if, on the contrary, the university is influenced by professional accounting associations and orders, in percussion of their selfish interests.

Keywords: professions, accounting, associations and professional orders, universities, accountants

1. Introduction

Studies on the role of professional associations in the field of democratic ideals are anchored in the thesis that professional associations are seen as one of the components of individual freedom through associative demands and one of the possible and democratic solutions to dealing with the administration of social complexity and the power of the state. In this environment, the premises of associativism, according to Luchman [1], in the context of democracy and individual freedoms, are not restricted to the meeting of individuals of the same trade, work, or profession.

Associations and professional orders and universities are public interest entities, and according to Freidson [2], both, together with the state, sustain professional power from three pillars: autonomy, monopoly of knowledge, and credentialism. Its activities have an emphasis on controlling the assets of physical and legal entities. Historically, the earliest associations of accounting professionals have emerged in Scotland in the 1770s. These associations are seen as the forerunners of the rise of accounting in Europe and later in America.

In turn, universities are entities that provide abstract knowledge and certify the technical skills that lead the individual to professional status [3]. Thus, in view of the autonomy envisaged which composes the concept of the university, the performance of professional accounting associations and orders, in order to interfere in the specific contents of the training of future accountants, as well as in the formulation and application of the tests of access to the professional category, is presented as a topic to be investigated. In view of this, in this chapter we will address the following dimensions underlying the theme:

- History of the first associations;
- Accounting profession and associative organization in the world;
- Access to the accounting profession in Brazil;
- Influences on the curricular contents that certify the accountants.

According to Berg and Lune [4], Bhattacherjee [5], and Beuren [6], this study, without social sciences context, is classified as exploratory and descriptive, qualitative, and bibliographic.

2. Theoretical framework

The professional associations, according to Abbott [7], are important social actors, seen through their leadership at a given moment, unleash a set of actions to improve the positioning of the profession in a given social and economic environment. Moreover, according to Willmott [8], although it is voluntary in nature, political bodies with purposes aimed at defining, organizing, securing, and representing the interests of its members, including through the construction of barriers to entry into its sphere of action, from the concession of the state.

Each of the professions has its own particular occupational culture, its founding heroes, and its own dialect, as well as myths and collective rituals of specific cultural resource which holds the monopoly that is attested by the possession of academic credentials, which, according to Diniz [9], operate as a rule of social exclusion, separating professionals from nonprofessionals.

2.1. Professional associations

Before the Industrial Revolution, the professional associations already performing their role, through activities equivalent to the Corporations of the Office. However, it was concluded in the Middle Ages—in the face of the supply of free labor from the countryside, due to the agricultural revolution and the weakening of feudal power—which was designed in contours of companies [10]. These and other circumstances have resulted in the growth of commerce and cities. Thus,in order to understand creation andits development, there is a need to connect these organizations and their influences not only in the context of capitalist and industrial society but also in their participation in regulating the social and economic life of the modern state.

In general, the maintenance of the first associations took place in a similar way to what is happening today: by collecting monthly or annual membership fees. In the structural aspect, they were organized under an established hierarchy, in which the masters occupied the highest positions and the associates, as apprentices, had to rise positions, improving their learning.

Although it is a widely accepted and recognized civil organization in today's society, it is still difficult to get a precise definition of the term "association." According to Luchman [1], it is difficult to establish, against the multiplicity of associative practices, a set of general characteristics that can determine some distinctions without running the risk of falling into reductions or simplifications. Such difficulty is present in the different theoretical currents and based on the interpretations about the importance of associations for life in society, but, although permeated by differences, notions about the concept of association are more or less common that resulted in no growth of trade and cities.

In this context, Luchman [1] rescues the influence of Tocqueville for the sedimentation of the modern conception, because of his vision of secondary associations, different from the primitive bonds.[1] In this perspective, the sense of association involves, to a large extent, the types of associative bonds that are fruit of personal choices but with weaker ties when compared to family associations. In practice, the existence and performance of a professional association are necessary components for the formalization of a particular profession, since it controls the rules of professional conduct through ethical and deontological codes, something that Durkheim [12] has already highlighted as an important link to establish the relationship of men to work and the community [13, 14].

If, on the other hand, there is a group of researchers who seek to find, definitively, the best definition of the term profession. Using even sophisticated terms for this, on the other, there is the view of authors, such as Brante [15], who proposed to abandon the proposed solutions in the last four decades. Brante [15] has focused his studies on one aspect that he considers as a basic problem, and that is behind many others: a simple definition of professions presupposes that these are based on their professional practice in greater systematized and often scientific knowledge. In an opposing view, Saks [16] understands that professions are constituted by their social power and by how they exclude, from a legal basis, individuals who do not hold the required knowledge.

Svensson and Evetts [17] share the view of Brante [15], regarding the relevance in maintaining the line that separates professions and occupations. When questioning the respective traditions,

[1]Cooley [11], in his work *Human Nature and Social Order*—1902, is attributed to the identification of the three types of associations, based on the nature and degree of the ties. Thus, family and friends are primary associations; the secondary ones—such as civic and religious associations and service clubs—are geared toward the collective; and the tertiary ones would be the interest groups and professionals, with a same specific proposal, but anonymous among themselves.

they seek to reposition the debate centered on the definition of the term profession and the efforts of conceptualization and relativization based on space-time references, in the incorporation of the most recent transformations of professional work and the organizational dimensions of its exercise, which delimit new theoretical and methodological questions and empirical manifestations, tributary to the convergence of such traditions.

It should also be noted that in the context of sociology and functionalist theory of professions, professional associations are placed as an important mechanism for protection and maintenance of professions, since they guarantee occupational control, autonomy, and regulation. However, Angelim [18] observes that in the context of professionalism, the professional association is created by the state and now represents the state policy. In the interactionist theory, professional associations are defined in the same way as Higher Education Institutions (HEIs), as institutions for the protection of diplomas, licenses, and mandates [3]. In this way, associations of this nature are intermediary institutions between the state and professionals and between them and the public, which participate in the game of rhetoric or speeches, aiming at public recognition and legal protection.

Historically, many of the professional associations founded on the European continent were able to exercise their effective power in the first half of the twentieth century. Many of them, whose constitution had been inspired by associations created according to the Italian fascist ideology, ended up in crisis, at the end of World War II, along with the victory of the democracies. If, on the one hand, the European institutions of social solidarity were able to find ground with an already existing mentality of historical origin, in other countries, such as Brazil, professional associations had the task of creating a psychological basis, through education, resulting in adaptations in the form of a corporatist model of its own, capable of sustaining the then anti-individualist tendency.

In particular, professional accounting associations and orders have different functions, among which are the access to the profession, the control and supervision of the activities of its affiliates, the promotion of research, and the advancement of science that involves the respective training. In the current context of professional associations, the position of Noordegraaf [19] stands out and moves the debate to a new direction, since it highlights connections between professional logics and external organizations, during the professional training processes. According to Muzio and Kirkpatrick [20], such pressures are forcing professional associations to seek new forms of reconstruction and classification, so that their behaviors become more organizational, including the possibility of a hybrid professionalism, combined with management principles.

Initially focused on the control of personal assets, the activity of the first accountants, in the modern history of mankind, brought accounting science to the organizations' environment, becoming essential to the management processes. Following the historical logic of meeting professionals in associations to defend their interests, early accountants also walked the path.

2.2. The accounting profession: brief history

The use of irrigation techniques by primitive people resulted in the emergence of surplus agricultural products. As a consequence of this new process, a part of the population began to be used in processes of commerce and manufacturing, marking the beginning of the urbanization period. Buesa [21] states that at the beginning of the cycle of urbanization, a ruling class emerged, which was enriched by the exploitation of labor, the collection of taxes and military, and the political and religious control. Considered as the science that controls the patrimony of entities and whose origin is as old as man, until the eighteenth century, accounting theories were practically the same as those considered in the pioneering work of Luca Pacioli: a printed book, dealing with arithmetic and containing only a treatise, composed of 36 chapters, on the accounting part, the distinction IX, treaty XI, Tractarus de computis et scripturis, dealing with the process of double matches.

Based on this treatise, presented by Pacioli, the main legacies for accounting emerged, among them the definition of inventory and guidelines of how to carry out the records; the organization of accounting entries in the memoriale (book in which transactions were recorded as they occurred), the giornale (diary book) and the book (reason book), and the authentication of these books as a means to avoid fraudulent records; the recording of expenses and revenues and a proposal on the financial result to be prepared at the end of the year; the confrontation between the entries of reason and the diary; and the system of double matches, among others, evidencing, first, the debtor and then the creditor.

The first complete record of a double entry bookkeeping system is from the Renaissance period, with the location of the City of Genoa in Italy. In addition to proposing a close connection with mathematics, Frei Pacioli's book *Summa de arithmetica, geometria, proportioni et proportionalitá* included a section on the double-start system and presented the reasoning that was based on accounting entries [22]. Following a process of shifting economic development from continental Europe to England, resulting from its pioneering process of industrialization, new needs linked to the controls in the entities are presented, which promoted the consolidation of the Anglo-Saxon model [8]. Similar to what occurred in Continental Europe, Italy was the cradle of accounting innovation during the long period when its city-states had a strong influence on the economy. England and later the USA are the influential territories for the development of contemporary accounting.

There is also the understanding that the origins of accounting professionals, as a component of corporate governance, are related to the creation of corporations and the legal requirement of auditing, which has led to the growth of accounting as a profession [22, 23]. Such growth, even if it has occurred differently in different countries, has brought about significant changes: it was the modern dimension of accounting. This dimension of modernity was the accounting response to the increase in information needs, resulting from the vast socioeconomic change, initially in the coal exploration business and later in the oil rush [24]. Later, the creation of technologies provoked the evolution of information quality and its influence on economic mediation, leaving behind the legacy inherited from the medieval past. This evolution occurred due to the flexibility and high degree of abstraction of the accounting, fundamental to inform about the diverse activities of the organizations, the scope, and complexity of the business.

In this environment of economic growth, leaving behind the old form of management and bookkeeping, a new demand for society of the time arises: the need for people with knowledge, skills, and qualifications to control wealth [25]. Therefore, it was natural for a space of action to emerge from those who held knowledge in accounting, leading to the creation of the profession. In such a scenario, the accounting profession was built on the contributions of individuals and then considered leaders, something important in the delimitation of jurisdictional boundaries, in professional organization, and in claims of legitimacy.

There is a perception, in the historical context that the emergence of the accounting profession has a close connection with the end of the restrictions that prevented the creation of corporate societies. Although there was a significant need for a capital in the period of the Industrial Revolution and in the early nineteenth century, legal impediments restricted the formation of limited liability companies, inhibiting the formation of these capitals, as well as the growth of the accounting profession [23].

On the other hand, in the period of much of the nineteenth and twentieth centuries, many countries were involved in military conflicts or economic disputes, often resulting from capitalist and ideological expansion and resistance to such expansions. At the time these restrictions were withdrawn, the field for accountants, as well as for the consolidation of the profession, was open.

2.3. First professional accountant associations

The formation of the first professional organizations, initially in Edinburgh and later in Glasgow, Scotland, though pioneering, did not originate from a desire of the accountants to elevate their status, to gain new privileges, or to promote monopolies [26]. What actually happened was a mobilization of these already prestigious professionals against the challenges of powerful London-based trading groups. In addition, class organization as an association served to raise awareness of the group and consolidates its identity, during ideological confrontations with hostile parties, such as the powerful mercantile groups.

In the early stages of the organization of the accounting profession, private sector institutes were responsible in Britain, and although they have been recognized by royal charters, they have not been formally regulated by the British state [23]. Unlike Britain in France, the regulation of professional accountants and auditors was divided between the *Ordre des Experts-Comptables* and the *Compagnie Nationale des Commissaires aux Comptes,*[2] both bodies being under strict state regulation. It is also necessary to reflect on the inclusion of the figure of the state as an ally of the professions, since it occurred by its authority to grant and impose monopolies or arrangements restrictive to the professions. Thus, according to Sudaby and Viale [27], professional projects, in addition to the support they seek from the state, so that they can initiate legal procedures and transform an occupation into a profession, bring with them institutionalization projects.

According to Willmott [8], the emergence of the modern state was an important condition for the development and organization of accounting practice. However, studies carried out in the context of the professions have neglected this practice or consider it as a neutral

[2]Accountants and statutory auditors, respectively.

influence. At other times, this role is perceived as relevant, at the moment it intervenes, limiting the autonomy of professions, and, traditionally, accountants have used the state to promote their interests, including in the expansion of their prerogatives and market closure, as in professionalization As auditors Ballas [28], as an example, the case of Greece between the years 1940 and 1950, where the state began the auditors' professionalization project, using audit as an instrument of economic and political control, as well as being a device for legitimizing the government itself.

Another point that deserves attention is the interference of the state in the regulatory processes, since accounting has not been regulated in the same way in different countries. One reason for such differences lies in the legal system, which differs internationally because there are two systems identified in the developed world: Code Law and the Common Law.

As for the Code Law, it is based on Roman Civil Law, which advocates intrinsically, with the government acting as regulator of all facts, and acts determined in the current legislation [29], and the Common Law tradition originates in medieval England, and it is a more diversified legal code, going back to the codifications of the nineteenth century. In its origin are customs and analysis of customary law, there is a process of creating laws in general, but the application of laws in specific cases, activities, or segments. Such a difference between the two systems lies in the particularity that company law or commercial codes establish in the form of detailed rules for accounting and financial reporting in Ref. [29]. With this, the nature of regulation and the rules of each country can be affected by the system, because where Common Law prevails, the development of the profession took place under a title, such as the *Certified Public Accountant* (CPA).

In relation to the Code Law countries, the accounting profession is dominated by state standards, and accounting and auditing have been developed as distinct professions with different designations. On the other hand, given the historical or cultural influences, it is possible to observe some exceptions, such as the Japan, Greece, and Bulgaria, where professional orders have acted to simplify the profession, in addition to reducing the number of titles, without success in such attempts.

Even if, at present, differences and similarities are observed in the attributions and the performance of the entity representative of accounting professionals, their origin is the same, from the first accountant societies, constituted from the 1500s in Europe.

2.3.1. Scotland and England: birthplace of professional accountants' associations

Although there is a mention of a society of accountants formed in the year 1581 in Venice, the greatest impetus to the profession occurred, according to Hendriksen and Breda [22], concomitant to the beginning of the Industrial Revolution, when the requirement of accounting specialists increased considerably. Scotland is presented as the country where the first professional associations were constituted, since the Edinburgh Municipal Directory for the year 1773 referred to the performance of seven accountants. Later, as early as the early nineteenth century, there were less than 50 public accountants registered and operating in the major cities of England and Scotland [22]. It was from a legal authorization, issued in 1854, allowing practitioners to present themselves as "authorized accountants," which established a society of accountants located in Edinburgh. Other local associations were then formed, culminating in the approval by Queen Victoria in 1880 of the Institute of Certified Accountants of England and Wales [25].

These professional associations of Scotland were the forerunners of the professional rise of the class, in the late nineteenth century, and beyond the Society of Accountants in Edinburgh (SAE), 1853; the Institute of Accountants and Actuaries in Glasgow (IAAG), from 1854; and the Society of Accountants in Aberdeen (SAA), 1866, can be taken as the earliest examples of associative control in Scottish accounting. To a certain extent, the formation of these associations was an attitude in response to the challenge of power and authority of Scottish public accountants in providing services related to the Court of Justice. The creation of the SAA, however, was related to local economic reasons, such as the railways and the banking sector, and after the formation of these three entities, its members faced challenges from competing organizations, concerned with the monopoly of the profession [25]. Despite the differences, the three associations joined forces to defend the professional status of accountants, including joint examinations, a review of national members, and professional registration.

The early organization of accountants in Scotland is explained by Walker [30] as a consequence of the Scottish legal separatist system, the rise of industrial society, and the attempt to achieve social closure and collective mobility. Vocational training in Edinburgh and Glasgow in 1853 was an organizational response to the activities of a powerful group of London merchants, whose demands for law reform emerged from the dominant economic philosophy of Victorian Britain. Such proposals ultimately threatened the interests of Scottish accountants but resulted in greater linkage between professional organizations in Scotland and England.

Another important milestone in the professionalization of accountants in Scotland occurred in 1854, when they came to hold the monopoly of accounting practice, through the sole acquisition of credentials as CA[3] [31]. At the time, the monopoly was challenged as being contrary to social and political philosophy and by employing a critical analysis of professional secrecy, which shows that it has assumed a functionalist interpretation of the role of the professions in society, receiving protection and help from superior resources, by their links with other professions and even by political circumstances. After the founding of the accountant associations in Scotland, similar formations emerged in England and Wales at the end of the nineteenth century [25]. As in Scotland, there were public accountants working in England and Wales, even though they were not linked to any professional associations [25, 32]. However, in line with Scotland, national legislation on the professional services of the Public Accountants of England and Wales created the need for a formally constituted group to establish associative control.

Since that time, the accounting profession already allowed to glimpse certain nuances in relation to the social context. Having its origin in trade practices, from the period beginning in the

[3]*Charter*. Term which is based on the designation "Chartered" of its associates, designation of professional prestige. In Scotland the Edinburgh charter, dating from 1854, gave rise to the designation of Chartered Accountant (CA) and then adopted in the royal diploma which in 1880 recognized in the Institute of Chartered Accountants in England and Wales (ICAEW).

http://dx.doi.org/10.5772/intechopen.68711

1870s, accounting in England and Wales leaves behind its poorly defined commercial occupation, becoming a profession established and recognized in the society [33]. At the same time that the accounting science extended its prestige and recognition, the occupation of secretary was losing importance and being identified like feminine function. At the end of the professionalization process, around 1930, the accountant had the recognition of being a function directed to the male professionals.

Currently, the associations that bring together accounting professionals in Britain, according to Altintas and Yilmaz [29], are Institute of Chartered Accountants in England and Wales (ICAEW), Institute of Chartered Accountants of Scotland (ICAS), Association of Chartered Certified Accountants (ACCA), Chartered Institute of Management Accountants (CIMA), Chartered Institute of Public Finance and Accountancy (CIPFA), Association of International Accountants (AIA), and Association of Accounting Technicians (AAT). Each has its own accreditation system and does not act in a joint and coordinated manner, but is under the supervision of the Accounting Organizations Advisory Committee (CCAB) [34]. Thus, the accounting standards are edited by a board, called Statement of Standard Accounting Practice (SSAP), and approved by professional bodies.

This pioneering role served as a model for other countries in Europe and also for the USA. In the European context, merchants' accounting had as one of the objectives to demonstrate the real value of debts, and an example of this is in France, where the French Commercial Code brings such a requirement since its implementation in 1673.

2.3.2. *Accounting associations in France and Germany*

The German school of accounting, together with the French school, is somewhat like classic examples of the Continental European model, as opposed to the Anglo-Saxon model. Regarding the legal and regulatory environment, the German Commercial Code in 1861, inspired by the French model and the corporate and tax legislation, is the backbone in accounting standardization. Still, according to Niyama [34] on the secondary level, there is the accountant profession and the stock exchange. The French Commercial Code is often cited in classical literature as the first document, in the world, to establish regulations for commercial activity. A determination, contained in that document, required traders who had double bookkeeping to prepare their balance sheets correctly for proper protection of creditors. The evolution of the accounting profession in France is based on the legal requirements for the appointment of various types of inspectors and auditors, ranging from inspectors, to syndics, to censeurs, and finally to commissaires [23].

Unlike the USA and Great Britain, accounting firms in France do not develop or enact accounting standards, and the accounting profession is represented by two entities:

- The Order of Account Specialists (Accountants): perform the accreditation of the profession and act under the jurisdiction of the Ministry of Economy and Finance. It was legitimized by the government in 1945, with the purpose of defending the honor and independence of the accounting profession.

- The National Commission of Independent Auditors (Auditors): they have the function of producing audit standards, revising the code of ethics and issuing technical guidelines. It is overseen by the Ministry of Justice, and, since 1966, auditing is mandatory for companies that fall into parameters, such as sales volume, total assets, and the number of functions.

To enter the profession, the classical career of the French accountant begins with an examination called baccalaureate, which grants the diploma of II Cycle. Obtaining this diploma, the aspiring professional can enter an accounting preparatory course, lasting up to 2 years. At the end of the course, he/she must carry out, together with the professional body, a series of written tests, with subjects, such as Tax Law, Mathematics, Accounting, and Informatics. The approval entitles the Preparatory Diploma of Accounting and Financial Studies (DPECF).

In order to be able to start the activities of general accountant and to obtain the maximum title of the profession (expert-comptable), the candidate undergoes a practical internship of 3 years in an audit firm, besides performing written tests and oral and thesis defense. At this point, you should already be affiliated with the bodies that regulate the profession, such as Ordre des Experts-Comptables [23, 35]. Therefore, they are around 10 years of study, and it is a difficult and time-consuming process but with a solid academic and practical background.

The birth of accounting in Germany came close to the 1900s, originating in business and trade schools (Wirtschaftshochschule, Handelshochschulen) and viewed as part of the discipline in business economics [35]. Six business schools were set up in Germany, Austria, and Switzerland: Leipzig, Aachen, St. Gallen, Vienna in 1898, Frankfurt and Köln in 1901, following the initiative of the companies and Chambers of Commerce. Others were founded in Berlin (1906), Mannhein (1908), and Munchen (1910), all created as a result of the Industrial Revolution, which brought changes to accounting, notably in terms of concepts, such as costs and depreciation.

Corporate law, as referred to by Altintas and Yilmaz [29], seems to have been the most influential factor on accounting in Germany, in view of the codified and prescriptive legal system adopted, as opposed to Anglo-American law. In addition to Germany, France, Greece, and Belgium restrict the creation of professional associations for accountants operating in the public domain. Evans and Honold [36] also share the view that German accounting, in its regulatory context, is a profession of lesser influence and much younger than in the case of Anglo-American countries, with strong state performance in professional development.

Like France, German legislation is based on legal codes, the so-called legalistic approach to accounting. In addition, the development of accounting principles and the editing of accounting standards in Germany are not influenced as strongly as in the USA and Great Britain. In addition, the role of the state differs greatly from that of the UK, with German professionals more likely to look at government and its regulation [36].

In the professional aspect, there are two categories in action in Germany. The first one is equivalent to Certified Public Accountant, which requires the approval of a professional qualification examination, through a university degree in finance, accounting, law, economics, and proof of minimum experience of 4–5 years for proper accreditation. The second one is as a category of licensed inspector and considered lower level, whose performance allows auditing small and medium enterprises. Both are legally authorized to perform audit work and act as members of the Board of Certified Auditors, which is the official German official body under the Ministry of Economy.

Just as in France, entry into the accounting profession in Germany is difficult because of the relevant degrees of knowledge required of the candidate. It is enough to remember that in the year 1931, the German government had already introduced the audit requirement for companies [35]. In addition, in France, 5 years of experience are required before the start of the examinations, in total of seven, in addition to the oral examination in front of an eight-member teacher's seat.

2.3.3. Profession and professional associations in Italy

In Italy, the influences of company law (Civil Code) and tax regulations in accounting are similar to those of a number of other Continental European countries, especially France, Belgium, and Spain. In view of the absence of an accounting standard setting body in Italy, accounting standards are set by the Civil Code. In the case of Italian-listed companies, these were subject to additional regulation, mainly by the CONSOB (*Commissione Nazionale per le Società e la Borsa*), which is an equivalent organ of the US SEC [29].

It should be noted that the regulation of the accounting profession in Italy was completely reformulated by Legislative Decree No. 1 39, June 2005. Since then, the accounting profession is subject to the general supervision of the Ministry of Justice. According to the new legal provisions, the accounting profession in Italy has two levels, which differ in relation to the scope and nature of professional activities: *Dottore Commercialista* and *Esperti Contabili*—Statutory Auditor and Accountant [37]. In the legal aspect, both levels have the requirement of a university degree, although with different periods of duration, which proposes a close link between the academic and the professional path. Still, the professionals who held the title of Ragioneri and Perito Commercial, on the occasion of the legal amendment of 2007, now have the registration of Ragioneri Commercialista, in the same professional group to which Dottore Commercialista belongs.

Regarding access to the profession, to obtain professional registration as Commercialist Dottore, candidates must obtain a 5-year diploma in Economic Sciences and Business Administration or in Economic Sciences [37]. There is also the requirement of practical experience, with a period of 18 months, with a registered profession. After obtaining the academic degree and the conclusion of the practice period, the candidate is able to take the state exam. Students of the 5-year university course are allowed to start the internship as of the fourth year of study. This training is carried out under the supervision of a Commercialist Dottore or an Esperti Contabili who have been registered for at least 5 years. This course, after graduation, aims to provide all theoretical and practical knowledge, as well as support the skills needed for the activity.

In relation to the state examination, the so-called proof of access to the professional category, for Commercialist Dottore, involves two stages: three written tests and one oral test.

The first written test covers the following subjects: general and applied accounting, technical banking, commercial and industrial auditing, financial management, and financial calculations. The second written test includes the following contents: Private Law, Commercial Law, Bankruptcy Law, Tax Law, Labor Law, and Social Security and Civil Procedural Law.

In addition, in relation to the application of the examinations to Italian professionals, universities have the competence to apply them graduates, being the responsibility of the Ministry of Justice when it is a matter for auditors. The same happens in their management, where the tests happen twice a year [37]. Given the set of requirements for access to the accounting profession in Italy, both in the academic context and the requirement of practice prior to the exams, the content of these, involving several areas, implies that one must be well prepared to obtain approval.

2.3.4. Regulation and accounting association in Portugal

Still in the European continent, accounting regulation in Portugal followed the model already adopted in France, where the CNC has an administrative and financial liaison with the Ministry of Finance, with the power to develop accounting standards, which are issued as decrees or decrees-laws. From this perspective, accounting in Portugal had its development closely linked to the state, an aspect that restricted the autonomy of the profession [38], and its beginning is linked to the Board of Trade, the Royal Decree of September 1755, and the Account of the Institution of the Class of Commerce, in 1779, both on the initiative of the Marquis of Pombal.

The Class of Commerce had the main objective to teach the Italian method of double matches to the children of the Portuguese merchants. This was the first establishment of the kind created officially in Portugal and aimed at professional education [39]. The Class of Commerce was a subordinate to the Board of Trade and was considered the first professional technical education course of accounting officially created in the world. According to Lira [40], the first teacher was I. Nancenti, a businessman who was ruined after the earthquake of 1755; the second teacher was an Italian named Avondano.

In the Portuguese accounting associative context, the association of the professional accounting class began in 1885, with the foundation of the Portuguese Accounting Association. Later, in 1894, the Association of Employees in Accounting was created, which, in 1900, was renamed the Institute of the Commercial Class of Lisbon [41]. When it was constituted, this accounting association organized a group, composed of associates able to work in higher accounting positions.

Carqueja [41] highlighted the founding of the Portuguese Accounting Society in 1945 and was legally recognized in 1946. For the author, Portuguese professionals owe this professional association representation and participation in international meetings and associations. In addition, some points had a negative impact on the accounting evolution in Portugal: the long period of validity of the Portuguese Commercial Code, instituted in 1833 and the period between 1928 and 1974 [38]. At that time, members of the associations could even elect their leader, but the elected person had his name approved by the Secretary of State for Corporations, and the unions depended on the Institute of Labor and Social Security.

In addition, journals published by associations could not circulate without the consent of the Secretary of State for Corporations.

In 1999, with Decree-Law No. 452, the Association of Chartered Accountants receives the name of the Chamber of Chartered Accountants. Then, at the beginning of 2000, the Code of Ethics enters into force, as a logical necessity to impose behavioral rules on all professionals, completing the requirements that define a regulated profession. To access the register as Certified Accountant (CA) —and to be a member of the Order of Certified Accountants (OCA)—the main requirements are to have the necessary academic qualification for enrollment, carry out a professional internship, and professional examination. Regarding academic qualification (undergraduate or higher), this must be obtained in one of the areas of Accounting, Management, Economics, Finance, Public Administration, or related, besides obtaining competences in nuclear and complementary areas.

In view of the trajectory of the accounting profession in Portugal, Caria and Rodrigues [38] observe that Portuguese professionals had little influence in the process of normalization through the representatives of the order in the CNC, something that is presented as a general characteristic of the European community, and in the continental model in addition to Portugal, Belgium, France, and Spain, they had a common legacy of tax reporting systems.

2.3.5. The Japanese model of the profession and accounting associativism

Japan is part of the group of countries that adopt the Code Law legal system, in which there is a high degree of detail of the rules that must be fulfilled. Similar to Germany and France, the Japanese system has less flexibility in structuring the financial statements, in addition to greater concern with creditors.

According to Niyama [34], until the end of World War II, Japan's economy was under the control of industrial and commercial conglomerates, known as zaibatsu, which often included banks. At the end of the American occupation, at the end of the conflict, the zaibatsus lost political power, notably by the implantation of antimonopoly law, signed in 1946.

Even though the USA tried to establish Securities and Exchange Commission (SEC) in Japan in 1948, it was dissolved in 1953, transferred under the Ministry of Finance, and encouraged the strengthening of the accounting profession through the Japan Institute of Certified Public Accountants, such initiatives have not been successful. Historically, Japan has brought from Europe many of the accounting laws implemented in the country, mainly Germany, as is the case of the Commercial Code, published in 1899, but with later revisions [29]. Thus, the Japanese accounting system was influenced by both Germany and the USA, but the government still exerts strong control over numerous activities, which results in high bureaucracy in business, the environment where accounting is embedded. In the history of Japanese associativism, the creation of the first class association dates back to 1927, and today the Japanese accounting profession originates from the Certified Public Accountants Act, enacted in 1948, aimed at ensuring the quality of accounting professionals at higher levels and in the USA and UK [34]. As a result of this law, the Japanese Institute of Certified Public Accountants (JICPA) [42] was established in 1949, currently the leading professional accounting organization in Japan.

In the professional trajectory, the path to becoming a Japanese CPA goes through academic training at the university level, in Accounting and Finance, Management Accounting, Auditing, or Business Law. Once this requirement is met, the next step is to pass the CPA exam, which is conducted by the *Certified Public Accountants and Auditing Oversight Board*, twice a year and in the Japanese language only. Upon successful completion, the applicant enters into a professional education program in accounting and a practical experience program; the requirement of which is the 3-year professional education program and program content provided by JICPA itself. In general terms, the curriculum that qualifies future accounting professionals in Japan is aligned with the requirements of the *International Accounting Education Standards* issued by the *International Federation of Accountants Board of International Standards of Education*. Completing the professional education program, the candidate will be able to perform the final tests, applied annually.

With regard to the practical experience required to obtain the CPA certificate in Japan, it covers the 2-year period, which can be done before or after the legal examination [42]. Complying with these requirements, the professional is able to obtain the registration as CPA, being able to carry out its activities and present itself as such in a public way. Therefore, it is a long training and with in-depth knowledge, but it results in a solid and rewarding career.

2.3.6. Development of the profession and associations in the USA

The development of accounting in the USA can be seen in line with the economic progress of the country, primarily due to the expansion of railways, which has boosted other activities and led to the emergence of large empires composed of refineries, oil pipelines, distribution stations, and other activities which accompanied the railway boom. As highlighted by Niyama [34], accounting issues involving depreciation, costs, dividends, and investments require conceptually sound solutions to investors.

In the context of the professionalization of accountants, it has been supported by strong associations, with accounting features from the UK, including the professional associative model [23]. Particularly, the evolution of accounting in the USA, as a profession in origin in the private sector, presents education and admission requirements, disciplinary practices, professional standards, auditing, and ethics. From the presence of accountancy professionals in the USA, from the UK, the associative movement in the USA did not remain unaware of the initiative of Scottish emigrants. According to Carqueja [41], the designation of *Certified Public Accountant* (CPA) originated in Law in 1896, in the state of New York, and then was adapted to the other states of the union, which resulted in the qualification that the CPAs had their prestige recognized.

Accounting associations in the USA began in 1887, when the American Association of Public Accountants (AAPA) was created and is now an American Institute of Certified Public Accountants [22]. At its foundation, the AAPA had the *Journal of Accountancy* as its official body, and its founders were in the number of 10, insignificant number before the thousands of members that it has at the present time. Although pioneering, the AAPA was not the only association of accountants in the USA. At the time, numerous independent state associations had been created by the country, aiming at the legal recognition of its members. This professional recognition as a CPA, obtained in 1896 by the professionals of the State of New York, entitled individuals to be called Certified Public Accountants (CPAs). To achieve such a degree, there was a need to obtain a certificate from the state university directors.

In the following decades, other states passed similar laws, and until 1922 all American states had such laws in place. However, divergences persisted because in state legislations it was possible to be a CPA without being a member of the AAPA and it was also possible to belong to the AAPA without being a CPA, which resulted in conflict because it was a matter of the states' rights [22, 29]. In addition, practitioners were concerned about the dominance of the New York State Association, which led to the reorganization of the AAPA in 1917, becoming an American Institute of Accountants (AIA), when educational requirements for admission were established, even though possession of a CPA certificate was not yet required.

The lack of mandatory certification as a CPA eventually led to dissent in 1921 with the formation of the American Society of Certified Public Accountants (ASCPA), and the only criterion for admission as a member was the possession of a certificate issued by the states. As observed by Hendriksen and Breda [22], during the next 15 years, ASCPA and AIA, after competing for the representation of the US accountants, opted for the merger, keeping the name of the institute and requiring a valid certificate—of being a registered public accountant. Those who want to become a Certified Public Accountant (CPA) in the USA need to initially do a set of tests called the Uniform CPA Examination, with a high level of requirement and difficulty.

The purpose of this examination is to protect the public interest in order to ensure that only qualified candidates become licensed as the US Certified Public Accountants [43]. Despite the degree of difficulty, approval in this examination alone is not enough to meet the requirements in obtaining certification, since they vary from one jurisdiction to another. In the most classical form, the CPA candidate must have completed a college undergraduate course, have a master's degree (MS or MBA), or a doctorate degree (PhD) [44].

In addition to the requirements for accounting content, the IES where the candidate has a baccalaureate degree must be registered in one of the six accredited educational institutions (US Regional Institutional Accreditation Agencies). There is also a need to pass the ethics exam and prove a minimum number of years of work experience in addition to the candidate obtaining a Social Security Number. This requirement is valid, even if the applicant is not a US citizen nor has he/she been working or residing in one of the jurisdictions.

2.3.7. Accounting association and accountancy profession in Brazil: Portuguese roots

In the period corresponding to the first 50 years after the discovery and Portuguese colonization in Brazil, there is no record of political, economic, or social activities. Through the failure of the hereditary captaincy system, the Portuguese government decided to take over directly the control of its colony and installed, in the year 1548, the system of general government. Regarding the history of the accounting profession in Brazil, as well as what happened in Portugal, the creation of the Aula do Comércio, based on the supervision of the Lisbon Commerce Board, is considered an important milestone, and its prediction is contained in Article XVI of the Statutes of the Board of Trade, established in Lisbon, approved by the decree of December 1756 [45].

In relation to the first higher courses in Brazil, these were created in 1808, upon the arrival of the Portuguese court. Despite the existence of these higher courses, the first university was only instituted in 1920, which is already in the period of the republic. It is perceived that it occurred somewhat late, compared with the Spanish-speaking countries, as was the case of Santo Domingo (1538), Mexico, Peru, Chile, and Argentina. Although it obtained its political independence in 1822, Brazil remained economically submissive to the European nations, with the permanence of the same colonial structure, based on slave labor, in contradiction to the rapidly expanding world capitalist system [45]. In the history of the Brazilian accounting profession, it was in 1945, when the commercial education reform was completed, that Decree No. 7988, formalized the creation of two higher courses: Economic Sciences and Accounting and Actuarial Sciences.

Concerning the associativism of the accounting profession, although the first movement with similar characteristics to that occurred in Europe and the USA has occurred in 1869, when the Court Bookkeepers Association was founded, the creation of the professional order, in the form of the Federal Accounting Council, occurred only in May 1946, when the country was already a republic. Since its inception, the Federal Accounting Council, as a professional order of accountants, besides supervising the exercise of the profession, was active in the regulation of accounting principles, in continuing education programs and in the edition of accounting standards of a technical and professional nature. There was also no application of the entrance exams to the professional category, which only occurred in 2010, in the form of the Examination of Sufficiency, which is compulsory for all postgraduate graduates of Accounting Sciences who wish to practice the profession counter.

In addition, higher education legislation in Brazil, regulated by the Ministry of Education, provides that Higher Education Institutions in the country, which offer a higher degree in Accounting Sciences, must follow the rule set forth in Resolution No. 10/2004, regarding the body of knowledge that makes up the future accountant. Regarding the training aspect, the future Brazilian accountants graduated by the Higher Education Institutions (HEIs), in periods ranging from 4–6 years, with the requirement, of practical internships and the application of knowledge tests, as part of the associations and professional orders, in order to guarantee access and professional practice.

In practice, the influences on the training of accountants in Brazil, mainly after the requirement of the examination of access to the professional category in 2010, considerably reduced the autonomy of Brazilian HEIs. This aspect is corroborated by a recent study, together with more than 900 higher courses in action in the country, aiming to know the organisms and their respective degrees of influence in relation to the curricular contents destined to diploma the accountants. Based on a study carried out by Bonzanini et al. [46], in addition to the professional order itself, other professional bodies, such as the United Nations (UN), IASB, and IFAC[4] seek to interfere, in a legal or contributory way, in the training of future Brazilian accountants.

[4]Respectively, International Accounting Standards Board and International Federation of Accountants.

2.3.8. Other professional associations and professional accounts: some particularities

In addition to the examples cited here, others may be brought, limited to the space of this text. One refers to the Netherlands, whose Commercial Code dates from 1837, the first document to contemplate the requirement of bookkeeping for the preparation of balance sheets of commercial establishments [34]. Although small in its geographic extent, the Netherlands became famous in the maritime trade, which provoked reflections in the accounting science. By dissociating itself from the Anglo-Saxon influence and the continental European model, due to its operations with foreign clients, its accountants and auditors needed to follow and integrate the evolution of the globalized market.

Currently, Dutch accounting is influenced by corporate law and the accounting profession, therefore, without the influence of tax legislation; there are regulations, both for the Registeraccountant (Chartered Accountant) and for the Administratieconsulent (Accounting Consultant) [34, 35]. As regards the exercise of the profession, the authority which oversees the two categories is the Netherlands Authority for the Financial Markets. For both functions, there is a need for a university degree (master's degree), 1–2 years of professional practice after the degree, and more than 3 years of practical training, in addition to passing the final exam.

In other countries, such as Australia, there has been a significant influence of the British Empire on the accounting profession since its inception as a result of exchanges since 1853, both in trade (import and export) and accounting professionals [47]. India can also be included in this example, as the colonies have in some way used the British model of qualification tests and exams, ultimately consolidating the influence of the accounting and membership principles hitherto used in the UK.

Based on the references presented in this text, the division of powers and attributions among the institutions that qualify future professionals—universities, institutes, and colleges—in relation to professional associations, orders, and councils becomes evident. According to Carvalho [48], the intervention of these entities in the space of so-called "schools" has been strongly criticized, in addition to violation of the separation of powers that must exist between academic training, professional competence of associations, and other professional bodies.

3. Disinterested action or the defense of interests?

According to Carnegie and Edwards [47], the process of professionalization does not start from the formation of an organizational body, although the organizational design is admittedly a key strategy in the pursuit of social closure recognized by the state, associated with the granting of occupational privileges and, not infrequently, to the monopoly powers, granted by the legislation. Rodrigues [3] observes that a fundamental question is related to the long period in which the conviction prevailed that the attribution in the definition of the codes of ethics and the institution of the mechanisms of self-regulation were sufficient for the defense of the public interest. However, the current perception is that it is necessary to discuss and institute new mechanisms for the external control of the professions, both in business ethics and in the ethics of accounting itself [3, 14]. However, practitioners often see such controls as threats to authority and trust in professions, resulting in social conflicts.

On the other hand, due to the recent efforts of occupations, including the use of various strategies to achieve the status of professional orders, the resumption of the teaching issue is important, and traditionally the education system is the only and necessary platform so that the future professional can ensure the credence of professional knowledge. Therefore, the professional orders have exerted the control, both directly and indirectly, on the educational contents of the academics, besides the other requirements of the professional accreditation. This relationship between the two systems of accreditation has resulted in professional closure in the form of a vicious circle, a questionable aspect, since it tends to foster forms of corporatism that are harmful to the public interest.

The primary role of the professional councils does not include the control and verification of the academic training of future professionals, whose role, as emphasized by Carvalho [48], is given to HEIs. Even if the academic title is officially accredited, it is up to the professional orders, as the last reserve of the competences, to expand certain knowledge, even after the academic formation. In this context, professional orders emerge as a controlling stakeholder in relation to universities, since they can determine the course of a profession, without entering into agreements with HEIs, which form professionals related to this professional order [49]. Once enrolled in the respective order, the members receive adequate training, in the scope of professional ethics, in relation to the legal aspects and the good practices necessary for the professional exercise, and functions that are not part of the competences of the university.

Given the need for more discussion, including the social importance of the work of professionals, something they themselves have neglected, Brint [50] affirms, in favor of the development of professional values and in particular association professionals, the importance of universities and intellectuals. This reinforces the importance of the prerogatives of associations, orders, and professional councils, as entities that guarantee the independence of the professions they represent. In this context, the first point that emerges regarding the performance of the orders and the professional councils is related to the role of inspector of the profession, granted by the state, aiming to guarantee access and professional exercise only to those who have completed all stages of training and qualification. However, the current liturgy has demonstrated the growing interest of the professional accounting associations and orders in the training of accountants.

In recent years, there have been a number of fundamental changes in accounting regulation, both in the substance of the rules and in the context of regulatory institutions [51]. Thus, accounting regulation institutions have shifted from the increasing worldwide adoption of International Financial Reporting Standards (IFRS), and in many jurisdictions, including European Union countries, this regulation has been replaced by government regulation or a private body responsible for new standards [52].

In the case of the USA, in addition to the strong performance of professional associations and boards, both in regulation and in the application of access tests, the Sarbanes-Oxley Act resulted in substantial changes in corporate governance until then acting in a self-regulated manner [53]. These changes imply adjustments in curricular content, since new laws, resolutions, and technical pronouncements have been sanctioned. Therefore, the composition of the curriculum, concomitant with the contents offered in the disciplines, can originate from several sources, such as the proposal presented by the United Nations Conference on Trade and Development (UNCTAD), from the Intergovernmental Working Group of Experts on International Standards of Accounting and Reporting (ISAR), in conjunction with the United Nations Conference on Trade and Development (UNCTAD), one of the United Nations (UN) sectors.

Other international organizations, such as the IASB and IFAC, propose regulation and accounting harmonization through a joint proposal for a global curriculum model, suggested as a benchmark for accounting professionals, aiming to standardize the qualification in all countries [51]. In several countries, among them Brazil, the preparation of a National Content Proposal for the undergraduate course in Accounting Sciences is underway, with the objective of creating a new curricular matrix.

Particularly, in relation to aspects to access to the profession, in countries such as Japan and France, there is a requirement for practical internships, defined and regulated by the respective professional order, as a requirement for effective access to the profession. In other countries, such as Germany and the Netherlands, although they do not act in the creation of accounting standards, professional associations are extremely demanding regarding the knowledge of the future professionals, aiming at the access to the respective category.

Thus, from the examples referenced in this text, it is observed that the performance of the professional accounting associations and orders is not limited to the control of professional practice, and there is evidence that it interferes, directly and indirectly, in the academic training given by HEI.

4. Conclusions

As a result of the creation of the professions, professional associations, and orders emerged as a meeting of individuals with the same job, aiming to guarantee, among other points, a private labor market, making it difficult for other members considered as not qualified for the activity. They are entities that do not have profitable activity, and their maintenance occurs through the contribution of their associates. Together with HEIs and the state, they sustain professional power from three pillars: autonomy, through the power to decide on one's own work; the expertise, or monopoly on knowledge; and credentialism, as a control in access to training provided by the state.

Associations and professional orders, in spite of their voluntary and associative nature, are political bodies whose purpose is to define, organize, ensure, and represent the interests of its members, including through the use of entry barriers within its scope of action, from the state concession.

The importance of HEIs in the formal structure that legitimates the professionalization process is emphasized in the theoretical framework of this study, together with professional associations and the state, based on the delegation of the latter. In relation to higher education, as an attribute of the professions and establishing the separation between these and occupations. Also, as central institutions that attribute licenses to work in an occupation, a point that distinguishes between laypeople and professionals.

Even in view of the autonomy envisaged for universities, in the construction of content designed to train accountants, the work of associations and professional orders, in addition to supervising the performance of its affiliates, establishes a series of requirements for the access to the profession and training in accredited schools. In addition to these requirements, in several countries, such as the USA, Germany, Japan, and Brazil, the application of professional access examinations is in charge of professional associations and professional accounting. In addition, numerous international bodies have significant influence over the content intended to train accountants. Among these, the work of the UN—by its agencies UNCTAD and ISAR, the IASB, and the IFAC—shows us that the performance of these entities goes beyond the purposes delegated by the state, directly and indirectly influencing the curricular contents taught in Higher Education Institutions.

Author details

Osmar Antonio Bonzanini[1*], Amélia Cristina Ferreira da Silva[2] and Teresa Gabriela Marques Leite[3]

*Address all correspondence to: bonzanini.prof@gmail.com

1 URI – Frederico Westphalen/RS – Brazil, Brazil

2 ISCAP, Porto, Portugal

3 ULP, Porto, Portugal

References

[1] Luchman L. Modelos Contemporâneos de Democracia e o Papel das Associações. Revista de Sociologia e Política, 2012;**20**(43):59-80

[2] Freidson E. The Professions and their Prospects. Newbury Park, USA: Sage; 2002

[3] Rodrigues M. Sociology of Professions. Oeiras, Portugal: Celta; 2002

[4] Berg B, Lune H. Qualitative Research Methods for the Social Sciences. 8th ed. Edinburgh: Pearson Education; 2014

[5] Bhattacherjee A. Social Science Research: Principles, Methods, and Pratices. 2nd ed. Tampa, Florida: Textbooks Collection; 2012

[6] Beuren I. Como Elaborar Trabalhos Monográficos em Contabilidade: Teoria e Prática. 3rd ed. São Paulo: Atlas; 2013

[7] Abbott A. The System of Professions. An Essay on the Division of Expert Labour. Chicago, USA: The University of Chicago Press; 1988

[8] Willmott H. Organising the profession: A theoretical and historical examination of the development of the major accounting bodies in the U.K. Accounting, Organizations and Society. 1986;**11**(06):555-580. Great Britain: Elsevier Science Ltd

[9] Diniz M. Os donos do saber: profissões e monopólios profissionais. Rio de Janeiro: Revan; 2001

[10] Passos T. Uma Análise dos Argumentos de Émile Durkheim e Oliveira Vianna a Respeito das Associações Profissionais. Revista Ciências Sociais em Perspectiva. Unioeste. 2014; **13**(24):161-173

[11] Cooley C. Human Nature and The Social Order. New York: Charles Scribner's Sons; 1902

[12] Durkheim E. The Division of Social in Society. New York: Macmillam; 1933

[13] Carr-Saunders A. The Profession. Oxford: Clarendon Press; 1982

[14] West A. After virtue and accounting ethics. Journal of Business Ethics. 2016,pp.1-16, Available at https://link.spinger.com /articles

[15] Brante T. Professional fields and truth regimes: In search of alternative approaches. Comparative Sociology. 2010;**9**(06):843-846. DOI: 10.1163/156913310X522615

[16] Saks M. Defining a profession: The role of knowledge and expertise. Professions & Professionalism, 2012;**02**(01):1-10

[17] Svensson K, Evetts J. Sociology of Professions, Continental and Anglo-Saxon Traditions. Sweden: Daidalos; 2010

[18] Angelim P. Profissionalismo e profissão: Teorias sociológicas e o processo de profissionalização no Brasil. Revista Espaço de Diálogo e Desconexão. 2010;**03**(01):31-46

[19] Noordegraaf M. Remaking professionals? How associations and Professional education connect professionalism and organizations. Current Sociology. 2011;**59**(4):465-488

[20] Muzio D, Kirkpatrick I. Introduction: Professions and organizations: A conceptual framework. Current Sociology. 2011;**59**(4):389-405

[21] Buesa N. A Evolução Histórica da Contabilidade como Ramo do Conhecimento. Revista Eletrônica Gestão e Negócios. 2010;**01**(01):01-16

[22] Hendriksen E, Breda M. Teoria da Contabilidade. 5th ed. São Paulo: Atlas; 2007

[23] Baker C. L'evolution d'une profession comptable globale: Une etude comparative historique en quelques pays europeens. In: Comptabilités et innovation, May 2012; Grenoble, France. pp. 01-27

[24] Miranti P. The emergence of accounting as a global profession: An introduction. Accounting History. 2014;**19**(1-2):3-11

[25] Lee T. Consolidating the public accountancy profession: The case of the proposed Institute of Chartered Accountants of Great Britain, 1988/1989. Accounting History. 2010;**15**(10):07-39

[26] Walker S. The genesis of professional organisation in English accountancy. Accounting, Organizations and Society. 1991;**29**(04):127-156

[27] Sudaby R, Viale, T. Professionals and field-level change: Institutional work and the professional project. Current Sociology. 2011;**59**(4):423-442

[28] Ballas A. The creation of the auditing profession in Greece. Accounting, Organizations and Society. 1998;**23**(08):715-736

[29] Altintas N, Yilmaz, F. The accounting profession: A descriptive study of the common and code law countries. Journal of Modern Accounting and Auditing. 2012;**8**(07):932-950

[30] Walker S. The genesis of professional organization in Scotland: A contextual analysis. Accounting, Organizations And Society. 1995;**20**(04):285-310

[31] Walker S. The defence of professional monopoly: Scottish chartered accountants and 'Satellites in The Accountancy Firmament' 1854-1914. Accounting, Organizations And Society. 1991;**16**(03):257-283

[32] Walker S. Men of small standing? Locating accountants in English society during the mid nineteenth century. European Accounting Review. 2002;**11**(02):377-399

[33] Kirkham L, Loft A. Gender and the construction of the professional accountant. Accounting Organization and Society. 1993;**18**(06):507-558

[34] Niyama J. Contabilidade Internacional. 2nd ed. São Paulo: Atlas; 2010

[35] Federation of European Accountats. Key Features on Structure and Organization of the Accountancy Profession across 30 European countries, 2012. Available from: www.fee.be

[36] Evans L, Honold K. The division of expert labour in the European audit market: The case of Germany. Critical Perspective on Accounting. 2007;**18**(01): 61-88

[37] Consiglio Nazional dei Dottori Commercialisti e Degli Esperti Contabili. The Italian Accountancy Profession; 2015. Available from: www.cndcec.it

[38] Caria A, Rodrigues L. The evolution of financial accounting in Portugal since the 1960s: A new institutional economics perspective. Accounting History. 2014;**19**(1-2):227-254

[39] Rodrigues L, Gomes D, Craig R. Corporativismo, liberalismo e a profissão contabilística em Portugal desde 1755. Revista da Câmara dos Técnicos Oficiais de Contas. 2004;**46**(01):24-39. Available from: www.academia.ed

[40] Lira M. A Importância da Aula Do Comércio Na História da Contabilidade Portuguesa. Revista Universo Contábil. 2011;**7**(02):97-113

[41] Carqueja H. As Associações e as Revistas de Contabilidade. Jornal do Técnico de Contas e da Empresa. 2002;**1**(445):296-300

[42] Japanese Institute of Certified Public Accountant. The process of Qualification as a CPA. 2015; Available from: http://www.hp.jicpa.or.jp

[43] National Association of State Boards of Accountancy. The Uniform CPA Examination. 2015; Available from: http://nasba.org/exams/cpaexam

[44] Tostes F. Formação do Contador: uma visão comparativa Brasil, França e Estados Unidos. Pensar Contábil. 2005;**07**(28):13-20

[45] Leite C. A evolução das Ciências Contábeis no Brasil. Rio de Janeiro: Editora FGV; 2005

[46] Bonzanini O, Silva A, Leite T. Critical Perspective on the Influence of Professional Organizations in the Construction of Curricula of Undergraduate Courses in Accounting. 3rd ISA Forum of Sociology – Professionalism in Education and Work. Vien, Austrian; July 2016, 2016

[47] Carnegie G, Edwards J. The construction of the professional accountant: The case of the Incorporated Institute of Accountants, Victoria (1886). Accounting, Organizations and Society. 2001;**26**(1):301-325

[48] Carvalho P. Ordens Profissionais, diferentes desafios, novas reflexões. Janus Online. 2006. Available from: www.janusonline.pt

[49] Mainardes E. Gestão de Universidades Baseada no Relacionamento com os seus Stakeholders. Tese de Doutoramento. Covilhã: Portugal: Universidade da Beira Interior; 2010

[50] Brint S. In an age of experts: The changing role of professionals ins politics and Professional life. Princeton, New Jersey: Princeton University Press; 1994.

[51] Wagenhofer A. Towards a theory of accounting regulation: A discussion of the politics of disclosure regulation along the economic cycle. Journal of Accounting and Economics. 2011;**52**(1):228-234

[52] Trabelsi R. International accounting normalization and harmonization processes across the world: History and overview. Journal on Business Review (GBR). 2015;**4**(02), p88.

[53] Gillis P, Petty R, Suddaby R. The transnational regulation of accounting: Insights, gaps and an agenda for future. Accounting, Auditing & Accountability Journal. 2014;**27**(06):894-902

Chapter 11

Behavioral Accounting and its Interactions

Filiz Angay Kutluk

Additional information is available at the end of the chapter

http://dx.doi.org/10.5772/intechopen.68972

Abstract

Behavioral accounting is a branch of accounting that is related to behavior besides the accounting knowledge. It deals with the attitude and behavior of people when they are encountered with an accounting phenomenon which determines the behavior that they will show in decision-making. This special area of accounting addresses such aspects as human information-processing behavior, judgment quality, accounting problems that are created by users and providers of accounting information, and accounting information users' and producers' decision-making skills. Behavioral research tries to find out how individuals make decisions and interact and influence other individuals, organizations, markets, and society. Behavioral accounting concept is examined under the topics of the influence of accounting information on behavior, managerial control (budget participation, nonfinancial measures, leadership, and balanced scorecard), auditing (auditor-client negotiations, auditor's judgment, and decision-making), and ethics (ethical decision-making, ethical orientation, and rationalizations on unethical behavior) in this chapter.

Keywords: behavioral accounting, accounting ethics, auditor, managerial control, influence of accounting information

1. Introduction

Behavioral accounting is a branch of accounting that is related to behavior besides the accounting knowledge. Accounting was recognized as a phenomenon that operated in contexts that forms, functioning, and consequences were interdependent with; now, it is recognized as a practice whose outcomes are mediated by the human and social contexts in which it operates [1]. It deals with the attitude and behavior of people when they are encountered with an accounting phenomenon which determines the behavior that they will show in decision-making [2].

The definition of *Behavioral Accounting* is "an offspring from the union of accounting and behavioral science; it represents the application of the method and outlook of behavioral science to accounting problems" and the *objective of Behavioral Accounting* is "to understand, explain, and predict human behavior in accounting situations or contexts" in Ref. [3] (pp. 127–128).

Behavioral accounting attempts to correct and enrich traditional approaches to accounting theory where preparer and user perceptions, attitudes, values, and behaviors are underemphasized [4]. Belkaoui defines it as "the application of behavioral science to accounting, with its basic objective being the explanation and prediction of human behavior in all possible accounting contexts" (p. 438).

"Not only does accounting summarize huge quantities of behavioral interactions, accounting measurements can become the object of behavior. Accountants account for behavior and accounting measurements can be the objective of behavior and so long as accountants make assumptions about human behavior in accounting, accountants should reexamine their behavioral assumptions be a greater understanding of and involvement in the behavioral sciences" [3] (p. 136).

Behavioral aspect of accounting is that segment of accounting which attends to develop an understanding of both cognitive (perceived) and affective (emotional) elements of human behavior that influence the decision-making process in all accounting contexts and settings. This special area of accounting addresses such aspects as human information-processing behavior, judgment quality, accounting problems that are created by users and providers of accounting information, and accounting information users' and producers' decision-making skills [5]. It was assumed that the decision-maker behaved basically as a profit maximizer in handling accounting problems; but today it is accepted that the individual exhibits psychological behavior also in accounting [6].

A well-known definition of behavioral accounting research appeared in Ref. [7] (p. 43) and was used in several studies such as in Refs. [8] and [9]: "The study of behavior of accountants or the behavior of non-accountants as they are influenced by accounting functions and reports." Behavioral accounting research contains the judgment of accountants and auditors, the influence of the accounting function and auditing function on behavior, and the influence of accounting information on judgment and decision-making of users [9].

Behavioral research tries to find out how individuals make decisions and interact and influence other individuals, organizations, markets, and society. Behavioral researchers who primarily study human actions in a variety of settings are behavioral economists and accountants, two groups of interest for this attempt. Laboratory experimentation, examination of naturally occurring (archival) data, verbal protocols, and theoretical models are from the methodologies employed [10].

The scope of behavioral accounting research has been heard from 1960s, the academic community began to examine the implications that accounting statements and information had upon decision-makers [8]. By the end of 1960s, interest in investigating the behavioral influences that accounting information on individuals and organizations grew rapidly and caused an increase in the number of published studies. In 1970s, the quality of the research was better and recognition of the behavior paradigm by the profession increased significantly [11]. In 1960s, the focus was on managerial accounting which was dealt with the accounting function on behavior; in 1970s, the focus on managerial accounting remained, but the emphasis changed to information processing by decision-makers [9]. Researchers examined judgment and decision-making and the research mainly focused on the auditors, their judgment, and the use of information. User characteristics, decision models, alternatives for communicating accounting information to users, and accounting policy-makers' behavior are also examined [12]. By the 1980s, the research was regarding all subject areas of accounting [9]. By 1997, a number of faculties taught and conducted research in behavioral paradigm, and identified their interest with the area of research application [11].

Behavioral accounting concept is examined in terms of the influence of accounting information on behavior, managerial control, auditing, and ethics in this chapter.

2. Influence of accounting information on behavior

"Accounting systems are often the most important formal sources of information in industrial organizations. They are designed to provide all levels of management with timely and reasonably accurate information to help them make decisions which *are* in agreement with their organization's goals"[13] (p. 156). While some organizations demand from accounting to assess the basis of tax or to follow up debits and credits only, some organizations demand to produce and report the information that meets the needs of the users [14].

According to Macharzina [6] (p. 5) "the process of influencing behavior through accounting information is conceived of as an interaction process, in the course of which an individual (accountant) attempts influence the behavior of one or more other individuals (focal persons) with the aid of appropriate reported information in order, as far as possible, to realize the reporter's or management's behavioral expectation."

Behavioral issues mainly appear through the communication process, not through the more traditional accounting issues such as data-processing methods. One of the domains of behavioral accounting research is the behavior of the recipient of accounting information and how variations in the information influence the behavior, because accounting communications are designed as the basis for behavior [7].

Accounting information influences decision-making mainly [15]. There are three decision-makers that decide by using accounting information:

- Decision-makers who decide concerning both activities and accounting system that prepares financial reports of the firm. This group is top management who is responsible for the preparation and presentation of financial reports and also any change in accounting system.
- Decision-makers who decide concerning activities, but do not decide concerning preparation of financial reports. They cannot change the content of accounting information, but

use it about the decisions of other activities; the result of their decisions may influence accounting system indirectly.

- People who are outside of the firm and influence the environment and activities of the firm, but who do not have direct control on the activities and works of the firm.

The behavioral research in this area examined information systems' structure, the influence of individual behavioral characteristics on the information usage and process, and the relationship between characteristics of decision task and information systems, in 1970s and 1980s [12].

Accounting information can be classified into two categories as financial information and nonfinancial information. Financial information is quantitative in nature, while nonfinancial information includes both quantitative and qualitative information. According to the managers' backgrounds and the nature of the decisions and problems they are facing, different types of accounting information are used in decision-making processes. Managers may also use financial and nonfinancial information simultaneously [16]. Financial information plays a key role in structural decision problems such as the evaluation of organizational performance, whereas nonfinancial information is considered to be more useful for unstructured decision problems like the identification of new business opportunities.

Accounting information can carry out two roles within decision-making: As decision-facilitating information and decision-influencing information [17]. Decision-facilitating information reduces decision-makers' pre-decision uncertainty and, thereby, enhance the probability to making better decisions with respect to the desired objectives. So, it is a direct input in decision-making and is supposed to improve the knowledge and anticipation to make decisions. Decision-influencing information, whose function is important only in multi-person contexts, affects (other) persons' behavior and influences managerial decision-making in the management context. Decision-influencing information enfolds its effects via behavior observation, performance measurement, and evaluation and rewarding or penalizing performance.

Two distinctive styles of information usage, namely diagnostic and interactive, are identified by prior studies [16]. A diagnostic use of the accounting information emphasizes the use of this for "diagnosis," for example, the observation of deviations of organizational processes from a preset norm which reflects a management style that relies on standard setting, measuring, comparing, and taking corrective actions, and which emphasizes monitoring, top-down control, and the pursuit of efficiency [18]. Interactive use of the accounting information emphasizes its role to engage in "interaction" with organizational participants which reflects a management style in which higher level managers involve themselves regularly and personally in the decision activities of subordinates. Managers should be experienced or trained in the use of nonfinancial accounting information in an interactive and participative style. Managers should be experienced in the typical "administrative" ways of dealing with the accounting information if they implement cost-reduction policies control.

Managers with a dominant administrative background tend to use accounting information more diagnostically than interactively, and seem to emphasize performance evaluation and prefer to use financial information for decision-making process [18]. By contrast, managers who adopt an interactive style of information usage tend to use nonfinancial information more than financial information in decision-making. Managers who have a balanced background may be most effective to resist pressures toward both cost reduction and quality enhancement. Different styles of information usage have direct implications on the behavior of managers. Senior managers who adopt a diagnostic style of information usage pay attention toward the achievement of planned outcomes [16]. They direct less attention to the tools adopted by lower level managers for achieving the outcomes. Most discussions on organizational outcomes are in formal reviews form and are conducted at the end of set operating periods. Within operating periods, exchanges of accounting information are limited. Continuous exchanges of information occur between organizational members when an interactive style of information usage is adopted by managers. Discussions on organizational outcomes tend to be less formal and can be held at any time.

The suitability of the styles of information usage to managers changes according to the types of decision problems they face; a diagnostic style of information usage is suitable for addressing routine, structural decision problems like organizational performance evaluation and the determination of rewards of the subordinates whereas an interactive style of information usage is more suitable for addressing unstructured decision problems [16].

Accounting information users' personal characteristics and their influence on decision-making should be well known by accounting information preparers and presenters [15]. Users' cognitive process and perceptions will influence the usage and interpretation of accounting information; it is supposed that decisions are influenced by prejudice of perceptions of decision-makers. Trust on decisions and information demand significantly link with the tolerance of uncertainty.

Behavior of accounting information producers depends on four major factors of quality of financial information [5]:

- Relevance: It means that accounting information should be relevant to decision-making.
- Faithful representation: Information should be complete, confirmable, and neutral.
- Comparability: It should enable that similarities in and differences between two sets of economic phenomena would be identified by the users.
- Understandability: It means that users with reasonable knowledge of business and economic activities or financial accounting should be able to realize the meaning of the information.

3. Managerial control

Many forms of empirical research have been taken and many topics analyzed over the years in management accounting research such as to what extent managers probably succeed with their management accounting and control systems in various settings [19]. The behavioral research in this area analyzed the impact of budgetary control on individual performance and how people affect budgets by analyzing individual differences, motivation, and risk aversion and helped us to understand the variability and complexity of people about work and performance. Since 1970s and 1980s, the objective of management accounting seemed to encourage and assist managers in making desirable decisions in organizations and motivating others to perform the results of the decisions [12]. The benefit of behavioral accounting research may be more probable to be seen in the managerial area than in any other aspect of accounting due to the direct and observable relationships between management accounting and behavior in organizations.

A significant portion of BAR also focuses on noneconomic dimensions such as trusting behavior, cooperation, and the expectation of a fair share of any rewards that influence decision-makers in directions at odds with the self-interest and wealth-maximizing assumptions These can lead to greater monetary returns to the decision-maker in certain settings, but they also can expose the decision-maker to greater risk. Other characteristics of the work environment including the national culture can also influence the expectations and behavior of the decision-maker [20].

3.1. Budget participation

Budgets and standards direct people to a certain target and motivate them and also create a criterion for performance evaluation. The extent to which budgets and standards have an influence on behavior depends on the difficulty level of budget targets and if these targets are prepared by the participation of decision-makers. Objectives, budgets, and standards affect human behavior, and the degree of this influence depends on the accessibility of the objectives [15].

One of the reasons that superiors decide to rely heavily on budget targets to evaluate their subordinates is the positive outcome which means that employee job satisfaction and performance are improved when a high budget emphasis evaluative style is accompanied by a high budgetary participation [21]. According to the prior studies, an evaluative style will probably be associated with favorable behavioral outcomes if it emphasizes the importance of budget targets used together with high budgetary participation. Brownell [22] referred that "superiors who exhibit a budget-constrained style and place primary emphasis in their evaluation of subordinates on budget achievement, will provide appropriate reinforcement only for those individuals who are heavy involved and influential in the budget-setting process" [21, 22]. This indicates that budgetary participation isn't independent of an evaluative style which emphasizes meeting budget targets, but rather it is a consequence of this type of evaluative style [21]. Budgetary participation moderates the impact of supervisory evaluative style on performance; it has a positive effect on performance [22].

Another reason that superiors decide to rely heavily on budget targets to evaluate their subordinates which is associated with high budgetary participation is based on the suggestion that it is fair [21]. If superiors choose a high emphasis on budget targets as an evaluation style, they will also choose high budgetary participation because of a forceful need. In this evaluative style, the level of budget targets is important to the subordinates because their performance will be assessed against these targets which may have important effects on the interest of subordinates; so it is only fair that they have a role in determining the levels of realistic and attainable budget targets. Generally, superiors care about to be seen as being fair among their subordinates; therefore, superiors who adopt an evaluative style that has a high emphasis on budget targets will decide to allow their subordinates high budgetary participation to be perceived as fairer.

The main purpose of subordinates' participation in the budgeting process, in superior's side, is to gain information from the subordinate that is useful to plan and coordinate production, reduce uncertainty, and thereby increase profitability [23]. Budgetary slack is "the result of employees misrepresenting their productive capabilities while participating in their budget setting process" [24]. This could result in overstatement of costs and understatement of revenues and profits and could be harmful for the financial well-being of the organization.

3.2. Nonfinancial measures

Performance evaluation is important to employees as their evaluations may be closely linked to their wages and promotions, so they are likely to be concerned with the fairness of the performance measures used [25]. Organizations are facing deep pressure to remain competitive and therefore adapt customer-driven strategies aimed at ensuring high levels of quality and innovation. So organizations expect from employees to perform and show success in possibly many diverse and complex roles. Nonfinancial performance measures such as defect rate, customer satisfaction rate, and number of new products launched may be suited to such contemporary situations as they are not linked to the annual reporting circles and need not be expressed in monetary terms. They may measure progressions in product quality and innovation necessary to maintain and improve customer satisfaction and retention.

Nonfinancial measures that are able to capture the long-term performance of employees' actions are suggested to be used in performance evaluations as they are more flexible, comprehensive, and therefore easier for the employees to associate with; by using them, employees may more likely to realize a long-term perspective of the position in the organization [26].

Employees are measured on the quality of their work, the initiatives they undertake, and in areas in which they have control and they are therefore likely to perceive the use of nonfinancial measures as a fair evaluation of their performance [25]. So, the use of nonfinancial performance measures is likely to be positively related to employee role clarity as it is a means of providing the necessary information to express the role of employees so that they are aware of what is expected of them.

Nonfinancial measures can be seen as a communication tool; the adoption of them as performance evaluation criteria will promote trust within the superior-subordinate relationship [25]. Procedural fairness perceptions are influenced by the trust in superior-subordinate relationships; subordinates are likely to believe that their supervisor will appraise their performance fairly, so the trust the employees have for their supervisors will likely be translated into faith in the performance evaluation system. However, if trust is not established between them, this would cause subordinates to suspect that their superiors may be deceptive and selfish and may lead to a perception that the performance evaluation procedures are unfair.

3.3. Leadership

Leadership, as a social influence process, only really works when people have faith that the manager is directing them toward a worthwhile goal and allow themselves to be led to achieve an organizational goal, which can be summed up in the concept of trust [27]. "Leadership involves activating and engaging the head, heart, hands, and spirit of employees for a purpose that is greater than the individual manager or any one employee that means developing behaviors that favorably impact tasks, build relationships, and bring about transformations" (p. 174).

In transactional leadership, managers create and maintain high-quality interactions with employees to meet the organizational goals by using rewards, power, and authorization. Transactional leadership isn't sufficient to engage and motivate most employees in the long term. Transformational leadership is about motivation of the employees by orienting them to a greater organizational goal beyond any individual short-term goals by creating a tough vision, enabling them to turn the vision into a personal reality, and empowering them to maintain the transformation. Transformational leadership can encourage the growth of a learning organization. An integrated approach is required for an effective management; managers will always make sure that employees receive rewards and recognitions in a transactional meaning, but leadership also requires the skill to provide employees looking beyond their current situation and focus on greater purpose.

3.4. Balanced scorecard

Senior executives realize that organization's measurement system affects the managers' and employees' behavior; in the 1990s, the traditional financial measure-oriented performance evaluation system was challenged by managers and academic researchers [28, 29]. Kaplan and Norton [30] claimed that financial measures were inadequate for the evaluation of the nonfinancial aspects of management performance, and managers may stress short-term financial goals rather than their organization's long-term interests in the case of exclusive use of financial measures in performance evaluations [29, 30]. They promoted using the balanced scorecard (BSC) to evaluate all aspects of managerial performance. A typical BSC has four measurement categories, including financial, customer, internal business process, and employee learning and growth perspectives; generally, the majority of the last three are made up of nonfinancial measures. Balanced scorecard uses both financial and nonfinancial measures with emphasizing nonfinancial measures; therefore, it is important for organizations to understand how the various performance measures can influence the behavior of employees by identifying the essential factors required for the success of performance evaluation systems [26].

If the top management uses both financial and nonfinancial measures in their performance evaluations when they evaluate the performance of middle-level managers, the middle-level managers are more likely to use both financial and nonfinancial measures in their subordinates' evaluation [29]. On the contrary, if the top management uses just financial measures and ignores nonfinancial measures in the evaluation of their middle-level managers' performance, their prejudice will spread to the next level of management via the contagion effect, who may put excessive emphasis on financial measures in performance evaluations as well (p. 104). As a result, top managers should use an evaluative style where all measures in the BSC are reflected in evaluating performance.

4. Auditing

Accounting information users need reliable and sufficient information for decision-making; it's the duty of the business management to provide this information [31]. But there may be a possibility that the information isn't reliable because of work load and sophistication in accounting transactions, distance of the users from business, and the tendency of the information providers. So the necessity arises to present audited financial statements to the users to decrease the risk of unreliable information. Some of the users may wish to invest, willing to loan money, or wish to merge; therefore, there must be a procedure to verify the accuracy of the company's financial status [32]. The independent auditor's task begins at this point.

"Auditing is an investigative and information-processing activity, which evolved in response to the need for independently verified stewardship reports" [33] (p. 89). Audit activity includes financial report data examination followed by an audit opinion on the report mainly compliance audit, internal audit, and operational audit. Our main focus will be on independent auditor who is responsible to examine and report the financial statements.

The auditor collects and evaluates relevant and reliable information, and applies professional judgment in choosing among alternatives also by consultation with other professionals who are knowledgeable in the area. The auditor should use critical-thinking skills in the development of a solution or an opinion on the financial statements. Conducting a proper audit requires professional judgment. Relevant knowledge and experience application to the facts and circumstances are essential for interpreting the relevant ethical requirements and GAAS and the informal decisions required during the audit process [34].

Independent auditors offer services to their clients and get payment from the clients for their services, but they may face conflicting loyalties because of the opposing interests between the public and clients; their main responsibility is to guarantee the interest of public [32]. "The auditor's obligations are to certify that public reports depicting a corporation's financial status fairly present its financial position and operations; shortly their fiduciary responsibility is to the public trust and "independence" from the client is fundamental in order for that trust to be honoured" (p. 118). The AICPA Code of Professional Conduct mentions two kinds of independence: Member who provides auditing and other attestation services should be independent in fact and appearance [32, 35].

4.1. Auditor-client negotiations

Financial statements are a product of auditor-client negotiations that is an important link between the audit and the quality of financial statement [36]. Unaudited financial statements of the clients are the first move of starting of negotiations. The first move is a key factor of the other side's actions and often estimates the first mover's attitude during the negotiation process, where client's signal becomes clear as negotiations progress. A client who refuses to post an adjustment proposed by the author may be viewed as being contentious or a client who willingly concedes on an issue after the initial proposal of an auditor may be viewed as concessionary by the author. These contentiousness and concession acts from both the auditor and client are viewed as tactics in a negotiation setting.

It is found that the negotiations are often influenced by negotiators who use tactics [36]. Many research about the use of concessionary tactics found that both auditors and clients reciprocate to concessionary negotiation tactics, such as a first move concession of an unreasonable item made by client may result as auditors probably waive material adjustment or to influence clients to be more likely to record adjusting entries, auditors may use concessions during negotiations. Findings of researches about the usage of contentious tactics show that clients indicated that they would use contentious position during a negotiation with an auditor, whereas auditors will be less likely to waive adjustments as responding to a client who was contentious in the past.

4.2. Auditor's judgment and decision-making

Auditors are required to exercise professional skepticism when making judgments based on audit evidence without being influenced by clients [37, 38]. But there are some evidences that clients may influence auditor judgment through ingratiation which can influence the judgment of the target in many settings [37]. Prior research stated that affect toward the client can influence auditor judgment; as an example, inexperienced auditors who felt negative affect toward the client assess a higher risk of inventory obsolescence than who did not experience affect toward the client. When the auditor likes the client, his/her fraud-risk assessments are lower than when he/she dislikes the client. Ingratiation is indicated as a successful influence tactic by many researches. When persuasiveness of ingratiation is examined, it can be said that sources with high incentive to influence the target have less influence on the target and are less persuasive than sources with low incentive. "When the client ingratiates, auditors are more likely to comply with the requests of clients with low incentive to influence the auditor than with requests of clients with high incentive. This result indicates that ingratiation magnifies the effect of client incentive on auditor judgment" (p. 70).

One of the most important parts of auditing contains decision-making and judgment which are the daily work role of auditors [33]. The ability to make judgments requires education, experience, and expertise, and a measure of auditor's judgmental quality is the degree of accuracy of his/her decisions. One of the factors that impact the auditor's decision-making may be firm size which is found by some researches that accounting disclosure decisions differed between auditors employed at large-size or small-size firms. Another factor that impacts the decision-making may be the auditor's psychological make-up such as tolerance to ambiguity which is closely linked to auditor decision-making. The authors who are tolerant of ambiguity may decide quickly and have more confidence in their decisions.

"When people make decisions in situations which are 'normatively ambiguous' their decision processes and decisions are influenced by knowing whether or not they are going to be accountable to another and suggests that the known view of the person they will be accountable to will influence their decision" [39].

When the judgment performance of experienced auditors versus inexperienced auditors is concerned, experienced auditors will outperform inexperienced auditors because of their domain-specific knowledge, if task and experience levels are properly matched [9].

A strong tone at the top that consists of the culture of control consciousness, integrity, and ethical values from upper level management affects ethical decision-making of mid- and lower level employees [40]. In organizations, upper level management is critical to establishing an ethical tone, but it is seen that ethical decision-making of the staff is also equally impacted by the ethical tones set by lower level supervisors. "The low ethical tone of supervisors at the top and/or bottom may cause entry level staff auditors to construe unethical situations as devoid of ethical implications, such that entry level staff auditors may act more unethically if either of their supervisors exhibit a low ethical tone" (p. 80). It is anticipated that entry-level staff auditors will follow their senior's tone rather than their partners tone as individuals will be more influenced by close in-group members who are similar to them than by out-group members who are dissimilar to them.

5. Ethics

"Ethics is a philosophical discipline that aims to apply actions and rules in keeping with the concepts of right and wrong. This notion is widely related to legitimacy, which is defined as the quality of legal, justice or equity. The legal bases, whether ethical or moral, are the root of legitimacy which is based on authority" [41].

Accounting uses ethics to provide the appropriate behavior of accountants who must adopt certain ethical values and expected to be honest, modest, just, dignified, prudent, zealous, responsible, loyal, innovative, respectful, tolerant, and independent [41]. Accountants must become ethically involved when they are aware that their figures have an effect; they cannot absolve themselves of the responsibility of effecting behavior [7].

5.1. Ethical decision-making

Ethical decision-making abilities and ethical behavior of accountants have been researched and found that the recognition of individual of his/her role as a moral agent is an important factor in ethical judgment and actions. "If a decision isn't recognized as ethical in nature, moral schemata will not be used to address the issue; this ability to recognize the ethical nature of a decision is referred to as ethical sensitivity" [42].

Several cognitive-based models of ethical decision-making have been borrowed mainly from psychology and extended into business and accounting paradigms. The foundation of these models is that Rest's (1986) four-stage model is the basis of these models which specifies four distinct sequential processes that individuals must take to involve an ethical dimension in their decisions, and behaviors are described below [43, 44, 45]:

- **Ethical sensitivity**: Refers to the interpretation of a particular situation, recognition of the ethical issue(s), awareness of what actions are possible, and determination of what the consequences may be on the parties involved.
- **Ethical judgment** (or ethical reasoning): It is about which manner is ethically justifiable; individual makes a moral judgment about the actions and chooses one of them as being morally right.
- **Ethical intention** (ethical motivation): Refers to intention to act in the morally right manner by giving primacy of ethical values higher than other values.
- **Ethical behavior**: Refers to constancy to follow through on the chosen course of action to perform in the morally right way.

"Researchers have found that the other people that an individual encounters in a professional environment influence ethical behavior significantly irrespective whether their behavior is consistent with the individual's ethics or not" [42]. The effect level may be influenced by the organizational distance between the parties and by their relative authority.

5.2. Ethical orientation

Accounting professionals' perceptions of the ethical environment of their firm may be influenced by their own ethical orientation which is driven by two characteristics: idealism and relativism [42, 45]. Idealism reflects the extent to which individuals attribute to universal moral rules and believes that desirable consequences can be generated without violating moral guidelines; by contrast, relativism reflects the degree to which individuals view moral decisions as a function of the particular situation and rejects absolute moral rules to guide behavior.

A direct link between ethical orientation and moral judgments was not present every time according to many researches, but significant relationships are found between ethical orientation and personal feelings about decisions and individual characteristics [45]. Results of some researches indicate that, subsequent to a moral violation, individuals low in relativism feel much more negatively about themselves than individuals high in relativism. Also, highly idealistic individuals feel much more positive about themselves than individuals low in idealism subsequent to a moral violation resulting in positive consequences for others.

5.3. Rationalizations of unethical behavior

The duty of the accountant within the firm is to portray the firm's financial situation correctly and truthfully. But sometimes, there may be misstatements. Managers may use some rationalizations as a guide to justify suspect behavior and to warn against misrepresentation of financial statements [31]:

- The first rationalization for unethical behavior may be the belief that an activity is within reasonable ethical and legal limits; in other words, it is (may) not actually illegal or immoral (p. 140). If there is a hesitation to perform the activity, it means there may be doubts about its accuracy; in this situation, the best way may be not to do it.

http://dx.doi.org/10.5772/intechopen.68972

- The second to justify unethical behavior may be the belief that an activity is in the best interest of the individual or the company; in other words, to undertake the activity would somehow be expected from the individual (pp. 141–142). The accountant is expected to be loyal to the company and it may require doing things for the interest of the company that he/she would not do as an objective individual. Even he/she must be loyal to the firm first, objectivity and obligation to the public is required by accountant's code of ethics.
- The third rationalization for unethical behavior may be the belief that an activity is safe because it will never be discovered by anyone (p. 143). Doing this activity with that belief is a rationalization, but not a justification and the behavior is wrong.
- The final reason to justify unethical behavior may be the belief that the company will condone the activity and even protect the person who attempts it because the activity helps the company (p. 144). This belief depends on the integrity of the leaders of the company; they excuse unethical activity, they will condone the loyalty of the accountant, but this lasts only if the unethical activity remains undiscovered. But being in a culture that expecting unethical behavior means that the integrity is in danger.

6. Conclusion

Accountants emphasize short-run measures and may not pay attention to the behavioral consequences because they have been conditioned by their education and organizational experience; this is similar with the focus of top management [12]. Behavioral accounting research is dealt with improving long-term performance. A major contribution on this point would be to include more variables such as human resource accounting in financial-reporting practices and less emphasis on short-run performance. The potential contributions of behavioral research in accounting will not be sufficiently realized until management attitudes change. Behavioral accountants should make great effort to prevail on their academic colleagues to realize the importance of the behavioral implications of accounting.

Accounting profession needs ethical professionals with ethical awareness and sensitivity and capable of considering various variables in decision-making. Various fields in behavioral accounting would improve their perspective [46]. Accounting academicians should consider inclusion behavioral accounting courses in postgraduate curriculum to train potential accounting professionals having a broad perspective.

Author details

Filiz Angay Kutluk

Address all correspondence to: angay@akdeniz.edu.tr

Department of Banking Finance, Faculty of Applied Sciences, Akdeniz University, Antalya, Turkey

References

[1] Hopwood AG. Behavioral accounting in retrospect and prospect. Behavioral Research in Accounting. 1989;**1**:1-22

[2] Usul H. Davranıssal Muhasebe. Ankara: Asil Yayın Dağıtım Ankara; 2007. p. 98

[3] Report of the Committee on the Relationship of Behavioral Science and Accounting. The Accounting Review. 1974;**49** (Committee Reports: Supplement to Volume XLIX of the Accounting Review):127-139. Available from: http://www.jstor.org/stable/pdf/244907.pdf [Accessed: March 13, 2017]

[4] Rogow R. Book Review of " Belkaoui, A. Behavioral Accounting: The Research and Practical Issues. Westport, CT: Ouorum Books; 1989. pp. 1-178" In: Kunin, T, Book Review Section. Personnel Psychology. 1990;**43**(2):438-442). Available from: http://web.b.ebscohost.com/ehost/pdfviewer/pdfviewer?sid=294653fc-d366-4f6b-a34b-31f284f61f75%40sessionmgr103&vid=0&hid=102 [Accessed: March 13, 2017

[5] Kurawa JM. Issues in behavioral aspects of accounting. In: Dandago KI, editor. Advanced Accounting Theory and Practice. 1st ed. London: Adonis & Abbey Publishers Ltd; 2009. pp. 221-233. ISBN: 9781906704223

[6] Macharzina K. On the integration of behavioural science into accounting theory. Management International Review (MIR). 1973;**13**(2/3):3-14

[7] Hofstedt TR, Kinard JC. A strategy for behavioral accounting research. The Accounting Review. 1970;**45**(1):38-54

[8] Lord AT. The development of behavioral thought in accounting, 1952-1981. Behavioral Research in Accounting. 1989;**1**:124-149

[9] Bamber EM. Opportunities in accounting behavioral research. Behavioral Research in Accounting. 1993;**5**:1-29

[10] Birnberg JG, Ganguly AR. Is neuro accounting waiting in the wings? An essay. Accounting, Organizations and Society. 2012;**37**:1-13

[11] Dyckman TR. The ascendancy of the behavioral paradigm in accounting: The last 20 years. Behavioral Research in Accounting. 1998;**10**(Suppl):1-10

[12] Caplan EH. Behavioral accounting: A personal view. Behavioral Research in Accounting. 1989;**1**:109-123

[13] Hopwood AG. An empirical study of the role of accounting data in performance evaluation. Empirical research in accounting: Selected studies. Journal of Accounting Research. 1972;**10**(Suppl):156-182

[14] Sevilengül O. Genel Muhasebe. 17th ed. Ankara: Gazi Kitabevi; 2014. p. 813

[15] Kısakürek MM, Pekcan A. The view of accounting information from different perspective. Cumhuriyet Üniversitesi İktisadi ve İdari Bilimler Dergisi. 2005;**6**(2):107-125

[16] Mohd Yusof NA, Hui WS, Rahman IKA, Alam NOS, Tse MSC. Style of information usage and use of accounting information: A Malaysian study. Asian Review of Accounting. 2012;**20**(1):20-33. DOI: 10.1108/13217341211224709

[17] Wall F, Greiling D. Accounting information for managerial decision-making in shareholder management versus stakeholder management. Review of Managerial Science. 2011;**5**:91-135. DOI: 10.1007/s11846-011-0063-8

[18] Naranjo-Gil D, Hartmann F. How CEOs use management information systems for strategy implementation in hospitals. Health Policy. 2007;**81**:29-41. DOI: 10.1016/j.healthpol.2006.05.009

[19] Kihn LA. Performance outcomes in empirical management accounting research: Recent developments and implications for future research. International Journal of Productivity and Performance Management. 2010;**59**(5):468-492

[20] Birnberg JG. A proposed framework for behavioral accounting research. Behavioral Research In Accounting. 2011;**23**(1):1-43. DOI: 10.2308/bria.2011.23.1.1

[21] Lau CM, Tan SLC. Budget targets as performance measures: The mediating role of participation and procedural fairness. In: Epstein MJ, Lee JY, editors. Advances in Management Accounting. 1st ed. Bingley, UK: Emerald Group Publishing; 2012. pp. 151-185

[22] Brownell P. The role of accounting data in performance evaluation, budgetary participation and organizational effectiveness. Journal of Accounting Research. 1982;**20**(1):12-27

[23] Hobson JL, Melone MJ, Stevens DE. Determinants of moral judgments regarding budgetary slack: An experimental examination of pay scheme and personal values. Behavioral Research in Accounting. 2011;**23**(1):87-107. DOI: 10.2308/bria.2011.23.1.87

[24] Venkatesh R. The budget participation-budgetary slack relationship: The role of psychological capital. Journal of Theoretical Accounting Research. 2014;**9**(2):1-20

[25] Lau CM, Berry E. Nonfinancial performance measures: How do they affect fairness of performance evaluation procedures? In: Epstein MJ, Manzoni JF, Davila A, editors. Performance Measurement and Management Control: Innovative Concepts and Practices. 1st ed. Bingley, UK: Emerald Group Publishing; 2010. pp. 285-308

[26] Chia DPS, Lau CM, Tan SLC. The relationships between performance measures and employee outcomes: the mediating roles of procedural fairness and trust. In: Davila A, Epstein MJ, Manzoni JF, editors. Performance Measurement and Management Control: Behavioral Implications and Human Actions. 1st ed. Bingley, UK: Emerald Group Publishing; 2014. pp. 203-232

[27] Reis M, Geller J. A Manager's Guide to Human Behavior. 5th ed. New York, NY: (American Management Association) AMACOM; 2010. p. 244

[28] Kaplan RS, Norton DP. The balanced scorecard-measures that drive performance. Harvard Business Review. 1992;**70**(1):71-79

[29] Kang GG, Roline AC. The contagion effect in performance evaluations in the context of balanced scorecards. In: Epstein MJ, Lee JY, editors. Advances in Management Accounting. 1st ed. Bingley, UK: Emerald Group Publishing; 2012. pp. 101-124

[30] Kaplan RS, Norton DP. Strategic learning & the balanced scorecard. Strategy & Leadership. 1996;**24**(5):18-24

[31] Bozkurt N. Muhasebe Denetimi. 6th ed. Istanbul: Alfa Basım Yayım; 2012. p. 379

[32] Duska R, Duska BS, Ragatz JA. Accounting Ethics. 2nd ed. West Sussex, UK: Wiley-Blackwell; 2011. p. 237

[33] Parker LD, Ferris KR, Otley DT. Accounting for the Human Factor. Australia: Prentice Hall; 1989. p. 212

[34] Weirich TR, Churyk NT, Pearson TC. Accounting & Auditing Research and Databases. New Jersey: John Wiley & Sons Inc.; 2012. p. 255

[35] American Institute of Certified Public Accountants (AICPA). 2002. Consideration of Fraud in a Financial Statement Audit. AU Section 316. Source: SAS No. 99; SAS No. 113. 2002. Available from: https://www.aicpa.org/Research/Standards/AuditAttest/DownloadableDocuments/AU-00316.pdf [Accessed: March 28, 2017]

[36] Bergner JM, Peffer SA, Ramsay RJ. Concession, contention and accountability in auditor client negotiations. Behavioral Research in Accounting. 2016;**28**(1):15-25. DOI:10.2308/bria-51146

[37] Robertson JC. The effects of ingratiation and client incentive on auditor judgment. Behavioral Research in Accounting. 2010;**22**(2):69-86. DOI: 0.2308/bria.2010.22.2.69

[38] American Institute of Certified Public Accountants (AICPA) Code of Professional Conduct. 2014. Available from: http://www.aicpa.org/Research/Standards/CodeofConduct/Down loadableDocuments/2014December15ContentAsof2016August31CodeofConduct.pdf [Accessed: March 28, 2017]

[39] Buchman TA, Tetlock PE, Reed RO. Accountability and auditors' judgments about contingent events. Journal of Business Finance & Accounting. 1996;**23**(3):379-398

[40] Pickerd JS, Summers SL, Wood DA. An examination of how entry-level staff auditors respond to tone at the top vis-a'-vis tone at the bottom. Behavioral Research in Accounting. 2015;**27**(1):79-98. DOI: 0.2308/bria-50918

[41] Youssef A, Rachid OM. Ethical basis of the international financial reporting standards (IFRS). Malaysian Accounting Review. 2015;**14**(1):1-24

[42] Shaub MK, Finn DW, Munter P. The effects of auditors' ethical orientation on commitment and ethical sensitivity. Behavioral Research in Accounting. 1993;**5**:145-169

[43] Rest, J. Moral Development: Advances in Research and Theory. New York: Praeger Publishers; 1986. 241 p

[44] Martinov-Bennie N, Mladenovic R. Investigation of the impact of an ethical framework and an integrated ethics education on accounting students' ethical sensitivity and judgment. Journal of Business Ethics. 2015;**127**:189-203. DOI: 10.1007/s10551-013-2007-5

[45] Patterson DM. Causal effects of regulatory, organizational and personal factors on ethical sensitivity. Journal of Business Ethics. 2001;**30**:123-159

[46] Bobek DD, Hageman AM, Radtke RR. The influence of roles and organizational fit on accounting professionals' perceptions of their firms' ethical environment. Journal of Business Ethics. 2015;**126**:125-141. DOI: 10.1007/s10551-013-1996-4

Chapter 12

The Future of Accounting Profession in an Era of Start-Ups

Burak Özdoğan

Additional information is available at the end of the chapter

http://dx.doi.org/10.5772/intechopen.69264

Abstract

With the help of the advancements in the field of communication and information technologies, the number of IT-based software has rapidly increased and the capabilities of high-budget enterprise resource planning (ERP) software widely used by large enterprises have begun to be offered to small and medium-sized enterprises (SMEs). In this chapter, cloud computing and other information technologies based accounting start-ups are covered, and the effects of these highly increasing start-ups on the profession of accounting have been addressed. In conclusion, it has been predicted that technology-based accounting start-ups with both accounting professionals and entrepreneurs having an expertise on information technologies will come together and will increase in the future, and cloud-based accounting initiatives will shape the future of the profession.

Keywords: accounting profession, technology, start-up, big data, accountant

1. Introduction

Accounting is a profound profession that has existed since the birth of civilizations, and its marks have been seen ever since BC and today people still use it [1]. Accounting, which is an essential business function and management tool, has always been able to restructure itself in all important transformations in enterprises and its forms in a new transformation today. This transformation includes both technological developments that transform the current form of the accounting and intellectual conversions that transform the purpose and ways in which accounting is used.

With the developments in communication technologies, accessing and investments costs are rapidly increased, and that situation led to the emergence of start-ups which enable small and medium-sized enterprises (SMEs) to benefit from many support systems of decisions that were previously available to large and institutional enterprises. Start-ups are newly established but have a high rate of growth and growth potential, have focused on especially SMEs in corporate services and have transformed accounting functions like operational functions into support-system of decisions for SMEs. In this process, start-ups, which use actively cloud computing, big data analysis and artificial intelligence technologies, have become a major opponent to the traditional business model and have influenced the future role of the accounting.

In this chapter, the predictions of the future of the accounting profession are shared by taking into account the technologies that are being used in today, reflections of these into business and effects on the accounting sector.

2. Technologies of today and their reflection to business

From 16 years now, it was 2001 when MIT Technology Review was announced 'Natural Language Processing' technology as one of the '10 Breakthrough Technology List' [2] of the year which is basically about the computers that can understand the daily language of humans and interact with them in a way as close as the natural communication of humans in between. It may seem familiar since we have 'Hey Siri!' or 'Okay Google!' in use today. It is not actually breakthrough today to interact with a computer in a very close way to the natural human interaction. Today, in the same list, there are immune engineering, reusable rockets, robots that teach each other and autonomous cars [3].

2.1. Technologies of today

All the technological advancements that we expect to have in future and that we used up already have transformational effects on the way we produce, buy, sell and consume. Technology is the major influencer of business and of its functions since the modern businesses that we establish today are strongly connected with technological advancements in many ways. The most important technological advancements that affect businesses directly can be listed shortly as follows:

- **Cloud computing and big data:** Cloud computing technology or simply referred as cloud is an on-demand server system that can be reached any time or anywhere to access or store data, applications or other services. Although it is not a brand-new technology which was also popular at the years of 'dotcom' bubble, with the help of advancements in communication technologies, infrastructure and the operational costs of cloud computing decreased significantly [4, 5]. Cloud technology has brought many advantages for businesses such as lower operating costs of working online, higher level of data security, access from anywhere and anytime [6]. On the other hand, with the advancements in both cloud and other information technologies, companies have faced with a stream of data from every aspect of their business and that stream allowed companies to analyse that big data and get insights that are hidden before [7, 8]. According to IBM, human being is creating 2.5 quintillion bytes of data every day and 90% of the world's data today has been created in the last

2 years alone [9]. Big data are defined by Gartner as 'high volume, high velocity and/or high variety information assets that demand cost-effective, innovative forms of information processing that enable enhanced insight, decision-making and process automation' [10]. IBM adds 'Veracity' to this definition as uncertainty of data [11]. The high volume, velocity, variety and veracity data can come in as company data, consumer data, sensor data or syndicated data [12]. According to the results of a research that conducted to the executives of 330 public North American companies, companies perform better on objective measures of financial and operational results when they characterize themselves as data-driven [13].

- **Artificial intelligence:** Artificial intelligence (AI) can be defined as using human intelligence elements by machines in order to complete tasks that require human intelligence. AI technology in today's context has a historical background that goes more than 70 years [14]. However, with the developments in the technology at last 10 years, the AI has become a strategic tool for businesses from smart devices to software. According to a report from Tractica, $40.6 billion will be spent on artificial intelligence systems for enterprises from 2015 to 2024 [15].

2.2. Technology-driven business and revenue models

The effect of technological advancements to the way of doing business is well known since the development of steam power machines [16]. Today, as a consequence of advancements in technologies mentioned above, new business models for traditional sectors have changed the way of competition [17, 18]. Hui claims that today's companies should reconsider their business models in order to stay in the competition [19].

With the wide spread use of cloud technology, many traditional software companies have changed their business model as subscribing the customers to the software service instead of selling the software. This new model is called as Software as a Service (SaaS). SaaS model creates an efficient and productive system for the customers and the software companies by decreasing the infrastructure investments, operating costs and making the data entry and monitoring activities seamlessly from anytime and anywhere with an internet-connected device [20, 21]. According to report of Gartner, SaaS cloud application services market growth 20.3% with $37.7 billion [22].

Janssen and Joha compare traditional software and SaaS characteristics as shown in **Table 1** [23]:

Characteristics	Traditional software	SaaS
Ownership	Buying of software	Renting of software without taking ownership
Pricing model	Up-front investments and costs for local installation/maintenance including licenses	Pay-per-use or pay-per-period
IT function	Buys, installs, develops, implements and maintains their own software	Subscribe, plug in and use; no need for an IT function and no concern of updates
Expertise needed	In-house software expertise needed for control and maintenance	Usage expertise required

Table 1. The Characteristics of Traditional Software and SaaS.

On the other hand, AI and machine-learning technologies allowed companies to create services like chatbots which can interact with humans and operate as the same as a human operator. Chatbots can be defined as a software for communicating with humans in a natural way in order to complete a task such as shop assistance or appointment schedule. Chatbots are getting more and more attention from businesses since it can reduce operating costs and increase customer satisfaction [24, 25].

The transformation in technology influenced the starting new era with business ideas and entrepreneurship. Many entrepreneurs have begun to build their business on the technologies detailed above. Businesses with cloud-based initiatives, SaaS revenue models, chatbots and other artificial intelligence applications are viewed as an important opportunity by entrepreneurs of the new generation. These small or medium-sized initiatives especially not so much paid attention by big companies, which have chosen the business as their market, have grown rapidly and led to the emergence of the entrepreneurial ecosystem within this market.

3. The effects of technology on accounting

Accounting is one of the professions that can adapt quickly to the requirements and competencies of the present times. It has a rooted tradition and historical background. The accounting profession, which has undertaken the necessary transformations without breaking away from its basic principles in coordination with all technological transformations since the period of record-keeping was occurring by hand, plays a critical role in the decision-making processes of enterprises as an important information system today [26]. The accounting information system can be defined as the collection, storage and processing of financial and non-financial accounting transactions through information processing technologies in order to support management decisions [27]. The accounting information system is integrated into the enterprise resource planning (ERP) flow. Thus, the stronger information-flow can be provided.

This transformation of accounting has led to the linking of information technology and the accounting profession to each other and strengthening this bond day by day. The relationship between IT and accounting affects the quantity and quality of information that will support decision-making processes [28, 29].

Enterprise resource planning systems that incorporate an accounting information system have not been very well suited for use in SMEs, which remain as systems that can be used only by large enterprises over a long period due to high installation and operating costs [30, 31]. With the technological developments, which have also been stated in the previous sections, and the transformation of these technologies into new business and income models by entrepreneurs as well as in many areas of the business, significant effects have also been seen in accounting field.

As mentioned above, today's small and medium-sized initiatives can benefit from the in-depth reports generated mainly from accounting data that are monopolized by large corporations in the past and interactions with other business units of the accountant. Mobile applications developed for use in smart devices enable the digitalization of bills, invoices and other traditional physical evidence and accelerate transactions. Through the mobile applications, many accounting transactions can be performed instantaneously without errors, and accounting processes are simplified and management is facilitated, especially for small businesses and freelance employees.

3.1. Big data, accounting and integrated reporting

Accounting is one of the most prepared business units for big data use as a unit in which intensive data flow and analysis have been carried out in the past, and reports have been filtered by these data. Big data, unlike the traditional data recording, processing, and interpretation processes, allow structured or unstructured data to be aggregated from many sources to produce meaningful results. Big data and accounting are two concepts that cannot be considered separately from each other in the near term.

In all areas of accounting, the use of big data in management accounting, financial accounting and financial reporting increases effectiveness and efficiency [32]. The audit processes are carried out in a data-focused manner and the more precise results are achieved through the big data [12]. Information results from big data analysis will reduce the risk of accounting processes, increase the accuracy of management decisions and enrich the meaning of accounting data. Big data allow the accountant to correlate financial measures with non-financial measures and improve their reporting capabilities [33]. Big data analysis can support business managers in predicting and managing the financial risks of the business.

The development of big data access in accordance with data processing, specialized algorithms and enhanced analysis methods enriched the reporting capabilities of businesses as well as the insights of reports for the use of management. Thus, it is enabled to reach more significant conclusions by using financial information and non-financial information together [33].

Related data are needed to measure, manage and create value from intellectual capital, human capital and other intangibles [34]. Value-based integrated reports that have been getting more attention from corporations in recent years are bringing light to value creation and change of businesses in today and in the future [35]. In order to improve the accuracy of integrated reports, big data analysis can be seen as an important opportunity. Businesses can define key performance indicators (KPIs) more accurately via big data analysis and enhance the performance measurements [36].

Big data analysis is a valuable asset that can enrich the effects of integrated reporting by providing more accurate forecasting, faster analysis capability and instant access to the critical data [37]. It helps the organizations to create the connectivity of information that supports integrated thinking by determining the relations between financial and non-financial performance of business functions, operational divisions and supply chains of businesses [38]. Along with developing models that can explain or predict what is happening and why, big data give the opportunity of creating value from that information via KPIs [39].

KPIs are tools that management use to understand how the organization performs in terms of critical success factors. These tools focus on the factors that are seen as the most important for the success of organization both in today and in the future [40]. Integrating big data analysis with performance monitoring and evaluating processes allows to uncover new motivational measures and to identify the harmful ones as well as producing correlations that can show management performance and value relation more clearly [41].

A significant competitive advantage can be gained by analysing all the data obtained from business units, shareholders and other related parties from internal and external environment of the business as big data on corporate reporting processes and on identifying and evaluating the KPIs. However, in order to convert big data to meaningful insights that are crucial for decision-making processes of the management, the organization should have adequate big data-analysis skills. In this sense, both accounting and finance units which are responsible from financial data and other units which are responsible from non-financial data should work in coordination with the focus of big data analysis.

3.2. Cloud computing and accounting

Cloud computing has become an essential technology that is more meaningful with big data technology and provides significant productivity increase and cost efficiency for businesses. As a result of supporting the relationship between accounting and data with cloud computing, the possibility of accessing desired information, report or analysis has emerged without noticing from time and place. The storage of accounting data in the cloud and the realization of analysis with cloud-assisted software also support accounting with real-time data and accelerate decision-making processes of managers [42, 43].

Cloud computing reduces operating costs by simplifying the technological infrastructure that businesses must have. The storage of accounting data in the cloud avoids risks that could lead to the loss of data such as accident, theft or loss that would occur in the physical condition of the business. Business models such as SaaS with cloud computing have distorted traditional software pricing strategies, making accounting and finance software much more accessible. This situation facilitated the use of accounting data as a critical management tool for businesses and increased the efficiency of accounting staff.

Cloud computing enables employees of accounting and finance doing their job simultaneously, as well as enable specialists from different business functions to access a report at the same time, or by supporting a report simultaneously with different data. In addition to all its benefits, data security is one of the most important issues that have slowed down or made a risk in the adaptation of cloud computing to businesses [44]. Contrary to traditional software, servers are owned by other organizations in cloud computing, and the limited number of intervention options in cloud computing users' to protect these data leads to increased security vulnerabilities.

3.3. Artificial intelligence and accounting

The widespread use of artificial intelligence and machine-learning technologies has led to the emergence of different collaborations and new effective management tools. The adaptation of artificial intelligence and machine-learning technologies into the areas of accounting and finance, and auditing is one of the areas of particular interest to businesses in the era we are in [45, 46]. A total of 1663 artificial intelligence initiatives, with a total investment of $12.35 billion [47], have been taken in 70 countries.

http://dx.doi.org/10.5772/intechopen.69264

KPMG announced last year that it would collaborate with IBM's artificial intelligence 'Watson' in its audit services to benefit from cognitive power [48]. IBM's artificial intelligence constantly analyses, learns and supports its users in their processes [49]. Similarly, Deloitte uses the artificial intelligence system developed by Kira systems to make audit processes more effective. Thanks to the system, hundreds of thousands of documents can be analysed within weeks and converted into meaningful results within the framework of defined criteria [50].

Data generated from accounting department are usually prepared in the framework of standards, policies, procedures and rules that are under control of legitimate authorities. Artificial intelligence technology can fulfil standardized accounting transactions without requiring human intervention, and even in non-standardized or interpretive works, make decisions like the human by learning former characteristics of decisions of the users. Besides comprehensive processes such as audit activities, artificial intelligence technology reduces the burden of businesses and improves productivity by reducing the error rate in basic accounting processes such as invoicing and tax applications.

Smacc, a Germany-based start-up, applies artificial intelligence technology to financial management processes and provides them to the sector. With the technology, invoices are automatically detected, their types are determined, tax processes are managed, records are made and the system develops itself by learning from past processes [51]. The use of artificial intelligence systems in accounting applications is one of the topics that the accounting academicians have studied for a long time [46, 52–54]. It is now apparent that these studies have been adopted by start-ups and big enterprises and contributed to the transformation of the profession.

4. Effects of the start-ups on the accounting profession

Companies that referred as start-ups with a great growth rate and make actual the business opportunities of the results from digitalization have affected disruptively on all traditional business models of traditional sectors like accounting. New-generation start-ups combine SaaS and similar business models with flexible working styles, focus on speed and simplicity, make these accessible for SMEs to high technology services that be taken apart from big corporate enterprises, thus creating a vital market.

Accounting profession has a key position for being both a function that internal structure of firms and external as support units like CPA offices. Accountancy that reflects all the transformations of technology on business for many years forced to a new transforming by technology-focused start-ups.

Micro-level accounting processes that SMEs must employ at least one accountant to make them real are detected as primary market for many start-ups that founded as accountancy-oriented and with the help of software that combines cloud, big data and artificial intelligence technologies, SMEs have become more effective and employee efficient.

In the past, enterprise resource planning software which was used mostly by corporate enterprises being served with SaaS model to small scaled enterprises; on the one hand, caused by increasing competition, on the other hand, started to threat traditional accounting processes and accountants which follow that processes. Accounting start-ups that combine complex accounting software with simple interfaces and mobile application supports enable businesses to track bills, invoices and other traditional accounting processes by digitally and destroy the traditional models of the accounting profession, and force to transforming present accounting companies.

Parasut.com, a start-up based in Turkey, that combines financial management of SMEs with cloud computing, was founded by three partners who do not have any accounting expertise or educational background. Among the 30 employees of Parasute.com that serves more than 3000 enterprises, there is no official accountant. It solves this need by receiving consultancy from public accountant companies in order to improve its products and services [55].

Today's accounting entrepreneurs are able to offer complete and efficient accounting systems for enterprises that can manage all the accounting processes of a company without employing any accountant. This situation also gives an important idea about the future of the accounting profession.

5. Conclusion

The survey, which was held in the USA, conducted with 400 CPA companies; 90% of participants agree with the digital future is approaching rapidly, while only 8% indicate the accounting profession is ready for the future. About 80% of the participants said they needed more knowledge about the developing technologies [56]. The technological developments mentioned and discussed in previous sections force the accountancy and accounting to an important shift, just as the example of parasut.com mentioned above. During this changing process, CPAs and other members of accounting profession do not have the opportunity to move to what they do today and the way of they doing those to the future.

According to a report published by Intuit, by 2016, 62% of small and medium-sized companies have completed cloud integration. This rate was 37% 2 years ago. This situation can be shown as a factor that obliges SME-CPA relations to be carried out entirely in the cloud in the near future. On the one hand, cloud computing and big data technologies are improving the efficiency of accounting and the quality of reporting analysis, on the other hand, increasing efficiency on the other side, promoting the need for fewer human resources. When these developments in communication technologies are combined with artificial intelligence and machine-learning technologies, it shows up all the tasks performed by traditional accounting professions can be performed by machines. This results in a shift in the roles of the accounting profession and accountants.

Future accountants have to focus on specialization and cooperation, enhance accounting skills in high value-added fields and adhere to technological innovations that affect the profession such as large data analysis and a focus on consulting. Especially, the rapid transformation of enterprises will bring new legal regulations and standards that must be followed. Professionals specialized in accounting may be responsible for managing the compliance process of an enterprise with the relevant conversions. In this entire transformation process, accounting companies which can follow the technology that affects closely to accounting, and can diversify their services by adapting to these technologies quickly, will continue to maintain their assets and continue to create value for businesses in the past as well.

The rapid increase in the number of start-ups and the expectation that this and discussed will continue in the near future brings an important opportunity for the accounting profession with it. Start-ups are constantly faced with investment and partnership transactions to manage the rapid growth process as micro-entrepreneurs built on specific expertise. The expertise of accountants in these micro-enterprises, with the ability to manage the investment and financing processes of start-ups, will bring CPAs into the position of CFOs for start-ups [57]. Similarly, fast-growing share economy as an ecosystem created by start-ups causes people who do not own any company to operate in different ways in the economic environment and to create financial transactions within the scope of the sharing economy. Accounting professionals may undertake the finance and tax advisor role of those who are getting crowded in the economy day by day without any financial competence.

Author details

Burak Özdoğan

Address all correspondence to: burak.ozdogan@cbu.edu.tr

Manisa Celal Bayar University, Manisa, Turkey

References

[1] Anandarajan M, Anandarajan A, Srinivasan CA, editors. Business Intelligence Techniques: A Perspective from Accounting and Finance. 1st ed. Berlin Heidelberg: Springer-Verlag; 2012. p. 268. DOI: 10.1007/978-3-540-24700-5

[2] MIT Technology Review. 10 Breakthrough Technologies 2001 [Internet]. 2003. Available from: http://www2.technologyreview.com/news/401767/natural-language-processing/ [Accessed: 15 February 2017]

[3] MIT Technology Review. 10 Breakthrough Technologies 2016 [Internet]. 2016. Available from: https://www.technologyreview.com/lists/technologies/2016/ [Accessed: 15 February 2017]

[4] Hayes B. Cloud computing. Communications of the ACM. 2008;**51**(7):9-11

[5] Buyya R, Yeo CS, Venugopal S, Broberg J, Brandic I. Cloud computing and emerging it platforms: Vision, hype, and reality for delivering computing as the 5th utility. Future Generation Computer Systems. 2009;**25**(6):599-616

[6] Assante D, Castro M, Hamburg I, Martin S. The use of cloud computing in SMEs. In: Second International Workshop on Mobile Cloud Computing Systems, Management, and Security (MCSMS-2016); Procedia Computer Science; 2016. pp. 1207-1212

[7] Côrte-Real N, Oliveira T, Ruivo P. Assessing business value of big data analytics in European firms. Journal of Business Research. 2017;**70**:379-390

[8] Ram J, Zhang C, Koronios A. The implications of big data analytics on business intelligence: A qualitative study in China. Procedia Computer Science. 2016;(87):221-226

[9] IBM. Bringing Big Data to the Enterprise [Internet]. Available from: https://www-01.ibm.com/software/data/bigdata/what-is-big-data.html [Accessed: 17 February 2017]

[10] Gartner. IT Glossary [Internet]. Available from: http://www.gartner.com/it-glossary/big-data/ [Accessed: 17 February 2017]

[11] IBM. IBM Big Data Hub [Internet]. Available from:http://www.ibmbigdatahub.com/sites/default/files/infographic_file/4-Vs-of-big-data.jpg?cm_mc_uid=02578212696914864077665&cm_mc_sid_50200000=1489318956 [Accessed: 17 February 2017]

[12] Hannan A. Big Data Meets Accounting [Internet]. 2016. Available from: http://www.beckerpinnacle.com/accounting-and-finance/continuing-professional-education/big-data-meets-accounting/2016 [Accessed: 18 February 2017]

[13] McAfee A, Brynjolfsson E, Davenport TH, Patil DJ, Barton D. Big data. The management revolution. Harvard Business Review. 2012;**90**(10):61-67

[14] Buchanan BG. A (very) brief history of artificial intelligence. Ai Magazine. 2005;**26**(4):53

[15] Tractica. Artificial Intelligence Market Forecasts [Internet]. 2016. Available from: https://www.tractica.com/research/artificial-intelligence-market-forecasts/ [Accessed: 18 February 2017]

[16] Baden-Fuller C, Haefliger S. Business models and technological innovation. Long Range Planning. 2013;**46**(6):419-426

[17] Pateli AG, Giaglis GM. Technology İnnovation-Induced business model change: A contingency approach. Journal of Organizational Change Management. 2005;**18**(2):167-183

[18] Amit R, Zott C. Business model innovation: Creating value in times of change. IESE Business School Working Paper. 2010;**870**:1-17. DOI: http://dx.doi.org/10.2139/ssrn.1701660

[19] Hui G. How the ınternet of things changes business models. Harvard Business Review. 2014;**29**:1-5.

[20] Ma D. The business model of software-as-a-service. In: Services Computing, SCC 2007. IEEE International Conference; 2007. pp. 701-702

[21] Lee SG, Chae SH, Cho KM. Drivers and inhibitors of SaaS adoption in Korea. International Journal of Information Management. 2013;**33**(3):429-440

[22] Gartner. Forecast: Public Cloud Services, Worldwide, 2013-2019, 4Q15 Update [Internet]. 2016. Available from: http://www.gartner.com/newsroom/id/3188817 [Accessed: 20 February 2017]

[23] Janssen M, Joha A. Challenges for adopting cloud-based software as a service (SaaS) in the public sector. In: ECIS 2011 Proceedings; 2011

[24] Reshmi S Balakrishnan K. Implementation of an inquisitive chatbot for database supported knowledge bases. Sādhanā. 2016;**41**(10):1173-1178

[25] Floyd SA. Do machines hold a key to business success? PM World Journal. 2016;**10**:1-10

[26] Ghasemi M, Shafeiepour V, Aslani M, Barvayeh E. The impact of information technology (IT) on modern accounting systems. Procedia-Social and Behavioral Sciences. 2011;**28**:112-116

[27] Trigo A, Belfo F, Estébanez RP. Accounting information systems: Evolving towards a business process oriented accounting. Procedia Computer Science. 2016;**100**:987-994

[28] Mancini D, Dameri RP, Bonollo E. Looking for synergies between accounting and information technologies. In: Mancini D, Dameri RP, Bonollo E, editors. Strengthening Information and Control Systems. Springer International Publishing; Switzerland 2016. pp. 1-12. DOI: 10.1007/978-3-319-26488-2

[29] Omoteso K. The application of artificial intelligence in auditing: Looking back to the future. Expert Systems with Application. 2012;**39**(9):8490-8495

[30] Haddara M, Elragal A. ERP adoption cost factors identification and classification: A study in SMEs. International Journal of Information Systems and Project Management. 2013;**1**(2):5-21

[31] Venkatraman S, Fahd K. Challenges and success factors of ERP systems in Australian SMEs. Systems. 2016;**4**(2):20

[32] Warren D, Moffitt KC, Byrnes P. How big data will change accounting. Accounting Horizons. 2015;**29**(2):397-407

[33] Hodgkinson R, Gillon K. The finance function and IT: A bigger picture. In: Management Accounting Research Conference; 22 March 2012; London School of Economics; 2012 https://www.icaew.com/~/media/corporate/files/about%20icaew/what%20we%20do/thought%20leadership/finance%20and%20it%20handout%20v5%20final.ashx

[34] Brynjolfsson E, Hitt LM, Kim HH. Strength in numbers: How does data-driven decision making affect firm performance? SSRN. 2011: DOI: http://dx.doi.org/10.2139/ssrn.1819486

[35] Moffitt KC, Vasarhelyi MA. AIS in an age of big data. Journal of Information Systems. 2013;**27**(2):1-19

[36] Cavey S How do Big Data and KPIs work together?. [Internet]. 2015. Available from: http://www.culturatech.com/blog/article/how-do-big-data-and-kpis-work-together#sthash.5CHy5jot.dpuf [Accessed: 05 March 2017]

[37] EY. Are You Prepared for Corporate Reporting's perfect Storm? [Internet]. 2015. Available from:http://www.eychile.cl/Content/pdf/Estudios/09022016153012_pdf_REPORT%20-%20FAAS%20Corporate%20Reporting%20Survey%202016%20(2).pdf

[38] Parmenter D. Key Performance Indicators: Developing, Implementing, and Using Winning KPIs. 2nd ed. John Wiley & Sons; New Jersey 2015. p. 7

[39] Gökten S. Entegre Raporlama Yaklaşımı için Uygulamaya Yönelik Sistematik Bir Öneri. World of Accounting Science. 2016;**18**(4):741-765

[40] Warren Jr JD, Moffitt KC, Byrnes P. How big data will change accounting. Accounting Horizons. 2015;**29**(2):397-407

[41] Eccles RG, Krzus MP. The Integrated Reporting Movement: Meaning, Momentum, Motives, and Materiality. John Wiley & Sons; New Jersey 2014

[42] KPMG. Have you looked at Finance & Accounting in the Cloud? Perhaps You Should [Internet]. 2012. Available from: https://home.kpmg.com/content/dam/kpmg/pdf/2013/03/have-you-looked-at-finance-accounting-cloud.pdf [Accessed: 21 February 2017]

[43] Brandas C, Megan O, Didraga O. Global perspectives on accounting information systems: Mobile and cloud approach. Procedia Economics and Finance. 2015;**20**:88-93

[44] Strauss E, Kristandl G, Quinn M. The effects of cloud technology on management accounting and decision-making. Management and Financial Accounting Report. 2015;**10**(6):1-12.

[45] Elliott RK. The third wave breaks on the shores of accounting. Accounting Horizons. 1992;**6**(2):61

[46] Baldwin AA, Brown CE, Trinkle BS. Opportunities for artificial intelligence development in the accounting domain: The case for auditing. Intelligent Systems in Accounting, Finance and Management. 2006;**14**(3):77-86

[47] Venture Scanner. Artificial Intelligence [Internet]. Available from: http://www.venturescanner.com/artificial-intelligence [Accessed: 21 February 2017]

[48] IBM. News Release [Internet]. 2016. Available from: https://www-03.ibm.com/press/us/en/pressrelease/49274.wss [Accessed: 21 February 2017]

[49] IBM. IBM Watson [Internet]. Available from: https://www.ibm.com/watson/?lnk=404 [Accessed: 21 February 2017]

[50] Kira. Deloitte [Internet]. Available from: http://info.kirasystems.com/partners-deloitte-alliance [Accessed: 21 February 2017]

[51] Smacc. AI-Enabled Financial Management [Internet]. Available from: https://www.smacc.io/en/ [Accessed: 01 March 2017]

[52] O'Leary DE, O'Keefe RM. The impact of artificial intelligence in accounting work: Expert systems use in auditing and tax. Ai & Society. 1997;**11**(1-2):36-47

[53] Connell NAD. Expert systems in accountancy: A review of some recent application. Accounting and Business Research. 1987;**17**:221-233

[54] Brown CE, Coakley JR. Artificial neural networks in accounting and finance: Modeling issues. International Journal of Intelligent Systems in Accounting, Finance and Management. 2000;**9**:119-144

[55] Parasut. Hakkimizda [Internet]. Available from: https://www.parasut.com/hakkimizda [Accessed: 03 March 2017]

[56] Canton J. Welcome to the fast future: Insight into the CPA of the future 2015 study. CPA. com Study. http://globalfuturist.com/wp-content/uploads/FastFuture-Study.pdf 2015 [Accessed: 03 March 2017]

[57] Sankar U. Journal of Accountancy. Trends that will Shape the CPA profession in 2016 [Internet]. 2016. Available from: http://www.journalofaccountancy.com/newsletters/2016/jan/2016-trends-accounting-profession.html [Accessed: 03 March 2017]

Chapter 13

Graphical and Textual Presentations in Financial Reports

Seedwell T.M. Sithole

Additional information is available at the end of the chapter

http://dx.doi.org/10.5772/68038

Abstract

The use of separate graphs and texts to disclose information is a frequent occurrence in corporate annual reports. Multiple sources of information does not enhance understanding of users of financial statements. This chapter compares spatially separated text and graphs with integrated presentations that aim at bringing text and graphs as close as possible to each other. The chapter begins by illustrating the concept of split attention. Cognitive load arises when disparate sources of accounting information need to be mentally integrated by users. An experiment using separate text and diagrams is then presented to demonstrate how participants can deal with cognitive overload when reading split-attention material. Using two instructional design formats, the split-attention format and the integrated format, first-year accounting students were used as surrogates for financial report user groups such as employees and shareholders. The presence of the split-attention effect in the financial accounting material was established. Effective use of text and diagrams in integrated reporting helps integrated thinking and assists the interconnectedness of information. The findings suggest that redesigning financial reports by integrating text and diagrams may make effective use of the available cognitive resources and possibly enhance investors and other stakeholders' decision-making process.

Keywords: accounting, cognitive load theory, financial reports, graph, split-attention

1. Introduction

Companies are increasingly using graphs, text and other visual representation methods to communicate financial information to their stakeholders. But do these forms of presentation enhance users understanding of the annual reports? In most cases, these companies augment the graphs with related notes below, above or on the side of the graph. While there is now a sizeable body of research on different aspects of presentations, such as the use of graphs in annual reports, graphs versus tables and numerous other narratives [1, 2], graphs and text proximity in corporate reports have received very little attention. Yet, graphs and texts are increasingly being used in annual financial reports. The purpose of the present chapter is to review the split-attention effect and present an experiment on graphs and text proximity, in order to identify a presentation format that enhances user understanding of corporate annual financial statements.

It is frequently suggested that graphs can aid the communication of accounting information [3]. Moreno et al. [4] study involving electrical engineering students as subjects revealed some interesting observations regarding concrete and abstract representations. Participants received instructions using abstract representations (e.g. electrical symbol for light bulbs), concrete representations (e.g. light bulbs) and both concrete and abstract representations. Moreno et al. [4] stated that in the past research studies, concrete representations had been shown to distract from learning compared to abstract representations. However, Moren, Ozogul and Reisslein's new study showed that the greatest learning occurred when a combination of concrete and abstract representations was used. Moren et al.'s study [4] revealed that visual representations play a critical role in learning and that visual representation is a vital tool of experts in problem solving and reasoning.

It is also suggested, however, that graphs can be misleading [5]. For example, graphs have been found to intentionally introduce distortions into the communication process, which misleads users of financial reports. Distortion of information is introduced by selectivity of some form and non-compliance with the principles of graph construction. This may involve a decision on whether or not to use graphs, and if they are used, a further selectivity could be in the particular choice of financial variables graphed [5]. Another distortion of graphs in annual reports is to reflect only one or two indicators, particularly favourable to the company instead of a number of indicators [6]. There are many ways a graph can be altered and would have the potential to affect users' perceptions mainly for the purpose of serving managerial interests rather than user interests [7]. Distortion of graphs results in the message conveyed as no longer being unbiased and neutral.

The effect of graph and text proximity in the context of financial reporting is largely unexplored. What is known is that graphs can aid the communication of accounting [8] and that preparers of accounting reports may intentionally create graphs that are misleading. The purpose of the present chapter is to conduct an experiment that compares spatially separated text and graphs with integrated presentations that aim at bringing text and graphs as close as possible to each other within the context of corporate annual reports. The three main research objectives are (1) to establish the existence of split-attention effect on graph and text presentations, (2) to investigate whether the integrated format group will outperform students in the split-attention format group on recall and transfer test items and (3) to investigate whether students in the integrated format group will report higher effort (cognitive load) than students in the split-attention format. Superiority of the integrated format will favour bringing text as close as possible to the related parts of the diagram in corporate financial reports.

http://dx.doi.org/10.5772/68038

The remainder of this chapter contains four sections. In the first section, we review the split-attention effect. Section 2 provides the study context. An outline of the experiment is given in the third section. Our results are presented in the final section, together with a discussion of the implications of our results.

2. Split-attention effect

Split-attention effect asserts that when designing instructional materials, it is important to avoid formats that require learners to split their attention between multiple sources of information. Existence of split attention would require the learner to mentally integrate the different sources of information, which has a negative effect on learning [9]. Since 1988, research into split attention investigated the effectiveness of worked examples as they had proven to be highly effective for learning algebra [10]. However, neither worked examples nor highly directed but not a full worked example (guided solutions) enhanced students' performance when compared with the conventional problem-solving strategies [11]. This led to the conclusion that the format of the worked examples, a diagram and separate text in the form of solution steps (such as that shown in **Table 1**), must increase cognitive load.

Over the years, presenting text and diagrams together rather than apart in instructional material has repeatedly been shown to enhance learning when compared to studying separate

Balance sheet		
Description	**Amount**	
Cash at bank	XX	**Assets** are resources controlled by an entity as a result of past events and from which future economic benefits are expected to flow to the entity. These economic benefits can be tangible (having physical characteristics) such as land buildings and equipment or intangible (assets without physical existence) such as legal claims or patent rights.
Accounts receivables	XX	
Building	XX	
Total assets	**XXXX**	
Liabilities	**XX**	
Accounts payable	XX	
Mortgage payable	XX	
Total liabilities	**XXXX**	
Net assets	**XX**	
EQUITY	XX	
XY, Capital	XX	
Total equity	**XXXX**	

Table 1. Format of the balance sheet normally found in textbooks.

text and diagrams [11]. **Table 1** illustrates split attention in financial accounting. The diagram is above the text which outlines the solution to the problem and in processing the information, the learner has to understand the solution steps presented as text and then match the steps with the diagrammatic representation [12]. This process requires mentally combining the two sources of information and a considerable amount of cognitive resources, not necessarily directly related to learning. Very little resources are then available for learning. In the case of undergraduate accounting learners, this is particularly important as most of them are meeting the instructional material for the first time and lack the proper schemas to integrate new information with their previous knowledge [13]. In the integrated worked example (see **Table 2**), the student focuses on the relational dimensions of the problem because the learners' mental capacity is released from the need to search and match the solution steps and link with the diagram [9].

Several studies have found that the searching and matching required by split-attention instructional material is inefficient and has a negative effect on learning [11, 14]. During their studies, students are likely to encounter various texts separated from diagrams in textbooks and other accounting instructional material. Integrating spatially separated information into successful problem solutions can be difficult [10].

Split-attention effect is guided by cognitive load theory (CLT). The use of CLT, as part of accounting instructional design, is compelling due to the robust way in which its general principles apply to a wide variety of instructional settings. There are various reports where

Balance sheet		
Description	**Amount**	
Cash at bank	XX	**Assets** are resources controlled by an entity as a result of past events and from which future economic benefits are expected to flow to the entity. These economic benefits can be tangible (having physical characteristics) such as land buildings and equipment or intangible (assets without physical existence) such as legal claims or patent rights.
Accounts receivables	XX	
Building	XX	
Total assets	**XXX**	
Liabilities	**XX**	
Accounts payable	XX	
Mortgage payable	XX	
Total liabilities	**XXX**	
Net assets	**XX**	
EQUITY	XX	
XY, Capital	XX	
Total equity	**XXX**	

Table 2. Integrated format of the balance sheet.

http://dx.doi.org/10.5772/68038

CLT-derived principles have improved learning outcomes [9, 15, 16]. Even though there is extensive empirical application of CLT principles in other disciplines, its use in accounting has been very limited.

3. Importance of split-attention effect to financial reports

Financial reports often consist of a statement of financial position, statement of comprehensive income, statement of cash flows, statement of changes in equity and notes to financial statements. Knowing basic principles in accounting provides the basis for understanding and interpreting accounting information, which is required in later years [10]. The basic principles comprise essential foundation for future applications by practitioners or for further study in the field of accounting. One of the main focuses of the financial statements is to illustrate how accounting information may be used in the decision-making process [16].

Financial reports usually have numerous diagrams and text [17]. A statement of financial position shows the state of a business on a particular date and is the result of a complex and long recording process that involves a record of transactions, posting to the respective ledger accounts and the preparation of a trial balance [18]. The users of the statement of financial position tend to regard it as proof of both the difficult nature of accounting and the technical competence and reliability of the accountants and auditors involved [9]. One of the reasons for the complication is the way the statement of financial position is presented. In most cases, the statement of financial position consists of a diagrammatic presentation followed by an explanation of each of the components, thus evoking the split-attention effect. A similar type of presentation is used for other financial statements, such as the statement of comprehensive income and the cash flow statement. As has been stated in the preceding sections, such separate text and diagrams require split attention, which does not enhance learning [4].

3.1. Integrated thinking, integrated reporting and integrated presentations

Integrated thinking is referred to as the "active consideration by an organization of the relationships between its various operating and functional units and the capitals that the organisation uses or affects. Integrated thinking leads to integrated decision-making and actions that consider the creation of value over the short, medium and long term" [19]. Integrated thinking is a key feature driving integrated reporting.

Proponents of integrated reporting suggest that traditional financial reporting has not kept pace with the changes in macro-economic value experienced over the years and that IR provides a richer picture [20]. Others argue that IR provides a concise, clear representation of how an organisation creates value and reveals sustainability [21]. The IR report provides information on financial and non-financial performance in a single document, showing the relationship between financial and non-financial performance and how these inter-related dimensions are creating or destroying value for shareholders and other stakeholders. Integrated reporting brings together information about an organisation's governance, performance, strategy and prospects in a way that it reflects the social, commercial and environmental context within which it operates [20]. Such IR supports better integrated thinking, which has the potential to be complimented by integrated text and diagrammatic presentations. Integrated thinking has a broader appeal than the traditional business decision-making, which tends to focus on short-term financial outcomes. The IR framework elicits multiple representations of information about organisational governance, strategy, performance and prospects in order to accomplish integrated thinking. Consistent with integrated thinking, the use of integrated text and diagrams makes such presentations more concise, clear and comparable.

Promoting user understanding of financial reports can only be brought about by well-designed text and diagrams. Providers of financial statements have attempted to expose users to a variety of presentations and in various ways, including online, to the extent of financial information overload. Information overload has widely been recognised to have adverse effects on decision quality [16]. To help overcome the information overload, users have to be exposed to alternative presentations, which have the potential to aid better understanding and decision-making. As illustrated, many financial statements require users to unnecessarily split their attention between diagrams and text. An alternative presentation, called the integrated format, is to have related diagrams and text as physically close as possible to avoid the extensive search-and-match behaviour. Various research studies have shown that text and diagrams need to be integrated in order to overcome the negative effects on understanding caused by split-attention design [22]. Consequently, this chapter presents an investigation on whether users (represented by students) can benefit more from integrated financial statements.

4. Study context

This study was conducted with accounting students at an Australian university. Undergraduate first-year students were used as suitable surrogates for employees, shareholders and other stakeholders as prior knowledge of accounting is not usually a prerequisite for users of financial reports. Prior research has demonstrated that studies requiring no prior knowledge can be completed by the surrogates [23]. According to Trotman [23], students may be suitable surrogates where the research does not rely solely on prior learning and the task can be completed by the surrogates. Liyanarachchi [24] supports their use in decision-making studies and suggests that maintaining the realism of experiments and replication of prior results is more critical with respect to generalisability than the use of real subjects. In the experiment reported in the current study, students were used as surrogates for the users of financial reports. Participants are assigned to two different formats in order to examine the effect of these formats on their understanding of financial reports. The first instructional format is split attention which is normally found in financial reports. The second is the integrated format, which involves bringing text and diagrams as close as possible to each other. The redesigning of financial reports to comply with integrated format was created in order for comparisons to be made.

The experiment sought to test the hypothesis that students in the integrated format would perform better than students in the split-attention format. Participants were randomly assigned to one of the two conditions. In the split-attention format, instructional materials were formatted in the same way as in the published financial statements. In the integrated format, the content was formatted in a different way to decrease split attention by bringing the diagram and text as close as possible to each other. Random assignments ensured that each student had an equal opportunity of being chosen to participate in the study [25]. A computerised random creation of participant numbers and allocation to groups based on the numbers generated were undertaken. The first 41 students were allocated to the split-attention group and the next 40 students were allocated to the integrated group.

Subjective rating scales were used to assess cognitive load and are the preferred method in most recent research. The rating of perceived task difficulty, which asks learners to rate the perceived difficulty of a task on a 9-point Likert scale, ranging from "very, very easy" to "very, very difficult," was used [26]. It was chosen as it is widely used in various cognitive load research studies since the early development of CLT [27]. Students rated task difficulties, for example, "How much mental effort did you invest to answer this question?" at the end of each test question. The rating scale consists of a line marked with nine anchor points, each accompanied by a descriptive label indicating a degree of effort. After every task in the test phase, students had to rate how much mental effort they invested.

How much mental effort did you invest to answer this question? (Please circle)

1----------2----------3---------4----------5-----------6---------7-----------8---------9

The tasks selected were diagrams and texts about ratios and the accounting equation. These tasks were selected because they have separate text and diagrams and were likely to exhibit clear associations with financial statements normally presented to users of financial statements.

5. Experiment

A pre-test questionnaire was first used to collect information about each student's age, gender, knowledge of accounting and language. In total, 45% female and 55% male students were randomly assigned to one of the two conditions. Thirty-six students in the first group were the split-attention group (Group 1: 13 females and 23 males, and M = 21 years old and standard deviation (SD) = 3.85) and 40 students were in the integrated group (Group 2: 14 females and 21 males, and M = 20 years old and SD = 1.84). The students were not paid and participated voluntarily in the study. With regard to performance, students in the integrated format group (Group 2) would be expected to outperform students in the split-attention format group (Group 1). This is due to the integrated materials requiring less mental effort than those in the split-attention group. This expectation follows from the fact that split attention requires that more working memory resources be utilised.

Students used pen and paper-based materials. In total, they were three pages of recall and transfer test questions to be answered which included a requirement to rate mental effort after answering every test question. Initially, participants reported their understanding of ratios and the accounting equation on a 5-grade category ranging from very poor to expert level. A one-way analysis of variance (ANOVA) was conducted on pre-test responses of age and basic knowledge of accounting to explore differences across the two groups involved in the experiment. Means and standard deviations are shown in **Table 3**. The one-way ANOVAs for pre-test questions demonstrate no significant main effect of group for age ($F(1, 70) = 0.851$, $p = 0.562$) and knowledge of accounting ($F(1, 70) = 0.655$, $p = 0.421$), thus enhancing the likelihood that any significant differences identified later are more likely due to the different treatment conditions.

5.1. Procedure

The demographic information was collected by using a pre-coded number on the learning materials and question papers for the split-attention group and the integrated group in order to guarantee anonymous data collection. Students were told that their information would be treated as confidential. Participants were then given the information sheets and consent forms, and they all indicated their agreement by signing the form.

A pilot study aimed at refining instructional guidance was conducted before the experiment. The pilot study informed the time that was to be allowed for each phase of the studies. Two students took part and they did not participate in the main experiment. Based on the pilot study, a time of 45 minutes for completion of the experiment was determined.

Instructional format	**Mean rating**	**Standard deviation**
Test phase–recall		
Split attention ($n = 36$)	57.61	12.13
Integrated ($n = 35$)	63.42	11.77
Test phase–transfer		
Split attention ($n = 36$)	31.47	20.54
Integrated ($n = 35$)	52.40	21.99
Learning phase		
Split attention ($n = 36$)	6.42	1.59
Integrated ($n = 35$)	4.74	1.92
Test phase–recall		
Split attention ($n = 36$)	6.55	0.96
Integrated ($n = 35$)	5.22	1.24
Test phase–recall		
Split attention ($n = 36$)	5.39	0.93
Integrated ($n = 35$)	4.37	1.33

Note: Actual raw score ranges were 0–28 for recall and 0–11 for transfer. The actual mental effort ratings were from 0 to 9 for cognitive load.

Table 3. Means and standard deviations for learning and test-phase mental effort ratings.

http://dx.doi.org/10.5772/68038

The experiment involved three phases. During the first phase, students completed their gender, language, knowledge of accounting and their age. The completion of this section took 10 minutes. During the next phase (learning phase), the participants were given 15 minutes to analyse the learning materials given to them. After the second phase, the test which consisted of transfer and recall question items was administered. The students were given 45 minutes to complete the test.

5.2. Results and discussions

5.2.1. Performance measures

A one-way ANOVA was conducted on test performance scores to explore differences between the two groups involved in the first experiment. Means and standard deviations are shown in **Table 3**. A one-way ANOVA for recall scores showed a statistically significant main effect for the recall test items ($F (1, 70) = 4.206$, $p < 0.05$, large effect size $d = 0.48$) [28]. The mean recall scores showed that the integrated group had higher scores than the split-attention group. The one-way ANOVA for transfer questions also demonstrated a significant main effect of group ($F (1, 70) = 17.185$, $p < 0.05$, and effect size $d = 0.98$). The integrated format group performed significantly better than the split-attention group.

5.2.2. Mental effort rating on instruction

The results from the one-way ANOVA for mental effort invested in the learning phase are shown in **Table 3**. They indicate significant differences across the two formats ($F (1, 70) = 16.07$, $p < 0.05$, with a large effect size, $d = 0.95$) [28]. Consistent with predictions, there were large and significant between-group differences of mean mental effort rating on learning results. The integrated group reported lower levels of cognitive load than the split-attention group.

A one-way ANOVA was conducted on the mental effort that the participants provided after each test question. **Table 3** shows the mean ratings and standard deviations for the ratings of the test phase. Again, there were large and significant between-group differences on mean recall results ($F (1, 70) = 25.349$, $p < 0.05$, large effect size, $d = 1.19$). Transfer items also revealed a significant effect between groups ($F (1, 70) = 13.972$, $p < 0.05$, large effect size, $d = 0.88$). The ratings for both the learning phase and the transfer phase showed that the integrated group reported a lower perceived amount of mental effort than the split-attention group.

5.2.3. General discussion

The experiment was designed to test whether participants in the integrated group would perform better than those in the conventional split-attention group. In addition, transfer test items were designed to establish whether the effect could be obtained with new, different and slightly more challenging questions. Students in the integrated group demonstrated higher performance than students in the split-attention group for both recall and transfer tasks.

As expected, in the experiment, students in the integrated group reported lower perceived cognitive load than students in the split-attention format group. Students in the split-attention group performed badly as compared to the integrated group in both the recall and transfer tasks. This was probably caused by requiring the split-attention group to refer to multiple sources of text and diagrams. This finding possibly illustrates that financial reports that integrate text into the diagrams in a manner which facilitates understanding may be more beneficial than split-attention financial reports. Apparently, the processes required to work during the test phase demanded different amounts of mental effort in all conditions. When the data are differentiated for recall and transfer, the results still revealed the same tendency, with the integrated group reporting the lowest level of cognitive load.

The major finding from this study relates to the participants' preference for integrated accounting material whether they were answering recall or transfer tasks. This is largely similar to financial reports which require users to split their attention between diagrams and text. Financial reports, similar to the text and diagrams used in this study material, do indeed demonstrate such split-source formats, and this has a negative effect on users of these reports. The most interesting outcome to emerge from this experiment is the consistency with which the integrated group outperformed the split-attention group. The participants in the integrated group did in fact maintain their high performance and reported lower cognitive load under both recall and transfer tasks. The superiority of integrated material seems to support Moreno et al.'s study [4] in engineering, which showed that the greatest learning occurred when a combination of concrete and abstract representations was used.

A further explanation of the results is that the superiority of the integrated condition might have resulted from the text which was already as close as possible to the relevant aspects of the diagram, which enhanced the students' learning. This is consistent with studies by Tindall-Ford et al. [29].

5.2.4. Implications of the findings and limitations and suggestions for future research

As discussed previously, the fundamental purpose of redesigning financial reports is to make an effective use of the available cognitive resources and possibly enhance investors and other stakeholders' decision-making process. The study reported in this chapter provides a first trend in this direction by reporting significantly better performance in the integrated format groups than in the split-attention format groups.

As demonstrated, the integrated format requires significantly lower cognitive load on the user of financial reports than the split-attention format. The evidence of the effectiveness of integrated financial materials adds to research into this effect in other domains. By demonstrating the very effective consequences of integration, the experiment suggests that preparers of financial statements should consider shifting focus away from "split-attention" format towards "integrated" format.

Integrated reporting has been heavily promoted during the past decade, as this chapter has demonstrated. It must be recognised that the concept demonstrates the linkages between an organisation's strategy, governance and financial performance and the social, environmental and economic context within which it operates. Such a framework would involve, in most instances, text and graphical presentations which have to be combined in order to

http://dx.doi.org/10.5772/68038

achieve "integrated thinking" [30]. Embedding integrated text and diagrams into the integrated reports would make the reports concise and clearer, facilitating the integrated thinking process.

There are a few important limitations of the chapter presented. Over the years, the measurement of mental effort has been a challenge [27]. The specific type of mental effort was not directly measured; future research might attempt to determine the precise type of mental effort reported by the students. In addition, there are possibly other factors that might have influenced students' performance and mental effort ratings. These could be emotional stress, levels of motivation and other non-cognitive factors may have confounded with the two cognitive load components. The use of students as surrogates may be another limitation. In this study, it appeared reasonable to use first-year undergraduate students as they may be perfect substitutes for employees and other stakeholders who may not be experts in accounting. Further research may use employees and other stakeholders. Finally, although split attention is found in ratios and T accounts instructional material, future research may use authentic financial reports that are given to employees and shareholders.

The experiment in this chapter has demonstrated to benefit from integrated financial reports and manage the cognitive load of the users of financial statements. Most importantly, the chapter has shown that such integrated presentations may be useful even for transfer tasks. The future research direction may include investigation of cognitive load measurement, in particular the measurement of each type of cognitive load.

Author details

Seedwell T.M. Sithole

Address all correspondence to: s.sithole@westernsydney.edu.au

Western Sydney University, Sydney, Australia

References

[1] Volkov A., Laing G. Assessing the value of graphical presentations in financial reports. Australasian Accounting Business and Finance Journal. 2012;**6**(3):85-108.

[2] Eisl C., Falschlunger L., Hofer P., Jungert M. Reporting design – a systematic literature review. Journal of Finance and Risk Perspectives. 2013;**2**(2):27-47.

[3] McCann L.M. Thinking outside the ledger: a visual representation project for accounting students. The Accounting Educators' Journal. 2016;**26**:61-84.

[4] Moreno R., Ozogul G., Reisslein M. Teaching with concrete and abstract visual representations: effects on students' problem solving, problem representations, and learning perceptions. Journal of Educational Psychology. 2011;**103**(1):32-47.

[5] Beattie V., Jones M.J. Corporate reporting using graphs: a review and synthesis. Journal of Accounting Literature. 2008;**27**:71-110.

[6] Burgess D.O., Dilla W.N., Steinbart P.J., Shank T.M. Does graph design matter to CPAs and financial statement readers? Journal of Business & Economics Research. 2008;**6**(5):111-124.

[7] Clatworthy M.A., Jones M.J. Financial reporting of good news and bad news: evidence from accounting narratives. Accounting and Business Research. 2003;**33**(3):171-185.

[8] McCann L.M. Thinking outside the ledger: a visual representation project for accounting students. The Accounting Educators' Journal. 2016;**26**, 61-84.

[9] Sithole S.T.M., Abeysekera I. Accounting education: a cognitive load theory perspective. New York, NY: Taylor and Francis; 2017, 152 p.

[10] Sithole S.T.M. The effects of presentation formats on understanding financial accounting: an experimental study. Australasian Accounting Business & Finance Journal. 2016;**10**(2):76-92. doi:10.14453/aabfj.v10i2.5

[11] Sithole S.T.M., Chandler P., Abeysekera I., Paas F. Benefits of guided self-management of attention on learning accounting. Journal of Educational Psychology. 2017;**109**(2):220-232. doi:10.1037/edu0000127

[12] Cooper G., Sweller J. The effects of schema acquisition and rule automation on mathematical problem-solving transfer. Journal of Educational Psychology. 1987;**79**:347-362.

[13] Tarmizi R., Sweller J. Guidance during mathematical problem solving. Journal of Educational Psychology. 1988;**80**:424-436.

[14] Morrison B.B., Dorn B., Guzdial M. Measuring cognitive load in introductory CS: adaptation of an instrument. In: Proceedings of the Tenth Annual Conference on International Computing Education Research; 2014, pp. 131-138. doi:10.1145/2632320.2632348.

[15] Agostinho S., Tindall-Ford S., Bokosmaty S. Adaptive diagrams: a research agenda to explore how learners can manipulate online diagrams to self-manage cognitive load. In: Huang W., editor. Handbook of human centric visualization. New York: Springer; 2014, pp. 529-550. doi:10.1007/978-1-4614-7485-2_21.

[16] Sithole S.T.M. Effect of instructional design on learning the accounting equation in an introductory accounting course. Journal of Accounting and Taxation. 2015;**7**(8):137-142. doi:10.5897/JAT2015.0192.

[17] Warren D.L., Young M.N. Integrated accounting principles: a best practices course for introductory accounting. Issues in Accounting Education. 2012;**27**(1):247-266. doi:10.2308/iace-50106.

[18] De Lange P., Jackling B., Gut A. Accounting graduates perceptions of skills emphasis in undergraduate courses: an investigation from two Victorian universities. Accounting and Finance. 2006;**46**(3):365-386. doi:10.1111/j.1467629X.2006.00173.x.

[19] IIRC. International <IR> Framework [Internet]. 2013. Available from: http://theiirc.org [Accessed 18 February 2017]

[20] Owen G. Integrated reporting: a review of developments and their implications for the accounting curriculum. Accounting Education. 2013;**22**(4):340-356. doi:10.1080/09639284.2013.817798

[21] Adams C.A. Understanding integrated reporting: the concise guide to integrated thinking and the future of corporate reporting. Oxford: Do Sustainability; 2013, 80 p.

[22] Tindal-Ford S., Agostinho S., Bokosmaty S., Paas F., Chandler P. Computer based learning of mathematical concepts by studying instructor-managed or self-managed split-attention materials. Education Technology and Society. 2015;**18**(40):88-89.

[23] Trotman K. Research methods for judgement and decision making studies in auditing (3rd ed.). Blackburn: Victorian Printing; 1996, 155 p.

[24] Liyanarachchi G. Feasibility of using student subjects in accounting experiments: a review. Pacific Accounting Review. 2007;**19**(1):47-67.

[25] Gall M.D., Gall J.P., Borg W.R. Educational research: an introduction (8th ed.). New York: Allyn and Bacon; 2006, 704 p.

[26] Paas F., Tuovinen J., Tabbers H., Van Gerven P.W.M. Cognitive load measurement as a means to advance cognitive load theory. Educational Psychologist. 2003;**38**(1):63-71. doi:10.1207/S15326985EP3801_8.

[27] Clark R., Nguyen F., Sweller J. Efficiency in learning: evidence-based guidelines to manage cognitive load. San Francisco: Pfeiffer; 2006, 416 p.

[28] Cohen J. Statistical power analysis for the behavioural sciences (2nd ed.). New Jersey: Lawrence Erlbaum Associates; 1988, 567 p.

[29] Tindall-Ford S., Agostinho S., Bokosmaty S., Paas F., Chandler P. Computer-based learning of geometry from integrated and split-attention worked examples: the power of self-management. Journal of Educational Technology & Society. 2015;**18**(4):89-99.

[30] Adams S., Simnett R. Integrated reporting: an opportunity for Australia's not-for-profit sector. Australian Accounting Review. 2011;**21**(3):292-301.

Section 5

Public Sector Accounting and Reporting

Chapter 14

Historical Development of Government Accounting

Mihriban Coşkun Arslan

Additional information is available at the end of the chapter

http://dx.doi.org/10.5772/intechopen.69121

Abstract

Government accounting aims at preventing waste in government services and establishing a balance between optimal expenditure and services by managing government assets and government sources in the most efficient way. This balance can be established only by obtaining complete and accurate information from government accounting system on time. Since the users have a low level of knowledge needs in government accounting system, it has been recorded for long years in a cash basis manner. However, as the government's area of operation expanded and the needs increased, it became obvious that cash basis system had lacking parts. So it started to focus on recording financial transactions and financial reporting. These lacking parts in the accounting system tried to be overcome through a new regulation by focusing on the areas where cash basis accounting system was insufficient; and a change was experienced with regard to applying the accrual basis in the areas of government accounting and financial reporting. This study aims to explain the historical development of government accounting by applications in countries and especially by detailed expressions for Turkey. As a result of the literature review and the examination of countries' government accounting practices, it has been determined that the government accounting practice has made the correct transition from cash basis to accrual basis.

Keywords: government accounting, cash basis government accounting, accrual government accounting, historical development of government accounting, applications of government accounting in country level

1. Introduction

As the economic boundaries between the countries started to be removed through globalization, the concept of an international competition emerged between them, and this concept forced the countries to experience an economic reconstruction. It also brought the necessity of the revision of the government's role and share in economic life as well as a reconstruction in government finance management which is appropriate for the new conditions within the framework of these developments. Reconstruction of government accounting systems is of high importance among reform movements in government finance management systems. Because accounting system is very important to establish financial transparency in government management, both for helping government managers to make correct decisions under the liability of accountability and about how the government sources are used in this area. Changes in the concept and perception of government, changes in the quality of goods and services, changes in government economy and changes in government budget systems had important effects on the development and importance of government accounting.

Government accounting used to monitor revenues and expenses, which were available only in the budget and excluded the payables, receivables and assets of the government as there was a limited area of operation for the government previously. As the area of operation of the government was expanded, government accounting became an accounting system, which monitored revenues and expenses determined through budget as well as the payables, receivables and assets of the government. However, there is currently no government accounting system, which is applied across the world. Government accounting systems also experienced some changes depending on the changes of the era. The need for knowledge regarding financial decisions and financial policies of the governments was relatively much more limited in the past, which led to the creation of simple and budget-oriented accounting systems. On the contrary, modern concept of government accounting goes far beyond being budget oriented and considers the changes in assets and includes cash flows into the accounting system.

For long years, government accounting systems have been recorded in a cash basis manner which includes allocations given by the budgets, expenditures from these allocations, total revenue for financing the expenditures, and some other information that may be needed and which principally represents for the record of collection of revenues and payment of expenditures. However, this budget-oriented recording system became insufficient to fulfill the needs of government management over time, and so, some new experiences were started to be looked for in the area of government accounting. Thus, there has been some studies recently to develop an accrual recording system which is recognized by all financial transactions which have already emerged or will emerge in the future including tangible assets of the government. In the selection of accounting systems which will be published in government area, there is a movement on a platform with cash basis accounting at one of the edges and accrual accounting at the other edge. This platform also includes the principle of undertaking, modified cash basis, and modified accrual basis.

This section explains how government accounting should be defined, what kind of a content it has, which important aspects it has for the country's economy, as well as the emergence and changes it has within its historical process in order to put forward the importance of government accounting for government managements and economies. It also evaluates studies which are carried out in different countries in the areas of government accounting and their reflections in Turkey as well as the studies which are carried out in Turkey.

2. Government accounting

Given that accounting is the recording, classifying, and reporting of financial transactions in monetary terms, this definition becomes valid for private sector. If the matter is government accounting, there is a different definition because the aim of government accounting ranges from being an instrument of financial management and control to the planning of national economy. Government institutions and organizations within the scope of government accounting record their transactions as efficiently as possible and facilitate accountability. This section explains how government accounting should be defined, what kind of a content it has, which important aspects it has for the country's economy, as well as the emergence and changes it has within its historical process in order to put forward the importance of government accounting for government managements and economies.

2.1. Definition, scope, and aim of government accounting

Government accounting is a process which enables recording, making decision analysis, classification, summarization, notification, and interpretation of government financial knowledge as well as including and reflecting all transactions which include purchasing, transferring, and allocation of government property in general [1].

When government accounting is described within the framework of financial accounting, it can be defined as recording and classifying all the monetary activities, assets, and liabilities of the government, which can be financial partially or wholly and reporting them to the authorized entities and institutions. Historical development of both financial and government accounting is in parallel with the political and economic development levels of the countries, because there are some changes in the concept of government management as a result of differentiation in economic and political organization types of the countries.

As the political regimes started to change, there were some important developments observed in the concept of government as well. Developments in government accounting also improved in accordance with these developments arising in the concept of government because government accounting is not an aim but an instrument for government management. Government activities started to change in parallel with the developments in the world, and traditional concept of government experienced a change. Within this process, firstly the concept of government budget emerged, and then the concept of accounting developed in budget-oriented manner. So government accounting system became a derivative of government budget system [2]. In this regard, the concept of government accounting is described in a budgetary point of view as follows: an accounting technique, which audits whether government activities are fulfilled in accordance with the determination of legislative power within time periods determined by budget laws or not, suggests the expenditures of government services and throws light upon forward decisions for the management [3].

Government accounting plays a key role in government finance management. Importance of government accounting lies behind the fact that countries trying to restructure government managements start their reforms by making adjustments in their accounting systems and making their systems to have the competency of producing more accurate, timelier, and more reliable knowledge [2]. Government that is liable to provide government services has to monitor government expenditures efficiently and account for it as well. It is not only the government expenditures that the government accounts for, but also has to keep transferred assets and observe any changes in their values [4].

Scope of government accounting is the general administration. Financial and nonfinancial government corporations compose the government sector in addition to general administration. However, these corporations are outside the scope of government accounting because they aim at making profit through their economic activities by producing goods and services in accordance with the accounting and reporting principles of private law for the market. So government accounting should aim at creating a framework which is practical for making comparisons with common accounting and reporting standards as well as consolidating them in central administrations, local administrations, and social security institutions which are included in the scope of general administration [5].

Issues which are handled based on the definition of government accounting are of high importance for the institutions and organizations which are included in government accounting. If we do not address to accounting to include general government services, it has a very limited scope, and there will be no account unity in government sector. So we need to address to the concept of government accounting in a broad sense and define it as an accounting which uses government sources as much as possible and shows the records of all government institutions and organizations. Because goods, services, and sources of the government are produced and used by people who create this organization, so it is important to provide transparency and accountability for these people. Liability of accountability, which is defined as displaying how efficiently they (people who are allocated with sources and provided with authority in this process) use the sources and authorization, is also important for the society to provide confidence toward the government. It will be beneficial with regard to government finance management to provide account unity, information accuracy, and common financial reporting in the government sector through the concept of government accounting, which we handle in a way that we include all the government sectors, not just a part of it [6].

Government accounting fundamentally aims at carrying out an audit for the results of the activities of government institutions and other government-affiliated institutions within a calendar year to determine their conformity with budgeted revenues and expenses. In this regard, government accounting accurately determines revenue and expenses within a financial year and reports the activity results [7]. Government accounting, as an instrument of financial management, also aims at creating a basis for productivity analyses by suggesting the costs of government services. In other words, it determines whether government activities are rational or not [5].

In conclusion, government accounting, as an instrument of financial management and control, aims at monitoring yearly and year-end accruals of budgeted revenues and expenses within a financial year as well as assets and sources of the government and executive bodies in addition to reporting the budget application results and activity results of executive bodies for specific periods to the relevant authorities in a way that is appropriate for information needs in order to provide information to the government sector which is necessary for planning and managing national economy [7]. In this regard, it is required to have budgetary accounts, assets, and capital accounts within the scope of government accounting, so that it can come up as an instrument which provides necessary data to the government in making efficient financial and economic decisions [8].

Government needs accounting more than private enterprises do because aim of the government is not to make profit just as in private enterprises, but to fulfill the needs of the society and provide wealth for them. So the government needs to spend the revenue which is gained from various sources in the most efficient way and to present some specific information about them [11].

Recording and monitoring the studies and activities of the governments regarding financial and economic policies, government accounting is the most important element of the principle of financial transparency and financial accountability in this regard. It checks whether or not government sources are managed efficiently and economically, and it provides the most important data in internal and external audits. Existence of government accounting is of high importance to provide government services efficiently in governments. Government accounting system contributes to information production, making them available for usage, determination of economic policies, and solution of budgetary applications [3].

2.2. Government accounting systems

Emergence and development of government accounting date back to the fifteenth century. Recording and development of government accounting started with cameral accounting system. Government accounting recorded through cameral accounting system was budget-oriented and handled the collection and expenditure of revenues and expenses of the budget [9].

There is currently no government accounting system that is applied across the world. Government accounting systems also experienced some changes depending on the changes of the era. The need for knowledge regarding financial decisions and financial policies of the governments was relatively much more limited in the past, which led to the creation of simple and budget-oriented accounting systems. On the contrary, modern concept of government accounting goes far beyond being budget-oriented and considers the changes in assets and includes cash flows into the accounting system [10].

There are two fundamental points of view in the historical development process of government accounting systems as traditional and modern views. cameral accounting system and Schneider accounting system were shaped within the framework of traditional view, while Constante accounting system and logismography accounting system were shaped within the framework of modern view.

2.2.1. Traditional government accounting system

Traditional government accounting system suggests that government accounting fundamentally aims at monitoring, recording, and controlling government revenues and expenses within the framework of budgetary provisions and procedures. It is possible to regard this system as "budget accounting" where tangible assets and intangible assets of the government as well as receivables and payables of the government are not monitored and recorded within the framework of accounting. Traditional view suggests that receivables, payables, and assets of the government should be excluded from the scope of government accounting because of the reasons below [12]:

- There is no power of disposition on the assets of the government (purchasing, renting, etc.). There can be no disposition on such government properties as ancient arts, palaces, and museums just as on private properties. Assets cannot be recorded as they are not an instrument of change for the government.
- Assets of the government belong to the community, not the government. So government is liable to prevent these assets by considering the interest of the community. Therefore, patrimuan (government's assets and enterprise revenues) accounting cannot be recorded through the assumption that government has no assets; items in the assets cannot be indicated in the balance sheet.
- Development of an accounting system regarding government properties brings out the idea of expanding government's assets. Traditional system suggests that government's function is to manage the existing assets in the best way, not to increase patrimuan.
- It is not possible to monitor cash account and asset account of the government technically. So there are many problems while presenting the facts about the balance sheet of the government.
- Patrimuan accounting requires making up a balance sheet. Assets and receivables in the balance sheet of the government and payables in the liabilities are not the same securities, so they cannot be compared. It is not possible to determine the liquidity of some values in the assets.
- Since there are many problems while presenting the facts about the balance sheet of the government, it is not possible to monitor the values. Accordingly, amortizing and managing the assets remain as utopic ideas.

Traditional government accounting systems are classified as cameral accounting system and Schneider accounting system.

2.2.1.1. Cameral accounting system

Being one of the leading accounting systems, cameral accounting system was designed as an internal audit assistant composed of cash tangible assets and derivatives, which have no systematic sustainability in financial management of the royalties (assets and treasury administration). Being called as simple cameral accounting between 1500 and 1750, this concept included classifying the revenues and expenses, monitoring personnel changes, and indicating the status of active assets. In other words, the cash basis which included recognition of budget values was applied. Today's accounting was founded between 1750 and 1810 with regard to government accounting. In 1763, Johann Mathias Puechberg, Australian Emperor's advisor, put forward the principles of cameral system in his book *Introduction to Development of Cameral Accounting*

Applied by the Kingdom. Defined also by Hung, the German Cameralist, this system started to keep the records of daily logs and larger books which were divided into subsections after 1786. Some arrangements also took place to include revenues and expenses between the accounts. So accrual basis gained much more importance in accounting. After 1810, revenue reports were prepared in conformity with commercial accounting model with the help of result-oriented transactions in accounting. After 1910, executors created cameral accounts, which will be indicated in inventory for expense items with the existence of government enterprises [13].

Cameral accounting system is divided into two as old cameral accounting system and new cameral accounting system with regard to historical development of accounting systems. Old cameral accounting system can only monitor the cash. It is not possible to monitor changes in the assets of the government and status of its receivables and payables. In this system, accounts are divided into two as revenue accounts and expense accounts. In cameral accounting system, there are two books as cash book and detailed book of revenues and expenses. Cash book is recorded by the cashier based on the documents of revenues and expenses. Detailed book of revenues and expenses is also recorded by the cashier based on revenue collections and expense payments in accordance with the phases and provisions in the budget [14].

New cameral accounting system is an updated version of old cameral accounting system created in order to remove some lacking parts of the old cameral accounting system in that the old version could not audit itself or the cash records, and it could not indicate the accrual balances of revenues and expenses [15]. In the new cameral accounting system, cash book and detailed book of revenues and expenses are kept by different people, which is something that facilitates audit of the accounts, and it can indicate the account balance of revenues and expenses. The only thing that makes the system insufficient is that it does not show the changes in assets of the government just as in cameral system [7].

2.2.1.2. *Schneider accounting system*

Both old and new cameral accounting systems only include cash and budget transactions in government accounting while excluding clearing transactions as well as off-budget receivables and payables accounts. Schneider accounting system is a more developed cameral system applied in order to remove these lacking parts [9].

In Schneider accounting system, accounting records are recorded in accordance with bilateral recording method: payables are recorded in the relevant column in the section of expenses, and receivables are recorded in the relevant column in the section of revenues. The most important benefit of this system is that it includes cash transactions as well as clearing and off-budget receivables and payables accounts. Furthermore, it enables balance sheet adjustments by making loss and profit accounts [7].

2.2.2. *Modern government accounting system*

Modern government accounting system suggests that government accounting should include and recognize the payables, receivables, and assets of the government as well as its revenues and expenses on the contrary to traditional view, because it is inevitable for a government to have assets, payables, and receivables because of the expansion of its area of operation. So it is incorrect to regard government accounting just as a budget accounting. It also means giving insufficient answers to the needs of government management. Views of modern government accounting system that are contrary to the budget accounting-oriented approach of traditional view are justified as follows [12]:

- Government's assets belong to the community. However, it does not remove the liability of the government. All kinds of changes in the government's assets should be recorded with regard to the principle of accountability of the government.
- There have been substantial increase in the government's assets with the increase in government functions today. Increase in the government's assets is a result of modern government concept. So assets should definitely be reflected in the accounting for an incredible presentation of the balance sheet of the government.
- It is not a rational approach to conclude that the view suggesting that existing assets should be recorded will definitely lead to an increase in the assets.
- Technically, budget accounts and patrimuan accounts should be addressed in different groups. It is not impossible to solve this problem by making an adjustment while considering this distinction in the account plan.
- Firstly, it is necessary to consider government budget and commercial budget separately. Even though it is not necessarily possible to evaluate some items in government budget sufficiently, it is not an obstacle for including these items into the balance sheet. For example, there are some problems while recording such items as museums, historical assets, and palaces. In this case, recording should be started after determining a method which will reflect the reality explicitly.
- It is absolutely correct that there will be major problems in the application of patrimuan accounting in large-scaled countries. However, existence of these difficulties is not an obstacle for the execution of the application. Large-scaled countries will lead to increase in the number of activities and even some changes in patrimuan. So it is an inevitable obligation to use patrimuan accounting.

Modern government accounting systems are classified as Constante accounting system and Logismography accounting system.

2.2.2.1. Constante accounting system

This system includes both budget accounts and asset accounts. System was founded in accordance with the principle of recording revenues and expenses in the budget in accrual phase. All transactions are recorded in accordance with bilateral recording method. Cash book and detailed book of revenues and expenses are recorded in the system. Cash book is used for monitoring the cash movements as usual, while detailed book of revenues and expenses is used for recording revenues and expenses in the relevant accounts in accrual phase. This system includes budget accounts and asset accounts. Since tangible asset accounts are also used in this system, there can be decreases and increases in the tangible assets of the government [7].

While the system enables determination of changes (increases and decreases) in the government's assets, it can also calculate loss and profit at the end of the financial year. Loss and profit balances of all the accounts are recorded in the capital account at the end of the year. Net balance of this account represents for the net assets of the government [11].

2.2.2.2. *Logismography accounting system*

Logismography accounting system also includes budget accounts and asset accounts just in Constante accounting system. In this system, there is a perception that there is one owner and one manager of the government's assets; so two accounts are kept as the owner (government) account and officer (civil servants) account. Logismography system can deliver budget accounts and asset accounts any time. It is also important and outstanding in that it brings new concepts to government accounting. It is one of the most important systems as it considers the cost of government transactions [16].

Owner (government) account shows all the goods and assets as well as any changes on them including the government's assets. Owner account is an account group, which shows the government's assets through its records, tables, and books [11]. On the other hand, officer account was created in order to notify the status of the assets of civil servants who keep and manage these assets on behalf of the government in accordance with specific laws, decrees, and regulations. So accounts of these officers are collected under the account of government officers [15].

2.3. Recording methods in government accounting

When political power had only a few duties in national economy in the past, there was not much need for information for economic administration. But today, political powers in some developed countries shoulder important roles in order to facilitate socioeconomic development of their communities for a direct management of economy. So it is of high priority and high importance for an efficient government finance management to adapt to new conditions in obtaining the necessary information. It is obliged to create a method which can respond to changes arising out of lack of information on account of relationships among the nations [17].

It is impossible to compare or consolidate financial reports which are produced in different accounting and reporting methods. For example, it would not be possible to consolidate EU financial statements if EU member countries applied different accounting systems. So international organizations launched studies in order to create the same accounting standards across the world. During these studies, there has been a shift from cash basis government accounting to accrual basis government accounting in government accounting systems [18].

Starting point of modern government accounting is the cash basis-oriented accounting system. Accrual basis accounting system which is the fundamental of modern government accounting system records all kinds of financial transactions regarding all the assets and liabilities, including tangible assets, regardless of collection and payment. For long years, government accounting systems have been recorded in a cash basis manner which includes allocations given by the budgets, expenditures from these allocations, total revenue for financing the expenditures, and some other information that may be needed and which principally represents for the record of collection of revenues and payment of expenditures. However, this budget-oriented recording system became insufficient to fulfill the needs of government management over time, and so, some new experiences were started to be looked for in the area of government accounting. Thus, there has been some studies recently to develop an accrual recording system which is recognized by all financial transactions which have already emerged or will emerge in the future including tangible assets of the government [19]. While recording methods in government accounting accept cash basis at one side and accrual basis at another side, there are other bases as well which are close to both sides. In other words, various regulations were developed within the specified boundaries in order to see the best accounting and reporting status of an asset [20].

2.3.1. Cash basis government accounting

Cash basis government accounting records are transactions arising out of cash purchases. In other words, financial transactions and cases are recognized upon purchasing or payment of cash. Cash basis accounting is not interested in when services and benefits which are derived from transactions have emerged. Financial reports lose budget revenues and expenses, cash inputs and outputs, and opening and closing cash assets in such an accounting system [21].

Cash basis government accounting does not record or report tangible assets, accrued revenues and expenses, expenditures on the assets which must be activated, and government payables as well as other liabilities, commitments, guarantees and changes in price, and quantity of the government's assets [7]. Cash basis accounting system is easy to understand and manage as it includes simple transactions. Since its scope is limited to cash flows, it does not serve for transparency and accountability purposes. So it is required for cash basis government accounting to include or be supported by commitments and liabilities arising out of budget applications at least. Moreover, cash basis government accounting can be strengthened through accrual budget accounting and recognition of some assets and liabilities such as security assets and deposit securities advances and financial assets [22]. Cash basis accounting system is easy to understand and manage as it includes simple transactions. Since its scope is limited to cash flows, it does not serve for transparency and accountability purposes [23]. Furthermore, it provides very little information which is beneficial for finance management as it is mainly focused on payments. It is not a single basis for performance evaluation in terms of prudence and efficiency or achievement of the targets, either [24]. It is possible to suggest the lacking parts of cash basis government accounting system [25].

Not making up a balance sheet: In this system, there is no balance sheet made up because there is no data regarding the payables, moveable and immoveable assets, liabilities, and equities of the government to make up a balance sheet. The fact that cash basis system does not record them and does not create data leads to some negative results. So users cannot obtain sufficient data regarding the financial information of government administrators, and they cannot make assessments.

Not revealing economic results: In this system, budget revenues, expenditures, budgetary and off-budget collections, and payment transactions are reported only based on cash flow.

Activity reports cannot be produced to indicate the results of activities of the institutions. So economic results of that institution cannot be indicated.

Not having economic and financial performance indicators: In this system, economic movements cannot be estimated. So there are some difficulties in evaluating the financial and economic performance of the institution because of lack of information in comparison of revenues and expenses of that period. Consequently, performance indicators cannot be determined.

Not producing information on service costs: Service cost information, pricing policy and control, and performance evaluation are beneficial and necessary instruments for decision-making process and government contract policies. However, since there is no necessary information which can be obtained regarding expenses and service cost in cash basis accounting system, it is not possible to get necessary information regarding decision-making process because revenues and expenses are recognized when the collections are made, not at their accrual time. Moreover, not recording the moveable assets and not calculating the amortizations are other reasons which make determination of service cost impossible.

Not fulfilling the liability of accountability and financial transparency: Liability of accountability, as a requirement of democracy, is the responsibility and necessity of making inquiries and calling somebody to account regarding fulfillment of the duties and use of government sources by people who are elected by the government and people who are appointed by these elected people. Financial transparency is the explicitness in which government accounts and economic targets can be observed by the government. Since government accounting is a method which records the use of all moveable and immoveable assets of the government as well as its sources and produced financial reports accordingly, it is the main element of accountability. However, this accounting system cannot produce necessary data for the fulfillment of liability of accountability and cannot produce the relevant reports. This system cannot sufficiently help financial transparency because it does not produce detailed and accurate financial data on the issues which are required to be within the knowledge of government.

Opinions of supporters and non-supporters of cash basis government accounting system can be summarized as follows [14]:

Cash basis government accounting system is the simplest method which is used for monitoring government accounts. Supporters of this system suggest that it easily determines the impacts of financial transactions on economy. They also suggest that actual payments by the government increase monetary revenues and revive economy, while payments to the government decrease cash position and society's demand for goods and services. Moreover, since the treasury works as a banker, this system enables evaluation of cash position which is required to be known. The most important function of cash basis accounting system is fund control and determination of liabilities. System also carries out the functions of feasibility and determination of economic impact through expenditure limitations in the short term.

On the other hand, non-supporters of cash basis system accept that cash basis system may have strong impacts on economy, but these impacts cannot be measured unless demands or liabilities are paid to the government. They believe that cash basis system is open to abuses, for example, postponing the payment of debts of current fiscal year to the upcoming year and going into unmatured debts such as advance payments and budget securities until the end of the year. Capacity of cash basis accounting system to help the managers to make decisions regarding administration and financing is limited only to the cash points while government's assets and charges are excluded.

Cash basis recording method, as it is explained above, includes information about the payments within the current fiscal year. However, since these payments do not reflect the actual value of real activity and used government sources, they are not accepted as expenses in reality. Moreover, since accounting records are recognized when the payments are made, not when services and goods are received, this method does not give any information regarding demands arising at the end of the year against a government administration.

2.3.2. Cash customized government accounting

In cash customized government accounting, financial transactions are recorded when the actual payment and collection are made regardless of their accrual periods just like in cash basis government accounting system [21].

The most important characteristic which differentiates cash customized accounting from cash basis accounting is that accounts are not closed by the last evening of the fiscal year; they are open for a specific period of time, generally one month, for the records of transactions of the previous fiscal year. Transactions of the previous period, especially invoices of the budget year, are accepted, and their accounting records are held within this additional period. In this method, transactions are recorded in the accounting records of that fiscal year, and they are reported in the relevant period [24].

2.3.3. Accrual customized government accounting

In accrual customized government accounting, transactions are recorded when an economic value is created, changed, exchanged, transferred, or eliminated regardless of time of cash flows. The most important characteristic which differentiates accrual customized government accounting from accrual basis is the scope of accounting transactions. In this basis, transactions regarding such tangible assets as land, estate, building, vehicles, inventories, forests, and monuments are not included in accounting system, and they are not reported. Therefore, it is easier to understand, apply, and manage compared to accrual basis accounting system because such transactions of determination of tangible assets, amortization, and reevaluation are excluded from accounting. Compared to cash basis, it does not produce deficient information, it records economic transactions as soon as they emerge regardless of cash flows, it is not budget oriented, it records and reports accrued receivables and payables, it creates a basis for activities and performance check, and it records and reports commitments and guarantees which may lead to liabilities in the future [7].

General characteristics of accrual customized government accounting and its distinctions from commitment basis, cash basis, and cash customized government accounting methods are as follows [24]:

- It does not have the weaknesses of cash basis in the production of information.
- It records commitments and liabilities, so it is one step further than commitment basis.
- It does not have the weaknesses of altered cash basis as inherited from cash basis in the production of information. Since liabilities are recorded when they are recognized, there is no need for set-off period in order to enable the principle of periodicity in this basis.
- It is more convenient for conformity with budget allocations and for liability audit.

It is also in conformity with cost accounting elements which are required by activity and performance audit.

2.3.4. Accrual basis government accounting

Accrual basis accounting fundamentally aims at comparing expenses and revenues accrued within a specific period of time and controlling the existing sources and liabilities to be fulfilled by the end of the period.

Accrual accounting was principally developed in order to make external financial reporting by high profit-oriented private enterprises. Government enterprises also experienced some changes as a result of distinctions of accrual basis. However, the idea that it could be applied in noncommercial sectors of the government had recently been very effective. While it was of high priority to increase profit performance in commercial enterprises, accrual accounting applications would be an instrument of decision-making for the managers in nonprofit governmental organizations and increase the management performance [26]. Liability of accountability, improvement of management, and providing savings would be enabled by increasing the management performance. Especially after 1990, it is seen that governments made progress in the issue of accrual accounting and started financial reporting, management systems, government financial reporting, and budgeting processes in accrual basis [27].

During accrual, transactions are recorded when they are recognized regardless of time of cash flows. Revenue account indicates revenue transactions which accrued throughout the fiscal year regardless of their being collected in cash and which are required to be recorded as revenues in accordance with the principles of accounting which are universally accepted, while expense account indicates sum of expenses which accrued throughout the fiscal year regardless of their being collected in cash. Given that, accrued revenues and expenses are included in the accounts and reports of their fiscal year. Such an approach records and reports these economic transactions in their fiscal year. So periodic financial reports exactly reflect the financial transactions regarding the relevant activity periods [28].

When there is an entitlement of using the sources, which are expected to provide benefit to the organization in the future, accrual basis government accounting system regards them as an asset and records them. Similarly, liabilities of the organization against third parties which are expected to be fulfilled in the future (firm, conditional, guarantee, etc.) are recorded as payables and liabilities. So if there is a positive difference between assets and payables, they are recorded and reported as the equities of the organization (net value) [29].

Important factors in the emergence of accrual accounting are to increase accountability, determine financial status of government sector better, and develop reporting studies as well as financing current expenditures by the taxpayers and making contributions to the assets to provide intergenerational equality. Being considered within the liability of accountability, accrual accounting provides large benefits to the governments with regard to showing actual costs of the use of sources [30].

When comparing with the other government accounting recording methods, accrual basis government accounting has some distinctions as follows [25]:

- *Making up a balance sheet*: Balance sheets which are prepared in accrual basis system and which include assets, payables, liabilities, and equities put forward the financial status and performance of the relevant government organization clearly, explicitly, and accurately instead of charts which are far beyond giving information prepared in cash basis government accounting. With the help of this characteristic, accrual basis government accounting system helps decision-making mechanisms of government management and external users. This system includes all payables and liabilities of the general government sector or the relevant government organization. In other words, it includes all economic results of the services and activities of the relevant government organization. It also helps us to evaluate the capacity of covering payables and liabilities of the government sector in the future through information on financial status obtained from balance sheet.
- *Preparing an activity sheet*: On the contrary to cash basis government accounting, accrual basis system can put forward and report the results of activities and services of the general government sector or the relevant government organization. Therefore, it gives us the opportunity of determining the costs of services or activities of the government and the relevant government organization. So it becomes possible to make a performance evaluation.
- *Determining performance indicators*: It is of high importance to record accrued revenues and expenses with regard to financial decision-making process and performance evaluation. In accrual basis government accounting, indicators and criteria can be determined for measuring economic and financial performance by using the produced reports.

There are some changes and adaptations experienced in the implementation of accrual basis government accounting system to overcome its difficulties. Approaches and modifications which were developed because of the obligation of this implementation in some countries using accrual basis government accounting system are as follows [31]:

- Approach which supports that assets and liabilities are recorded in accrual basis while revenues are recorded in cash basis because of difficulty in calculating the amount of collection.
- Approach which supports that all the liabilities are recorded in accrual basis except for some payable items (social security payments funded by budget revenues).
- Approach which supports that all the assets are recorded in accrual basis except for some asset items (infrastructure, defense and cultural assets, etc., which are recognized as an expense when they are acquired or constructed)

- Approach which supports that all tangible asset items are recorded when they are acquired manufactured or constructed

Financial reports which are produced in accordance with accrual basis accounting system include revenues, expenses (including amortization expenses), assets (financial assets, physical assets, capital assets), liabilities, and other economic flows. Accrual basis accounting records and reports all the program costs including amortization expenses. So it creates a strong basis which measures whether or not government sources are used efficiently and economically or in other words whether or not government managers are good managers with good performances [22].

2.4. International developments

Developments in government accounting were principally brought in as a result of the need for creating financial statistics and reports for the governments by international financial institutions such as United Nations, OECD, IMF, World Bank, and regional economic and political units such as European Union. Since it is impossible to compare and consolidate financial reports that are produced in various accounting reporting systems, it has become necessary to make adjustments which will enable comparison and consolidation in the field of financial statistics and reporting [7].

International organizations and institutions, economically developed countries, and especially European Union carry out important studies in the field of government accounting in international level. Thus, System of National Accounts (SNA93), Government Finance Statistics Manual (GFSM2001), European System of Accounts (ESA95), and International Public Sector Accounting Standards Board (IPSAS) are the fundamental outputs of these studies and projects carried out in this area.

2.4.1. System of National Accounts (SNA93)

SNA93 was founded in order to establish standards and rules regarding measurement of national economy such as classification of national economies in corporates, sector and subsector level, flows, rules of stocks and accounting, production account, income distribution, capital account, financial accounts, balance sheet, economic activities with the foreign world, changes in prices and values, population and labor force inputs, and functional classification which are prepared by the European Union, International Monetary Fund (IMF), Organization for Economic Co-operation and Development (OECD), International Bank for Reconstruction and Development (IBRD), and United Nations (UN) jointly. This system includes principles, which should be taken into consideration while creating systems of accounting and reporting with regard to issues specified above [28].

SNA93 aims at handling scopes and definitions which have recently emerged regarding economy and removing the difference between definitions and scopes of these concepts which are observed in the reports and governmentations of various institutions and organizations [32]. SNA93 is composed of a set of meaningful, consistent, and integrated set of macroeconomic accounts, balance sheets, and statements based on a set of concepts, definitions, classifications, and accounting rules, which are internationally accepted [33]. In this regard, this system aims at recording an economy in full [34].

There were important developments in macroeconomic concepts across the world especially after World War II. Many economists were satisfied with a few economic variables in the past, while they need more detailed economic data in statistical analyses today. Collection of this data is only possible by collecting more detailed statistical data. So current System of National Accounts is a complicated system which is composed of many economic variables which are associated with each other beyond calculating gross domestic product today. There is too much detailed information in the accounts in System of National Accounts (SNA93) depending on the rules of economy and perception of their operation manner. Moreover, these accounts provide more comprehensive and detailed records about economic relationships between complicated economic activities and various economic elements within an economy [32].

2.4.2. Government Finance Statistics Manual (GFSM2001)

Government Finance Statistics Manual (GFSM2001) is a regulation which is prepared by IMF with the participation of the experts from such countries as Australia, Canada, America, and the USA which made progress in the field of accrual basis accounting and reporting as well as International Bank for Reconstruction and Development (IBRD), United Nations, Organization for Economic Co-operation and Development (OECD), and European Commission and which aims at preparing government financial reports such as balance sheets and activity reports as well as classifying and reporting stocks, liabilities, revenues, and expenses in the same manner in every country in accordance with the accrual basis. It includes points which should be taken into consideration while creating accounting and reporting systems especially such as the classification of assets, revenues, and expenses with regard to its scope and rules. GFSM2001 fundamentally aims at creating a comprehensive concept and an accounting framework which enable analysis and evaluation of financial policies, as well as the performance of general administration, in specific terms, and government sector, in broad sense [35].

Basic definitions, concepts, and classifications in GFSM2001—regardless of the conditions in the country where they are applied—are based on economic ideas and principles, which are universally validated. So GFSM2001 can be applied on all the economies regardless of corporate or legal structure of the country where it is applied, complexity of its statistical system, its accounting system, or expansion of its government administration. Unfortunately, some sections of GFSM2001 will not represent for the same meanings and results for the countries, which have important differences in terms of administrative and economic structure.

GFSM2001, as SNA93 is described, was designed and published for general administration and government sector. These sectors are defined based on corporate units, which can acquire assets, go into liabilities, and deal with economic activities on their own. An important difference of GFSM2001 from SNA93 is that it is focused on financial transactions of Government System of Financial Statistics such as taxes, expenditures, and payables, while it also includes production and consumption of goods and services of System of National Accounts [35].

2.4.3. *European System of Accounts (ESA95)*

European System of Accounts (ESA95) is a study prepared by EUROSTAT, a sub-institution of the European Union, carrying out studies in the field of statistics aiming at creating statistics, which can be compared and consolidated in the member states and candidate states of the Union at the same level. ESA95 is a substitute for European Integrated System of Economic Accounts published in 1970. ESA95 was prepared and published in complete conformity with SNA93 which is a worldwide guidance regarding national accounting systems. However, ESA95 is heavily focused on the provisions of European Union as well as information and data, which are required in integration. Just like SNA93, ESA95 also enables uniformity in concepts and classifications of such various economic and social statistics as employment statistics, production statistics, and foreign trade statistics. So ESA95 is a core reference for the European Union and member states regarding economic and social statistics. Framework of ESA95 is composed of two basic sets of table [36]:

- Sector accounts
- Framework of input-output and industrial accounts

Accounts are classified under three categories:

- Current accounts include acquisition, distribution, redistribution, and the use of revenues for final consumption. These accounts also enable saving calculation, which is a necessary transaction for saving (capital) accounts.
- Saving (capital) accounts analyze changes in the assets and liabilities of different units and enable recording of changes among net values (differences between assets and liabilities).
- Balance sheets indicate assets and liabilities of different units as well as net values as from the beginning and end of the fiscal year.

2.4.4. *International Public Sector Accounting Standards Board (IFAC-PS Standards)*

The International Federation of Accountants is the most executive and comprehensive organization of the accounting profession in the world. It carries out global studies and provides services in the field of accounting through various subdepartments, councils, committees, and independent advisory boards. As it is specified in the decree of the organization as well, it fundamentally aims at providing service for government interests, strengthening the profession of accounting across the world, and making contributions to the development of international powerful economies [37].

A subdepartment of IFAC, International Public Sector Accounting Standards Board, carries out studies in order to create worldwide standards for government accounting and reporting. These studies are recognized by international financial institutions, regional economic and political unions, and developed countries. There are 21 accounting standards that are published by IFAC so far, and the new ones are under work for the time being [19].

International Public Sector Accounting Standards (IPSAS) no. 1 standard which is prepared by PS of IFAC fundamentally aims at explaining the principles of financial statements prepared by government institutions and organizations as well as types of these financial statements. Aims of government financial statements are classified in two categories in the relevant standard [37]:

- Providing information regarding sources, assets, and changes in them as well as results of government works.
- Providing necessary data in order to analyze cash flows which can emerge in the future.

These activities are not so different from each other. Especially GFSM2001, SNA93, and ESA95 have similar applications with regard to the scope of government statistics and division of accounts. The first point to be considered is the issue of scope of government accounting. National economy is classified in sector level in the international studies, which are carried out in order to determine the scope, so government accounting system is based on social security institutions as well as local and central administrations [22].

3. Government accounting applications in Turkey and in the world

Many countries shifted from cash basis accounting system to accrual basis accounting system as a government accounting method in order to give a response to the pressures regarding efficiency and effectiveness of government sector. However, some other countries rejected this change because they supported that harmful and beneficial aspects of this system varied depending on the special cases of the countries [39]. In this regard, we firstly examined countries which had important developments in shifting to accrual basis accounting system as it threw light upon the developments in the world and which made the first applications of this system. After explaining government accounting applications in the world, we detailed government accounting applications in Turkey.

3.1. Government accounting applications in the world

It is remarkable that countries shifted from cash basis to accrual basis in the applications of government accounting in the world. Even though some countries did not approve this shift, they still advocate its benefits. In this section, we will brief the exemplary applications in some countries and explain the implementation of government accounting systems by the countries.

3.1.1. New Zealand

Developments regarding government accounting which started in the 1980s were not still completed at the beginning of the 1990s. Countries which started to work on this issue were mainly in designing or conceptual phases in 1993 [20]. However, government departments in New Zealand shifted to accrual basis in the issues of budgeting and accounting in 1991, and New Zealand became the first country to produce government accounts in accrual basis in 1992. A government reporting was carried out in 1993 to include approximately 3000 institutions ranging from the largest government enterprise to the smallest primary school (including all assets of the government). New adjustments were brought in the operation of budget system through Liability Insurance Act of 1994. Through these adjustments, combined plans were made which included the ministries in strategical areas (education, health, social aid, social security, environmental protection, and economic development) after 1995 [40].

When the government shifted to accrual basis accounting, it had the competence of preparing balance sheets which can be consolidated and had the opportunity of calculating the actual value of its assets for the first time. Prestige of financial policy in New Zealand increased provided that accounting and budgeting would be made in accordance with all the widely accepted principles of accounting. A private institution acting independently from the government was authorized to control the prosecution and application of these accounting standards so that the government lost its opportunity to make explanations on behalf of itself. New Zealand broke taboos by granting the financial reporting authority of the government to an independent institution through this application [38].

After shifting to the new financial management system, it was possible to see integrated financial reports of the government in New Zealand. New series of widely accepted standards of accounting which are based on the government's financial statements were produced within the scope of a basic project which included the following seven factors [41]:

- Creating accounting policies.
- Collecting information from departments, government institutions, and state economic enterprises.
- Combining (consolidating) the information.
- Validating the information.
- Interpretation and analysis.
- Governmentation and presentation of financial information.
- Communication and marketing.

Studies for improving government finance management were carried out in three directions as creating government accounts, preparing accrual reports, and reporting which includes other independent institutions and enterprises of the government. Accounts and contents were determined through these adjustments. These accounts are "enterprise account" which indicates revenues and expenses of the government, "financial status account" which indicates assets and liabilities of the government, "cash flow account" which indicates cash flows arising out of the activities of enterprises and other institutions, as well as "borrowing and commitment account" and "receivable account". In fact, it was required to be in conformity with generally accepted accounting practice (GAAP) in New Zealand for the accounts which were applied in the central and local administration. Basic element of GAAP is accrual basis in accounting [20].

Adoption of widely accepted accounting standards facilitated the establishment of accounting policies in New Zealand. Approaches which are used by private sector in many areas could easily be applied. Since accounting policies of the government suggested a methodology for preparing financial statements and affected all the government institutions, development of accounting policies was highly emphasized. These accounting policies were also analyzed by the accounting specialists in detail [41].

3.1.2. *Australia*

Developments in the field of government accounting were maintained within the scope of government management reforms in Australia, just like in New Zealand [20]. Governments made progress in accrual accounting especially after 1995, and they brought a vision to accrual accounting in the issues of financial reporting, management systems, government reporting, and budgeting. However, government managers were warned against the issue of accrual basis accounting starting from the mid-1980s indeed. In the 1980s, Australian Accounting Research Foundation, Australian Accounting Standards Board, and Public Sector Accounting Standards Board developed the idea of general-purpose financial accounts both for private and government sectors [27]. Large-scaled financial and administrative reforms in Australia include two basic themes [42]:

- Focusing on management control system by developing information obtained from accounting system and defining and determining roles and responsibilities.
- Providing economic balance by bringing the concept of competition in the government sector.

In general, financial reforms include financial reporting, accrual basis accounting, complete cost, reconciliation between supplier and buyer, and management of the assets, while administrative reforms include structural reforms, operational reforms, revision of information systems, and other reforms regarding responsibilities. However, administrative reforms are not limited to the foregoings [32]. These reforms were put into practice through two law proposals: "Improvement Plan for Financial Management" and "Program management and Budgeting". In addition to these laws, "Financial Management and Responsibility Law" was enacted in 1997. Government institutions started to apply accrual basis budget and accounting as a result of these reforms. Accrual basis accounting system was applied, and accrual basis financial statements were created in Australia for 1999–2000 budget year for the first time [42]. A "working group" was also created in order to develop accrual accounting and bring it in the government sector. Enterprise accounts, asset and liability accounts, cash flow accounts, and bond accounts were included in the account plan which covers the whole central administration [20].

3.1.3. *Canada*

The Government of Canada has applied cash basis in budgeting and recognition of financial transactions until the 1980s. It also used "creative accounting" (overvaluation) methods in reporting and measuring some financial information just like some governments. So that cash basis accounting was used as an instrument of showing false financial reality. However, evaluating financial assets as differently from the reality did not satisfy the need for information which would help correct estimations for the future. So the Government of Canada was highly indebted through its financial statements and budgets obtained through cash basis accounting, could not see the real financial status, and could not take the necessary precautions. The Government of Canada gave up using cash basis accounting application and decided to shift to accrual basis accounting application in order to remove this negativeness. The Government of Canada made important changes in financial reporting applications and shifted from cash basis to accrual basis and financial statements consolidated from separate accounting reports from the beginning to the end of the 1980s. These changes were partly encouraged by Public Sector Accounting and Auditing Board (PSAAB) of Canadian Institution of Chartered Accountants as well [43].

3.1.4. England

There are reform studies regarding the functions, operations, and structure of central administrations in England. The most important reform in this scope is that some authorities and duties of central administration units which provide government services have been transferred to autonomous institutions and agencies [44]. "Resource Accounting and Budgeting (RAB)" is applied in budget and accounting system in England. RAB is a term used for the application of accrual basis in government budgeting and accounting system. It includes the use of "Resource Accounting" knowledge for the control and planning of "Resource Budgeting" government expenditures. Although benefits of accrual basis accounting for the countries could not be understood by many countries in the 1990s, it was understood in England that accrual basis was efficient in both budget and accounting. Accrual basis accounting system was used primarily for government health services at the beginning of the 1990s [45]. England pays much attention to record budgeting and accounting in accrual basis. RAB transforms political priorities of the government into department strategies and budgets, so that the parliament can be reported about productivity and efficiency of the services. It fundamentally aims at enriching the services which are provided by the government. RAB was first founded in 1982 in England through "financial management principles" based on "Financial Management Legislation (FML)". Then, "Green Paper" and "White Paper" published in England included important developments about RAB. There was also an important progress regarding the announcement of RAB after July 11, 2000 [46]:

- "Spending Review" was prepared in order to plan government expenditures on July 18, 2000.
- On July 19–20, 2000, two parliamentary election committees (Government Accounting Committee and Cooperation Committee) authorized the Parliament to make the Treasury apply accrual basis accounting for 2001–2002 fiscal year.
- On July 28, 2000, "Government Resources and Accounts Act (GRAA) 2000" abolished the laws which had been applied since 1866 and provided legal assistance to the parliament both for applying RAB and consolidating all the accounts of the government.

There are financial statements in England, which is similar to the ones produced by government institutions and private sector institutions. However, budgeting process is still regarded as one of the fundamental aspects of financial control.

3.1.5. The United States of America

Developments in government accounting in the USA started with the government sector reforms. The Federal Government prepared a large program for the development of management as from 1981. It was specifically emphasized to facilitate government management and decrease the costs, increase the efficiency of service programs in government sector, and develop financial system to the extent that it can be compared to private sector. In 1990, Federal Accounting Standards Board was founded in order to strengthen the relationship between reporting and accounting upon the agreement of budget office, treasury, and general accounting office. This board has a mission to make advices in accounting standards [20]. This board would be making contributions to development and the use of accrual basis accounting in the next years. As a result of the studies, Administrative Financial Accounting applications made it possible to analyze and report the way of using and controlling the sources as well as collection and measurement of the information which is produced [30]. In 1993, US Senate enacted "Government Performance and Results Act" (GPRA). This act aims at establishing a system of strategic planning and performance measurement within the Federal Government and emphasizes preventing waste and enabling efficiency in the use of government sources in order to fulfill the common needs and demands of the citizens sufficiently. Within this scope, it includes strategic plan, performance plans, and performance reports which are the documents that will be used for getting objective information regarding determination and achievement of performance measurement, aims, and targets; meanwhile procedures and principles regarding the elements which are needed to be available in these documents as well as qualifications and preparation of the documents are also indicated [47].

3.1.6. European Union member states

EU member states, except for Germany and Denmark, prepare their financial reports in accrual basis. Moreover, many member states do not prepare their consolidated financial statements for the whole of government. There are different applications in studies of the countries to shift to accrual basis. Firstly, Holland and Sweden prepared their financial statements in accrual basis and then reflected these statements in their budgets. On the other hand, France and Spain apply accrual basis only in their financial statements while adjusting their budgets in cash basis. Prepared by government management committee, 2002 OECD Study put forward that only three member states prepared their government financial statements based on accrual accounting. Statements prepared in corporation level suggest that there are three member states more in this group. So only 6 member states among 15 member states use accrual basis though in different levels [48]. Spain has been using cash basis accounting system and unilateral record method with regard to government accounting since 1977. It enacted "General Budget Act" for government sector and laid the foundations of new accounting information system. Then, it started "Government Chart of Accounts Plan" (PGCP) for the assets of the government. First studies regarding the government chart of accounts were published in 1983 and remained in force until January 1, 1995 when the new PGCP was put into effect. Then, "System of Information for Accounting and Budget" (SICOP) was published in 1986 in order to put these reforms enacted in the 1980s into force efficiently. This system includes the following: chart of accounts for the general government, detailed accounting lists, and financial statement models regarding the rules of determination and valuation of prices. After all this progress, Spain published Government Accounting Principles of "General Internal Audit and Accounting Offices" (IGAE) in 1991 and accepted the new government chart of accounts in 1994. So Spain shifted to accrual basis accounting with regard to government accounting and adjusted the principles of accounting for the government institutions in a way that they would not be different from the principles of accounting for private sector [49]. The most outstanding characteristic of Sweden government model is that decisions made by the government are jointly made by all the ministers. While daily activities are carried out by a large number of independent units and authorities in different scales, structures, and types, the cabinet determines and makes the policies. Upon the approval of government budget by the parliament, all the allocations are submitted to the use of the government, while the government transfers its responsibilities and funds to its bodies. All accounting applications are carried out in the level of independent units (in this sense, ministries are regarded as independent units). In 1979, "Regulation on Government Accounting" was published by putting forward the accounting principles of independent units. However, some exceptions from accrual basis accounting which are specified in the regulation were applied for a majority of the independent units, while old methods and standards were allowed to be used. Regulation was changed in 1991, and all the exceptions were abolished in 1994 when one-third of independent units changed their accounting methods every year. The parliament also decided to apply these accounting regulation adjustments and accounting principles for the whole government sector. These principles were also standardized in local and regional institutions, but there was no obligation imposed. So that it became possible for Sweden to execute annual accounts in the basis of operational balance sheet, certificate of revenues-expenses, and universal accounting principles which include application balance sheet for sources and funds [50].

Shifting to accrual basis accounting system was regarded as a fundamental step for the managers to derive benefit from total flexibility in input selections. So it was required to see the costs of each input in order to have a more efficient management. Accrual basis accounting system increases the quality of cost information. Also budget and all allocation accounts are also cash basis. Moreover, Sweden brought the obligation of publishing annual reports for the government institutions in 1993. These annual reports include not only financial reports but also performance reports [51]. Studies on accrual basis in Holland started in 1997 when the Ministry of Finance submitted a study titled "From Expenditures to Costs" to the parliament. The government aims at getting the best cost and benefit by using accrual accounting and budgeting in all government services. Having been used in private sector until 1997, accrual accounting also became important in budget classification with the help of these studies after the discussions of full accrual or half accrual [52].

3.2. Applications in Turkey

This section firstly explains the historical development of government accounting applications regarding the application process of government accounting in Turkey. Then, it will address to the reform of government accounting applications in Turkey.

3.2.1. Historical development process in Turkey

Government accounting applications in Turkey date back to pubic accounting system in Ottoman Period. In the fifteenth century, Ottoman Empire firstly made financial legal regulations and then aimed at developing accounting regulations within this legal framework. So a strong government accounting order and organization emerged in the mid-fifteenth century when financial management was structured within the government organization. Government accounting was regarded as a place to hide the secrets for Ottoman Empire. It also emphasizes the importance of government accounting. In the mid-seventeenth century, when there were no budget applications in the west; the idea of government budgets was brought in Ottoman Empire. Budget expenditures were higher than budget revenues at that period. This deficit became chronic as the wars were longer and more expensive. When Europe became richer and stronger in the seventeenth and eighteenth centuries, Ottoman Empire fell behind in economic and military terms. Being a part of the reforms, Imperial Edict of Reorganization in Ottoman Empire was announced in 1839. This edict brought reforms in the field of law, and then the most important reforms were made in the field of finance. Works of writing the legislation of expenses which started toward the end of Period of Reorganization continued until Constitutionalist Period and ended in this period. Subsistence, salary, and retirement laws were put into force in this period by completing the legislation of expenses and starting to keep the records of government officers working in provinces and at the headquarters. These legislations of expenses created the basis of current legislations of expenses in Turkey. After 1876 Constitution was put in legal basis again and Second Constitutionalist Period was announced, the First Parliament and Assembly of Notables accepted the budget of that year in 1909. This budget is of high importance to create the basis of the budgets in the other years in Republic Period. After the announcement of Second Constitutionalist Period in 1910, the first "General Accounting Law" and "By-Law on Restrictions on Accounts to be kept in Subdivisions of Treasury" was put into practice. This main law was practiced until 1910 abolished in 1927 through the Law No. 1050 upon the enactment of General Accounting Law [53].

The first difference in government accounting applications in Turkey is composed of government accounting and budget system in Ottoman Period, while the second difference is composed of government accounting which is applied by the regulations in the field of government accounting throughout Regovernmentan Period. There are important differences in terms of state organization and legality of regulations between Ottoman and Regovernmentan Periods. From this point of view, it is more appropriate to analyze the development process of current government accounting applications in Turkey within the scope of Regovernmentan Period.

After the announcement of Regovernment, there has been important progress in development of government accounting and commercial accounting in our country. While there were progresses in commercial accounting depending on the share of the statist economic policies and so the government in the production of goods and services, there were also important studies in the field of government accounting. As a result of these studies and efforts, General Accounting Law No. 1050 which is regarded as excellent was enacted on May 26, 1927, in early Regovernmentan Period. This law includes authorities and duties of accrual departments, government officers, and accountants of the ministries as well as government budget and other relevant issues [54]. Law No. 1050 had been the legal basis of government accounting system in our country for 76 years until 2003 when Government Finance Management and Control Law No. 5018 was enacted. However, as a natural result of changes in government management concept and government organization structure, Law No. 1050 became insufficient, so the Law No. 5018 was put into force in 2003 as the main law which regulated government financial management. Law No. 1050 fundamentally aimed at basing on the existing administrative structure and establishing financial structure on it. Financial system which is composed of this fundamental structure is as follows [55]:

- Legislation and judicial institutions affiliated with sole government legal entity as well as ministries and organizations are affiliated to a ministry, while their allocations are included in general budget of general administrations (departments) as a separate division.
- Defined in state organization, independent administrations having separate legal entities which are not included in sole government legal entity (service place administration) are included in government budget in the name of value-added administrations. Value-added administrations have their own budgets on account of their separate legal entities. So government budget includes general budget which represents the budget of administrations within the scope of central administration and added budget which represents the budget of the administrations within the scope of service place administration. On the other hand, budget of local administrations named as special budget is excluded from government budget [56].

General Accounting Law which regulates the decisions to determine the officers who are responsible from spending the government expenses, collecting the government revenues, and regulating the final accounts was enacted in 1927. Then, By-Law on Procedures of Treasury Account was put into force in 1928. This bylaw facilitated accounting transactions; abolished Principal Register, which was previously recorded; and put Classification Journal into use. After that, remittances, allocations, and general revenue accounts of current treasury account were also abolished, and money accounts from treasury and branches, collection accounts on behalf of other treasuries, and dispatch account from treasury branches were brought. Moreover, this bylaw abolished the accounts regarding the accrual of budget expenses and revenues, decreased the number of accounts, left the control of the accounts through bilateral recording method, and adopted the control with subsidiary ledgers. In other words, a new system was created by combining the cameral accounting system and the bilateral recording system with the said instruction [56].

"General Regulations of Government Accounting and Regulation on Government Accounting Procedures" have been put into effect since January 1, 1948. The operation of accounts has been explained with General Regulations of Government Accounting, and accounting documentation to be used has been included with Regulation on Government Accounting Procedures. These regulations, which went into effect in 1948, became part of regulations and joints in 1953, 1974, 1975, 1977, 1981, 1986, 1987, and 1989; the number of accounts has been multiplied; accrual and commitment accounts have been added; and the number of off-balance sheet accounts that are available has been increased. Despite the existence of important documents in this regulation such as period end and goods accounting transactions, the abovementioned additives have come to an extreme mixed state with the issuance of regulations, and the new generation of officials is having difficulty with the spelling language. Both regulations were then merged and entered into force as of January 1, 1990 under the title "Government Accounting Regulation" [56].

According to the application of Law No. 1050 in Turkey, an accounting system other than the accounting logic was established structurally aiming to record and report the results of the budget implementation in the units which are included in the general and annexed budgets. Later, when General Regulations of Government Accounting entered into force, entities that are not included in cash-based and noncash-generating debts, affiliates, loans, assets such as extra-budgetary capital, and record of income accruals have also begun to be included in the accounting system in addition to the cash-based accounting system which records budget results. As it is known, all accounts based on cash are closed on December 31. However, after the regulation accounts were not closed on this date and kept open for one month so that past year's accounts can be completed. As it is seen, past practice is neither a totally cash basis nor an accrual accounting system. The application is seen as a system between the adapted cash basis and the accrual basis.

When Government Accounting Regulation is examined, it is seen that the accounting system applied in the general and annexed budgetary administrations accounted for transactions such as deposits and cash capital formations, which are not based on cash basis and income accruals in addition to cash-based budget applications. In addition, accounts are not closed on December 31, the end of the fiscal year, and are kept open for 1 month to complete the budget process for the previous year. When assessed with these characteristics, the government accounting applied for units with general and annexed budgets can be expressed as a system between the adapted cash basis and the accrual basis [24].

3.2.2. Reforming government accounting practices in Turkey

The reform studies in the field of government accounting in Turkey were initiated in 1995 under the name of "Government Financial Management Project" with loan support of the World Bank and maintained in 1999 with the "Regulation on the Accounting of Companies with Circulating Capital". Within the scope of the project, on March 2, 1999, it was planned to be transferred to automation in all the accounts, and the pilot accountancy for Say2000i "Web-Based Accountancy Automation Project" was selected and the first application started. The Say2000i project is a bill management automation system aiming at transparent, fast, and secure service on a virtual network that links all the accounts to each other centrally and across the country. The Say2000i system was started to be implemented in all the accountancies as of December 31, 2001 [57].

Following this, in 2003, "General Regulations of Government Accounting" entered into force, and the accounting plan created according to this regulation also resulted in the change of accounting method. As an accounting method, accrual accounting method has been adopted instead of the government accounting method, which is somewhere between the adjusted cash basis and the accrual basis [11].

Pilot applications were made following the General Regulations on Government Accounting, and all information could be obtained from central computers by providing transparency in government accounts. The pilot works of accrual-based government accounting were initiated in 47 accounting departments carrying out the transactions of 6 pilot institutions selected in 2002 (under Secretariat of Treasury, General Directorate of Highways, Ege University, Hacettepe University, Ministry of Energy and Natural Resources, and Coast Guard command). The transactions carried out in these accounts were recorded according to the cash-based accounting system from one side and according to the accrual accounting system. These records were made in a systematic and accurate basis with around 6000 detail codes classified according to their qualifications. The developments in the accounts and registration methods in the government accounting continued with the abolition of the "General Accounting Law" Law No. 1050 in December 2003, and the "Government Financial Management and Control Law" No. 5018 was put into effect [58].

The criticisms of this system applied in Turkey before 2003 are as follows [24]:

- Since the government accounting system focuses only on the budget, only the budgetary operations are accounted, and government activities that are out of the budget are not monitored.

- The current accounting system is based on cash basis. In the accounting system based on the cash basis, information about the assets and responsibilities of the state cannot be recorded in full and on time. This situation causes much information that is important for financial reporting not to be recorded and lost.

- Government accounting system is limited by scope. Government Accounting Regulation includes annexed budget administrations, without prejudice to the provisions of general budget departments and special legislation. However, there are also institutions in the government sector that hold and use financial resources in their hands such as municipalities, private administrations, funds, and social security institutions.

- There is no accounting unit in the government. Since the existing accounting system includes general budget administrations and annexed budget institutions, institutions outside of them have created their own special accounting systems. Because of this multi-structure, it is not possible to consolidate accounts across all the government sectors.

- Accounts do not have a systematic code, and there are no time separator accounts in the current accounting system. Accounts are classified according to their qualifications. The qualifications of the accounts and the meanings they bear are only understood by the experts in this field. For this reason, financial reports and information that all users can understand and interpret from the existing accounting system cannot be produced, and government accounting remains a specialty.

- Continuity is one of the basic accounting principles. In the current accounting system, activity and budget practices remain in their respective years, while assets such as government assets, liabilities, and receivables are not transferred to the new fiscal year. The results of government action and budget implementation cannot be carried to forwarding years.

This removes the continuity of current government accounting and the comparability of these accounting-generated reports.

- The government accounting system is not as detailed as its competence. The current accounting system is not suitable for generating detailed information both because of the coding system and because it is not fully automated. Since the accounts are not divided into subaccounts, different and detailed information within an account cannot be decomposed and displayed and reported by the accounting system.
- The government accounting system is not suitable for reporting and generating results in this situation. Due to the problems mentioned above, the current system recognizes the transactions of general and annexed budgets and is only able to produce information in the form of rules that can be prepared by non-accounting transactions related to budget implementation results; it is unable to issue financial reports covering the government sector.
- The treasury general account and final account law, which the state is liable for accountability of the budget implementation results, does not have a similar financial reporting feature, and since they are communicated together with the new fiscal year budget in plan budget committee and the general assembly, they are voted and accepted in about 15 min and thus completely loses its effectiveness.
- Many accounts used in the account plan have lost the sense of accounting; different transactions by nature have been recorded on the same account. Reasons for this situation, especially occurred in payable accounts, are that some of government debts are monitored out of budget and a cash basis accounting cannot respond to the accounting needs of emerging borrowing instruments.
- In this accounting system, the government's assets are not recognized and cannot be reported.
- Most semi-fiscal transactions are carried out outside the accounting system, the ones that the system registers are lost in bag accounts which are emerged as the result of not using the accounts in accordance with their qualifications; as a result semi-fiscal transactions cannot be reported.
- Since this accounting system, in which the financial transactions of the government are recorded and therefore the financial reports are generated, does not register enlisted commitments, cannot separate noncash flows from cash-generating flows, cannot show pending expenses, it is not eligible for making allocations and cash projections.
- Accounting of budget implementation and reporting it at both local and central levels is usually carried out manually. This affects the accuracy and speed of information in a negative way.
- The manager should be able to access the information as soon as possible in order to make the right decisions. Information provided with day delay is not sufficient for good and effective management.

"General Regulations of Government Accounting" which is one of the products of "Government Financial Management Project" and regulates accounting and reporting standards and framework account plan for units included in the scope of general management has been published in the Official Gazette on November 19, 2003 with the decision of the Council of Ministers dated October 16, 2003 and No. 2003/6334. However, it has been stated that this regulation will be postponed until the enforcement date of regulations to be made in accordance with the Law No. 5018 dated December 10, 2003. "Accounting Regulation of Units Included in General Budget and Added Budget Administrations" which was included in the units within the central government in 2004 and is on accrual basis has entered into force on February 20, 2004. This regulation terminated the "Government Accounting Regulation" which entered into force in 1990 [59].

Government Financial Management and Control Law No. 5018 was issued in 2004 in order to harmonize Turkish government financial management system with contemporary financial management principles and practices such as efficient, economical, and the effective use of government resources; transparency; accountability; accrual-based government accounting; analytical budget system; and internal control. This law, which is fulfilled with the General Accounting Law No. 1050, was adopted in the Turkish Grand National Assembly on December 10, 2003 and was started to be implemented on January 1, 2006 with all its provisions. Following the governmentation of some provisions of Law No. 5018 in 2003, "General Management Accounting Regulation" which was entered into force by being published on the Official Gazette dated June 8, 2005 with the decision of the Council of Ministers dated May 3, 2005 and No. 2005/8844 abolished General Regulations on Government Accounting dated 2003 from the date of enforcement. The purpose of this regulation has been expanded according to "General Regulation on Government Accounting". Accountability, which is an indispensable element of financial transparency, has been added to the text of the regulation. Furthermore, "General Budget Accounting Regulation" was issued in 2005 and put into force as of 2006. With the governmentation of the said regulations, General Regulations on Government Accounting issued in 2003 and "Accounting Regulation of Units Included in General Budget and Added Budget Administrations" issued in 2004 have been abolished. Finally, General Budget Accounting Regulation has been abolished with "Central Administration Accounting Regulation" which is prepared for administrations within the scope of central government in line with the amendments made in the Law No. 5018 with Law No. 5436 and has been effective as of January 1, 2007. In the first article of the Law No. 5018, which is formed within the scope of the government accounting reform implementations in Turkey, the aim of the law is expressed as follows: the mission that the law is undertaken is emphasized by telling "The purpose of this Law is to regulate the structure and functioning of government financial management, preparation and implementation of government budgets, the accounting, reporting and financial control of all financial transactions to ensure accountability and financial transparency to obtain and use goverment resources effectively, economically and efficiently in line with the policies and targets contained in the development plans and programs" [60].

The scope of the law is shown in the second article of the Government Financial Management and Control Law No. 5018: "This Law includes the financial management and control of government administrations that are within the scope of general management which constitutes of government administrations within the scope of central government, social security institutions, and local administrations". The use and control of resources provided by the European Union funds to government administrations from within and outside the country is also subject to the provisions of this Law, provided that the provisions of international agreements are reserved. The domain of financial management and control is set forth by telling that "regulatory and supervisory agencies are subject to articles 3, 7, 8, 12, 15, 17, 18, 19, 25, 42, 43, 44, 47, 48, 49, 50, 51, 52, 53, 54, 68, 76, and 78 of this Law" [60]. The accounting system prescribed by Government Financial Management Control Law No. 5018 includes the following matters [61]:

- Taking the overall management sector and all of economic transactions into full coverage.
- Enabling officers and officials to account and be controlled.
- To be detailed enough to be able to produce data suited to the needs of administrators and staff.
- Allowing the preparation of final accounts and financial reports.
- Accrual accounting of all financial transactions and at the same time recording the budgetary transactions in cash basis.
- Determination of accounting and reporting standards by a board—preparation of financial reports and financial statistics in line with international standards.
- Governmentation of financial reports and financial statistics by the Ministry of Finance for specified periods.

Government financial management system in Turkey is fundamentally changing with Law 5018; especially the boundaries of government financial management have been specified; common terminology has been prepared; financial reporting, financial statistics, and government accounting have been rearranged; new arrangements have been introduced in parallel with international developments in the scope, implementation, and realization of the central governed budget. By this law, provisions relating to government accounting and government financial statistics have been arranged between 49 and 54 articles of the fourth part of the law entitled "Government Accounts and Financial Statistics" [57].

In Article 49 of the Law, the government accounting system is defined as to ensure that making decisions, controlling, and giving accountability steps are effective and to be established and implemented in such a way that it will be based on a quick calculation of the final account and financial reports. In the second paragraph of Article 49, the features of the government accounting transactions are introduced, and the reasons for the recording of accounts related to accounting transactions are explained. In the said article, it is said that "Records are kept to provide information to the government by the authorities in the control and management in government accounting accounts by taking into account the commitments and trusts in a predetermined system for the assets of government institutions with financial transactions that have any financial consequences and which cause the equity to decrease or increase" [61].

The time and conditions under which accounting transactions are to be recorded are set out in Article 50 of Law No. 5018. In accordance with this article, accounting transaction is "When any economic asset emerges, is converted to a different style, sold or completely left out, it is taken into account. It is essential that all financial transactions are included in accounting and all accounting entries are made based on absolute documents" [61]. Regarding budget expenditures and revenues, it is stated in Article 51 of Law No. 5018 "Government expenditure and income must be shown in the accounts of the accrued year, budget expenditures and revenues must be collected in the accounting records of the year in which the collection is made". In this article government revenue costs and related accounting records are tracked in the accounts of the fiscal year accrued according to the accrual-based registration system. However, recording of budget transactions continues to be recorded on a cash basis as it was in the past [61].

According to the regulations regarding financial statistics made by Article 54 of the Law No. 5018, the provision "Financial statistics for a year are examined by the Court of Accounts for regulation, reality, governmentation, reliability, suitability for predetermined measures and then the conclusion of the review is sent to the Ministry of Finance, to the Turkish Grand National Assembly. The Ministry of Finance takes necessary measures regarding the evaluation of the report" is available [61].

Consequently, while the government accounting system applied in Turkey until 2004 was based on cash basis, Law No. 5018 was published in 2003 within the framework of the studies initiated in 2001, and with the regulation introduced in 2004, the accrual-based government accounting system was introduced.

Within the scope of secondary legislation regulations of the Government Financial Management and Control Law No. 5018, "General Management Accounting Regulation" and "General Budget Accounting Regulation" were issued in 2005 and put into force as of 2006. With the governmentation of the said regulations, General Regulations of Government Accounting issued in 2003 and Accounting Regulation of Units Included in General Budget and Added Budget Administrations issued in 2004 were abolished. Finally, together with "Central Management Accounting Regulation" issued in 2006 and put into force as of 2007, General Budget Accounting Regulation has been abolished.

4. Conclusion

Government accounting assumes the most important role in taking forward rational and sound decisions as a means of providing budgetary control. It is therefore a fundamental task of government accounting to keep records of financial policy transactions and to report them in a manner that is understandable to everyone, by providing the control of the state and other government institutions' compliance with the budgeted revenue and expenditure outcomes of a fiscal year.

Studies that started at the beginning of the 1980s in the world with the purpose of providing efficiency in government financial management, performing accountability to society, making financial reports, and making information transparent resulted in the change of the structure and functioning of government accounting. In general, government financial management, in private, especially developments and changes in government accounting continue. In government financial management, international organizations contribute to government accounting, national accounting, and budgeting. It has been important in the development of accounting that IMF, OECD, the World Bank, and the European Commission have contributed in national accounting subject, but in fact the United Nations has pioneered this issue, IMF has pioneered in budgeting, and International Accountants Federation has leaded on the accounting discipline. Especially the work of the International Accountants Federation and the government sector committee within that continues to meet the new demands expected from accounting. International developments in government financial management and accounting caused countries to review their financial management and accounting systems. Developments that were started in this direction in New Zealand and Australia continued in the USA, Canada, Sweden, the Netherlands, England, Germany, Switzerland, Korea, and Turkey although the starting years were different. New Zealand, the country where first developments in government financial management were experienced, started working in 1989 and has become to record state accounts with accrual-based accounting in 1992. We believe that New Zealand thinks of these things as things that should be in their own internal structure rather than thinking internationally. In other words, we think that the importance of the effective use of government resources and the integration of accountability are socially integrated and work is started in this direction. New Zealand practices led to other countries. The studies carried out by other countries were also carried out for the same purpose in order to gain a certain discipline in government financial management and to realize government accountability.

Cash-based government accounting based on the Accounting Government Law number 1050, which has been implemented for many years in the government sector after the Regovernmentan period in Turkey, was kept totally based on the budget. Only the results of the budget implementation could be seen; it could not ensure that the results of the original work of the government were visible. While the transactions related to the budget were being recorded, the transactions out of that could not be recorded. A simple accounting system was used to record only the cash inflows and outflows from financial transactions regardless of when the benefits from financial transactions come into play. Since the changes that have taken place in the commodities owned by the state have not been recorded in the accounting records, the account of these goods could not be kept, and therefore the borrowing capacity of the state is kept hidden; the actual size of the state could not be determined. For this reason, government-owned assets and accrued income and expenses, commencing commitments, payables, and receivables could not be recorded and reported. It was not possible to obtain financial reports and healthy information from this system. In addition, global and scientific developments emerged in the world have increased the social requirements. State that determines revenue and expenditure according to budget realizations had to pay unnecessary interest by borrowing extemporaneously.

Due to all these reasons, the Law on Accounting Government Law No. 1050 was insufficient against the changing conditions. For this reason, government financial management reform initiatives have been initiated starting from 1995. The first step in the reform of government accounting was taken at the beginning of 2002 with pilot applications made to test accrual-based government accounting by creating a working group within the General Directorate of Accounts. The results of testing the account plan prepared as a result of pilot applications have been successful. It has been seen that it is possible to produce financial reports in accordance with international classification, data can be collected on the basis of institutions, and reports can be produced as classified institutional. It has been understood that budget applications can be reported daily through the Say2000i system. Successful results as a result of pilot applications have shown that accrual-based accounting and reporting system could be implemented.

"General Regulations of Government Accounting" has been prepared after these studies for the transition to accrual-based state accounting in 2003. Then, in 2004, the "Accounting Regulation of Units Included in General Budget and Added Budget Administrations" was put into effect. The regulation, which was in force for 2 years, underwent some amendments under the Government Administration and Control Law No. 5018. "General Management Accounting Regulation" which aims to cover the entire government sector pursuant to this law was published in the Official Gazette on June 8, 2005 and entered into force as of January 1, 2006.

A number of problems were encountered during the transition to accrual-based accounting system that enabled more effective fiscal management and drastic changes in the government accounting system, and it is inevitable that problems will be experienced in the following period. However, with the arrangements made, government accounting has come to be able to fulfill the functions expected from accounting. This used system will be more effective over time by eliminating the deficiencies in implementation and by increasing the knowledge of the staff with better adaptation to the system and will fully fulfill the benefits expected from it.

Author details

Mihriban Coşkun Arslan

Address all correspondence to: mihriban.arslan@gop.edu.tr

Department of Business Administration, Faculty of Economics and Administrative Sciences, Gaziosmanpasa University, Tokat, Turkey

References

[1] Dean P.N. Government Accounting in Developing Countries, Policy Studies and Developing Nations, A Multi-Volume Treatise Volume: 3. In: Nagel SS, editor., Routledge, United Kingdom, JAS Press Inc; 1996. pp. 265-283

[2] Güngör A. Azmi, Yönetim Aracı Olarak Türk Devlet Muhasebe Sistemi. No: 1981/231. Ankara: Maliye Bakanlığı Tetkik Kurulu Yayını; 1981

[3] Bulutoğlu K, Kurtuluş E. Bütçe ve Kamu Harcamaları. İstanbul: Kent Basımevi; 1981

[4] Akarçay V. Türkiye'de Devlet Muhasebesi ve Uygulaması. İstanbul, Marmara Üniversitesi Yayınları; 1980

[5] Devlet Muhasebesinde Reform Çalışmaları: Nakit Esasından Tahakkuk Esasına, Ankara: Muhasebat Genel Müdürlüğü; 2002

[6] Demirbaş T. Sayıştaylar Tarafından Gerçekleştirilen Performans Denetimleri ve Türk Sayıştayı Uygulaması. Sayıştay Araştırma, İnceleme. 2001; Çeviri Dizisi: 17, Ankara

[7] Karaarslan E. Devlet Muhasebesi Olgusu ve Ülkemizde Devlet Muhasebesi Standartları. Ankara; 2005

[8] Akmut Ö. Türkiye'de Devlet Muhasebesi. No: 170. Ankara: Atatürk Üniversitesi Yayınları; 1973

[9] Çetinkaya Ö. Devlet Muhasebesi Alanındaki Gelişmeler ve Türkiye'de Yapılan Çalışmaların Değerlendirilmesi. İstanbul Üniversitesi İktisat Fakültesi Maliye Araştırma Merkezi Konferansları Sayı: 46. 2004. pp. 83-98

[10] Sipahi B, Yanık S, Topal C. Devlet Muhasebesi. İstanbul: Nobel Basımevi; 2007

[11] Yıldırım, Z, Çetinkaya Ö. Devlet Muhasebesi Teori ve Uygulama. Bursa, Ekin Kitabevi; 2006

[12] Giray A. Milli Muhasebe ve Devlet Muhasebesi. Ankara; 1997

[13] Monsen N. The case for cameral accounting. Financial Accountability & Management. February 2002;**18**(1):39-72

[14] Gökçen G. Devlet Muhasebesi. İstanbul: Türkmen Kitabevi; 2003

[15] Şahin N. Devlet Muhasebesi. Ankara: Ankara İktisadi ve Ticari İlimler Akademisi; 1968

[16] Tügen K. Devlet Bütçesi. İzmir: Anadolu Matbaası; 1999

[17] DPT. Kamu Mali Yönetiminin Yeniden Yapılandırılması ve Mali Saydamlık Özel İhtisas Komisyonu Raporu. Sekizinci Beş Yıllık Kalkınma Planı. Ankara: T.C. Devlet Planlama Teşkilatı Yayınları; 2000

[18] Karaarslan E. Merkezi Yönetim Kapsamındaki Kamu İdareleri İçin Devlet Muhasebesi. Ankara, Muhasebat Kontrolörleri Derneği Yayınları; 2007

[19] Maliye Bakanlığı TC. Muhasebat Genel Müdürlüğü. Devlet Muhasebesinde Reform Çalışmaları: Nakit Esasından Tahakkuk Esasına. Ankara; Muhasebat Kontrolörleri Derneği Yayınları, 2002

[20] OECD. Accounting for What?: The value of accrual accounting to the government sector. Occasional Paper on Government Management. Paris, OECD; 1993

[21] Dişli M, İpek M, Aydın B. Merkezi Yönetim Muhasebesi. Ankara, ISBN. : 9786056168604, Mayıs 2007

[22] Kerimoğlu B. Devlet Muhasebesinde Reform Çalışmaları, Mali Kılavuz Dergisi, No. 17. Ankara: Muhasebat Kontrolörleri Derneği Yayını, 2002

[23] Karaarslan E. Tahakkuk Esaslı Muhasebe ve Devlet Hesaplarında Şeffaflık, Mali Kılavuz Dergisi, No: 15. Ankara: Muhasebat Kontrolörleri Derneği Yayını, Ocak 2002

[24] T.C. Başbakanlık Devlet Planlama Teşkilatı. VIII. Beş Yıllık Kalkınma Planı: Kamu Mali Yönetiminin Yeniden Yapılandırılması ve Mali Saydamlık Özel İhtisas Komisyonu Raporu. Ankara, T.C. Başbakanlık Hazine Müsteşarlığı Yayınları; 2000

[25] Montesinos J.V., Vela Bargues, J.M., Governmental Accounting in Spain. Research in Governmental and Non-profit Accounting, 9, 1996, pp: 219-238.

[26] Maliye Bakanlığı Muhasebat Genel Müdürlüğü Devlet Muhasebesinde Reform Çalışmaları: Nakit Esasından Tahakkuk Esasına. Ankara, T.C.Maliye Bakanlığı Muhasebat Genel Müdürlüğü Yayını; Kasım 2002

[27] Guthrie J. Application of accrual accounting in the Austalian government sector—Rhetoric or reality? Financial Accountability & Management. February 1998;**14**:1-19

[28] Gören İ.. Kamu Mali Yönetiminin Yeniden Yapılandırılması Bağlamında Performans Yönetimi. Türk Kamu Mali Yönetiminin Yeniden Yapılandırılması ve Bu Yapılandırmada Performans Yönetimi ve Denetiminin Yeri. XV. Türkiye Maliye Sempozyumu. Akdeniz Üniversitesi, İ.İ.B.F. Maliye Bölümü. 15-17 Mayıs 2000; pp. 227-266

[29] Ainsworth P., Denıes D., Plumlee RD, Larson CX. Introduction to Accounting: An Integrated Approach. A.B.D.; 1997

[30] Robinson M. Accrual accounting and the efficiency of the core government sector. Financial Accountability Management. February, 1998; **14**(1):21-37

[31] Allen R, Tommasi D. Managing Government Expenditure; A Referance Book for Transition Countries, Paris, OECD-SIGMA; 2001

[32] Unur K, İçöz O. Turizm Uydu Hesapları. Dokuz Eylül Üniversitesi Sosyal Bilimler Enstitüsü Dergisi İzmir. 2004;**6**(1):304-327.

[33] T.C. Başbakanlık Devlet İstatistik Enstitüsü. Uydu Hesapları Turizm: 1996-1998. Ankara, Devlet İstatistik Enstitüsü Matbaası; 2002

[34] Jackson D. The New National Accounts: An İntroduction To The System of National Accounts 1993 and The European System of Accounts 1995, Cheltenham, Edward Elgar; 2000

[35] Government Finance Statistics Manual. 2001. Companion Material, CLASSIFICATION OF GFSM 1986 DATA TO THE GFSM 2001 FRAMEWORK, International Monetary Fund, www.imf.org, October 2002

[36] European System of Accounts (ESA95). http://forum.europa.eu.int

[37] Handbook of International Government Sector Accounting Standards. www.ifac.org, ISBN 978-1-60815-264-3, December 2015.

[38] Chang J, Chen G, Chow C. Exploring the desirabilitiy and feasibility of reforming China's governmental accounting system. Journal of Government Budgeting, Accounting & Financial Management. Winter, 2008;**20**(4):482-509

[39] Pallot J. A decade in review; New Zeland's experience with resource accounting and budgeting. Financial Accountability & Management. November 2001;**17**(4):383-400

[40] Rıchardson R. Opening and balancing the books: The New Zealand experience. Perspectives on Accrual Accounting: IFAC Occasional Paper 3, New York: Public Sector Committee;1996

[41] Warren K. Implementing accrual accounting in government: The New Zealand experince. IFAC Occasional Paper. October 1994;1:1-19.**1**

[42] Hoque Z. Moll J. Government sector reform ımplications for accounting, accountability and performance of state owned entities an Australian perspective. The International Journal of Government Sector Management. 2001;**14**(4):304-326

[43] Hillier, D. From cash to accrual: Canadian experience. Perspectives on Accrual Accounting: edited by International Federation of Accountants, Public Sector Committee, Occasional Paper 3. Newyork, 1996:15-22

[44] Skelcher C. The Appointed State, Buckingham: Open University Press; 1998

[45] Jones G. Resource accounting and budgeting: Another false trail? Perspectives on Accrual Accounting: IFAC Occasional Paper 3. ISBN 1-887464-22-0, 1996:33-37

[46] Resource Accounting Framework of Accounting Standart Setting in the UK Central Government Sector. IFAC Government Sector Committee , United Kingdom, No: 5; 2002

[47] Yılmaz S. Performans Esaslı Bütçenin Gelişimi ve Uygulanması. Bütçe Dünyası Dergisi. 2007;**3**(27):35-43

[48] OECD. Accurual accounting and budgeting key ıssues and recent developments. Twenty-third Annual Meeting of OECD Senior Budget Officials. Washington, DC. 3-4 June 2002

[49] Montesınos V, Bargues JV. Bases of accounting and reporting foci in Spanish governmental accounting. Perspectives on Accrual Accounting: IFAC Occasional Paper 3. ISBN 1-887464-22-0, 1996: 17-24.

[50] Ström S. Full accrual government accounting in Sweden. Perspectives on Accrual Accounting: IFAC Occasional Paper 3. ISBN 1-887464-22-0, 1996: 25-32.

[51] BlöndaL JR. Budgeting in Sweden. OECD Journal on Budgeting. 2001;**1**(1):27-57

[52] OECD. Accrual Accounting in the Netherlands and the United Kingdom. 1997. www.oecd.org./puma

[53] Öner E. Osmanlı İmparatorluğu ve Cumhuriyet Döneminde Malî İdare. Ankara, Maliye Bakanlığı Araştırma – Planlama – Koordinasyon (APK) Daire Başkanlığı Yayınları, Yayın No: 369.; 2005

[54] Çoşan MH. Devlet Muhasebesi. Ankara, Yeni Uğur Matbaası; 1980

[55] Bayar D. Kamu Mali Yönetim ve Kontrol Kanunu Ne Getir(m)iyor? Maliye Dergisi. Eylül-Aralık 2003;144: 47-61

[56] Karaarslan E. Ülkemizde Devlet Muhasebesinin Serüveni. Sayıştay Dergisi, Ankara. Temmuz- Eylül:2004;54; 37-76

[57] Gökgöz A. Say2000i Web Tabanlı Saymanlık Otomasyon Sistemi Üzerine. Kamu Hesaplarına Uzman Bakış Dergisi. 2001;**1**(1):52-56

[58] T.C.MALİYE BAKANLIĞI Muhasebat Genel Müdürlüğü. Tahakkuk Esaslı Devlet Muhasebesi Pilot Uygulama Sonuçları. Ankara, T.C. Maliye Bakanlığı, Muhasebat Genel Müdürlüğü Yayını; Mayıs 2003

[59] Dişli M. Tahakkuk Esaslı Devlet Muhasebesi Açıklamalı-Çözümlü, No: 6. Ankara: Muhasebat Kontrolörleri Derneği Yayın; 2004

[60] Resmi Gazete. 24.12.2003; 25326

[61] Kızılkaya E. Yeni Devlet Muhasebesi Sistemi. Mali Kılavuz Dergisi, Ankara. 2007;35: 91-112

Chapter 15

Public Accounting Reform from Institutional Theory Perspectives: Case of Turkey

Ceray Aldemir and Tuğba Uçma Uysal

Additional information is available at the end of the chapter

http://dx.doi.org/10.5772/intechopen.68778

Abstract

In the literature, it is often found that institutional theory is used as the theoretical framework to explain the development and application of accounting. By means of these studies, it becomes easier to understand accounting as a social and political activity within itself and thus to be able to understand the economic, institutional, political and social environment of the turnover of the practices. In this regard, the main aim of this study is to explain the development of the public accounting system in Turkey with the help of institutional theory. Thus, it is aimed to explain all the dynamics that provide the institutionalization of state account in the national sense, together with the economic, political and social processes of the period in question. It is revealed that the regulatory arrangements directly contribute to the institutionalization of a field, and as a result, how the public organizations directly contribute to the institutionalization process.

Keywords: public accounting, institutional theory, public administration reform

1. Introduction

Historical processes have shown that states, which are powerful central structures in the collection and dissemination of incomes, are more successful in shaping internal and external politics than other states [1–3]. Such a centralization will not prevent the increase in tax revenues, but will prevent the lost income from being lost in middle-man stages. This is the most important influence underlying the search for a transparent and accountable state that continues to increase in importance throughout history. Nowadays, public institutions need to provide a rational accountability in order to be able to sustain an accountable, effective and efficient state structure. For this, there is a need for an accounting system that facilitates accountability, whether it is a strong and controlled state or a state structure that is maintained at a minimum level of control.

According to Hopwood [4], accounting has a vital role both in organizations-states and in social relationships. Accounting knowledge can affect perceptions, change languages and offer new possibilities for new actions. In this case, accounting also plays an active role in the realization of economic action. Abstracts and objectifications in the field of accounting are created within the economy. For this reason, the economic information that forms also shapes organizational activities, interests and preferences. From Hopwood's point of view, it can be said that there is a close relationship between accounting and organizational theory. This brings about the convergence of the two areas that are seen as far apart. Namely, it is possible that the approaches used in the theory of organization can be used to explain the accounting applications. Especially since the 1980s, this situation is often encountered.

Dillard et al. [5] explains this situation by the failure of the accounting discipline to empirically fail to explain the emerging accounting techniques and systems of theory, such as efficient market theory and theory of power of attorney. According to them, the accounting discipline needs to be re-conceptualized. Also, they add that as a result of this, the questions in the accounting researches have changed and the researchers have started to work interdisciplinary and applied the theories in different disciplines in order to be able to search for better answers to the questions such as how accounting is affected and how it affects. One of the theories that have been used to answer these questions has been institutional theory. Thus, accounting practices and change processes can become more expressible.

In the literature, it is often found that institutional theory is used as the theoretical framework to explain the development and application of accounting [1]. Some pieces of the literature indicate that accounting researchers investigate the development of accounting idea, explain how and why it changes, and discuss the social, economic, environmental and individual factors that influence changes. By means of these studies, it becomes easier to understand accounting as a social and political activity within itself and thus to be able to understand the economic, institutional, political and social environment of the turnover of the practices [2].

In this regard, the main aim of this study is to explain the development of the public accounting system in Turkey with the help of institutional theory. In this chapter, the standardization studies of the accounting system, especially the nineteenth century and the Republican period, which are experienced from the day to the day, are handled, and the transfers to the public accounting system, which is directly affected by the regulations and the conditions of the day, are studied. Thus, it is aimed to explain all the dynamics that provide the institutionalization of state account in the national sense, together with the economic, political and social processes of the period in question. It is revealed that the regulatory arrangements directly contribute to the institutionalization of a field, and as a result, how the public organizations directly contribute to the institutionalization process.

This study more specifically highlights the institutionalization process and institutional isomorphism and legitimization process. On the basis of this—as explained above—is the process of institutionalization that the accountant has as an occupational field and the contribution of this process to the institutionalization of the organizations. Globally, countries in the institutionalization process can adjust their own regulatory accounting systems and standards according to regulations in the actor countries [6]. As a result of this process, accounting specialization is provided. Especially in a sophisticated combination of theoretical knowledge, universality in the global context of a field of expertise, such as accounting, which incorporates analytical power and decision-making capability, offers the advantage of socio-political growth and potential advantage in terms of potential conceptual diffusion in this area [7].

However, this process can occur differently in different countries. Sometimes, the cultural environment [7] and sometimes the economic and political situation of the period (such as the war period) can be decisive in terms of ensuring and maintaining professional development. For example, such an environment can occur which needs a new cost-accounting system—after First World War [8]—or may occur as a result of dual regulations such as the one between the USA and Canada [6]. Or, as it happened in Turkey, it can be done with national reforms which are direct transfers from decisive countries. In this case, it is the subject of observing all of the figures considered. In short, the scope of this work is the public accounting reform in Turkey. Thus, the study evaluates the institutional theory of the public account ing reform process in Turkey from 1800s to 1950s.

2. The conceptual framework of institutional theory

As Dillard et al. defines institutional theory is, in general, a way of thinking about the relationship between formal organizational structures and the social processes that contribute to the development of these structures [5]. On this basis, the phenomenon of institutionalization is defined as the merging of new norms, values and structures with existing norms, values and constructions [9]. This process provides equilibrium and predictability in social relations, and accordingly these relations continue to occur [10]. The main reason for this is that institutionalization is seen as a social process [11]. In short, the foundation of the theory of institutionalization is the tendency of organizations—states to adapt to changing norms and social influences—processes of institutionalization. If they do not, naturally they will lose their legitimacy. This encourages organizations to homogenize their organizational structures and practices [6]. This is the starting point of many studies in the literature that explains the institutional theory.

As is known, the development of this theory involves more than half a century. Özen [12] examines the historical development process, the years of the 1980s were the beginning of the theory; the end of the 1980s and beginning of the 1990s were the years when the differences between the approaches explaining the institutional theory are being questioned and the effects of the 1990s on the organizations of the state and professional organizations as the years in which empirical studies continue. Within the development process of the theory, there are five different approaches that explain the institutional theory in the literature. These approaches are summarized in **Table 1**.

Year	Researchers	Institutionalization approaches	The way of institutionalization	Organizational goal
1957	Selznick	Adaptation tool	By creating values	Balance Legality
1977	Zucker	Formation of social order	By developing joint appropriate and meaningful behaviour together with the environment and transferring them to other individuals	Relevance Legitimacy
1977	Meyer and Rowan	Formation of social order	By creating a shared value system	Legitimacy Increasing resources Continue your life
1983	DiMaggio and Powell	Adaptation tool	Imitating successful organizations	Escaping uncertainty
1987	Friedland and Alford	Affect conscious and normative pressures	Changing corporate environment to protect interests	Follow-up of benefits

Source: Ref. [10].

Table 1. Institutionalization approaches.

Based on the pioneering work that contributes to the formation of institutional theory,[1] it forms the basic thesis of theory, the structures and processes of organizations by adapting them to the institutional environment they are in. In other words, in order for organizations to survive, they need to be productive not only in technical terms but also to legitimize themselves [12]. In order to do this, organizations need to respond to pressures from their institutional environment and adapt their organizational choices to socially accepted constructs or procedures [13]. This finding is the common point in all studies. The main difference in the studies is the form of institutionalization and institutionalization process. The question of these fundamental differences, together with the institutional theory itself, causes disagreements within it. This situation brings to mind the old and new concepts of institutional theory.

The piece of DiMaggio and Powell in these studies is shown as a study explaining the new institutional theory. The most important contribution of this work to the new institutional theory is the clarification of the concepts of isomorphism and organizational domain. DiMaggio and Powell argue that with modern life, organizations—even public institutions—are becoming more and more like each other. This process is expressed as the structural change process that the state and the professions shape as the greatest rationalizers, and as a result, the organizations according to the process are similar to each other [12].

[1]For detailed reading, please see Ucma T. (2012). Türkiye'deki Muhasebe Sisteminin Gelisiminin Kurumsal Teori Çerçevesinde Açiklanmasi, Muhasebe ve Finans Tarihi Arastirmalari Dergisi, MUFAD Yayinlari, Sayi: 2, Ocak, S. 145–178.

DiMaggio and Powell [14] call it isomorphism as long as organizations tend to adapt to the same constructs and practices. Isomorphism is often expressed as a similarity in the organizational and institutional context as a term used in mathematics, chemistry and biology [6]. According to DiMaggio and Powell [14], the concept of isomorphism is the best expression of the homogenization process and is expressed as the process of resembling others in a population with the same environmental conditions. It is understood that organizations should change themselves according to their characteristics.

DiMaggio and Powell describe their work as a process of isomorphism. Two types of isomorphism are mentioned in this process. The second one is competitive isomorphism. According to DiMaggio and Powell [14], institutional isomorphism occurs in three mechanisms. These are as follows:

> *Coercive isomorphism: It emerges from political influences and legitimacy problems. The coercive isomorphism arises from the official or non-official pressures of other organizations and the cultural expectations of the community they are in. These pressures can sometimes be in the form of a force, a means of persuasion or an invitation. Under certain conditions, however, organizations respond to this pressure. In other words, the organization directly affects the behaviour and structure of the organization in many ways around the periphery. For example, legal and technical requirements such as annual reports, budget, financial reporting requirements in a country shape organizations. In this case, the organizations are becoming increasingly homogenous [14].*
>
> *Mimetic isomorphism: In such isomorphism uncertainty is a force that pushes organizations to imitate. When goals are ambiguous and the environment creates symbolic uncertainty, organizations can model themselves to other organizations. Thus, the uncertainty is answered. The model received does not know that it is sometimes modeled or even does not want to be imitated. As a result, organizations in this kind of isomorphism make themselves more similar to other organizations and thus become more legitimate or more successful [14].*
>
> *Normative isomorphism: The third source of organizational isomorphic changes is normative isomorphism. It means here that all members of a profession, expressed by specialization, can jointly define the conditions and methods of work and contribute to the legitimacy of the profession and its foundations. Both aspects of the specialization are important in terms of isomorphism. While the educational and cognitive-based legitimacy provided by the universities is mainly provided, the second is the establishment and expansion of professional relations and therefore the dissemination. Universities and vocational training institutions are important for the development of organizational norms [14].*

Regardless of what mechanism occurs, institutional isomorphism refers to the cohesion of an organizational practice with other organizations. Institutional environmental structure is one of the main determinants of isomorphic process formation [5], and organizations are becoming isomorphic, that is, uniform, with the institutions of the public institutions adopting them [12].

It is possible to discuss the process of isomorphism in public organizations in terms of public accounting. Even though the theory of organization and the theory of accounting are reflected as far apart, they have an effective role in the rationalization of accounting organizations. It can be shown that the main reason for this is that the accountant is determinative of the legitimacy and transparency of the public organizations. In particular, it is considered that the concept of isomorphism that best expresses the international standardization in the field of accounting, namely homogenization, isomorphism, imitator, normative or compulsive isomorphic tendencies that arise due to institutional environment structure, causes institutional theory to constitute the theoretical basis of study. This approach, which is included in institutional theory, is expected to facilitate the understanding of the development or formation of the national accounting system, which is specifically described in subsequent parts.

3. Public accounting transformation between 1800 and 1950: reasons, implications and insights

An examination of the transformation in an area based on institutional theory is possible by evaluating the environmental, economic and political factors that emerged during the transformation process. In order to be able to interpret the historical development of the Ottoman reforms on public accounting, it is necessary to examine the aforementioned factors. When the history of public accounting in Turkey is examined, it is known that the history is based on ancient periods of Ottoman. According to information obtained from the accounting historians and the Prime Ministry archives, it seems that the public accountancy in the Ottoman Empire came into existence in the first years of the establishment of the Empire. The Ottoman Empire's first regular taxes based on traditional taxing regulations—*tımar ve zeamet*—were made by Çandarlı Kara Halil Pasha during the Sultan Orhan, the second sultan of the state. According to this method, a land conquered by the Ottoman armies was shared among the state treasury and soldiers; and, in the General Directorate of the Archives, the books, which are still known as the examples of them, are recorded and the taxes are allocated on them. It is possible, however, to find out that the expenses of the empire from the time of its establishment were regularly recorded on the day of the day.

Historical records also include budgetary examples that are not modern. During the reign of Sultan Mehmed IV, Tarhoncu Ahmet Pasha presented the state budget of 1651, which shows the state's income and expenditures and the precautions to be taken due to the budget deficit. Later on, these revenues were recorded in the books called *Ruznamçe* which are still stored in the General Directorate of the Archives, and tax is allocated on them. It is possible, however, to find out that the expenses of the Empire from the time of its establishment were regularly recorded on the day of the day. Historical records also include budgetary examples that are not modern. During the reign of Sultan Mehmed IV, Tarhoncu Ahmet Pasha presented the state budget of 1651, which shows the state's income and expenditures and the precautions to be taken due to the budget deficit [15].

The most striking point in this budget, which belongs to the seventeenth century, is the budget deficit. In order to assess the budget deficit, it is necessary to look at the characteristics of the period before this century. The financial problems that could lead to budget deficits in the Ottoman Empire began in the middle of the sixteenth century and continued to increase in the seventeenth and eighteenth centuries, reaching a summit in the nineteenth century that would lead to the demise of the empire. In order to get there from above, external borrowing was done in the empire. This has caused the Ottomans to become a good market in terms of Europe [16]. The process of overcoming the increasing financial strains in the Ottoman

Empire, especially through external borrowing, has been one of the most important triggers of public accounting reform in the empire. Raccagni [17] expresses the process in this period as follows:

> *"The situation in the Ottoman Empire was favorable to the expansion of French business. The Commercial Agreement of 1838 enabled France and Great Britain to sell their manufactured goods all over the Ottoman Empire without being hampered by customs regulations. The Capitulations were used to its ever-increasing detriment. By the late eighteenth century, members of the religious minorities of the Empire came to establish close ties with their foreign coreligionists, and, by adopting the latter's citizenship, were able to enjoy legal immunities and fiscal advantages denied their Muslim countrymen by the ruling authorities (Raccagni, 1980: 340)".*

In terms of being influential on state policies, France plays the most active role in the Ottoman market. However, France's influence over the Ottomans was not only limited with public financial reform but also encapsulated the military and education. Raccagni (1980) expresses this in the following way:

> *"The Ottoman government often welcomed French assistance. Military and educational reforms were carried on French patterns, often under the supervision of French officers and teachers sent by the Government of Louis-Phi- lippe.11 The leaders of the Tanzimat period (1839-1876), who had been exposed to French influence during their formative years in Europe, resorted to French collaboration in order to counterbalance the influence of Russia and Austria, who had gnawed at Turkish territories for more than a hundred years, and of England, who already had a strong incentive to get a foothold in their realm to secure her imperial communications (Raccagni, 1980: 340-341)".*

Although the Ottoman Empire had similar practices with Europe until the eighteenth century, after that date, the greatest cause in the differentiation and influence of Europe is the decentralized tax systems. According to Karaman and Pamuk [3], taxation is the distribution of resources in centralized states in Europe early in the modern era. These states have tried to increase the effectiveness of internal sources with a more efficient centralized tax system and to achieve military success in the international arena. In addition, some of these states have provided a great deal of financial centralization, and since the second half of the eighteenth century, they have made considerable differences both financially and militarily compared to other states. This is because the centralization of income is a financial phenomenon and the differences in this century can be seen clearly in the countries that cannot manage this financial phenomenon.

For example, it is known that in the sixteenth century the Ottomans showed similarities with France in many respects when the European influence in the nineteenth century was assessed on the Ottoman public financial system. Both countries were not very complex and centralized. By the seventeenth century, both the Ottoman and French tax systems had developed at significant levels. War and financial needs have been the driving forces of change in early public funding. In particular, the increase in the wartime financial deficits caused changes in French and Ottoman financial institutions. In this respect, the tax systems applied to centralize both France and the Ottomans in the first half of the seventeenth century appeared in various forms. The system applied as a tax-farming system was effective in the eighteenth century when it was operated in France, but did not find a successful application area in the Ottoman Empire [18].

In the direction of these developments, nineteenth century has been the period of significant changes in terms of financial and monetary policies in the Ottoman Empire. This century was not only the period when the reforms in financial systems took place but also the period in which the results of the different periods of Ottoman financial structure were taken due to internal and external borrowings [19]. The basic statements mentioned were influential in the selection of the period of study focus. This is because the need for reform of the public accounting in the Ottoman Empire came about not in a single century but in the evaluation of the results of more than one hundred centuries. In other words, it is possible to relate the dynamic of the changes that took place in the Ottoman period in the nineteenth century to the problems that have been effective since the fourteenth century [20].

Nineteenth century was a period when the foreign influence increased due to the policies applied in the Ottoman Empire. Reform Edict (Tanzimat Fermanı-Gülhane Hatt-i Humayunu) was declared on 3 November 1839, in order to manage this perception that occurred in the international arena and to restrict Europe's intervention areas on the Ottoman side. The word reform has been chosen in particular and has been used in order to prevent chaos in the country and to regulate it in terms of the state mechanism. Therefore, between 1839 and 1876, it was defined as the *Reform Era* in the Ottoman Empire [16]. In the Ottoman Empire, innovation movements, which had started at the time of Selim III (1789–1808), and increasingly continued during the period of Mahmut II (1808–1839), did not give much importance to the financial management. However, those movements had been manifested in the military and administrative field. Especially after 1830, developments were seen in this area, and a year before Tanzimat, in 1838 the foundations of the current centralized financial management were established [12].

One of the most important innovations in this period was realized on the tax collection system. In the Ottoman Empire, the greatest failure of the state occurred during the tax collection process. Only certain taxes were collected by the Taxman and linked to a tax collection system called *iltizam*. In this process, Taxman brought his tax obligations to increase his income and sent certain parts of the collected tax to the state [21]. Taxes from foreign merchants, however, were gradually declining—initially as a result of agreements made with the United Kingdom and later with other western countries. In order to prevent this, it was stated that the taxpayers would collect the people according to their income and that the soldiers could only take part in this process as observers [16].

Another innovation in the reform period is related to the budget. Looking at the historical development of the budget, it is not possible to mention a modern budget estimating the general income and expenses of the state before the reform period in the Ottoman Empire. Only income was collected from various sources for specific services. In the reform process of 1839, there is no clear statement of the budget. However, there are explanations about the fact that the expenses are determined by law. For the first time in 1845, the decision to prepare a modern budget is announced in accordance with the estimation and collection principles. In the Ministry of Finance, a decision was taken every year to start budgeting in 1846. A framework has been presented taking Western models into consideration.

After this date, the Finance of Treasury has published annual books called the *Muvazene* (Balance). The first legal arrangement in the name of the budget was realized in 1855 [16]. *Bütçe Nizamnamesi* (the Budget Ordinance) published with the 1856 Islahat Fermanı brought important provisions about the budget. With this regulation, every year the income and expenditures of the state will be determined and a notebook called *Muvazene* will be presented to the Sultan. Even though this regulation has introduced the principles of budgetary technique, a parliament has been given to the commission, instead of a parliament representing the nation who has authority to prepare and approve the budget.

In 1859, the Islahat-ı Maliye Komisyonu (Finance Reform Commission)—consisting of four Turkish and three foreign members—was established and a year later the name of this commission was changed to the Treasury Assembly. The Commission faced great difficulties; hence the desired information about the financial and economic situation of the country has not been reached. However, based on the figures and information gathered in the relevant departments, the first budget could be prepared in 1863–1864. At the beginning of the 1860s, British Hobart and Foster, who came to Istanbul to study the Ottoman state's financial situation on a new debt request, spoke of the necessity of making a realistic budget in their reports. The first budget was set, but the system and necessary organizational structure was not established. The budget has been prepared to allow the state to obtain foreign debt more and to show the financial status of the state to the foreign states. In other words, the first budgets and then the other budgets that follow these budgets have not gained much importance. It was the documents that were approved by the persons who were brought to the administration by appointment and presented to the absolute will of the Sultan.

In 1872, a new regulation was issued in the name of 'Budget Regulation of the State Treasurer'. An important difference brought by this regulation is that the Budget Commission should examine the budget before it is sent to parliament [22]. In 1874, the second legal regulation on the budget was made accordingly. The second regulation, which has the same framework as the first regulation, includes the submission of the budget proposal prepared by the Ministry of Finance to the approval of the Sultan by the Board of Ministers after being discussed in the budget commission. One of the most important ones in the budget regulation during the reform period is to make the Julian Calendar (financial year) for the budget preparation according to the Islamic order [16].

In this respect, the first law concerning the Ottoman budget was the 1876 Constitution. The state budget was defined on the basis of the provisions of the French constitution. The annual income of taxpayers, the approval of income and expenditures in terms of departments and the annual principles of the budget were included; the Court of Accounts Law and the final account law were adopted [22]: 1876 Constitution (Kanun-i Esasi). Kanun-ı Esasî has given the budget right to the Assembly and the Assembly established by the Parliament and Ayan Parliament. In the Kanun-i Esasî, it is stated that (1) the money cannot be collected from anyone under the name of tax, charge without legal foundation, (2) the state revenues and expenditures will be executed every year after being approved by the Muvâzen-i Umumiye Law and (3) the recognition of income and expenditure as separate items. However, these principles were not practically applicable until the declaration of Second Constitutionalist Period in 1908, and taxpayers continued to gather with the will of the sultans and spend the places that the sultan approves. Until 1880, there were no institutions related to accounting and auditing in the Ottoman Empire. Because of this lack of organization, an undecided and ineffective tax collection system has emerged, and as a result, the state has lost its high income [23]. This has led to a debated and criticized state mechanism.

The publication of the first law on Ottoman public accounting also took place in this process. The first public accounting law in the Ottoman Empire was dated 1880. This law has been put into practice since 1881 and has been transformed into a system that shows the system of *Kameral Accounting*, that is, income and expense accrual depending on the budget [15]. As it is mentioned above, Kanun-i Esasi (The Constitution), which was put into effect with the Second Constitutional Monarchy in 1908, has also established the budget system that has been implemented to this day. Later on, in 1910, the first budget of the Mesrutiyet was accepted and a new accounting system without classical budget rules was established. The first public accounting law, which was drafted by the French and Belgian government accounting laws, was enacted in 1910. In the next 2 years after the application of this law, the problems in practice were revealed and the Accounting-Public Law was adopted on 26 May 1927 as a result of a 15-year study of the French, Italian and Belgian public accounting laws. This law not only describes the procedures for maintaining records in the field of public accounting but also contains some rules regulating tax, budget and commercial life with the state [24].

With the arrangement made, since the accounting system in the new system is required to be maintained in the *Kameral System*, it is not fully compatible with the two-sided recording system. In 1923, there was a transition to a new law and budget accounting to be applied according to the bilateral registration system. After the new arrangement, it is worth noting that the features of the books in the American accounting system have been utilized [15]. This law was another important step for a modern and established financial structure and formed the basis of the financial order to be established during the Republican era [22]. In 1928, with the guidelines issued, the accounts used in the public accounting system have been simplified and some kind of cameral dual-sided registration system has begun to be used. With this arrangement, the public accounting system that was started to be implemented was criticized and the system was re-opted [15]. Because, in 1927, with the Accounting-General Law, it was aimed to prepare a budget, to formulate a solid basis for financial affairs by arranging provisions, allocations and form conditions to be included in the budget.

From the 1930s onwards, the influence of the big economic crises experienced by the capitalist system around the world has shifted to the politics of the statist economy, and a change in the understanding of the equivalent budget has been experienced. In this period, the balance of the economy has become more important than the budget. In other words, the budget deficit or surplus of the budget is considered insignificant as long as it contributes to the balance in the economy. New ideologies that affected the whole world after the Second World War also had an effect in Turkey. In this process, social state and understanding of social welfare have gained importance. This approach tried to find its place in the classical budget, but as a result of the change experienced in the country, the reconstruction of the financial landscape came to the forefront [22].

http://dx.doi.org/10.5772/intechopen.68778

For this reason, the new accounting system, which was started to be used on 1 January 1948, fully adopted double-sided registration and budgetary accounting. However, it is seen that the accounting system still does not include accrued expenses, and modern public accounting is not introduced. A more cash-based budget accounting explains the public accounting system in 1948. For this reason, the issue that is mostly discussed in this period is whether Turkey's state account is composed of a budgetary account. Because if the goal is only budget, then the system used at that time is the *Kameral Accounting* system. However, there are also parties that are separated from budgetary accounting within the system [15]. A more rational public accounting system has been established than in previous periods, but it has not been able to switch to a public accounting system that covers incomes and expenses fully accrued.

The Ottoman financial organization can be examined in two ways as the central finance and the autonomous provincial finance. This binary system is generally supported by external treasury, but in special cases, some transfers can be made in the interior with the permission from the sultan [25]. One can say that this financial system is operated by a budget tradition and there are about 50 budget examples from that day [26]. Unlike today's budgets, these budgets do not have the income item in detail, but they cover the costs in detail [25]. When the nineteenth century came, the integration of the western world began to transform the economic and financial life of the Ottoman State and all the dynamics that regulated them. In general, the public financial system, in particular, the budget system, is at the forefront of transforming areas.

Briefly, Turkey is one of the late countries in terms of modern budgeting and application of techniques. The passage of budget preparation, reparations and control rights to the national representatives became possible only after the great difficulties and delays in the late nineteenth century [27]. Reform movements have started in Tanzimat Term but these have remained in the administrative and military areas. Today's centralized financial management can be called beginning at that time. Although reforms have introduced financial management provisions such as taking gore tax for heroic financial power, bringing in the salary system, converting the Sultan's treasury and expenditures to state treasury instead of the bargaining and dues methods, there has never been a mention in the budget of the financial power [28]. Moreover, as it is stated above the development of accounting principles in the era of the Turkish Republican (1923-present) can be understood from various historical perspectives. From 1923 onwards, there have been several attempts to develop well-established principles in the accounting system.

The most important factor in the transformation between 1923 and 1950 is the establishment of the Republic of Turkey. In this period, most of the state regulations were aligned with the practices of the developed Anglo-Saxon and Continental Europe. Besides, in the period between 1950 and 1980 (1980 was the beginning of the economic liberalization in Turkey), it is seen that Jewish Professors such as Fritz Neumark, who fled from Hitler's Nazi Germany and took refuge in Turkey, constitute the public financial system. In the post-1980 period, a standard accounting system was introduced. After 1980, an understanding of performance management, aimed at improving management performance, including items such as efficiency, effectiveness, frugality, service quality, performance measurement, etc., has become a key element in many countries' reform programmes—Turkey is one of them. In the performance management framework that characterizes the results-based management system, it has become important to maintain public accounting efficient and to increase aggregate accountability for all public account and public accounts together with it.

4. Conclusion and discussion

In this study, it is aimed to explain the transition period of the public accounting system of the Ottoman from the nineteenth century to the first half of the twentieth century within the frame of institutional theory. In the Ottoman Empire, which had a similar financial system to many European countries until the middle of the eighteenth century, there was a need to analyse the budget deficits caused by internal and external borrowing in the midst of a financial crisis. The process specified in line with this requirement initiated a serious reform process in the Ottoman Empire and triggered the need to maintain the tax collection system and public accountancy. There are various reasons behind the lack of a centralized tax collection system in the Ottoman Empire. According to Balla and Johnson [18], the main reason for this is that taxmen (tax collectors) are more heterogeneous due to the breadth of the Ottoman land.

In other words, the different ethnic and religious roots of tax collectors in the Ottoman Empire hinder the centralization of the tax collection system. According to Karaman and Pamuk [3], factors such as difficult terrain conditions, differences in capital distribution and low urbanization rates made tax collection difficult compared to the smaller and more urbanized Western European countries in the Ottoman Empire. The differences in per capita national income have also caused difficulties in total taxation. In addition, wrong money policies applied in the Ottoman Empire also caused the acceleration of the effects of the process. Because foreign borrowing in the Ottoman Empire was first taken in 1854 during the Crimea War, the type of money called Kaime entered into force in 1840 and was abolished in 1862. When it came to 1861, internal and external debts were realized at 1/8 of the state expenditures [16]. The stated reasons have led tax incomes to not be able to generate the income mechanism of the state well and therefore to follow their expenses effectively.

Various improvements have been made in order to get out of this process. Ozekicioglu and Ozekicoglu [16] summarize the improvements in five basic topics. The first one is to maintain records more regularly. The second is to prepare a detailed budget. The third is the improvement of the money system. The fourth is the simplification of the tax system and the centralization of the financial centre and the improvement of the treasury and the budget. The fifth amendment is to make arrangements for the establishment of banks and similar financial institutions on 18 February 1856 in order to understand the banking sector. There was also a need to establish a state bank. Thus, the negative effects on the value of the money were tried to be prevented by the mechanism of the state bank. Each remedy made was aimed at balancing budget deficits with money and financial policies. It can be said that the most useful point of view for monitoring the financial transformation process in the mentioned Ottoman period is to evaluate the state budgets and the changes made in this area.

Table 2 summarizes the transformation process of the Ottomans which was prepared in line with the explanations made in this study. **Table 2** also maps each reformist regime to the type of institutional theory involved. The type of institutional theory in the table is designed taking into account the structure and the reasons for the reformist arrangements made. This is because DiMaggio and Powell [14], who point to the isomorphism approach in institutional theory, tend to show the social and economic cohesion of states—especially those with ambiguous

Date	Underpinnings of the reforms	Reason(s)	Application area	Type of institutional theory
Between seventeenth and nineteenth centuries	The necessity of reformer developments	Decentralized tax system, wrong monetary policy, Internal and external debt increase	Military system	Coercive isomorphism
		Ottoman turn into an open-bazaar in terms of European market	Education policies Financial system	Mimetic isomorphism
1839	Reform Edit (Tanzimat Fermanı)	To reduce the Western influence in the Ottoman Empire	The foundations of current centralist financial management have been laid	Coercive isomorphism Mimetic isomorphism Normative isomorphism
1856	Royal Edict of Reform (Islahat Fermanı)	Publication of the Budget Ordinance: the need to keep the state's income and expenditures annually and the need to make budget-related adjustments	Financial system	Coercive isomorphism Mimetic isomorphism Normative isomorphism
1859	Finance Reform Commission (Islahat-ı Maliye Komisyonu)	The commission formed by the French and English members due to the regulatory reforms in the reform period to activate the tax system and to achieve the desired result in the prevention of the economic crisis	Financial system	Mimetic isomorphism
1872	Government Budget Ordinance (Devlet-i Aliyenin Bütçe Nizamnamesi)	It is a budget law prepared in line with the need to develop and renew the tax system in line with the proposal of the Reform Commission. Based on the provisions of the French constitution, the state budget was defined and presented in 1876 constitution	Financial system	Mimetic isomorphism

Date	Underpinnings of the reforms	Reason(s)	Application area	Type of institutional theory
1880	Publication of Public Accounting Law	The First Public Accounting Law: The Kameral Accounting System has been adopted in line with the influence of the developed Western States of the time	Financial system	Mimetic isomorphism
1910	Establishment of a First Budget and a new accounting system during the Constitutional Period	The first law, inspired by the French and Belgian Public Accounts Act, is the state budget	Financial system	Mimetic isomorphism
1927	General Accounting Law	France, Italy and Belgium Government Accounting Laws were taken into account again. And the problems of the first law have been tried to be solved	Financial system Trade laws	Mimetic isomorphism
1948	Transition to Double-Sided Recording Accounting System	Acceptance of a state accounting system that is compatible with capitalist new world order under Anglo-Saxon influence	Financial system	Coercive isomorphism Mimetic isomorphism Normative isomorphism

Source: This table is adopted from the related literature by the authors.

Table 2. Historical evolution of the public accounting reforms in Turkey.

aims and unreliable performance measures. In order to ensure the institutionalization of the states, the first of the manifestos constitutes a large proportion of specialized knowledge and adapts to them [13]. From this point of view, it is also easy to understand the transfer processes that are living in the national sense. It seems that isomorphic tendencies prevail in applications which are based on responding to the uncertainty that is at first economic and social in nature, that is to say those which are shaped according to the institutional environment.

Thus, the effects of ambiguity are reduced and the required application environment is prepared for the future. The level of uncertainty in such practices constitutes a driving force in terms of imitation [29]. There can be many reasons for the ambiguity that exists. The most important dynamics of the uncertainty that betray Turkey are the need to make adjustments in the decentralized tax collection system, the economic downturn after the war period, the reformist practices, economic policies, the declaration of the Republic and the industrialization efforts of the capitalist system. Turkey has tried to overcome the effects of this environment primarily with French, later German and American systems. Regulations in Turkey show that the actively taking part in the state takes place on the basis of coercive isomorphism. However, the regulations are the same as the transfer. In the later period, the emergence of the standardization phenomenon as a necessity in the whole world, and the phenomenon of globalization that accelerates it, manifests itself in the practice of sometimes coercive and sometimes normative isomorphic tendencies for a country that is trying to achieve political harmony within the global system.

Author details

Ceray Aldemir and Tuğba Uçma Uysal*

*Address all correspondence to: utugba@mu.edu.tr

Muğla Sıtkı Koçman University, Muğla, Turkey

References

[1] Barbu EM, Farcane N, Popa A. Looking for an accounting identity: The case of Romania during the 20th century. Cahier de recherche. 2010;**03**(E2):1-23. DOI: http://hal.archivesouvertes.fr/docs/00/53/47/41/PDF/cr_2010_03_E2.pdf

[2] Previts GJ, Parker LD, Coffmann ED. An accounting historiography: subject matter and methodology. Abacus. 1990;**26**(2):136-158.

[3] Karaman KK, Pamuk S. Ottoman state finances in European perspective, 1500-1914. The Journal of Economic History. 2010;**70**(03):593-629.

[4] Hopwood AG. Accounting and organisation change. Accounting, Auditing & Accountability Journal. 1988;**3**(1):7-17.

[5] Dillard JF, Rigsby JT, Goodman C. The making and remarking of organization context—duality and the institutional context. Accounting, Auditing & Accountability Journal. 2004;**17**(4):506-542.

[6] Rodrigues LL, Craig R. Assessing international accounting harmonization using hegelian dialectic, isomorphism and Foucault. Critical Perspectives on Accounting. 2007;**18**: 739-757.

[7] Covaleski MA, Dirsmith MW, Rittenberg L. Jurisdictional disputes over professional work: The institutionalization of the global knowledge expert. Accounting, Organizations and Society. 2003;**28**:323-355.

[8] Loft A. Accountancy and the First World War. In: Anthony GH, Miller P, editors. Accounting As Social and Institutional Practice. Cambridge Studies in Management. USA: Cambridge University Press; 1994. pp. 116-137.

[9] Tamer B and Seymen OA. Yönetim ve Örgüt Düsüncesinde Kurumsalcılık, Yeni Kurumsalcılık ve Kurumsal Esbiçimlilik. Fırat Üniversitesi Sosyal Bilimler Dergisi. 2006; **16**(1):223-254.

[10] Apaydın F. Kurumsal Teori ve İsletmelerin Kurumsallasması. C.Ü. İktisadi ve İdari Bilimler Dergisi. 2009;**10**(1):1-22.

[11] Scott WR. The adolescence of institutional theory. Administrative Science Quarterly. 1987;**32**(4, December):493-511.

[12] Özen S. Yeni Kurumsal Kuram: Örgütleri Çözümlemede Yeni Ufuklar ve Yeni Sorunlar. In: A. Selami Sargut ve Sükrü Özen, editor. Örgüt Kuramları. 2nd ed. Ankara: İmge Kitabevi; 2007.

[13] Carpenter VL, Feroz EH. Institutional theory and accounting rule choice: An analysis of four US state governments' decisions to adopt generally accepted accounting principles. Accounting, Organizations and Society. 2001;**26**:565-596.

[14] DiMaggio PJ, Powell WW. The iron cage revisited: Institutional isomorphism and collective rationality in organizational fields. American Sociological Review. 1983;**48**(2, April):147-160.

[15] Akdeniz G. Devlet Muhasebesi. İstanbul: İsmail Akgün Matbaası; 1948

[16] Ozekicioglu S, Ozekicioglu H. First borrowing period at Ottoman Empire (1854-1876): Budget policies and consequences. Business and Economic Horizons. 2010;**3**(3):28-46.

[17] Raccagni M. The French economic interests in the Ottoman Empire. International Journal of Middle East Studies. 1980;**11**(03):339-376.

[18] Balla E, Johnson ND. Fiscal crisis and institutional change in the Ottoman Empire and France. The Journal of Economic History. 2009;**69**(03):809-845.

[19] Buluttekin MB. The assortment of agriculture In Istanbul glimpses from Istanbul Ahkâm registers in the eighteenth-century (1757-1760). Dicle Üniversitesi Sosyal Bilimler Enstitüsü Dergisi (DÜSBED). 2015;**7**:55-89.

[20] Quataert D. The Ottoman Empire, 1700-1922. 2nd ed. UK: Cambridge University Press; 2005

[21] Cosgel MM, Miceli TJ. Tax collection in history: Public institutions and institutional change in the Ottoman Empire. In: 2006 August; Helsinki. 2006

[22] Özsen U. Cumhuriyet Dönemi Bütçe Yönetimi Üzerine Bir İnceleme [thesis]. Ankara: Ankara Üniversitesi, SBE, Kamu Yönetimi ve Siyaset Bilimi Anabilim Dalı; 2006

[23] Ecchia S. The Economic Policy of the Ottoman Empire (1876-1922) [Internet]. 2010. Available from: https://mpra.ub.uni-muenchen.de/42603/ [Accessed: 22 February 2017]

[24] Nihat S. Devlet Muhasebesi Usulü. İstanbul: Arkadas Matbaası; 1935

[25] Bulus A. Türk İktisat Politikalarının Tarihi Temelleri. 4th ed. Konya: Çizgi Yayınevi; 2015

[26] Karaman K, Pamuk S. Avrupa devletleriyle Bir Karsılastırma: Osmanlı Bütçeleri ve Mali Yapının Evrimi. Toplumsal Tarih. 2009;**Kasım**(191):26-33.

[27] Edizdoğan N. Kamu Bütçesi. 4th ed. Bursa: Ekin Yayınevi; 1998

[28] Coskun G. Devlet Bütçesi Türk Bütçe Sistemi. 6th ed. Ankara: Turhan Kitbevi; 2000

[29] Gyasi AK. Adoption of International Financial Standards in Developing Countries—The Case of Ghana [dissertation]. 2010. Available from: https://publications.theseus.fi/bitstream/handle/10024/15526/ANTWI_KOFI_GYASI.pdf?sequence=1

Section 6

Managerial Accounting

Chapter 16

The Factors Used to Create Performance-Based Budgeting: A Research on Turkey

Hakan Vahit Erkutlu, Şükran Güngör Tanç and Seyhan Çil Koçyiğit

Additional information is available at the end of the chapter

http://dx.doi.org/10.5772/intechopen.68920

Abstract

Performance-based budgeting (PBB) is the practice of developing flexible financial management tools to increase the efficiency and productivity of public institutions both in developed and developing countries such as Turkey. It can be seen from international literature gathered as a result of researches that developing countries have come a long way in developing performance-based budgeting activities. In developed economies, successful international institutions such as Organization for Economic Cooperation and Development (OECD) and International Monetary Fund (IMF) promote the implementation of performance-based budgeting for a developing world. Fiscal transparency, medium-term expenditure framework, and other institutional arrangements are factors effective in developing performance-based budgeting. Budget experts regard these factors as important factors, and the view that it is difficult to implement these prevails. Within the context of this theory, the main purpose of this study is to determine the preparation and implementation of performance-based budgeting in public institutions of developing countries such as Turkey, which has an important economy in the world, and to measure the perception levels of employees working in these institutions. As a result of the confirmatory factor analysis (CFA) based on the main findings of the study, goodness-of-fit values of the measurement model were found to be sufficient. Independent t test and one-way ANOVA analyses were conducted to find out the perception levels of the participants in the study. As a result of the analyses, significant differences were found between demographic features and perception levels.

Keywords: confirmatory factor analysis, performance-based budgeting, perception, fiscal transparency, Turkey

1. Introduction

Performance-based budgeting (PBB) has been developed in many countries within the frame of a new administrative mentality based on the performance of public sector as of 1980s, which included primary objectives such as increasing the quality of public services, reinforcing decision-making processes by getting more information about the activities of the state, and ensuring accountability and fiscal transparency. With the aforementioned objectives, governments focused on the effective and productive use of public funding and, within this context, tended toward allocation of resources in line with the results reached through goods and services produced rather than information regarding the input in budget processes Although it does not have only one accepted model in the world, performance-based budgeting, which is defined as a type of budgeting that associates resources with measureable objectives in the widest sense, has found area of implementation in many developed countries in various forms with its outcome-oriented mode of management. Within this context, while some countries followed a transition process that included all the public administration gradually, other countries allowed public administration to switch to the application in process on a volunteer basis [1].

New Zealand and Australia at the end of 1980s, Canada, Denmark, Finland, France, Holland, Sweden, England, and the USA in 1990s, and Austria, Germany, and Switzerland at the beginning of 2000s started various practices of performance-based management, budgeting, and reporting.

"The law no. 5018 on public financial management and control" issued at the end of 2003 in Turkey is about the efficient, economic, and effective use of public resources. With the efficient and effective use of resources, accountability and fiscal transparency will also increase in institutions. Performance-based budgeting practices started with the Article 9 of the Law no. 5018 on public financial management and control, which makes the statement that public institutions prepare their budgets in line with the mission, vision, strategic goals, and targets in strategic plans and based on performance.

The reasons for switching to performance-based budgeting system include public financial crises, inefficient use of public resources, increase in the amount and quality of public expenditures, rapid changes in technology, and the new mode of public administration [2].

With the development of democratic systems in the whole world, public services are performed in line with the needs of society. Accordingly, there has been an increase and variety in demands from administrators directed at public services. The increase in the expectations of the society for public services has led to an increase in public spending and tax load, which in turn made it imperative to ensure efficiency in the use of resources.

Strategic planning-oriented PBB model: the model makes it imperative for public institutions to prepare strategic plan, and these plans constitute the basis of preparing the budgets of public institution [3].

- Performance agreement-oriented PBB model: in this model in which it is not imperative to prepare strategic planning in terms of public institutions, performance agreements have to be made with the top executives of the institution in order to be able to maximize the performance of employees.

- Budget format PBB model: unlike the other two models, no document is prepared to measure performance except the budget text in this model. Thus, the budget has information about only performance and allowance. In addition, there is no independent performance report.

Performance programs bring an output and result-oriented budgeting system to the forefront by making performance information available as well as fiscal information in the budget documents and thus bring fiscal transparency and accountability principles into force to which our new public financial administration system depends on [1].

The items in the questionnaire given to employees in this study were designed on four basic factors. Confirmatory factor analysis (CFA) analysis results show that the goodness-of-fit values of measurement model are sufficient. Significant differences were found between the genders and education levels of the participants in terms of performance-based budgeting practices level of perception.

2. Literature review

Some of the national and international literature studies about performance-based budgeting practices and researches and the key findings of these are explained below.

In Egeli et al.'s study [5], titled "Analysis of Critical Control Points of Strategic Planning Oriented Performance Based Budgeting System: The Applications of Turkey's Public Institutions," a general conclusion was reached that the system may not be effectively applied before the completion of all steps toward the performance-based budgeting within the framework of the results obtained from the critical control points and analysis of public institutions in Turkey [5].

According to Kim and Park's study [6] titled "Performance Budgeting in Korea," Korea is in the initial stages of implementing performance-based budgeting; it is therefore too early to form an assessment. However, it has been concluded that it should be noted that having introduced performance-based budgeting as one component within a broader range of comprehensive reforms has helped to lower resistance and resolve institutional problems [6].

Jordan and Hackbart's study [7], titled "The Goals and Implementation Success of State Performance Based Budgeting," concluded that accountability can be seen as a goal, rather than budget allocation, makes a stronger foundation for determining performance-based budget success [7].

In Çildir's study [8] titled "An Assessment of United Kingdom's Performance Based Budgeting System," since the application of Public Service Agreement started in England in 1998, a lot of changes have occurred. Each expenditure analysis underwent some changes in terms of their structure. Ever since it began to be applied, the Public Services Agreement framework has guided the government in terms of the increases in public expenditures. The Public Services Agreement places importance on focusing on the data that create a problem for those who make use of management inputs and public services, prioritizing public services that should specifically be conducted and providing more flexibility [8].

In their study titled "Theoretical and Practical Problems of Performance-Based Budgeting System," Çelebi and Kovancılar [9] stated that advantages of performance-based budget system in terms of public fiscal management were effective in their being preferred by other countries. However, it was also stated that the aforementioned system included some theoretical and practical problems and difficulties within the structure of the system [9].

In their study titled "Performance-Based Budgeting Process in Turkey: Kocaeli University Case," Badem et al. [10] concluded that if the performance-based budgeting system is fully applied in Turkey, an awareness of transparency and calling to account will be developed in the society; policies and strategic goals will be evaluated by everyone; and the performances and policies of top executives in both the government and the public institutions will become questionable. In addition, by means of PBB, institutions' expenditures will be questioned through performance auditing, and it will be possible to find out whether public resources are used economically and effectively. In terms of Turkey, time, interest, care, raising an awareness of questioning in the public, and increasing the legal sanctions of this are evaluated as what is needed for a full implementation of PBB [10].

In Liu's study [4] titled "What Drives Performance Budgeting to Perform? A Survey Examination in Taiwan," it was found that while there was high consensus over international experiences in Taiwan, respondents in different categories featured slightly different attitude. The survey results revealed that experts in academia were more affirmative toward auxiliary institutional arrangements for performance budgeting compared to the practitioners in selective government's agencies [4].

Demirel's [11] study titled "The Financial Aspect of Performance: Performance Based Budget" aimed to ensure fiscal transparency and accountability through performance-based budgeting. Performance-based budgeting, which is indispensable in popularizing performance-based practices in public administration, is also closely related with a great number of concepts. One of these concepts, strategic planning, contributes to the preparation process of performance-based budgeting through missions which clearly reveal the duties and functions of the institution with future visions. Performance programs and indicators reveal the adaptation capacity of an institution to specified strategies. Announcement of activity reports prepares the basis for a healthy comparison of past and future results [11].

In their study titled "Performance-Based Budget Arrangements, the Implementation Process and Advancements in Turkey," Karacan and Yazıcı [12] stated that the Law no. 5018 brought radical changes in the financial management and control system, the findings, evaluations, and suggestions related to the ownership, coordination, role of the parliament, capacity, calendar, reporting, and budget connections in Turkey undergone during the 10-year period. They stated that the public management sector is a sector where the outputs and results are seen in the long term. They also added that the best practices are experienced for long years in planning and nearly 30 years in management and PBB. As a result, when the best practices and other applications in the world are considered, they concluded that we can be optimist about the future of the PBB in Turkey [12].

In Ciubotaru and Hincu's study [13], titled "Implementing Performance-Based Budgeting in Republic of Moldova," the researches stated that the analysis of performance indicators shows the linkages between the policies, and budgeting, as well as budgeting performance in compliance with European principles in this area [13].

3. Budget reform in Turkey Law no. 5018

Public Financial Management and Control Law no. 5018 foresees public administrations to prepare strategic plans which include their medium- and long-term objectives, basic principles and policies, targets and priorities, performance criteria, the methods to reach these, and their resource distributions and also to prepare these in line with and based on the missions, visions, strategic goals, and targets included in the strategic plans of budgets [1].

Public administrations prepare strategic plans with participatory methods in order to create future missions and visions, to find out strategic objectives and measureable targets, to measure performance in line with present indicators, and to follow and evaluate this process within the framework of development plans, programs, applicable law, and adapted basic principles. Public institutions prepare their budgets in line with the mission, vision, strategic goal, and targets in their strategic plans and also based on performance. The Ministry of Finance is authorized to audit the suitability of public institutions' budgets to the performance indicators in strategic plans and other issues related with the activities of institutions and their performance-based budgeting. Performance indicators, which are determined by the Ministry of Finance, the under secretariat of state planning organization, and the relevant public administration appear in the budgets of institutions. Performance audits take place within the framework of these indicators [14].

Performance planning has been predicted to take place through strategic plan. Strategic plan, according to its definition in Article 3 of Law no. 5018, refers to the plan which includes medium- and long-term goals, basic principles and policies, objectives and priorities, and performance indicators of public administrations, as well as the methods and the resource distribution to achieve these. In the legislation, the period of strategic plans has been predicted as a period of 5 years within the scope of regulations related to the period, updating and renewing. Updating of strategic plans has been made possible only 2 years after they have been implemented. Updating has been defined as quantitative changes in goals without changing the mission, vision, and goals of the strategic plan [15].

Performance-based budgeting, proposed by Law no. 5018, has been defined as the kind of budgeting that shows the information about what public institutions will do with the budget allocated to them. The basic expectations of countries which have adapted or which are about to adapt performance-based budgeting from this system are classified as follows [16]:

- Effective distribution and use of resources,
- Establishing a mode of administration based on targets,
- Reinforcement of the processes of preparing, implementing, and auditing a budget,
- Increasing the quality of service, and
- Ensuring fiscal transparency.

Fiscal transparency allows a better analysis and assessment of the government's budget policies. This in turn allows development of programs and more efficient use of resources. Thus, one of the eventual objectives of reforms in budget systems, maybe the most important, is fiscal transparency [17].

The concept of fiscal transparency entered into application with performance-based budgeting. Fiscal transparency makes it obligatory to provide flow of information to those concerned and the public about the performances of public institutions. To do this, public institutions prepare activity reports, and they present these for public use in electronic or printed version. The objective of fiscal transparency is to prevent exploitation and waste in public resources. However, activity reports prepared by public institutions cannot provide the expected benefits. In addition to having too much information, these reports are far from reflecting the performance of public institutions [18].

Performance-based budgeting assumes that all the officers, administrators, and executives in the process have the necessary skills and equipment. A full implementation of a real performance-based budgeting will take years, and it requires administrative capacity. Most of the countries, especially developing countries, seem to be deprived of institutional capacity in this sense. Within this context, the perception levels of employees working in institutions and departments, in which it is essential to implement performance-based budgeting, will be examined. In addition, employees' fiscal transparency and medium-term expenditure frameworks and their views about other factors will be analyzed.

4. Research design

Fiscal transparency, medium-term expenditure framework, and other institutional arrangements are factors effective in developing performance-based budgeting. Budget experts regard these factors as important factors, and the view that it is difficult to implement these prevails. Within the context of this theory, the main purpose of this study is to determine the preparation and implementation of performance-based budgeting in public institutions of developing countries such as Turkey, which has an important economy in the world, and to measure the perception levels of employees working in these institutions. In the study, a questionnaire was given to employees of public institutions in Turkey through question forms. The question forms were prepared by using a study from Taiwan (Liu [4]), which is a developing country like Turkey. The question forms were designed on four basic factors. The first factor is about measuring the comprehension or perception level of performance-based budgeting activity. The second factor is about the role of performance-based budgeting on fiscal transparency. The third factor is about how performance-based budgeting influences medium-term expenditure frameworks. The fourth factor consists of elements that in performance-based budgeting implementation, other institutional organizations may be necessary. The factors in the question forms were formed with five Likert scale. The universe of the study consists of institutions within the body of the Ministry of Finance, which implement performance-based budgeting, universities, provincial special administrations, and municipalities, which have a level of information about performance-based budgeting practices.

Since the number of staff working in institutions which have performance-based budgeting is unknown and it was not possible to reach the employees in the universe and due to limitations such as the cost of data collection and time, sampling was thought to be appropriate. The exact number of the employees in the universe of this study is unknown. Thus, the following formula was used to find out the sample size [19]:

$$n = \frac{z^2(pq)}{e^2} \tag{1}$$

In this formula,

n is the sample size,

p is the incidence of the phenomenon examined, the probability of occurrence (50%),

q is the non-incidence of the phenomenon examined, the probability of non-occurrence $(1 - p)$,

e is the level of acceptable error (±5%), and

z is the standard error within the specified confidence interval (95%).

Since the universe is unknown in this study, the incidence (p) and non-incidence (q) of the phenomenon examined was taken as 0.5. Error tolerance was accepted as 0.05, while the level of confidence was accepted as 95%. When these values are inserted in the formula, the sample size was calculated as follows:

$$\frac{1.96^2(0.5 \times 0.5)}{0.05^2} = 385 \tag{2}$$

The sample size consists of 385 people. In this study, the first factor is about measuring the comprehension or perception level of performance-based budgeting activity. The second factor is about the role of performance-based budgeting on fiscal transparency. The third factor is about how performance-based budgeting influences medium-term expenditure frameworks. The fourth factor consists of elements that in performance-based budgeting implementation, other institutional organizations may be necessary. After the sample size was determined as 385, in order to reach the desired sample size, samples were gathered from different public institutions that use performance-based budgeting and 416 questionnaire data were obtained for analysis from different cities and public institutions as much as possible. The confirmatory factor analysis (CFA) method was used to test the suitability of each dimension of the factors used in performance-based budgeting practice in the study.

The confirmatory factor analysis (CFA) is an analysis method that is frequently used in developing measurement models, and it provides significant conveniences. The CFA is used in both scale development and validity analysis as well as in the verification of a present structure [20].

5. Empirical results

In terms of the demographic features of the data obtained from the study, data about the individuals' genders, educational status, occupational experiences, and working positions were collected, and the data obtained were shown in **Table 1** with frequency and percentages.

According to the descriptive analysis results, 66% of the participants are males, while 34% are females. In terms of education, it can be seen that 72% are undergraduates, while 17% have master's degree. In terms of professional experience, 57% have 1–5 years of professional experience, 21% have 6–10 years of professional experience, 9% have 11–15 years of professional experience, and 13% have 16 and over years of professional experience. About 41% of the participants are staff directly responsible for the performance-based budgeting activities, 6% are executives, 7% are auditors, and 46% are assistant qualified personnel for performance-based budgeting activities. In **Table 2**, sub-dimensions related to performance-based budgeting are given.

The confirmatory factor analysis (CFA) was conducted for the performance-based budgeting scale used in the study (**Figure 1**). As a result of CFA, goodness-of-fit values such as Chi-square statistics (χ^2), Chi-square/Degree of freedom (χ^2/df), root mean square error of approximation (RMSEA), comparative fit index (CFI), goodness-of-fit index (GFI), and AGFI were checked first, and the fitness of the model was found.

As a result of CFA, goodness-of-fit values of the measurement model were found to be sufficient ($\chi^2 = 227.360$; sd = 84; χ^2/sd = 2.707; CFI = 0.87; GFI = 0.93; AGFI = 0.89; RMSEA = 0.067). The most commonly used goodness-of-fit indices are Chi-square statistics (χ^2), Chi-square/degree of freedom (χ^2/df), RMSEA (root mean square error of approximation) and CFI (comparative fit index), goodness-of-fit index (GFI), and adjusted goodness of fit. (χ^2/df), an acceptable model fit value less than 3, a value equal to or less than 0.05 for RMSEA means perfect fit and a value equal to or less than 0.08 means acceptable fit. For AGFI, GFI, and CFI, values equal to and more than show perfect fit, while values between 0.85 and 0.95 show acceptable fit [21–23]. In addition, according to another method that examines whether discriminant validity is met, correlation coefficients between the specified dimensions differ between −0.110 and 0.602. Since these values are less than 80, it can be said that discriminant validity is met [24].

Independent *t* test and one-way ANOVA analysis were used to show whether the perceptions of the participants differed on performance-based budgeting.

In **Table 3**, significant difference was found between female employees and male employees in terms of *level of perception about performance budgeting* [$t_{(414)} = -2.145$; $P < 0.05$]. When the

Demographic features	Frequency	Percentage
Gender		
Female	143	34
Male	273	66
Education		
High school	21	5
Two-year degree	21	5
Undergraduate	299	72
Master's	72	17
Doctorate	2	1
Professional experience		
1–5 years	238	57
6–10 years	87	21
11–15 years	37	9
16 years and above	54	13
Professional field		
Executive	25	6
Staff directly responsible for the performance-based budgeting activities	171	41
Auditor	29	7
Assistant qualified personnel for performance-based budgeting activities	191	46

Table 1. Results of demographic features.

reason for this difference was examined, it was found that when compared with male employees ($\mu = 3.68$; sd = 0.876), female employees ($\mu = 3.48$; sd = 0.933) agreed less with the thought that their level of perception about performance-based budgeting was insufficient.

Similarly, when the Independent *t* test results about the expression "Ministry of Finance should develop medium-term expenditure ceilings in all ministries for performance-based budgeting to be successful" were analyzed in terms of gender, a significant difference was found between female employees and male employees in terms of this expression ($t_{(414)} = 3.067$; $P < 0.005$). When the reason for this difference was examined, it was found that when compared with male employees ($\mu = 3.23$; sd = 0.841), female employees ($\mu = 3.13$; sd = 0.887) agreed less with the thought that the Ministry of Finance should develop medium-term expenditure ceilings in all ministries for performance-based budgeting to be successful.

Under the assumption that the data obtained from the employees were homogeneous, when the ANOVA analysis results were examined in terms of level of education in **Table 4**,

Level of perception	A1	Your level of perception about performance-based budgeting
	A2	Your opinion about the implementation of performance-based budgeting in OECD countries, in which Turkey is a member
	A3	Your opinion about the implementation of performance-based budgeting in Turkey
Fiscal transparency	B1	Public sector should explain the policies that will be implemented clearly to the public for performance-based budgeting to be successful
	B2	The state's asset-liability management policy should be clearly defined for performance-based budgeting to be successful
	B3	Same policies should be used in preparing fiscal reports for performance-based budgeting to be successful
	B4	The state's activities and finance should be audited with transparency by national audit firms for performance-based budgeting to be successful
Medium-term expenditure frameworks	C1	Medium-term income and expenditure frameworks should be prepared with macroeconomic models for performance-based budgeting to be successful
	C2	All ministries should develop a medium-term expenditure ceiling to present to the Ministry of Finance for performance-based budgeting to be successful
	C3	Ministry of Finance should develop medium-term expenditure ceilings in all ministries for performance-based budgeting to be successful
	C4	Ministry of Finance should hold regular meetings periodically for all ministries about medium-term expenditure ceilings for performance-based budgeting to be successful
Other institutional organizations	D1	The support and assurance of agency leaders are essential for performance-based budgeting to be successful
	D2	Professional skills of employees of the institution are essential for performance-based budgeting to be successful
	D3	A customer-oriented organizational culture of the institution is essential for performance-based budgeting to be successful
	D4	Performance evaluation involving citizen participation is essential for performance-based budgeting to be successful
Staff information	E1	Gender?
	E2	Level of education?
	E3	Professional experience with budgeting activities?
	E4	Professional field (work position)

Table 2. Distribution of items in sub-dimensions.

a significant difference was found between participants with undergraduate and master's degree and participants with doctorate degree [$F_{(4\text{-}411)} = 3.459$; $P < 0.05$] in terms of *"opinion about the implementation of performance-based budgeting in OECD countries, in which Turkey is a member."* When the reason for this difference was analyzed according to the Tukey test, it was found that compared with employees with undergraduate degree ($\mu = 3.14$)

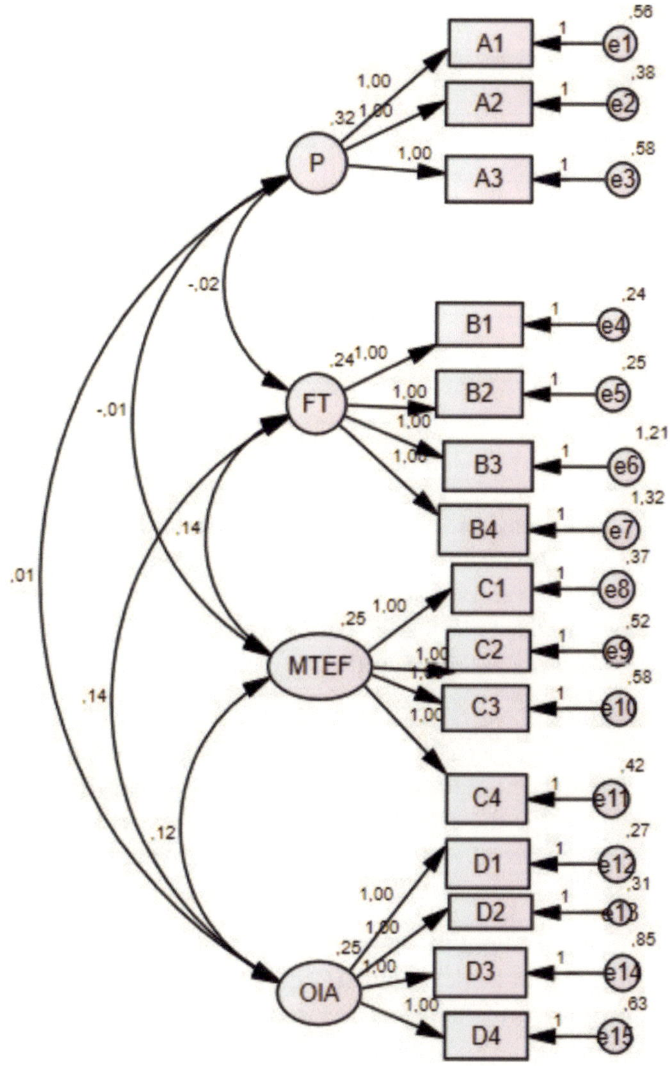

Figure 1. General CFA model goodness of fit.

and employees with master's degree (μ = 3.14), employees with doctorate degree (μ = 5) thought that the implementation of performance-based budgeting in Organization for Economic Cooperation and Development (OECD) countries, in which Turkey is a member, is very sufficient.

In terms of Turkey's performance-based budgeting implementations, significant differences were found between both high school graduate employees and employees with undergraduate and master's degree and between employees with master's degree and employees with doctorate degree [$F_{(4\text{-}411)}$ = 6.238; $P < 0.01$]. According to Tukey test results, which was conducted to show the reason of differences, it was found that when high school graduate

Items		Levene's test for equality of variances				
		F	*Sig.*	*t*	*df*	*Sig. (2-tailed)*
Your level of perception about performance budgeting	Equal variances assumed	1.450	0.229	-2.188	414	0.029
	Equal variances not assumed			−2.145*	273.037	0.033
Ministry of Finance should develop medium-term expenditure ceilings in all ministries for performance-based budgeting to be successful	Equal variances assumed	22.898	0.000	2.876	414	0.004
	Equal variances not assumed			3.067	343.883	0.002
	Equal variances not assumed			0.114	314.385	0.910

*$P < 0.05$; $N = 414$.

Table 3. Independent *t* test statistics of performance-based budgeting in terms of gender.

employees (μ = 3.52) were compared with employees with undergraduate degree (μ = 2.76) and master's degree (μ = 2.76), they thought that performance-based budgeting implementations in Turkey are very sufficient. In addition, employees with doctorate degree (μ = 3.50) rather than employees with master's degree (μ = 2.76) accept that performance-based budgeting implementations in Turkey are more sufficient.

As can be seen from **Table 5**, "level of perception about performance-based budgeting" differs in terms of work position [$F_{(4\text{-}412)} = 6.410$; $P < 0.01$]. According to the Tukey test, the reason for the difference is the fact that the staff directly responsible for performance-based budgeting activities (μ = 3.73) believe that their level of perception about performance-based budgeting is more sufficient when compared with assistant qualified personnel for performance-based budgeting activities (μ = 3.33).

On the other hand, "opinion about the implementation of performance-based budgeting in Turkey" also differs in terms of work position [$F_{(4\text{-}412)} = 2.631$; $P < 0.05$]. According to the Tukey test, the reason for the difference is the fact that the staff directly responsible for performance-based budgeting activities (μ = 2.65) think that the implementation of performance-based budgeting in Turkey is more sufficient when compared with assistant qualified personnel for performance-based budgeting activities (μ = 2.92).

The perceptions about the expression "Ministry of Finance should develop medium-term expenditure ceilings in all ministries for performance-based budgeting to be successful" also differ in terms of work position [$F_{(4\text{-}412)} = 3.091$; $P < 0.05$]. When Tukey test results are examined, the reason for this difference is the fact that auditors (μ = 3.31) agree with this view less than assistant qualified personnel for performance-based budgeting activities (μ = 3.81).

Finally, the perceptions about the expression *"Performance evaluation involving citizen participation is essential for performance-based budgeting to be successful"* also differ in terms of work position [$F_{(4\text{-}412)} = 6.065$; $P < 0.05$]. When Tukey test results are examined, the reason for this difference is the fact the auditors (μ = 3.20) agree with the approach less when compared with executives (μ = 3.96), staff directly responsible for performance-based budgeting

ANOVA

		Sum of squares	*df*	Mean square	*F*	*Sig.*
Your opinion about the implementation of performance-based budgeting in OECD countries, in which Turkey is a member	Between groups	9940	4	2.485	3.459	0.009
	Within groups	295.288	411	0.718		
	Total	305.228	415			
Your opinion about the implementation of performance-based budgeting in Turkey	Between groups	22.966	4	5.741	6.238	0.000
	Within groups	378.262	411	0.920		
	Total	401.228	415			

Table 4. Statistics of one-way ANOVA for education level.

ANOVA

		Sum of squares	*df*	Mean square	*F*	*Sig.*
Your level of perception about performance-based budgeting	Between groups	15.394	3	5.131	6.410	0.000
	Within groups	329.828	412	0.801		
	Total	345.221	415			
Your opinion about the implementation of performance-based budgeting in Turkey	Between groups	7.541	3	2.514	2.631	0.050
	Within groups	393.687	412	0.956		
	Total	401.228	415			
	Within groups	605.186	412	1.469		
	Total	607.962	415			
	Within groups	356.565	412	0.865		
	Total	359.094	415			
Ministry of Finance should develop medium-term expenditure ceilings in all ministries for performance-based budgeting to be successful	Between groups	8970	3	2.990	3.091	0.027
	Within groups	398.509	412	0.967		
	Total	407.478	415			
Performance evaluation involving citizen participation is essential for performance-based budgeting to be successful	Between groups	18.191	3	6.064	6.065	0.000
	Within groups	411.941	412	1.000		
	Total	430.132	415			

Table 5. Statistics of one-way ANOVA for work position.

activities (μ = 4.02) and assistant qualified personnel for performance-based budgeting activities (μ = 3.96).

No differences were found in other expressions about performance-based budgeting in terms of gender, level of education, work position, and professional experience.

6. Conclusion and evaluations

According to key findings obtained as a result of the study, the confirmatory factor analysis showed that goodness-of-fit values were sufficient for the measurement model. Independent *t* test and one-way ANOVA analysis were conducted to show whether the perception levels of the participants differed. According to the findings, a significant difference was found between female employees and male employees in terms of the perception levels about performance-based budgeting. When the Independent *t* test results were examined about the expression "Ministry of Finance should develop medium-term expenditure ceilings in all ministries for performance-based budgeting to be successful," significant difference was found between female employees and male employees in terms of this expression. When the ANOVA analysis results were examined in terms of the level of education, significant difference was found between participants with undergraduate and master's degree and participants with doctorate degree in terms of "opinion about the implementation of performance-based budgeting in OECD countries, in which Turkey is a member." Perception levels about performance-based budgeting differ in terms of work position.

In terms of Turkey's performance-based budgeting implementations, significant differences were found between both high school graduate employees and employees with undergraduate and master's degree and between employees with master's degree and employees with doctorate degree. Finally, perceptions about the expression "Performance evaluation involving citizen participation is essential for performance-based budgeting to be successful" also differed in terms of work position.

No differences were found in other expressions about performance-based budgeting in terms of gender, level of education, work position, and professional experience.

Importance should be attached to performance-based budgeting in public institutions, and institutions should organize meetings and briefings to emphasize the importance of performance-based budgeting. Especially at the end of the year, expenditures of institutions should be presented online in detail in terms of transparency and accountability. Public audition should be made independent, and its activities should be increased. Legislation should be developed for these. Performance-based wage for employees will increase the efficiency of performance-based budgeting. It is also thought that public institutions should be audited by a national audit firm in terms of fiscal transparency. It has been stated that only the necessities of the legislation are realized in public institutions within the context of performance-based budgeting. In terms of medium-term expenditure frameworks, in case of a change in the policies of the institution, institutions should be able to update their activities and expenditure frameworks, and there should not be strict rules about updates. Performance-based budgeting activities should be seen not as written works on documents, but as policies with which institutions can realize their missions, analyze their visions, and be eager about providing service. At this stage, it seems important both to adopt the process and to control it with audit mechanisms.

Author details

Hakan Vahit Erkutlu[1]*, Şükran Güngör Tanç[1] and Seyhan Çil Koçyiğit[2]

*Address all correspondence to: erkutlu@nevsehir.edu.tr

1 Faculty of Economics and Administrative Sciences, Nevsehir Haci Bektas Veli University, Nevsehir, Turkey

2 Faculty of Economics and Administrative Sciences, Gazi University, Ankara, Turkey

References

[1] Performans Programı Hazırlama Rehberi [Internet]. 2009. Available from: www.bumko.gov.tr/PEBhttp://peb.bumko.gov.tr/Eklenti/4587,performansrehberfinalpdf.pdf [Accessed: October 2, 2017]

[2] Bal T. Applicability of alternative models in Turkey within the framework of performance based budgeting (PBB) system. Sayıştay Journal. 2015;**96**:25-54

[3] Erüz E. 5018 Sayılı kanuna göre performans esaslı bütçeleme. In: Aktan C C, editor. Kamu mali yönetiminde stratejik planlama ve performans esaslı bütçeleme. Ankara: Seçkin; 2006. pp. 217-236

[4] Liu LC. What drives performance budgeting to perform? A survey examination in Taiwan. Public Administration Research. 2013;**2**:58-72

[5] Egeli, H, Akdeniz A, Aksaraylı M, Tüğen K, Özen A. Analysis of critical control points of strategic planning oriented performance based budgeting system: The applications of Turkey's public institutions. Dokuz Eylül Üniversitesi I.I.B.F. Journal. 2007;**1**:27-47

[6] Kim JM, Nowook P. Performance budgeting in Korea. OECD Journal on Budgeting. 2007;**4**:1-11. ISSN 1608-7143

[7] Jordan MM, Hackbart M. The goals and implementation success of state performance-based budgeting. Journal of Public Budgeting Accounting & Financial Management. 2005;**17**(4):471-487

[8] Çildir M. An assessment of United Kingdom's performance based budgeting system. Eskişehir Osmangazi University SBE Journal. 2010;**11**(2):217-228

[9] Çelebi AK, Kovancılar B. Theoretical and practical problems of performance-based budgeting system. Yönetim ve Ekonomi. 2012;**19**(1):1-18

[10] Badem A. C, Kılınç Y. Kavas T. Performance based budgeting process in Turkey: Kocaeli University case", Kocaeli University SBE Journal. 2013;**26**:77-104

[11] Demokaan D. The financial aspect of performance: Performance based budget. Atatürk Üniversitesi Sosyal Bilimler Enstitüsü Dergisi. 2015;**19**(1):265-282

[12] Karacan E, Yazıcı K. Performance based budget arrangements, the implementation process and advancements in Turkey. International Journal of Business and Social Science. 2015;**4**(1):62-79

[13] Ciubotaru, M, Hinc V. Implementing performance-based budgeting in republic of Moldova. Risk in the Contemporary Economy, Proceedings Conference. 2016. pp. 267-272. ISSN-L 2067-0532 ISSN online 2344-5386

[14] Aktan CC, Tüğen K. Performance based budgeting systems. Aktan CC, editor. Kamu mali yönetiminde stratejik planlama ve performans esaslı bütçeleme. Ankara: Seçkin. 2006. pp. 205-216

[15] Şahin İpek EA. Kamu Kesiminde performans yönetim aracı olarak büyükşehir belediyeleri örneği performans esaslı bütçeleme sistemi: Büyükşehir belediyesi örneği. Ankara: Türkiye Belediyeler Birliği; 2013. ISBN: 978-975-6311-75-2

[16] OECD. Public sector modernization: Governing for performance. OECD Policy Brief. OECD Observer. 2004:1-7

[17] Cura S. Türkiye'de saydamlığı sağlamaya yönelik bir uygulama: Analitik bütçe sınıflandırılması. Aktan CC, editor. Kamu mali yönetiminde stratejik planlama ve performans esaslı bütçeleme. Ankara: Seçkin; 2006. pp. 238-255

[18] Tüğen K, Özen A. Türkiye'de performans esaslı bütçeleme sistemi uygulamasının değerlendirilmesi. Kamu Mali Yönetim ve Denetim Sempozyumu Kitabı; Ege Üniversitesi 25-27 Mart 2011; pp. 110-119

[19] Chi CGQ, Qu H. Examining the structural relationships of destination image, tourist satisfaction and destination loyalty: An integrated approach. Journal of Tourism Management. 2008;**29**:624-636

[20] Aytaç M, Öngen B. Doğrulayıcı faktör analizi ile yeni çevresel paradigma ölçeğinin yapı geçerliliğinin incelenmesi. İstatistikçiler Dergisi. 2012;**5**:14-22

[21] Jöreskog K, Sörbom D. Structural Equation Modeling with the Simplis Command Language. Hillsdale, NJ: Lawrence Erlbaum Associates; 1993

[22] Çalık M, Altunışık R, Sütütemiz N. Bütünleşik pazarlama iletişimi, marka performansı ve pazar performansı ilişkisinin incelenmesi. International Journal of Management Economics and Business. 2013;**9**(19):137-162. ISSN:2147-9208 E-ISSN:2147-9194

[23] Schermelleh EK, Mossbrugger H, Müller H. Evaluating the fit of structural equation models: Test of significance and descriptive goodness of fit measures. Methods of Psychological Research Online. 2003;**8**(2):23-74

[24] Kline RB. Principles and Practice of Structural Equation Modeling. 3rd ed. New York/London: The Guilford Press; 2011. ISBN 978-1-60623-876-9

Chapter 17

The Managerial Perspective and Systems of Accountability in Judicial Offices

Ubaldo Comite

Additional information is available at the end of the chapter

http://dx.doi.org/10.5772/67555

Abstract

In Italy, the machinery of justice has been, on more than one occasion, the subject of criticism. For the most part, the criticism has been relative to the slowness of trials and the inadequacy of the judicial system, deemed not capable of confronting the request for continuously evolving justice in an exhaustive manner, whose characteristics change in time based on the emerging needs of society. The analysis of the justice system was, in fact, generally not subject to enquiries on offices' productivity and to evaluation of the management of resources invested in the sector. The same centres of data elaboration and the related departments at the Ministry of Justice, for example, have not gone much further than collecting the statistical data and creating the generic indicators of service quality. Such parameters, though, are often revealed to be too bureaucratic and of little use in proposing ameliorative solutions of the service offered to citizens, who desire levels of protection that are more responsive to their expectations. In this sense, the application of the system of accountability within the judicial system can contribute to the managerialization of the service.

Keywords: judicial administration, business, accountability, Ministry of Justice, service

1. Introduction

An efficient and effective operation of the judicial system in which a request put forward by the citizens and an offer from the judicial institution represents one of the indispensable conditions for promoting and guaranteeing the proper operation of an economic and social system [1].

At first glance, the use of the criteria of efficiency, effectiveness and economy, which are typical economic business parameters in the study of the operations carried out by the courts, can be surprising.

The analysis of the justice system was, in fact, generally not subject to inquiries on offices productivity and to evaluations of the management of resources invested in the sector [2].

The same centres of data elaboration and the related departments at the Ministry of Justice, for example, have not gone much further than collecting the statistical data and creating the generic indicators of service quality. Such parameters, though, are often revealed to be too bureaucratic and of little use in proposing ameliorative solutions of the service offered to citizens, who desire levels of protection that are more responsive to their expectations.

Not infrequently one speaks of inefficiency in the justice sector as well as of the excessive delays in proceedings which are required to give replies to public and private interest derived from the acknowledgement of the interests recognized in court. Usually, however, the support of the considerations expressed is omitted with a suitable analytical technique to formulate corrective solutions. Instead, the attempt to apply criteria typical of the economic business analysis to the study of trials (civil and criminal) and to the organization of judicial offices could prove useful [3].

The observation of the offices and the concrete verification of the organization of the solutions adoptable for improving it would become, therefore, useful instruments with which to study reality, even if it is as complex as the courts.

Only if the reasons that determine a disadvantageous or a crisis situation are known can there be an intervention in some form to orient it, considering the judicial organization as a single productive unit that aims to maximize the beneficiary who could draw from the resources available (thus reaching the efficiency of the office itself or through a more parsimonious use of at least one input, for the same output, or through the increase of the amount of output, for the same input) [4].

In view of the progress achieved by other sectors in public administration, where the application of economic business criteria has registered considerable results in terms of the optimization of resources and good performance of the service (local health-care authorities, local authorities, universities, chambers of commerce, etc.), virtually as much concreteness is not found within the justice system. This environment, in fact, has always drawn out objective problems of conceptual order connected, first of all, to the difficulty of reaching a definition that is not contrary to the judicial function itself (or jurisdictional) and secondly to the particular nature of the principles and values involved. Repression of crime, sense of safety and legality, substantial equality for all citizens before the law, presumption of innocence until tried, reasonable length of trial, guarantee of defence for the defendant, judicial protection for victims, and separation of power are some of the values for which only effectiveness is looked at, instead of implementing them in an efficient manner [5].

This has produced, not infrequently, a result conversant with measures and provisions that are neither effective nor efficient.

The judiciary organization, as a whole, and singularly of all those who operate within it (clerks, public ministers and judges, civil or defence lawyers, witnesses or consultants, assessors and judicial officials, investigative police, etc.) uses considerable resources in carrying out the proper functions [6].

http://dx.doi.org/10.5772/67555

It is often from the resource entities themselves who choose to assign one activity rather than another on which the outcome of the action plan depends; just as it is from the entity and the nature of the resources available that certain strategic choice can depend. Each strategic option, in fact, has a cost that is also represented by the alternative that is renounced in order to go with preferences, and even the choice between different procedural stances must be studied on the base of cost opportunity that each determines.

To this logic, one certainly cannot take away anyone involved in the judicial sector, but without a doubt nor does it take away the legislators, who must face budget constraints, problems connected with the managerialization of the service and with the costs and opportunities of each policy [7].

2. Public administration and corporatization

The definition of new functions, services and development strategies of which public administrations are recipients (*id est* judicial administrations) necessitates a reflection in regard to the process of corporatization of public administration [8].

The starting point of the important changes that have interested public administration in the last few years is made up of reform processes that can be defined 'as explicit modifications of the operating rules of the systems' [9]. A positive change of a determined situation is implicit in the achievement of these reforms. With reference to public administrations, the necessity to carry out these transformations emerges from various motivations, traceable to a gap that was progressively growing between what public administration should have done from an institutional point of view and what it actually did do, in view of an always greater quantity of resources absorbed.

In short, reform functions as a factor that produces, promotes or facilitates change, in that the system that is the subject of the reform manifests a motion of development that is inferior in respect to that necessary. The regulation consists of a fundamental passage to institutionally accredit innovation in planning and oversight functions and the introduction of new organizational and managerial instruments.

Public administration, besides Administrative Law, has for a number of years been considered a subject in Business Administration, a discipline that puts into practice a unified study with the theme of economic activity, independently from the nature of those involved in its practice, from its dimensional characteristics or from its legal background.

Even in public administration, in fact, all those requisites of Business Administration that qualify a business are recognized. These are autonomy, continuity, dynamism and coordination, reason for being and social legitimization to be constantly achieved in the interaction with the environment.

Autonomy of a business intends its ability of self-determination. This requirement allows business activities to be distinguished from all the economic activities conducted within an institution, but bound by a relationship of accessoriness. Speaking of autonomy, it is also necessary to recall its three main specifications. One speaks, in fact, of decision-making autonomy, which is the ability of self-legislation, of choosing conduct and behavioural guidelines; of asset autonomy, such as conditions of self-determination in economic choices in the administration of its own resources; finally, of economic autonomy, such as the power to control the flow of resources that characterize carrying out the activity of management [10].

It can be absolutely agreed upon that all three of the specifications indicated belong to the public context. To safeguard these forms of autonomy, the Law itself and the Constitution are in place.

The second aspect, continuity, manages to translate the necessary continuity of existence of the public authorities foreseen in different constitutional and administrative ordinances into economic—business terms. If on the one side there is a necessity for continuity for legal and political motives, on the other side, a balance that allows for the correct economic and financial survival of these authorities should be necessarily guaranteed.

It is, therefore, a continuity that is characterized by dynamism and subject to evolutionary phenomena and adaption (coordination) to the requests of the service users.

The reason of being and the social legitimization of the public authority, furthermore, are phenomena that do not lend themselves to particular objections, from the moment that they find their origins not only in the law but also in the social contract of a country [11].

So, if the public authority takes on all the characteristics typical of a business, it is a business itself, and, as such, can be studied in a homogeneous manner, prescinding from characteristics of form that distinguish the typologies.

Moreover, discussing public businesses only means putting together two terms of a diverse nature: the first is of a business origin, the second of a judicial origin.

Business [12] is a typical concept of Business Administration that answers the theoretical constructions and the relative operative indications, while public is the qualification that represents a particular mode of being of the business phenomenon.

This allows for the public authority (administration) to be put into a framework as a business equipped with specificities and, as such, characterized by communal rules independently of its dimensional, organizational or regulative characteristics.

Its process of administration and control becomes, therefore, identifiable with that of an activity with all the typical connotations of a business, with respect to the principles and laws of Business Administration.

All this brings about the recognition of two different operating dimensions within public administration:

- a political dimension, adopted in a determined moment and in a determined space by institutional bodies and by logic that controls the operation of economic governance, within which the interpretations of the aims of the authority are expressed and where the concept of the institution itself is explicated;

http://dx.doi.org/10.5772/67555

- a business dimension through which the carrying out of the operations of production and consumption, as well as administration of the assets are assured.

For this reason, it is necessary to classify the various authorities of public administration based on the different relationships between the two dimensions and the different contributions that they variably will give in time to the achievement of the primary aims, analysing the so-called *level of corporativity* that it characterizes, in other words, the role that the objectives take on in an economic business nature in which they reside.

The presence of such different levels will depend on two factors:

- a political-institutional factor, that is, the choices that the Legislator has made on these types of authorities and the degree of financial and proprietary autonomy that each will recognize;
- a factor pertaining to the economic situation, that is, the economic-financial characteristics of a single entity and the needs that they set down [13].

Corporatization has the objective of bringing the essential and indispensable qualities of private companies into any public enterprise. Amongst them, these play a primary role: (1) the decision-making autonomy and the correlated taking on of responsibility for the decisions made, as well as for the results attained, (2) the effectiveness, efficiency and economy of management and (3) the professionalism of the managers and the workers and the formation of a corporate culture.

The terms effectiveness, efficiency and economy are keywords in the economic-business dictionary; it is not by chance that the search for such conditions is communal and indispensable objectives for all enterprises. A brief description would be that effectiveness identifies the capacity to reach set objectives, efficiency is that of reaching a given goal with the minimum waste (optimizing, namely, the use of resources and therefore improving the input-output relationship), economy identifies a situation of balanced and complete valorization of the economic, organizational and professional resources of a company.

Within the process of corporatization, the concept of effectiveness is tied to that of the quality of services. The public enterprise carries out its activities at an advantage over other enterprises of singles users or groups, to each of which it must assure the satisfaction of the needs expressed. Contemporarily, such enterprises must also commit themselves to the achievement of technical and economic efficiency, namely reaching their managerial goals by reducing the degree of the means used and, compatibly with its size, the level of costs.

While the considerations expressed above on the concepts of effectiveness and efficiency are valid for both private enterprises and public, there are some differences for economy. Indubitably, reaching a balance that has value over time is an indispensable objective for all enterprises on par with that of effectiveness; however, from the public characterization of the economic subject and with the aims of general socio-economic interest pursued, they carry constraints and requests that are different in respect to private enterprises which, in fact, can limit their profitability in a brief period.

Nevertheless, the actions of public enterprises must always be brought back to the principles of maximum efficiency, economic rationality and the achievement of the conditions necessary for economic self-sufficiency as well as global and total quality.

In summary, the public admiration-business system relationship develops through the re-establishment, or the introduction, of the managerial perspective, which in turn is based on (a) the search for consonance amongst the aims, the objectives and the constraints, in order to guarantee the unity of the management, (b) the adoption of a strategic perspective, which combines long-term needs with those derived from everyday management which then contributes to guaranteeing a lasting operation of the organization and (c) the orientation towards effectiveness, efficiency and economy (**Figure 1**).

For this reason, for more than two decades by now, institutional, regulative and managerial reforms are significantly modifying the face of public administration, pushing to be closer to citizens and for better quality of the services offered. This sometimes entails the redesign of institutional structuring and calls for innovative organizational models to respond to new demand.

Therefore, the path to reform undertaken by public administration has tried to outline a new 'public administration model' oriented towards understanding the principles of 'business management' [14].

In this context, the planning of the activity of direction and guidance of the entire system can be seen, or rather the activity through which the objectives of their own actions as a 'business' are identified and decided, activating adequate and correct decisions capable of reaching the set objectives in the execution phases.

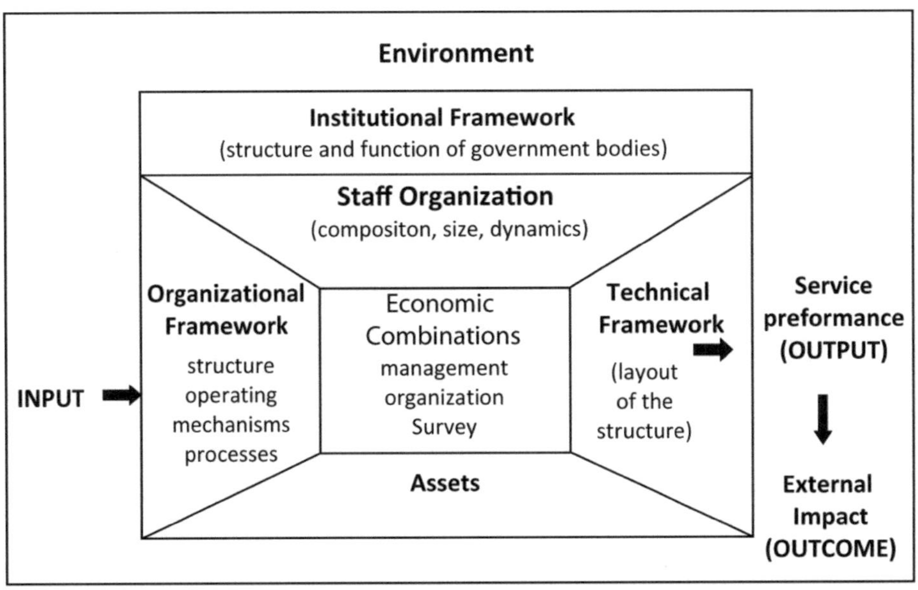

Figure 1. The dynamic system of public administrations. Source: personal elaboration.

Consequently, the activity of control consistent in the survey, analysis and valuation of the results obtained and of the connection between these and the set objectives or decisions of the enterprise bodies appears of undeniable relevance.

In this direction, legislation has done much, forming an unavoidable constraint which must be necessarily taken into consideration, essentially looking towards the aims indicated by the legislator without, though, creating a 'regulative guide' [15].

The business paradigm, even if it intervened late in offering its contribution to the study of public administrations, represents a third dimension, alongside political and institutional, that guides the behaviour of public businesses in the pursuit of their own institutional goals. The consensus and the legitimization on the part of the stakeholders cannot prescind from the ability of the public business [16] to operate according to the principles of economic rationality and, in particular, that of economy [17].

In this sense, the authority of the resources absorbed by the public sector, the extent of the tasks and the competences entrusted to them impose the daily confrontation, upon political, economic and administrative players, scholars and researchers, with a managerial approach, of problems connected to efficiency, effectiveness and economy of the administrative acts and of management that characterize the daily behaviour of even judicial administrations.

3. Judicial administration and managerial perspectives

A new paradigm has imposed itself onto judicial administration: obtaining and managing consent both externally, by obtaining the trust of the stakeholders, and internally, through values that can consolidate the various organizational levels.

In light of the considerations carried out, it is possible to identify certain criteria that in substance reconnects itself to the principles of business economy and that in their organic whole make up a system of 'values', which by integrating themselves into the operative plan and if knowingly made up of all the institutional participants (stakeholders) are capable of obtaining, in an economic-business and managerial sense, judicial administrative management.

Schematically, the previously mentioned system of values refers to the following concepts [18]:

- economy of management: as the judicial system is an economic 'institute' with the purpose of enduring in time, economy of management is placed at the apex, meaning that its operations must be based on criteria of 'economy' geared towards results. Here, as opposed to the enterprise that produces for the market, economy is not measured by profit, but rather by utility, which is reached by 'efficiently' producing goods and services which are capable of 'effectively' satisfying the needs of the citizen user. This means that in judicial administration, the quantification of results, which cannot be entrusted towards a sole indicator of profit, is reached for in other indicators that are different based on the type of production of goods or services, entrusting the budget specifications to a model that, in respect to the conditions of efficiency and effectiveness [19], can concretely inform the entire business activity, focalizing attention on reengineering and on simplification, with the objective of reducing waste, re-thinking and re-inventing the so-called Judicial Government, with the intent to increasing the effectiveness of the services.

- planning and oversight: these two elements make up an essential value in judicial administration, in that planning allows for, on the one side, the rationalization of the behaviour of the 'deciders' and, on the other side, the defining of the model capable of stabilizing the economic conditions that must guide the business activity. Oversight allows for the verification of the manner and measure that the economic conditions are realized in the effective carrying out of the business management.

- the information system: intended as an interrelated whole of elements, it attributes operational concreteness to planning and oversight, in that it allows the identification, through the handling of information, of the parameter of economy, offering a base, as objective and rationale as possible, to the management of the business. The managerial data acquire economic and juridical value, thus becoming information, only if they are properly organized and actually used in the decision-making processes in relation to their identification abilities.

It is a shift from the exclusive use of top-down-type logic promoted by the 'centre' through laws that reward and punishment systems could be associated, to bottom-up-type logic characterized by voluntary experimentation on part of single tribunals and by the subsequent diffusion in the public administration system of the emergent models. Consolidating, therefore, the action coordinated between the policies of support promoted on a central level and the promotion and diffusion from the bottom of innovative experiences and best practices, such as good-quality projects, innovation rewards and the systematic benchmarking of results and processes.

- the organizational culture: it interests above all the valorization of human resources, the personal qualification of the managers, the involvement of the staff, who must be made responsible for the expected results. The process of gradual re-orientation of the staff towards the business values, which in the general public are more difficult to learn, often reducing itself to mere formal acts, entails a symmetrical and equally gradual overcoming of the typical bureaucratic-administrative culture (government), characterized by exclusively juridical knowledge, oriented towards the oversight of the acts more than the results, fraught with formal responsibility in the direction of respecting the regulations as such without the due attention for the results that the same regulation aims to achieve (governance), without stimuli in the direction of change imposed by the constant reform of public administration.

- social control and the ethical dimension: the first value permeates judicial administration from the political-social point of view, as it is exercised by the people interested in the business itself, that is, the citizen users, or by who represents them, that is, the determined body (Ministry of Justice, magistrates). The ethical dimension, instead, re-enforces social control in the sense that the economic rationality and the ethical values in operating in the public administration are complementary aspects of a single 'system of values', adopted as a model of operation of the judicial administration, founded on values that are necessarily both ethical and economical [20].

http://dx.doi.org/10.5772/67555

The whole of these values outlines a virtuous cycle capable of distinguishing the actions of the judicial administration [21].

4. Judicial accountability and its application

Accountability in public administration proposes a report that is geared not only towards a higher-level public body, a monitoring body or, generically, to the administrative community, but also to all the principle categories of stakeholders, in the knowledge that all are interested in the business activity, or benefit from the results, and furthermore that all, with their active and reactive behaviour, have the ability to influence the activity itself, collaborating positively, or posing obstacles which would hinder the possibility of the business reaching their planned objectives [22].

The concept of accountability is considered as one of basic principles in the process of change and reform in public administrations that, even in an Italian context where it has not found a specific translation, it has been interpreted in its acceptance of attitudes of being accountable, of transparency and responsibility, distinguishing the aims and the external or internal focus to the business [23].

Despite the proliferation of definitions proposed on the concept of accountability, they seem to be accumulated:

1. from the greater complexity of the contextualized concept in the public sector in respect to its application in the private sphere;
2. from necessity, in order to speak about accountability, of the presence on one part (accountee) that must wait for another (accountor), responsible for accounting for how to respond to the same.

Specifically, the concept of accountability in judicial offices requires a transfer of information from the accountor (judicial office) to the accountee (citizen, political body, etc.) to whom the possibility of assessment of the public action based on the information obtained is recognized [24].

It can be stated that the aim is to create a 'relationship' between public administration and general stakeholders (stakeholder relationship), through a process of one-to-one communication (**Figure 2**).

In particular, in order to speak of judicial accountability, not only is the availability of information a necessity but they must also have the characteristics of reliability, comprehension, accessibility, diffusion and distribution.

Finally, the process of accountability must foresee the possible judgement expressed by the accountee that represents feedback on the part of who receives the information towards who sends it.

Figure 2. Relationship management with stakeholders. Source: personal elaboration.

In merit of the focus that addresses the process of accountability, a relevant distinction is highlighted among

a) an external orientation. In this case, the judicial offices should demonstrate that they are accountable, assuming responsibility for their actions and the results obtained, communicating them to the stakeholders, denoting transparency on the acquisition and the use of resources and on the performance achieved;

b) an internal orientation. In this hypothesis, accountability has a value as internal decision-making support entailing utility towards managers and magistrates. This would allow these figures to assume responsibility in a conscious manner, acquiring greater awareness about the objectives to be reached and regarding the necessity of accounting for the choices made and the results reached.

In order to better illustrate the different dimensions that can assume responsibility in judicial offices, it can be useful to consider a matrix analysis model composed of two principle dimensions of analysis (**Table 1**): (a) the recipient of accountability (internal or external) and (b) the type of results on which accountability is founded (financial-economical or meta-economical).

As it can be easily inferred from this model, accountability applied to judicial offices appears as a complex concept characterized by numerous aspects. In an environment with 'the need to account', in fact, a multitude of functions and tasks are included.

In other words, therefore, the manner with which judicial administration 'accounts' to the citizens can be varied.

As has happened for various types of public administration, even for judicial offices, the evident gap created in the years between user expectation and the services actually delivered has contributed to raise awareness of the nature of public service, which must be delivered with efficiency and economy.

The need for reform processes that are capable, on one hand, of developing a greater consistency between demand and supply of the services, and, on the other hand, of favouring the recovery of administrative action transparency and of the oversight on behalf of all the stakeholders is thus rendered evident.

	Financial-economic dimension	Social dimension
Internal accountability	**Function** Taking responsibility for the financial-economic results and the articulation of authority costs **Instruments** Oversight of management, ABC, remuneration tied to performance, etc.	**Function** Taking internal responsibility for the strategic objectives **Instruments** Balanced score card, MBO, etc.
External accountability	**Function** Accountability and representation of costs and income of a financial nature **Instruments** Financial accounting	**Function** Accountability and representation of effectiveness, social impact and mission consistency **Instruments** Social balance

Source: modified by F. Monteduro (Ed.) Amministrazione Pubbliche: principi e sistemi contabili. Aracne, Rome, 2006.

Table 1. The dimensions of judicial accountability.

In other words, an evident need for new governance mechanisms and accountability logic in judicial offices that are compatible with the independence of the magistrature was created.

Intended in terms of taking on responsibility, as well as reporting accounts, accountability represents, therefore, a necessity in the public sector in general, and in the judicial system in particular.

Anywhere resources are used in order to guarantee the attainment of a result, be it of public interest, or in the interest of a few, there is the need to take on responsibility for the results and accounting for them, to verity if, and in what way, the awaited results were met.

From the above-mentioned considerations emerge, therefore, the particular significance of the process of accountability in judicial offices.

If, in fact, transparency and reporting accounts through methods that go beyond those imposed by law are useful for enterprises and can produce important benefits for them (trust, image, shares, etc.), for judicial office it is a duty towards the recipients of the accountability process, in respect to the purpose of collective interest of this type of 'business' and the relationship of trust on which their actions are based, namely, as the need for reporting accounts and taking on responsibility not only for the efficient use of resources but also for the result obtained in terms of output and outcome.

5. Conclusion

The attempt of adopting a managerial logic in the judicial sector is certainly more complex because the service rendered by the courts is characterized by publicity and by specific needs and rules that make it more peculiar.

It is this character, however, that renders worthwhile each analytical attempt that aims to obtain a higher and higher level of satisfaction for the user.

Despite the evident need, the diffusion in the judicial offices (and therefore the same throughout the judicial system) of accountability logic and managerial orientation that could promote the recovery of higher levels of efficiency is often opposed by constant reminders of the necessity to guarantee the independence of magistrates. This independence is considered the most important ruling posed by the Constitution to guarantee individual freedom but, translating it into reality it is the principle element of a more complex immunization strategy put into place to oppose change.

Making the justice system more efficient with the knowledge that even justice is a stimulus factor for the economy and, moreover, can contribute to leading the country out of this crisis does not undermine the independence of the magistrate. On the contrary, the independence of the magistrate is reserved for exercising its function, but the magistrature must also understand that it is part of a complex organization, whose rules of efficiency must be toughened and made binding.

In the countries in which the managerialization process of the justice system is more evolved, substantial compatibility between independence and accountability has been established. Both, in fact, represent fundamental presuppositions of the public action of Judicial Administrations, in view of safeguarding collective interests.

Reducing the influx of judicial demand, increasing the adaptability of the judicial instruments and increasing the efficiency of the judicial organization: these are the three guidelines that can inspire a period of reform to address the emergency that involves justice in a manner that is no less worrisome than the economy.

In the knowledge that courthouses are not temples for novices, but a crossroads of social-economic development of a country, it can be concluded that even a judicial office can no longer avoid the responsibility that is typical in every public institution of reporting the results achieved by reconciling a business approach with the provisions, the regulations and the directives that daily regulate judicial activity.

Author details

Ubaldo Comite

Address all correspondence to: ubaldo.comite@libero.it

University 'Giustino Fortunato', Benevento, Italy

References

[1] Comite U. (2010a). The efficiency, effectiveness and economy of the Italian Judicial System: The economic-business perspective. In 2010 International Conference on Public

Administration (6^ ICPA), "Public Administration Challenges and Opportunities: Serving Citizens in a Globalized World", Canberra, Australia, 22-24 September 2010 (Vol. I, pp. 337-348, ISBN 978-7-5647-0624-1).

[2] Kostoris R. (2003). Giustizia, garanzie ed efficienza: delicati equilibri e suggestioni. Diritto & Giustizia no. 25. Milan: Giuffrè.

[3] Comite U. (2010b). Management and social balance in the Italian courts: Methods and operative proposals. In 2010 Oxford Business and Economics Conference (OBEC) Proceedings, St. Hugh's College- Oxford University, England, 28-30 June 2010 (ISBN 978-0-9742114-1-9).

[4] Alvino F., Lepore L. (2009). Court management: inquadramento dottrinale e strumenti operativi. Rome: Quaderni Monografici RIREA.

[5] Comite U. (2010c). The entrance of court management in the courts through the use of social balance: The Italian experience. In Global Conference on Business and Finance, online, 1931-0285 on CD, The Institute for Business and Finance Research, Hilo, HI, 3-6 January 2010, Keauhou Beach Resort, Kailua-Kona, Hawaii (Vol. 5, no. 1, ISSN 1941-9589).

[6] Caperchione E., Pezzani F. (Ed.). (2000). Responsabilità e trasparenza nella gestione dell'ente locale. Milan: Egea.

[7] Elder H. W. (1989). Trial and settlements in the criminal courts: An empirical analysis of dispositions and sentencing. The Journal of Legal Studies, Vol. XVIII, pp. 191-208, Chicago University Press.

[8] Anselmi L. (1995). Il processo di trasformazione della pubblica amministrazione. Turin: Giappichelli.

[9] Borgonovi E. (2005). Principi e sistemi aziendali per le amministrazioni pubbliche. Milan: Egea.

[10] Cavazzoni G. (2004). Il sistema del controllo di gestione. Strumenti per le decisioni operative aziendali. Turin: Giappichelli.

[11] Anselmi L. (Ed.). (2005). Principi e metodologie economico-aziendali per gli enti locali. Milan: Giuffrè.

[12] Hinna L. (Ed.). (2008). Appunti di Economia Aziendale. Padua: Cedam.

[13] Comite U. (2009). Business economy profiles of financial difficulties in local corporation: From default to financial renewal. Journal of International Finance and Economic (JIFE), Vol. 9, number 1, pp. 66-76.

[14] D'Alessio L. et al. (2008). Gruppo di studio e attenzione dell'Accademia Italiana di Economia Aziendale. In Innovazione e Accountability nella Amministrazione pubblica. I drivers del cambiamento. Rome.

[15] Alford J. (1993). Towards a new public management model: Beyond managerialism and its critics. American Journal of Public Administration, Vol. 52, Issue 2. pp. 135-148

[16] Farneti G. (2004). Ragioneria Pubblica. Il nuovo sistema informativo delle aziende pubbliche. Milan: F. Angeli.

[17] Borgonovi E., Fattore G., Longo G. (2009). Management delle istituzioni pubbliche. Milan: Egea.

[18] Persiani N. (2002). Modelli di programmazione e sistemi di controllo interno nella pubblica amministrazione. Milan: F. Angeli.

[19] Sforza V. (2005). L'economia delle aziende sanitarie pubbliche. Logiche di gestione e strumenti di analisi dei risultati aziendali. Padua: Cedam.

[20] Comite U. (2009). Creazione di valore e sussidiarietà nell'amministrazione pubblica: un approccio economico-aziendale. In G.P. Calabrò (Ed.). La nozione di sussidiarietà tra teoria e prassi. Naples: Edizioni Scientifiche Italiane.

[21] Moore M. H. (2003). La creazione di valore pubblico. La gestione strategica nella pubblica amministrazione. Milan: Guerini e associati.

[22] Bertocchi M., Bisio L. (2005). Bilancio sociale: dalla rendicontazione al dialogo. "Il Sole 24 Ore", Guida agli Enti Locali no. 43. Milan.

[23] De Matteis F. (2011). Il bilancio per il cittadino negli enti locali. Padua: Cedam.

[24] Steccolini I. (2004). Accountability a sistemi informativi negli enti locali. Turin: Giappichelli.